Buddha in the Marketplace

Traditions and Transformations in Tibetan Buddhism

David Germano & Michael Sheehy, Editorss

Buddha in the Marketplace

The Commodification of Buddhist Objects in Tibet

ALEX JOHN CATANESE

University of Virginia Press | *Charlottesville and London*

University of Virginia Press

Printed in the United States of America on acid-free paper

First published 2019

9 8 7 6 5 4 3 2 1

Library of Congress Cataloging-in-Publication Data
Names: Catanese, Alex John, author.
Title: Buddha in the marketplace : the commodification of buddhist objects in Tibet / Alex John Catanese.
Description: Charlottesville : University of Virginia Press, 2019. | Series: Traditions and transformations in Tibetan Buddhism | Includes bibliographical references and index.
Identifiers: LCCN 2019025042 (print) | LCCN 2019025043 (ebook) | ISBN 9780813943176 (hardback) | ISBN 9780813943183 (paperback) | ISBN 9780813943190 (ebook)
Subjects: LCSH: Buddhist religious articles—China—Tibet Region. | Buddhist religious articles—Marketing.
Classification: LCC BQ5070 .C38 2019 (print) | LCC BQ5070 (ebook) | DDC 294.3/92309515—dc23
LC record available at https://lccn.loc.gov/2019025042
LC ebook record available at https://lccn.loc.gov/2019025043

Photographs not otherwise credited are by the author.

Cover art: Watercolor painting (Buddha) courtesy of Joy Lynn Davis, Joylynndavis.com (with Arabic Floral Seamless Border [Azat1976/Shutterstock] below and Ornament black white card with mandala [An Vino/Shutterstock] in background)

For my brother Tony

Contents

Illustrations

Acknowledgments

There are a number of people I would like to thank without whom this book would not have been possible. First and foremost, I would like to thank all of the Tibetans in Amdo—artists, merchants, and monks—who allowed me into their places of work and residences, who gave generously of their time, and who allowed me to ask them sensitive religious questions. Next, I could not have done much without the assistance my very talented interpreter, Pema Gyatso, who not only patiently assisted me during long, often repetitive interviews but who also helped me with clarifying the transcriptions afterward. Many thanks also to Alyson Prude for providing my initial contacts in Amdo and to Tsering Samdrup, who helped me get oriented to Xining and who assisted me with the first several interviews there. I would, of course, also like to thank José Cabezón for his encouragement and guidance throughout this project and particularly for his editorial contributions and translation assistance. I am also grateful to the UC Pacific Rim Research Program for funding my research and for their flexibility during my fieldwork. Additionally, I'd also like to thank Vesna Wallace for suggesting the Amdo region as a prime location for my research and Mayfair Yang for her support and feedback. A hearty thank you as well goes to my dear friend Nathaniel "the Dude" Rich for making valuable editorial suggestions, to Karl Musser for creating my maps, to Joy Lynn Davis for painting the beautiful Buddha image for the cover, and to Siobhan Drummond for her superb editing of the final manuscript. I'd also like to express my gratitude to the series editors, David Germano and Michael Sheehy, for giving me the opportunity to publish my research, and to the staff at UVA Press, particularly Eric Brandt, Mark Mones, and Helen Marie Chandler, for their support throughout the process of creating this book. Finally, and most importantly, I'd like to thank my family, especially my wife, Krysten, and daughter, Francesca, for their love, support, and encouragement throughout what has been a very long process. Thanks also to my mother, Joan, and sister, Annette, for continuing to cheer me on.

Buddha in the Marketplace

Introduction

Well over a decade ago, while perusing the religion section of a bookstore in Santa Barbara, California, I came across a sight which, while I did not know it at the time, would be the catalyst for a course of study that would preoccupy me for a number of years. What I saw was a product called "Buddha in a Box," which purported to be a miniature portable altar that one could use for religious practice. It contained a small Buddha image and a book that introduced the Buddha's life and teachings. It wasn't my desire to purchase this product that made me pick it up and examine it. Rather, it was the way in which Buddhism seemed to be prepackaged and mass-produced for sale that grabbed my attention. For me, this particular product seemed to epitomize the commodification of Buddhism, something that I had been noticing more frequently in the markets and in the media in general. My immediate reaction to "Buddha in a Box" was that the existence of this object was just as much about making money and taking advantage of market trends as it was about imparting the actual teachings of Buddhism. At the same time, I also began to notice that the advertising industry was becoming particularly fond of using the Buddha's image in order to sell certain products. While the continued appearance of "Buddhafied" items in the marketplace suggested that nobody was seriously considering what the religious response to such things might be, I often wondered what actual Buddhists would think if they saw the image of the founder of their religion being used in such a way. How would they

FIG. 1. "Buddha in a Box," or "The Buddha Box," published in 1988.

respond to the Buddha's picture on a pair of shoes or on a bikini, or its use to sell merchandise that was totally unrelated to Buddhism? All of these uses of Buddhist images were being reflected in the American marketplace, and some of them were beginning to generate particularly negative reactions from overseas Buddhist groups.

It wasn't until I began to study what Buddhists, particularly Tibetan Buddhists, thought about such activity that I learned that the concerns of the Tibetan tradition went much further than the so-called cultural misappropriation of Buddhist objects and images. In fact, I soon discovered that,

FIG. 2. The cover of an Earth Shoes catalog from 2005 depicts shoes on top of a Buddha statue that is being caressed by a woman. (Image courtesy of Earth Brands)

FIG. 3. A Dean & DeLuca catalog from 2006 advertises a chocolate Buddha as part of a collection for the serious chocolate connoisseur.

FIG. 4. As part of a large campaign to end the misuse of Buddha images, a billboard in Bangkok sponsored by the Knowing Buddha Organization reminds citizens and tourists alike to respect Buddha images and not to treat them as decorative items.

traditionally speaking, Tibetan Buddhists believed that the mere selling of Buddhist images and religious texts—objects considered receptacles of the body, speech, and mind of the Buddha (*sku gsung thugs kyi rten*)—was a sin (*dikpa, sdig pa*), and not just a small sin but a big one that had serious negative karmic consequences. Having continued my investigations into this topic and having traveled to Tibetan cultural areas, I also discovered three additional details about the issue of selling Tibetan Buddhist objects. First, I learned that there was a vast body of Buddhist literature that contains statements that explicitly prohibit the selling of Buddhist images and texts. Second, I learned that such objects were, in fact, sold everywhere by Tibetans themselves. And third, I learned that this commercial activity was said to be a relatively recent phenomenon, beginning to appear only in the 1980s after the introduction of market reforms and the easing of restrictions on religious practice that were implemented during the Cultural Revolution (1966–76). Before this time, in premodern Tibet, religious objects were typically acquired by commissioning artists.

Given the persecution of Tibetan Buddhism and the destruction of its religious material culture during the Cultural Revolution, Tibetans' current participation in the commercialization of their religious goods made a lot of sense to me. After all, Tibetans needed religious objects to resume their religious practices. Still, I wondered about what seemed to be an obvious contradiction between what was said to be the traditional Tibetan thinking on this issue, on the one hand, and what was happening on the ground in the marketplaces of Tibetan cultural areas, on the other. Why, now, were Tibetans openly selling religious objects when their religious tradition condemned such activities in the strongest possible terms? What had happened to the religious proscriptions against their sale? How did Tibetans themselves make sense of these religious proscriptions vis-à-vis their own selling activities? Furthermore, how should we as observers understand Tibetans' current sale of religious goods? Tibetans' commodification of Buddhist religious objects—that is, the process by which such objects have become items for sale on the open market—is the topic of this book. Its aims are to understand the importance of the religious proscriptions against the sale of Buddhist objects in the Tibetan Buddhist tradition, the forces that have contributed to Tibetans' commodification of religious goods in the contemporary context of modern China, Tibetan perceptions of the religious prohibitions against their sale, and the outcomes or effects that the transition of Buddhist objects from noncommodity to commodity have had on Tibetan religion and society.

In pursuing answers to the above questions, this study takes a broad historical and contextual approach and draws upon a number of sources, including classical religious texts, secondary historical works, and ethnographic research conducted in the region of Amdo (A mdo). Amdo, located on the northeastern part of the Tibetan Plateau, is traditionally understood as one of three regions of Tibet along with Ü-Tsang (Dbus gtsang)—that is, Central and Western Tibet—and Kham (Khams) in the southeast. Today, Amdo makes up the entire province of Qinghai, part of Gansu Province, and northern Aba, Tibet Autonomous Prefecture (TAP), Sichuan Province. The region of Amdo provided a prime location for fieldwork on this issue, as Amdo was and remains famous as a center of artistic production. The art of Rebkong (Reb gong; Ch. Tongren), one of the main urban centers of Amdo, became institutionalized within several neighboring Gelukpa (Dge lugs pa) monasteries, flourishing from the mid-seventeenth century until the middle of the twentieth century.[1] The monks and lay artists who lived in and around Rebkong dominated arts production and accepted commissions from all over the Tibetan world (Stevenson 2002, 198). Today, not only has this artistic production been restored to its former glory in what many scholars have recognized as an artistic renaissance, but the sale of ready-made—that is, noncommissioned—religious objects in shops and galleries is also flourishing and has become a new source of livelihood for a number of Tibetans.

Fieldwork for this study was carried out over a period of four months (April–May and October–November) in 2010 and consisted of interviews with three different groups of Tibetan informants: merchants of religious objects; artists—most of whom were painters of the traditional Tibetan art form known as *thangka* (*thang ka*), or scroll paintings, which depict images of various buddhas and bodhisattvas; and monks.[2] During this period, I visited several markets where religious objects were sold, as well as monasteries, in order to find out what Tibetans generally thought about the current sale of religious goods and the traditional religious proscriptions against selling them. Merchants included both men and women. Artists (all male) included laypersons, monks, and former monks. And monks who were not artists included those who held the degree of *Geshé* (*dge bshes*), one of the highest monastic degrees in the Gelukpa scholastic tradition. Research for this study took place primarily in Qinghai Province in Xining, Haidong, and Huangnan Prefectures, with one location in Gansu Province. Locations included the Xining Tibetan market, Kumbum Monastery and its surrounding market (Sku 'bum byams pa gling, Ta'er Si), Jakhyung Gonpa (Bya khyung dgon pa, Xiaqun Si), Gur Gonpa (Mgur dgon pa or Rma mgur dgon, Gulu Si) in Chentsa County (Gcan tsha, Jianzha), the marketplace of the town of Chentsa, Gasar Gonpa (Ska sar sgar 'dus bzang chos gling, Gashari Si), Sengeshong Mango Gonpa (Seng ge gshong ma mgo dgon pa, or Lower Sengeshong, Wutun Xiazhuang), Sengeshong Yango Gonpa (Seng ge gshong ya mgo dgon pa, or Upper Sengeshong, Wutun Shangzhuang), Rongwo Gönchen (Rong bo dgon chen, Long wu), Nyentok Village (Gnyan thog), Maksar Gonpa (Mag gsar sman re'i bshad sgrub smin grol gling, Muhesha Ga-er Si), and the market near Labrang Monastery (Bla brang bkra shis 'khyil, Lapuleng Si) in Gannan Prefecture, Gansu Province.

In total, I interviewed forty-five individuals: fifteen artists, eighteen merchants, and twelve monks. Interviews were conducted in the residences and workplaces of informants with the assistance of a multilingual interpreter. These interviews were recorded and later transcribed into English. Because some participants' responses had political overtones, I have excluded the names of my informants. Also, because of the number of informants and the difficult task of keeping track of a large number of testimonies, I have chosen not to substitute my informants' names with pseudonyms. Instead, I have de-

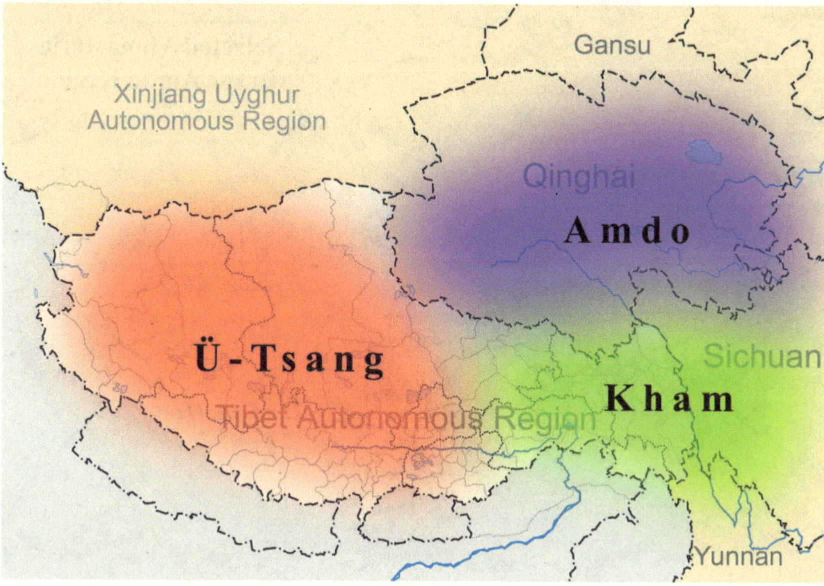

FIG. 5. The areas of Ü-Tsang, Kham, and Amdo. (Map by Karl Musser)

cided to use generic references.[3] Several individuals declined to participate in this study. My interpretation of their decision not to participate is that such discussions either made them feel uncomfortable from a religious standpoint or, alternatively, that they did not want to be seen speaking at length to a foreigner out of concern for their own safety.[4]

In many ways, a broader study of the issue of the commodification of religious objects in the Tibetan context is long overdue. Although there have been valuable scholarly articles on the commodification of Tibetan thangka paintings in Kathmandu (Bentor 1993), Dharamsala (McGuckin 1996), and in the Rebkong cultural area (Reynolds 2011), and while some authors have indeed noted that the sale of religious objects is proscribed by the Tibetan Buddhist tradition (Kolås 2008), no study has yet to thoroughly examine the issue of selling religious objects in Tibet from a historical perspective or engage specifically with the question of how Tibetans have dealt with (and are continuing to deal with) the religious prohibitions against the sale of such goods. By taking a textual, historical, and ethnographic approach to the religious issue of selling Buddhist objects in Tibet, this study aims to contribute to our understanding of how such ideas functioned historically in Tibetan

FIG. 6. A map illustrating the various locations of fieldwork in Qinghai and Gansu Provinces. (Map by Karl Musser)

society and how they continue to be relevant in contemporary times as Tibetans grapple with the moral questions surrounding the sale of their religious objects.

While this study is relatively broad in scope, it is also, perhaps inevitably, partial. There are many areas within the "business" of selling religious objects that this study does not cover. For example, my research could have benefited from gaining access to the factories that mass-produce Buddhist objects, the traders who supply many of the retail merchants whom I interviewed, and the painters who paint from home and who are said to supply the majority of images for the open market.[5] In addition, conducting more research among the older generation of Tibetans about the market availability of religious goods in the past and the attitudes toward selling such goods, both before the Cultural Revolution and today, would have enriched this study. These various gaps reveal that there is still much more research to carry out on this issue.

In terms of theory, my research is influenced primarily by Arjun Appadurai's work on the commodity in *The Social Life of Things* (1986). Appadurai argues for a vision of the commodity as an object that is primarily social in nature and one that is in a process of becoming rather than being a certain *type* of object. Appadurai's use of the concept of commodity "paths and diversions"—the notion that in all societies objects are regulated according to prescribed paths, which may then be disrupted by various forms of diversion—is especially important to the organization of this study. Utilizing this processual approach, I follow the trajectory of the commodification of religious objects, tracing them from their status as non-commodities—as objects that are withheld from the market and exchanged according to prescribed normative pathways or protocols—to the point at which these objects are "diverted" toward their increased commodification.[6] Also important to my discussion and closely related to the idea of paths and diversions is Appadurai's notion of an object's "commodity context"—that is, the conditions (social, economic, political, etc.) which tend to give rise to or which tend to curtail an object's commodification. Considering the commodity context of Tibetan religious objects in present-day Amdo, I attempt to illustrate the various forces which have helped to bring about, or which have encouraged, Tibetans' sale of their religious goods.

This book is divided into seven chapters. Chapter 1 traces the origins of the prohibitive statements against the sale of Buddhist objects as they are found in Indian and Chinese Buddhist texts and traces how these ideas reached Tibet. Chapter 2 provides a substantive textual background for these proscriptive statements as they come to be articulated in Tibet in a number of literary genres. It explores the parameters of these statements and traces how these proscriptions are perceived and articulated by Tibetan scholars up to modern times. Chapter 3 examines how religious objects (namely statues, thangkas, and texts) were exchanged historically in Tibet up to the Cultural Revolution and how such exchange practices were influenced by religious ideas and traditions. In presenting these transactions, I survey a number of historical works, including literature on trade, travel narratives, and secondary scholarship on Tibetan arts, and I outline the typical or normative means of exchange for religious objects in pre-1960s Tibet. In doing so, I attempt to historicize the commodification of religious objects in the Tibetan context.

Next, I turn to the current context and the post-Mao era and inquire into the possible causes and conditions that have led Tibetans to engage in the commercialization of their religious goods. Here, the impact of the capitalist free market and other forces present in Tibetans' socioeconomic and sociopolitical context are considered and explored. Drawing upon relevant sociological research as well as informants' testimony, chapter 4 explores the possible factors that derive from Tibetans' socioeconomic environment. Chapter 5 similarly examines factors related to Tibetans' sociopolitical position as an ethnic minority in China. Although the economic and political issues addressed in these chapters are of course intertwined, these discussions have been treated separately for organizational purposes. Chapter 6 explores and outlines how Tibetan painters, merchants, and monks currently view the sale of religious goods and the proscriptive statements against this practice. Finally, chapter 7 seeks to offer an analysis of the effects or outcomes of Tibetans' commodification of religious objects by addressing the social, cultural, economic, and religious ramifications of this activity.

Based on my review of the above materials, I argue that we must understand Tibetans' commodification of religious objects not only as a response to the introduction of free market capitalism in China but also as a response to the socioeconomic and political conditions and circumstances resulting from particular policies of the Chinese Communist Party. Furthermore, while Tibetans' commodification of religious objects has contributed to important economic and cultural outcomes, such practices are also contributing to a number of transformations in religious traditions, practices, and values (i.e., the *moral economy*) associated with religious objects as well as to transformations in traditional notions of Tibetan Buddhist identity.

1 | Early Prohibitions against Selling Buddhist Objects

Indian and Chinese Sources

The sale of Buddhist religious objects is ubiquitous throughout Tibet today; such objects have become part of the everyday commercial environment. The contemporary marketplace, therefore, hardly gives any indication that such goods were ever prohibited from being sold or that their sale, according to religious texts, is believed to constitute a sinful act. Yet, textual statements proscribing the sale of Buddhist objects—specifically, statues, paintings, and religious texts—have a long history, originating in India centuries before Buddhism entered Tibet in the eighth century and persisting up to the present day. There is, likewise, a substantial body of evidence that these concerns extended from India into China where they took on a life of their own, appearing in what are considered by scholars to be indigenous Chinese Buddhist works. Statements pertaining to these prohibitions later emerged in Tibet within a variety of literary genres: hagiography (*rnam tar*), artistic manuals, ritual texts, treasure literature (*gter ma*), and especially the stages of the path, or lamrim (*lam rim*), literature. Today, such prohibitions continue in the writings and discourses of popular Tibetan teachers, including those of the Fourteenth Dalai Lama. In order to provide a foundation for a discussion of these proscriptions in the Tibetan tradition, this chapter outlines the possible origins of these statements and focuses primarily on where and how they become articulated within the Indian and (to a lesser extent) Chinese Buddhist contexts. Although early explicit statements proscribing the sale of Buddhist religious objects are relatively scarce, the available literature suggests that such statements may have begun as early as the first or second centuries of the Common Era and as the primary concern of monks. Furthermore, it will be shown that this early literature contains at least two distinct themes. One theme reflects prohibitions against selling religious goods conceived of as the *property* of the monastery or of the Three Jewels (the Buddha, Dharma, and Saṅgha). Here, a moral infraction occurs as a result of wrongly appropriating, stealing, or selling this property. Another theme is reflective of more general prohibitions against selling religious objects that portray such acts as a form of immoral behavior or of wrong livelihood, in which (while not always stated explicitly) the sale of such objects is seen to violate the intended purpose, specialness, or sacrality of the object. While these two themes are closely related insofar as they both deal with objects that are proscribed from commercial activity, I suggest that they represent two separate doctrinal concerns, each following their own logic and reasoning. Such a distinction is important to the present discussion, for as will be observed later on, it is the latter theme which becomes emphasized and more fully elaborated in Tibetan articulations of proscriptions against the sale of Buddhist objects.

SELLING RELIGIOUS OBJECTS—EARLY INDIAN PROSCRIPTIONS

Early Indian *vinaya* texts, which contain the monastic disciplinary codes and regulations for monks, frame the selling of the property of the Three Jewels as an infraction to be avoided and as having serious negative consequences. Rules pertaining to divisions and uses of monastic property prohibit the personal appropriation and sale of those things owned by or dedicated to the Buddha, Dharma, and Saṅgha. Scholars working on various vinayas have long recognized that the Buddha was conceived of as a property owner, represented by the *stūpa* and by his image, and that the Saṅgha maintained rigorous rules with respect to the use or misuse of this property and the property held in common by the Saṅgha. According to Gregory Schopen, "ownership rights were clearly divided in a *Mūlasarvāstivādin* monastery: property belonged to the Buddha, the Dharma, or the Community. In each case such property could be used only for specific purposes and normally could not be transferred to another unit or purpose. This tripartite division of property rights, or some form of it, is recognized by virtually all the *vinayas*" (2004, 104–5). An alternative method of conceptualizing these monastic property divisions has been put forth by Joseph Walser (2005), who divides monastic property into three categories. First, according to Walser, there is "cultic property" (sometimes referred to as the "property of the Buddha" or the "property of the stūpa," depending upon the particular vinaya text), which includes any objects used in ritual or worship (139). Next, there is "property of the Saṅgha," which includes such things as monastic buildings, a monk's bedding, and boats. And finally there is "personal property," which includes the personal items of a monk, such as his robes, his bowl, his mat, and so forth. Commenting on the vinaya texts in general, Walser notes that a monk could sell, trade, or barter items considered his own personal property as he wished (141). Yet, the personal ownership of goods considered communal property or the property of the Buddha (or stūpa) was not permitted. Furthermore, the personal appropriation and/or sale of this property had its own respective consequences:

> Whereas unlawfully appropriating property of the *saṅgha* as one's own was a *niḥsargika-pāccatika* (an infraction requiring confession and relinquishment of the appropriated item), the separation of the *saṅgha's* property from cultic property was much more rigid. Any monk caught using the property of the Buddha (or, in the case of the *Mahāsāṅghika vinaya,* "the property of the *stūpa*") for the purposes of the *saṅgha* or selling the Buddha's property to purchase property of the *saṅgha* was guilty of a *parājika,* an offense requiring expulsion. (Walser 2005, 142)

Thus, according to vinaya texts, any monk who was caught misusing or selling the property of the Buddha (which, here, would have included cultic property such as Buddha statues, paintings, and presumably any offerings made to such objects) was seen to be transgressing vinaya laws.

As for religious texts, evidence from the *Mūlasarvāstivāda vinaya* in particular suggests that Buddhist scriptures were likewise considered to be the property of the monastery and, as such, were prohibited from being owned by individual monks or sold. In one section of the *Cīvaravastu* of the *Mūlasarvāstivāda vinaya,* which discusses rules governing the death and distribution of the estate of a shaven-headed householder, the Buddha himself is made to proclaim that any texts designated as the "word of the Buddha" (*buddhavācana*) found to be in the possession of the deceased were not to be sold but were to be placed in the storehouse as common property of the entire monastic community.[1] After describing what should be done with the property of such an individual—property such as children, animals, and spirituous liquor—the text describes what is to be done with any books:

> With regard to precious objects, with the exception of pearls, divide all gems, [pieces of] lapis lazuli, and conch shells spiraling to the right, and so forth, into two parts. Give one to the Dharma and the other one to the Saṅgha. As for [the portion that was given to] the Dharma, it should be used to copy the word of the Buddha and to adorn the lion throne. As for [the portion that was given to] the Saṅgha, it must be divided by the monks. From among his books, those books that are the word of the Buddha are not to be distributed [among monks but] must remain in the general storehouse for the sake of the Saṅgha of the four directions. Books which are the treatises of non-Buddhists must be distributed by being put up for sale.[2]

Here, our passage suggests that only those books containing the views of non-Buddhist sects (which happened to be in the possession of the deceased) are permitted to be sold and the profits distributed. The word of the Buddha, on the other hand, is to become (or to remain) the property of the community.

Within Indian vinaya literature, therefore, not only do we observe prohibitions against selling Buddhist religious objects, such statements appear to be closely tied to prohibitions against taking the property belonging to the Three Jewels. In the case of religious objects, a monk could "possess" and/or use certain items that were considered communal or cultic property—as in the case of a Buddhist text—but he could neither appropriate them as his own nor sell them, for they were not considered his property but that of the Buddha, Dharma, or Saṅgha.

The idea that religious objects could not be sold because they were to be considered the property of the Three Jewels is also supported by statements pertaining to the movement and liquidation of property in some early Mahāyāna sūtras. For example, the *Heap of Jewels Sūtra* (*Ratnarāśi Sūtra, 'Phags pa rin po che'i phung po zhes bya ba theg pa chen po'i mdo*), one of the forty-nine texts belonging to the larger *Jewel Peak* (*Ratnakūṭa*) collection of sūtras, explains how an administrative monk must neither combine various types of monastic property nor tamper with the property or assets dedicated or belonging to stūpas. According to this text:

A monk should not think of himself as having power over [*dbang bya ba*] any wealth. And any action that is done, even a small one, must be done in accordance with the advice of the Saṅgha, and not done on one's own. Whatever articles belonging to the local Saṅgha, the Saṅgha of the four directions [*dge 'dun gyi phyogs bzhi*], or the stūpa [*mchod rten*], should be left alone just as they are. [The wealth] of the Saṅgha of the four directions should not be mixed with that of the [local] Saṅgha; neither should the wealth of the local Saṅgha be mixed up with the wealth of the Saṅgha of the four directions. [Similarly], the wealth of local Saṅgha and of the Saṅgha of the four directions must not be combined with the wealth of the stūpa; and the wealth of the stūpa should not be combined with that of the local Saṅgha and of the Saṅgha of the four directions. [But] if the Saṅgha of the four directions becomes impoverished, and if the wealth of the [local] Saṅgha has become great, [then] the administering monk, at a gathering of the monastic assembly, by means of a vote, may transfer the wealth of the local Saṅgha to the Saṅgha of the four directions. Also, in a case where a stūpa for the Tathāgata should fall into ruin, if the wealth of the local Saṅgha and the Saṅgha of the four directions has become large, the administering monk, gathering the entire assembly of monks and then putting it to a vote, says, "This stūpa of the Tathāgata has fallen into ruin. Given that the wealth of the local Saṅgha and the Saṅgha of the four directions has become great, if, venerable ones, you see no harm in this, and if you accept it and grant your consent, I will take a little bit of the wealth from the wealth of the local Saṅgha and the Saṅgha of the four directions to mend this stūpa for the Tathāgata." If the local Saṅgha allows it, that administering monk should do so accordingly. If, however, it is refused by the [local] Saṅgha, that administering monk should repair the stūpa for the Tathāgata, obtaining [the funds] by asking donors and patrons. Kāśyapa, whatever the wealth of the stūpa, even if it becomes abundant, the administering monk must not transfer [*bshugs pa*] it to the local Saṅgha or the Saṅgha of the four directions.[3] Why? Because that which is offered to the stūpa by many faithful and sincere people, even merely a single thread of fabric, [belongs to] the stūpa [that is the property] of the entire world, including the gods. If that is the case, what need is there to say anything about jewels or precious substances [that are also dedicated to the stūpa]. In a case where cloth is offered to the stūpa, even if it has become deteriorated by wind, sun, and rain on that same stūpa for the Tathāgata, the

> cloth that is offered to the stūpa, which is a basis [for merit,] cannot be exchanged for the value of a jewel or [other] precious object. Why so? Because there is no price, not even in the slightest, [that can be placed] on the property of the stūpa, and the stūpa is not a matter for business in any case.[4]

Here, in a continuation of the same argument observed above, a monk is not allowed to sell something that is dedicated to or owned by the stūpa, for that which is so dedicated becomes its property and cannot be sold. Not only were these acts potentially grounds for a monk's expulsion from the monastery, but the outcome of such actions is described as having grave karmic repercussions. In a passage that follows the one presented above, our text goes on to provide us with a clue as to the results of selling stūpa property by describing the consequences for a monk who keeps the property of the monastery for himself:

> Kāśyapa, whatever administering monk collects the wealth of the Saṅgha and having brought it together does not give it [to the monks] from time to time, or if he gives it with an [attitude] of contempt, or if he gives away some of it and [then] does not give some of it away, or if he gives it to certain people, but does not give it to others, that person, on account of those nonvirtuous acts, will be born in the realm of hungry ghosts [*yi dwags*] in that [place] known as "sinking to the knee in mud and excrement" [*rgyag 'jim byin pa nub*]. Having been reborn in that place, he will be made to beg for food from other hungry ghosts. When it is shown to him, at the time it is displayed, he will look at that food with both eyes wide open, and enduring the feeling of suffering that is the pain [caused by] hunger and thirst, will not attain that food again for one thousand years. Even if he obtains that food at some time in the future, it will become vomit and pus and blood.[5]

Statements such as these likely served as a strategy to both preserve the wealth (and perhaps the legitimacy) of the monastery or Saṅgha and strike fear into the hearts of unscrupulous monks.[6]

The notion that Buddhist religious objects ultimately belonged to or were to be considered the property of the Three Jewels is also supported by particular statements surrounding the issue of the theft of monastic property found within the bodhisattva vow literature. For example, within the

Ākāśagarbha Sūtra (*'Phags pa nam mkha'i snying po zhes bya ba theg pa chen po'i mdo*) and Asaṅga's *Bodhisattvabhūmi,* or *Bodhisattva Stages* (*Byang chub sems dpa'i sa*), the theft of the property of the Three Jewels is articulated as a root transgression for an individual who has accepted the bodhisattva vows. In the *Ākāśagarbha Sūtra,* for example, a text which became the primary source for the bodhisattva transgressions in the Tibetan Buddhist tradition, and which may have in fact acted as a source for the *Bodhisattvabhūmi* (Tatz 1986, 30), the theft of monastic property is described as a root transgression for Kṣatriya-rulers, ministers, and beginner bodhisattvas who have accepted the vow. Such a transgression is described as leading to the forfeiture of all accumulated virtue and to rebirth in the lower realms. In the following passage, the Buddha reveals to the bodhisattva Ākāśagarbha and a monastic assembly how the theft of monastic property becomes a root transgression for beginner bodhisattvas:

> Furthermore, son of a noble family, in the future, there will arise servants of the ministers of the kṣatriyas, servants of their state officials, servants of their heroes, and servants of their medical personnel—fools, who, proud of their false skills, are nonetheless rich and exceedingly wealthy. Appearing to engage in many different acts of meritorious giving, having become proud and haughty due to [that] giving, they will cause divisions between kṣatriyas, and cause divisions between monks and kṣatriyas. They will use those kṣatriyas to punish monks by stealing [from them] through [imposing] monetary fines. As a result of that harm, those monks will steal from whatever individual, [local] Saṅgha, Saṅgha of the four directions, or shrine [they can], and, having done that, will offer the gifts to those [servants of ministers etc.] Similarly, those dishonorable ones will present [that] to the kṣatriyas. Both of these [actions] will become root downfalls. This is the seventh root downfall.[7]

Aside from the very interesting context in which the act of theft is said to take place in this passage (one of extortion), here the association between the wealth of the shrine (which we might reasonably assume included religious or "cultic" objects) and its status as monastic property seems clear. Moreover, if the taking of monastic property by bodhisattva-monks in order to pay fines is prohibited and constitutes a root transgression, it follows that the sale of such property by monks or others (an act which would seem to require the theft of property in the first instance) was likely considered to be a kind of stealing of the wealth or property of the Three Jewels and was similarly condemned.

The view that the monastery or the Three Jewels was the sole proprietor of religious wealth and objects is further reinforced by yet another set of issues discussed in the bodhisattva vow literature. In his "Chapter on Ethics" in the *Bodhisattvabhūmi* (*Rnal 'byor spyod pa'i sa las byang chub sems dpa'i sa*), Asaṅga, after laying out what constitutes the breaking of the bodhisattva vows (which includes the theft of monastery property), explains that there are cases when bodhisattvas are obligated to transgress these vows when motivated by a concern for another's welfare. In a discussion of what is and is not considered a fault for a bodhisattva, Asaṅga turns to how a bodhisattva may transgress the vow against theft by stealing monastic property back from those who have taken it for their own enjoyment:

> Thus, a bodhisattva, if he is capable, with the thought of doing benefit and with a mind of compassion, removes those in power, rulers of the kingdom, [those] kings and high officials, those who carry out many nonvirtuous acts on the basis of their position, who set out to do harm to others, who are exceedingly cruel and truly merciless toward sentient beings. A bodhisattva steals back the wealth from bandits and thieves, those who steal the wealth of others, who steal a great deal of wealth of the Saṅgha and stūpa, taking it into their possession, and from those who desire to utilize [this wealth]. Thinking, "the enjoyment of that wealth is not proper when, by that [enjoyment], it only prolongs harm and misfortune for them . . ." he gives [back] what belongs to the Saṅgha to the Saṅgha and what belongs to the stūpa to the stūpa. A bodhisattva individually investigates [monetary] requests [*dgos 'dun*] [made] by park custodians, those who improperly waste the wealth of the stūpa, and those who use it for themselves. Thinking, "it is not proper if this leads to prolonged harm and misfortune for them due to that wrongful enjoyment," he removes those in power. In this way, with respect to that kind of [action], a bodhisattva, while taking what has not been given, does not incur a fault. [Instead], his merit will greatly increase.[8]

While the main purpose of this passage concerns how a bodhisattva (by maintaining a compassionate motivation) may transgress the vow against stealing without incurring fault, it also suggests more broadly that objects associated with the Saṅgha and, specifically, the stūpa, that may be found outside of the monastery and in another's possession, are ultimately objects which are to be considered the property of the Three Jewels and, therefore, should be returned by any (skillful) means.

The above examples, drawn from various early Indian sources, not only condemn the sale of religious goods as a nonvirtuous act, they also strongly imply that Buddhist religious objects are not to be sold because they are, in the end, the property of the monastery or the property of the Three Jewels. Yet, while the textual statements above read as those in which property and ownership rights figure prominently, other early Mahāyāna sūtras articulate similar prohibitions by suggesting, alternatively, that selling objects such as statues, paintings, or texts is an act that is generally considered immoral or one of wrong livelihood.

Condemnations of selling Buddha images that appear to follow this logic may be observed, for example, in the *Mindfulness of the Excellent Teaching Sūtra* (*Smṛtyupasthāna Sūtra*), the original Sanskrit version of which belongs to the Mūlasarvāstivādin school and is believed to date to as early as the first or second centuries CE.[9] The following excerpt from the Tibetan translation made between the eleventh and twelfth centuries criticizes the selling of Buddha images not because such objects constitute monastic or Buddha property but, seemingly, because such an act constitutes a negative desire (*'dod pa*) that is not conducive to progress on the spiritual path. Following a presentation of a verse on desire, and within an explication of the verse's meaning, our author(s) presents the selling of Buddhist images as being one example of despicable desires. Below is a portion of the verse and its gloss:

> Why is desire the worst of defilements? It is because it is a stain that generates deceit. Individuals who are infected with those stains rush headlong into hell. Then, at that time, the Lord Tsuktorchen said this verse:
>
> Anyone who steals another's wealth
> Through business that is deceitful
> Experiences more covetousness,
> Thinking to constantly harm [others].
> In their heart they experience no happiness
> Either day or night.
> Their minds, having been overpowered by desire,

Crave others' wealth.
Those who have this terrible nature
May appear to befriend people
But they actually destroy everyone
Like a terrible poisonous snake.
Men who have come under the influence
Of this terrible desire
Go to hell after they die.
Or to the realm of pretas [. . .][10]

What is the meaning of these [lines]? Intense desires are pointless in every way; they do not accomplish one's needs. In fact, [quite the opposite]: the intense desires of the world act as obstacles to people because they habituate them to [more] intense desires. They also increase. Just as a fire that comes into contact with firewood causes it to flare up, in precisely the same way, whenever intense desire finds wealth, it flares up; it causes one to act with a covetous mind. Hence, those individuals who practice Dharma ought to, with great efforts, destroy intense desires.

[For example, once] the gods gave something to some individuals and, overjoyed, they sold it and used a small portion of the price [that they received for it] to acquire food and drink for the sake of making an offering to ascetics and brahmins. But because it was filled with [so many] special qualities, they had sold something that was actually priceless. [Those to whom they sold it] in turn sold it for four times the original amount, then for eight times, and then for ten times the previous amount. This is an action of despicable people who suffer from inordinate desire.

Another case of inordinate desire involves Dharma preachers who take money for teaching the Dharma [and who do not] dedicate that wealth to the Three Jewels . . .

. . . Another example of a despicable desire is as follows. It involves someone who became a renunciant and then sold a statue of the Lord made from earth, made from ivory, made from wood, or made from silver. Their desire is utterly despicable. They did not dedicate the wealth [they accumulated from selling the image] to the Dharma.

In this way, those [who want to] obtain the transcendental qualities [of an *ārya*] regard intense desires as despicable, blameworthy, and disgusting. Desire [for wealth] is always and perpetually vile [lit. ugly, lacking in any beauty].[11]

By its reference to Dharma preachers and renunciants, the passage above appears to be intended for the monastic community. But what is significant here is that we see direct statements deriding the selling of Buddha images in a manner which appears separate from the idea of selling as a form of misappropriation of Buddha, Dharma, or Saṅgha property (to which, according to the preceding discussion, such images supposedly belong). Rather, the rationale underlying why one should not sell a Buddha image (and use that wealth for oneself) is that the desire for the wealth from the sale of a Buddha image is a negative one, is only the cause for the cultivation of more greed, and is ultimately destructive to one's own spiritual development as a Buddhist practitioner. Furthermore, at a still more basic level, and with respect to the statements made about Dharma preachers who accept money for teaching the Dharma (a whole other issue that is certainly worthy of a separate study), our passage also seems to be condemning those monks who would make selling Buddha images a means of livelihood.

Other passages from the *Lion's Roar of Maitreya Sūtra* (*Maitreyasiṃhanāda Sūtra, Byams pa'i seng ge'i sgra'i mdo*), which according to Schopen may also date from the first or second centuries, condemn the selling of Buddha images more directly as a source of personal income.[12] In one particular passage, the Buddha, in a conversation with his disciple Mahākāśyapa, speaks disapprovingly of monks who would seek to make a living from painting his image:

> Kāśyapa, during the end times, in the final five-hundred-year period [of the Dharma], some monks will appear who have not cultivated their bodies, who have not cultivated their minds, who have not cultivated ethical conduct, and who have not cultivated wisdom. They will paint the image of the Tathāgata on cotton, on walls, and on courtyard fences and, moreover, by doing that, will intend to make their livelihood. That work causes them to become proud and to praise [themselves] and to despise and disparage others.
>
> The Venerable Mahākāśyapa then said to the Lord . . . "Oh Blessed One, didn't you, Lord, say to King Prasenajit [the king of Kosala], 'Having made an image of the Tathāgata, you will generate such and such an amount of merit?'"[13]
>
> The Lord replied, "Kāśyapa, it is like this. It is because King Prasenajit wears the white dress of a householder that I encouraged him to make images of the Tathāgata, so that that [image] may be [an object of] worship for him. But it was only so that it could be used for worship, and not so

> that those objects would lead to satisfying desires—whether for monks' robes, alms food, or some trifling gain. But Kāśyapa, foolish people think to earn their living by that object, thinking, 'I am doing something meaningful,' when, in fact, their action is without any purpose. Kāśyapa, the sons and daughters of the lineage, who only desire merit, if they are encouraged to make the image of the Tathāgata, will create immeasurable merit. Kāśyapa, if it is not proper to sell the bodies of those born as animals, how much more must we condemn those who sell the image of the Tathāgata. But these foolish people, having been encouraged to create images of the Tathāgata, sell them to the hands of laypeople, and by that, intend to make a living. Oh Kāśyapa, it is like this, for example, there are some immature beings who are by nature devoid of wisdom: they refuse nectar and instead eat poison. Kāśyapa, I think that, likewise, whatever fool sets out to create Buddha images for the sake of material gain [*zang zing*] is himself or herself like someone who has ingested poison. Kāśyapa, what is called "poison" in this Dharma-vinaya is that which, obtained, causes foolish people to compete out of anger, to quarrel, fight with, and criticize each other. These individuals, while [on the surface] making offerings to the Tathāgata, are on their way to hell. Kāśyapa, it is like, for example, when men who are unskilled in warfare go into battle, they strike themselves with their own weapons. [In the same way], Kāśyapa, those foolish ones will become hell-beings by means of the excellent Dharma teachings.[14]

In this passage, the creation of Buddha images for the purposes of worship is celebrated as a meritorious act, and those who would create such images for the purposes of making a living are clearly condemned. Moreover, as in the *Mindfulness of the Excellent Teaching Sūtra* above, the denunciation of the sale of Buddha images follows not the logic of property or ownership rights. In this context, the sin of selling the Buddha image is compared to the sin of selling animals, an action that (along with the sale of humans) is portrayed in the Aṅguttara Nikāya, for example, as one of wrong livelihood (Harvey 2000, 188). Concerning why the sale of images should be seen as wrong livelihood, the above passage suggests further that images of the Buddha that were manufactured by monks or laypeople were considered to be "special" or sacred objects and, as such, were to be respected and not to be sold. To use such objects for commercial purposes, according to the text, is like utilizing something intended for spiritual benefit for the sake of worldly benefit, an action, we are told, that brings only harm.

According to Schopen, the *Lion's Roar of Maitreya Sūtra* remained a relatively obscure and unimportant scripture in the Indian context. Furthermore, he argues that because contemporary vinaya sources were very much concerned with image processions and with the donations made from such processions, and because some contemporary inscriptions appear to have, in fact, promoted the cult of images, the argument against selling Buddha images expressed in the *Lion's Roar of Maitreya Sūtra* may indicate a conservative Mahāyāna "polemic" against what may have been a mainstream monastic practice (2005, 65). Moreover, according to Schopen, because monastic involvement with images only increased after the Kushan period (first to third centuries CE), the argument against the sale of Buddha images within the text may be seen as a marginal one. However, these observations notwithstanding, and while the *Lion's Roar of Maitreya Sūtra* itself may have remained relatively unknown in the Indian milieu, the argument against making Buddhist images and texts a source of one's livelihood would become very much a part of textual and popular religious discourse both within the Chinese and Tibetan religious contexts and more than merely a marginal or "conservative" religious view.

CHINESE PROSCRIPTIONS AGAINST SELLING BUDDHIST OBJECTS

In China, proscriptive statements against selling Buddhist objects show up in the textual record as early as the fifth century CE and reflect the same two themes described above. For example, while not influential in Tibet, the *Brahma's Net Sūtra,* or *Brahmajāla Sūtra* (*Fanwang jing*), considered an apocryphal work and a text which served as the primary source for the bodhisattva *prātimokṣa* vows for early Mahāyānists (Hanh 2008, 18), contains statements which indicate that the selling of Buddha images and texts is an infraction against rules pertaining to monastic property.[15] The statement presented in the *Brahma's Net Sūtra* is similar (although with some variation) to Asaṅga's passage from his "Chapter on Ethics" in the *Bodhisattvabhūmi,* in which he describes how a bodhisattva may (by maintaining a compassionate motivation) transgress the vows with respect to theft. However, the statement in the *Brahma's Net Sūtra,* which is located within its forty-eight minor bodhisattva precepts, suggests more definitively that religious objects are to be considered the property of the monastery or of the Three Jewels and therefore should not be sold. Point 31, entitled "Pay ransom and rescue people from their difficulties," reads as follows:

> The Buddha said: "If, in this evil world which exists after the Nirvana of the Buddha, a disciple of the Buddha should see an outsider, a wicked person or a thief selling images of the Buddha, bodhisattvas, or their parents; trading in sutras or books of *vinaya;* or, having sold bhikhsus, bhikhsunis, bodhisattvas who have given rise to the mind of enlightenment, or men of the Way, making them become slaves or the servants of government officials, then with a compassionate mind he must use all possible skilful [*sic*] means in order to rescue them. Wherever one goes one must teach and transform others and try to raise the money needed to redeem the images of the Buddhas and bodhisattvas, and the sutras and *vinaya* texts, and to rescue the bhikshus, bhikshunis, and bodhisattvas who have given rise to the mind of enlightenment. To fail to do so results in breaking a secondary precept and committing a defiling offence." (Batchelor 2004, 75–76)[16]

Here, like Asaṅga's statement above, this minor precept clearly condemns the sale of statues and texts as a negative activity. Moreover, it implies that the reasoning that underlies this criticism is that the rightful owners of *all* Buddha statues and texts found outside the monastery are, in fact, the monastery itself or the Three Jewels. Still other early Chinese Buddhist sources appear to maintain this same rationale with respect to the sale of Buddhist objects. For example, in a similar vein, Erik Zürcher (1995, 7) notes that in the *Sarvāstivādavinayavibhāṣā* (*Sapoduo pini piposha,* T1440), another fifth-century text, we are told that those Buddha statues which are stolen for the purposes of worship do not result in a fault, but those which are stolen for the purposes of sale amount to a sin.[17] Although Zürcher does not speculate as to why the latter acts become sinful, such a statement, being located in a vinaya text and intended for monks, is likely reflective of the aforementioned concerns surrounding the personal appropriation of monastic property and its unauthorized use. That the theft of Buddha images for the purposes of worship is sanctioned also appears closely akin to statements in the bodhisattva vow literature, in which a bodhisattva may transgress the vow against theft in order to return the property of the monastery to the monastery.[18]

While proscriptions against the sale of Buddhist objects and their association with property or ownership rights are indeed represented in early Chinese Buddhist literature, other extant Chinese Buddhist sources appear to reflect our secondary theme, condemning the sale of such objects as either an immoral act or as an improper means of livelihood. For example, several

Chinese Buddhist apocryphal works reveal the existence of this now familiar alternative logic. In a work known as the *Scripture of Maudgalyāyana's Questions about Five Hundred Light and Heavy Sins in the Monastic Discipline* (*Mulian wen jielüzhong wubai qingzhongshi jing,* T1483), a text which, according to Funayama Tōru, may have been derived from a lecture delivered by Vimalākṣa between 412 and 415 shortly before his death (2006, 42–43), the authors frame the sale of Buddha images more broadly as a negative act that is comparable to the selling of one's parents. According to one passage:

> He [Mahāmaudgalyāyana] asked: "What is the sin committed by a *bhikṣu* who sells a Buddha image?" He [Buddha] answered: "It is equal to the sin of selling one's father and mother!" (Zürcher 1995, 8)[19]

While this statement is brief and slightly obscure, here the comparison between selling a Buddha image and selling one's mother and father may be unique to the Chinese context. In this instance, the author(s) compares the sale of a Buddha image to something recognizably immoral in Chinese culture, where the practice of filial piety (*xiao*) is pervasive. In other words, the logic operative in this case appears to be that if one would not commit the (obviously) shameful act of selling one's parents, those who are deserving of high honor and utmost respect, so too must one not sell images of the Buddha, who is also deserving of the same reverence. Alternatively, one may also interpret the underlying rationale of this statement as involving the notion of wrong livelihood. In this case, just as one would not sell one's mother and father—the trafficking in people being a stated form of wrong livelihood—so too must one not sell a Buddha image, which is seen here to be the equivalent to human trafficking. Furthermore, while it may be tempting, given the concern of this text with vinaya rules, to assign this statement to those that reflect matters of monastic property, this same reasoning for not engaging in the sale of Buddha images appears in another Chinese apocryphal text which Zürcher notes for its strict attitude toward selling Buddha images. In a work known as *The Scripture [Spoken by] the Buddha in His Golden Coffin about the Merit of Devotion* (*Fo zai jin guan jing fu jing*), one passage, referring to the artist and citing the fact that the artist will be greatly rewarded with merit, proclaims, "He shall not accept any wages; [if he does], it is like becoming rich by selling his father and mother" (9).[20] Thus, in both of these works, the rationale proscribing the sale of Buddha images appears to have to do with the notion that selling Buddha images is morally reprehensible in its own right, given the status of the Buddha image as a special or sacred object deserving of respect.

Still other Chinese works that contain injunctions against selling Buddha images promote the idea that their sale is a form of wrong livelihood. For example, the *Scripture Solving Points of Doubt Concerning Sin and Merit* (*Zuifu jue yi jing*) forthrightly "threatens those who make images 'for a living' (*jingying*) with terrible karmic punishment" (Zürcher 1995, 9).[21] Similarly, within Chinese Buddhist eschatological literature, the *Book of Resolving Doubts Concerning the Semblance Dharma* (*Foshuo xiangfa jueyi jing*), a mid-sixth-century Chinese apocryphal text which claims to be the Buddha's final sermon (Tokuno 1995, 257), describes the occupation of selling Buddha images as a negative activity and remarks that those who both sell and purchase images will incur demerit:

> Then the World-honored One told the bodhisattva Constant Donor: "Son of good family! In future generations, among the clergy and laity, there will be various wicked people who construct images of me or of bodhisattvas and sell them for profit in order to support themselves. All the clergy and laity, not knowing [what constitutes] merit and demerit, will purchase those images and make offerings to them. Both [those who sell and purchase] images incur demerit [as a result of which] they will be constantly sold by others for as long as five hundred generations." (Tokuno 1995, 267)[22]

Here, the crux of the problem clearly appears to be one of living on the profits from the sale of religious goods or, in other words, making a livelihood of this practice. Furthermore, in what seems to be a unique twist, this text suggests that both those who sell and those who purchase images incur demerit, as (we might assume) both parties are complicit in the commercial transaction. As for the reason the sale of Buddhist images should become a nonvirtuous act or an improper means of livelihood, this passage points implicitly to the special nature of the Buddha image as the rationale underlying these prohibitions. That is, Buddha images (it is suggested) are deserving of respect and are thus not to be submitted to commercial activity.

Finally, Jacques Gernet's (1995) work on the economic history of China from the fifth to the tenth centuries likewise illustrates that trafficking in

Buddhist religious goods was condemned in China not only within religious texts but also in state proclamations on the grounds that selling them constituted a form of improper livelihood. For example, Gernet himself (1995, 25) cites the passage (noted above) from the *Book of Resolving Doubts,* a text which, in contrast to Tokuno, he attributes to the eighth or ninth century and to the Sect of the Three Stages (San Jie Jiao), a group whose teachings were heavily influenced by the notion of the degeneration of Buddhism.[23] Yet, Gernet also notes that particular statements regarding the sale of Buddhist images and scriptures came to circulate at the level of state discourse. From the beginning of the Tang dynasty (618–907), according to Gernet, following a decline in a trend in the construction of monumental Buddha images, both wealthy and common people began to purchase images for use in private home worship, a state of affairs, he implies, which prompted Emperor T'ai-tsung (r. 626–49) to issue a decree prohibiting their sale. According to the decree:

> Families of skilled artisans frequently cast statues. Those wishing to do homage to the Buddha come vying with one another to buy these. They assess by touch the artistry or clumsiness of the work and try to estimate its weight. The buyers are scarcely concerned with accomplishing an act of merit, but only seek to obtain the object at the lowest price. As for the sellers, who from the outset had no other aim but to enrich themselves, they think only of selling as dearly as possible. The accumulation of sins [resulting from this mercantile spirit applied to religious objects] is such that the merit acquired by these acts is reduced to nothing. Since the teachings of the sacred texts are thereby violated, We have decided to prohibit such dealings. From now on, artisans are no longer permitted to fabricate Buddhist or Taoist statues for sale. However, those that have already been completed at the present time shall not be refounded: they are to be distributed to the Buddhist and Taoist monasteries, the communities of which shall pay their price. The administrators of each prefecture and county shall see to the implementation of this order, which is to be carried out within ten days. (Gernet 1995, 24)[24]

In addition, Gernet goes on to cite another, similar decree issued in 714 decrying the selling of these same objects. The decree, as he recounts it, reads:

> It has come to Our attention that shops are opened in the streets where sutra are copied and Buddhist statues are cast in broad daylight. Alcohol and meat are consumed in these places. . . . From now on, in the village streets and markets, it shall be forbidden to do business casting statues and copying sacred texts. (25)[25]

According to Gernet, these proscriptive statements against the sale of Buddhist images and texts, including those within the *Book of Resolving Doubts,* had much to do with attempts at curbing the commercial exploitation of commoners' religious piety. Continuing, he explains that religious fervor had reached such a height during this period that farmers would frequently take to melting down their farm implements in order to cast statues or would even go hungry in an effort to create merit, prompting such a reaction from both the ruling and religious segments of society. However, while it is possible that such statements aimed to quell the exploitation of religious devotion, it should be noted that the appeals to halt these commercial activities do not follow an economic logic but rather a religious one that opposes the submission of Buddhist objects to a commercial environment on religious grounds. In other words, given the preceding discussion, such statements may be better read as a continuation of the religious argument against the sale of Buddhist paraphernalia, one which aims to proscribe the sale of Buddha images and sūtras because making a livelihood from their sale is considered a negative act according to Buddhist teachings themselves. Regardless of the motivation behind the appearance of such proscriptions, the above examples illustrate that in China, both within religious literature and at the level of state discourse, the rationale underlying the proscriptions against selling Buddha images and scriptures often followed a logic in which their sale was seen to be a form of wrong livelihood, an act which violates the special character or status of such objects.

The question of the relationship between the above two proscriptive themes—those which revolve around issues of monastic property or ownership, on the one hand, and those that frame the sale of religious objects as a matter of wrong livelihood or as an otherwise immoral act, on the other—is an interesting one, and further research would undoubtedly shed light on their connection and historical development. It is tempting to conclude that the proscriptions against stealing or selling monastic property or the property of the Three Jewels evolved historically, eventually becoming those in which selling representations of the Three Jewels more broadly (i.e., those which came to circulate outside the confines of the monastery) became similarly prohibited and framed as a sinful act. The affinity shared between the two types of statements as well as the fact that the vinaya literature likely represents the earliest instances of such proscriptions, would seem to indicate the probability of this scenario. However, such a hypothesis also seems to imply that at some historical point all Buddhist images and texts, regardless of whether they were owned by or located within a monastery, came to be conceived of as the inherent property or wealth of the Three Jewels. Moreover, it suggests that the logic which would come to underlie the prohibitions against selling these representations followed this same understanding. Selling religious objects would then become an infraction whereby "one cannot sell what one does not own."[26] Yet, while the association between appropriating monastic property and selling such property indeed shows up in the textual record, the idea that selling *any and all* Buddhist religious objects constitutes the stealing of the wealth or property of the Three Jewels is neither clear nor consistent historically.[27] As we have seen throughout this discussion, the proscriptive statements themselves reveal the existence of another, or second, rationale for prohibiting the sale of religious objects, one which places an emphasis on the problematic nature of earning one's livelihood from their sale or on the idea that selling them constitutes an affront to their special or sacred character. This suggests the existence of a class of objects that maintained an independent status as sacred objects apart from notions of property, and that, for that very reason alone, they were to be respected and were not to be sold. This conclusion seems to be represented most poignantly by the *Lion's Roar of Maitreya Sūtra,* in which selling paintings of the Buddha is clearly framed as a form of wrong livelihood and compared to the improper act of selling animals, and by several articulations of these proscriptions in the Chinese context.

Early textual sources, therefore, seem to suggest the existence of two separate doctrinal issues reflecting two different contexts or social realities. The first appears to be related exclusively to the problem of the theft or the misappropriation (by monks or others) of goods considered the property of the Three Jewels or the actual material property of the monastery. Such statements were presumably aimed at keeping this property both in order and intact and likely sought to protect the reputation of the Saṅgha as an institution, which, by the beginning of the so-called Middle Period (first to fifth or sixth centuries)—as evidenced by the numerous rules and regulations for handling loans, property, and donations in the *Mūlasarvāstivāda vinaya*—had amassed considerable wealth (Schopen 2005). The second doctrinal concern appears to address another problem that arose either simultaneously to these concerns or shortly afterward—that is, the problem of monks, and presumably laypeople, who attempted to make their livelihood from the sale of religious objects. This occurrence, which, following Gernet, may have indeed been driven by a growing trend in the desire for the private ownership of such objects, likely prompted (or required) yet another type of proscriptive statement, only this time one based on a different rationale, one rooted in the notion that peddling in such objects violated their intended purpose and/or their very sacrality; what was to be revered and respected was not to become a mere item of merchandise.

CONCLUSION

The above discussion has illustrated that the proscriptive statements against the sale of Buddhist objects—that such activity was seen as a sinful act with negative consequences—occurred quite early on. Based on evidence from the vinaya literature and on evidence from the *Mindfulness of the Excellent Teaching Sūtra* and the *Lion's Roar of Maitreya Sūtra,* we may be able to date such statements to at least as early as the first or second centuries of the Common Era. In India, these early statements appear to primarily reflect the concerns of monks who, on the one hand, sought to prevent other monks from wrongfully appropriating, stealing, or selling the property of the Three Jewels and, on the other, attempted to prevent the manufacture of religious goods from becoming a means of personal income. In the Chinese context, in particular, it is clear that by the fifth century CE these same concerns were also present, and such prohibitions not only applied to monastics but also to the laity, both those who attempted to make a living from selling religious objects and, in some cases, even those who would seek to purchase them. Thus, by the eighth century, when Buddhism entered Tibet more systematically, owing to the work of the first wave of Indian and Tibetan translators headed by Śāntarakṣita (725–788), we have very clear articulations of two kinds of proscriptions against selling Buddhist objects circulating both in India and in China. It is perhaps no surprise then that we find statements proscribing the sale of statues, paintings, and texts in various genres of Tibetan literature in the centuries that follow. However, although both types of proscriptive statements—those that sought to prohibit the sale of Buddhist objects conceived of as monastic property and those which condemn the sale of such goods as a form of wrong livelihood—came to appear in the Tibetan context, it is the latter reasoning and variations on this particular theme that would become the predominant way in which the prohibitions against selling Buddhist objects were expressed historically in Tibet. Moreover, it is this particular logic that has been continuously invoked by Tibetan scholars for these proscriptive statements on down to the present day.

2 | Selling Buddhist Objects in Tibetan Buddhist Literature

Perhaps the earliest narrative utilized by Tibetans to illustrate the priceless nature of the Buddha image derives from a story about two Indian kings that recalls the creation of the first paintings of the Buddha during the Buddha's own lifetime. In this story King Utrāyaṇa (the king of Roruka, Sgra sgrogs), in a gesture of friendship, gives King Bimbisāra (543–491 BCE), the ruler of Magadha, a precious jewel (or, in some versions of the story, jeweled armor). This gift is determined by Bimbisāra's ministers to be priceless, for not only is it breathtakingly beautiful, it also contains healing properties. Despondent that he could not possibly reciprocate what he perceives to be such a precious gift, Bimbisāra consults the Buddha, who then determines that he should send Utrāyaṇa an image of him—i.e., the Buddha. The artists who try to paint the Buddha are so enraptured by his radiance that they must instead paint from his reflection. Some narratives relate that the artists painted from the Buddha's image as reflected in a pond; others suggest that the Buddha projected his image onto the artists' canvases (Jamgön Kongtrul Lodrö Tayé 2010, 396). Eventually, the paintings are completed, the best one selected, and the gift is given to Utrāyaṇa. According to this story, upon opening his painting, Utrāyaṇa is awestruck, and awakening positive karmic imprints, he perceives the truth and achieves arhatship (i.e., sainthood). While this story has been retold for various purposes within the Tibetan Buddhist tradition, including as a means to illustrate how merely seeing a Buddha image can remove previously accumulated negative karma, one of the fundamental themes of this narrative is the notion that representations of the Buddha are beyond all worldly value. Such is the heritage that Tibet received from India regarding Buddhist sacred objects and the significance of their value, a heritage that shows up repeatedly in statements and stories about Buddhist objects and the issue of their sale within a number of Tibetan literary genres.[1]

Among texts influential in Tibetan Buddhist traditions, statements condemning the sale of religious goods that evoke the sacred and/or priceless nature of Buddhist images (as well as texts) are abundant. A significant amount of the information related to this topic is narrative and anecdotal in nature, while, in contrast, in the stages of the path (*lamrim*) literature, for example, we find systematic treatments of this issue within more formal explications of the refuge precepts (*skyabs 'gro*) and/or preliminary practices (*sngon 'gro*). Specifically, such statements are usually found within descriptions of how one who has taken refuge in the Three Jewels should treat or respect their representations. Taken together, both types of statements—those that are more narrative and those that are more purely doctrinal—reveal the parameters of Tibetans' understanding of this issue. While the proscriptive statements related to the sale of Buddhist religious goods within Tibetan literature are not always consistent on every point, the literature as a whole reveals the widespread existence of these proscriptions across teaching lineages and schools and their remarkable continuity over a period of almost a millennium. The relative continuity of perspectives between disparate Tibetan personalities and different traditions (i.e., that all commentators on this topic seem to agree that selling religious objects for a living is a negative activity) is likely reflective of the fact that these statements are associated with the refuge precepts and thus form part of the ethical foundation of all Tibetan Buddhist practice. It is also likely reflective of the emphasis the Tibetan tradition places on maintaining all of the sets of vows (i.e., the prātimokṣa, bodhisattva, and vajrayāna vows) as "stages of the path," a philosophical synthesis which occurred in Tibet from the eleventh century onward and one that is reflected in the lamrim literature, beginning most notably with Atīśa. One who held the vajrayāna vows was also expected to uphold the trainings associated with the refuge precepts, prātimokṣa vows, and bodhisattva vows. Thus, adherence to the refuge vows, which contain prohibitions against selling religious objects, were as relevant for the unconventional yogi as they were for the scholar-monk.

HAGIOGRAPHY

Within Tibetan hagiographical literature, or *namtar* (*rnam thar*), we find numerous statements attributed to a variety of important religious figures which frame the selling of religious objects as a negative activity. For example, one narrative statement proscribing the sale of religious goods is attributed to Nāropa (956–1041), the former abbot of the great Buddhist university of Nālandā, who would later become a known as a *mahāsiddha* and one of forefathers of the Kagyu school. In a collection of Drigung Kagyu hagiographies by Dorje Dze Ö (Rdo rje mdzes 'od), titled *The Great Biographies of the Kagyu* (*Bka' brgyud kyi rnam thar chen mo*), selling religious texts is described in Nāropa's hagiography as one of the worst actions one can perform.[2] Here, Nāropa's remarks on this topic come when he is asked by a local king about the actions King Aśoka took to remove his negative karma. The following passage contains a verse with several notes, or *chan* (*mchan*), many of which have been included here:

> [The king asked Nāropa], among the Dharma king Aśoka's meritorious acts, which was the greatest? [And Nāropa said], "It was the fact that through a single order he had millions of stūpas built, had millions of the Buddha's relics placed in them, and had them consecrated by millions of arhats; this was the greatest."
>
> "And what are the greatest sins?" [asked the king].
>
> And Lord Nāropa replied, "It is to cause division in the teachings or the community, or to burn them with fire; the fire [that comes] at the end of the eon;[3]
>
> To burn one's own mind with the fire of grasping and fixation [is also a great evil].
>
> To despise or slander the lama [is also a great evil];
>
> [So is] to have no antidotes regarding (mchan: *i.e., to have no restraint regarding*) the Saṅgha's wealth.
>
> Being disputatious (mchan: *that is, causing divisions within the community*) and, with respect to the teachings, (mchan: *eating the ransom payment given for the scriptures*), and allowing the antidotes to degenerate (mchan: *which is a wrong view and definitely results in rebirth in hell*).
>
> You ought to know not to harm others.
>
> (mchan: [*if one does these things, one*] *will be born in hell for a length of time equal to 72,500 eons).*

> [For] those who are realized, those who cannot speak (mchan: *i.e., someone who is mute and deaf*), those who possess a greater objective (mchan: *such as reciting hundreds of scriptures*) or who have no way of being able to accomplish [these things], these are not recognized as faults; and (mchan: *even though they act consciously while they are disrupting the community, they are not reborn in hell, but are said to be burdened with obscurations*). Those who seek refuge (mchan: *if they apologize in the manner of a confession*) and diminish [these sins] (mchan: *engaging in repentance*) will understand the meaning of the unborn always."[4]

While the meritorious actions by King Aśoka enumerated here are obvious exaggerations, and the consequences of wrong actions extreme, this rich passage reveals some very interesting points and distinctions about the sale of religious objects, many of which we find repeated elsewhere within Tibetan literature. First, we see that "eating the ransom" for religious texts (*gsung rab kyi glud zos pa*)—ransom being a common Tibetan euphemism for the payment or donation offered for a religious object—is among those actions which may cause one to be reborn in hell. Hence, we are told that one is not to use the monies offered for scriptures for personal use, and definitely not for food, a key point that becomes central to explanations of these proscriptions by later commentators. Second, the wrongful use of the wealth of the Saṅgha (i.e., having no restraint regarding this wealth) appears to be distinguished from the act of utilizing the money gained from religious scriptures. In short, they appear as two separate offenses. Thus, Nāropa (or rather, the authors here) appear to reinforce the point made above by suggesting that religious texts are not to be sold because of their sacred status and not because they are necessarily considered the property of the Saṅgha. Also intriguing are the final statements, which serve to qualify these negative actions. While the conditions and circumstances mentioned of those who would engage in such activities may lessen the negative consequences of these acts (those who operate under these circumstances are not born in hell), they do not have the power to completely circumvent them, as mental obscurations are still accumulated. Such is the heavy karmic weight that is believed to be associated with selling religious texts that is often described within Tibetan Buddhist literature. Here, according to this passage, even those who are realized, āryas or bodhisattvas, for instance, must experience to some degree the negative consequences of such actions.

We also find related statements in the biography of Machik Labdrön (Ma gcig lab sgron, 1055–1149), the great Tibetan yoginī and chöd practitioner. In hagiographical portions of *Machik's Complete Explanation: Clarifying the Meaning of Chöd* (*Phung po gzan skyur gyi rnam bshad gcod kyi don gsal byed*), her comments are found within prophetic statements about the decline of the Dharma. From a section entitled "Future Deterioration of Religious Ethics," Machik answers questions from a girl named Sönam Gyen and relates her vision of the downfall of the Dharma, which includes comments on the behavior of monks. It is here that Machik describes selling statues as a form of "wrong livelihood":

> Lazily procrastinating their practice of the ten virtues, they will jump at the chance to exert themselves in evil. Thinking that the general wealth of the Saṅgha [belongs to them], they will abscond with it, using it to support [*gsos*] others, evil men and women. Desiring connections and profit for the sake of fame, they will have great zeal for giving away food and wealth. They will sell those who possess yellow robes and ritual objects [i.e., monks, nuns, and tantric priests] as merchandise and hoard the accumulated [wealth]. The prescribed rules of the training will disappear and be abandoned. They will acquire wealth and food from the wrong livelihood [*log 'tsho*] of charging for [*gla*] statues.[5]

In the first portion of this passage, Machik seems to be predicting the fact that monks will sell off the Saṅgha's property in order to gain money so as to ingratiate themselves with (influential?) laypeople, an activity she clearly condemns. However, for Machik, the treatment and sale of statues and robes as common goods (i.e., as merchandise) also constitutes "wrong livelihood." Furthermore, we also see the suggestion, similar to Nāropa's statements above, that living off of the proceeds gained from this activity (here, using the profits for food) is wrong. In other words, this passage suggests that it is unethical to accept or acquire food as a result of the sale of statues. Nevertheless, with Machik's statements, and perhaps even those of Nāropa, we are tempted to assume that these prohibitions applied exclusively to monks and that they extended only to sacred objects that were owned by the Saṅgha or monastery. However, other contemporaneous narratives confirm that they extended to laypersons as well and to Buddhist religious goods outside the monastery more generally.

The life story of Gampopa Sonam Rinchen (Sgam po pa sod nams rin chen,

1079–1153), another forefather of the Kagyu lineage, illustrates that even at the level of lay commerce the treatment of religious goods as merchandise and the practice of living off of the profits thereby gained was considered a sinful activity. In a popular anecdotal story that illustrates this, Gampopa deals briefly with a disciple who had made his living from selling religious objects:

> Once a businessperson became a follower of Gampopa, Milarepa's successor. The trader confessed to Gampopa that for many years he had earned his livelihood by trading in religious statues, scroll paintings, sacred texts, and ritual implements. He was well aware that this type of commerce was not what the Buddha had in mind when he exhorted laypeople to practice "right livelihood." Therefore, the trader asked his teacher how to purify the bad karma associated with such unwholesome activities, which could only hinder him on the path to freedom and enlightenment. (Surya Das 1992, 214)[6]

This statement neither suggests that the goods in question are owned by the Saṅgha or a particular monastery, nor does it suggest that they are believed to have been stolen. Rather, we are left to envision these goods as being simply in circulation, perhaps produced by artisans outside of the monastery. The very act of selling these goods, regardless of their ownership, constitutes a sin and, moreover, a form of wrong livelihood. In response to the seller's question about how he may remove these karmic impurities, Gampopa "advised him to earn *by another means* as much as he had gained by his previous business and then use the profits to build a temple" (Surya Das 1992, 214; emphasis mine). The method of purification prescribed by Gampopa is interesting: the sin, it would seem, can be annulled by performing meritorious actions, in this case by donating legitimately earned money for the sake of religion.[7] Upon the completion of his task, the disciple returns to Gampopa only to complain that now that he has built the temple, he has to work to furnish it, a task that will only take more of his time and energy away from meditation practice. Gampopa responds by telling his disciple that the faithful will provide all of the furnishings for the temple, and he concludes by saying, "If you can sustain an understanding of the dharmatā even for a moment, this will purify a whole mountain of non-virtue" (Stewart 1995, 103). Gampopa's story, in contrast to the comments attributed to Nāropa, illustrates that the negative karma from these actions can indeed be removed.[8]

Still another story about the negative consequences resulting from the sale of religious texts may be found in the biographical material of Jigten Gonpo Rinchen Pel ('Jig rten mgon po rin chen dpal, or Jigten Sumgön, 1143–1217), one of the main disciples of Phagmodrupa and the founder of the Drigung Kagyu lineage. In a biographical sketch of his life, Dan Martin relates how Jigten Gonpo regretfully tells a story of how his father, a Vajrabhairava practitioner and teacher in his own right, once sold his religious texts. Jigten Gonpo would later warn others not to do the same. According to Martin's account:

> Already as a young child, Tsunpa Kyab [one of Jigten Gonpo's earlier names] demonstrated an aptitude for memorization, reading and meditation. It is said that by age eight he had clear visions of deities, and in the following year he started instructing others in meditation. Biographies describe him as the sort of person who simply could not bear to see other beings in distress. Once he found a dog that had nearly died of hunger. No other food being available, Tsunpa Kyab vomited out the contents of his stomach in order to feed it. He was even known to offer massages to lepers. When there was a widespread famine, his father was forced to sell his Vajrabhairava texts in exchange for barley to feed his family. Years later Jikten Gonpo would tell this story with the comment, "Never get married. If you do you will have children, and if you are unable to feed them you will end up selling all your refuges like my father did, since eating is necessary." (2008, par. 2)

In this brief biographical snippet we are told several interesting details with regard to Jigten Gonpo's perception of the sale of religious texts. Not only does he paint the sale of scriptures in negative light, as something to be avoided, he also suggests that the act itself constitutes a breach and relinquishing of one's refuge vows, making the sale of religious texts a particularly non-Buddhist act.

Other *namtars,* or biographies, contain stories about painters and their practices, stories reminiscent of the attitudes toward commercializing paintings found in the *Lion's Roar of Maitreya Sūtra*—that is, that one is not to paint in order to make a living. Janice and David Jackson, for example, in their research on the history of Tibetan thangka painting, find that historically "skilled and famous painters could and sometimes did enrich themselves by peddling their work for the highest possible fees" (1984, 13). Such practices provoked the following comments from the fifteenth-century "mad yogi" Drukpa Künlé ('Brug pa kun legs, 1455–1529):

> As for those painters of deities who are "divinely emanated"—Phooey!
> Their images are shaky and possess neither [correct] shape nor proportions—Phooey!
> Without distinguishing the opening of the eye through color and shading, they open [the eye], shading on the vital life force [*bla'i*] with dark lac dye—Phooey!
> Not thinking of the donation [they receive] as a basis for [generating] virtue,
> They set [the price] at one drey [*bre*] for each deity—Phooey!
> Not refreshing the murals in the temples, they sell for profit thangkas that they doodle—Phooey!
> I have still more meaningless talk of many kinds, [but] I will not speak of them, [even though] I really want to.[9]

While the first few lines of this passage are comments on the poor execution of paintings and the lack of attention to prescribed iconographic measurements, actions which are described in artistic literature as having serious karmic repercussions, here we notice not only a condemnation of setting a price for thangka paintings but also concerns with profiting from their sale. Such critiques were espoused not only by nonartist "crazy yogis," however. The setting of a price for religious goods is also condemned in artistic literature and in other narratives as well.

NONCANONICAL LORE

A similar critique of those who would seek to monetize religious objects is found in the work of the Mongolian scholar/artist Ngawang Khedrup (Ngag dbang mkhas grub, 1779–1838), the abbot of the Hevajra Practice College of Urga (presently Ulaanbaatar). In a text found in his collected works entitled *A Commentary on a Literary Text Composed in the Form of Instructions for Artists* (*Lha 'bri ba'i man ngag lag len du sbyar ba'i gsung rtsom gyi 'grel pa*), Ngawang Khedrup explains why one should never evaluate the price of, or sell, paintings:

> As for the fourth point: It is said that even images of deities which are created for the purpose of child's play should be considered to be the actual body of the Buddha and worthy of worship. When this is so, evaluating the price of an image of a deity is foolish. Who dares to evaluate or [put] a price on a manifest body of compassion, wisdom, and the enlightened mind? The Buddha said, "At the site of one atom, there are as many buddhas and gods as there are atoms in the universe." This means that if, for example, a Buddha image which is created for the sake of play by children is recognized as the body of the actual Buddha and then worshipped, one obtains benefits which are similar to worshipping the Buddha himself. When this is so, those who set the price of an image and then haggle back and forth over this are utterly foolish. This is because [such individuals] have not understood even the refuge precepts. It is images that serve, as it were, as the representatives of the Buddha's corporeal manifestations of knowledge, compassion, and power. What intelligent person would dare—that is, no one would dare—set a price for something like this? It is said that in the space of a single atom, buddhas equal to the number of atoms of the universe can abide and engage in various magical activities, like preaching the Dharma. Because they have obtained such qualities, from the very moment that someone completes a simple drawing of the Buddha, wisdom beings are already residing therein, bringing mounds of blessings. Who then would dare to put a price on such a thing?[10]

This passage provides us with reasons for why one should never set the price of a Buddha image or "haggle" over the price. It has little to do with it being the property of the Three Jewels or with the fact that its sale somehow constitutes the theft of the wealth of their property. Rather, the explanation is overwhelmingly concerned with the sacredness of the image, which contains buddhas in every atom and whose worship is similar to worshiping the Buddha himself. In other words, from this perspective, we are encouraged to see the Buddha image, even those created for the sake of child's play, as the Buddha himself, and for these very reasons it is impossible to set the price of an image of the Buddha. Furthermore, while the karmic repercussions of doing so are not stated, they are implied by the question, "who . . . would dare?" to do such a thing.

The concern over placing a monetary value on representations of the

Buddha is also found in *Blazing Splendor,* the memoirs of Tulku Urgyen Rinpoche (1920–1996). There we find the story of a master named Jamdrak (nineteenth century), who lived in a hollow tree and who was renowned for his knowledge and teaching of Padmasambhava's text *Light of Wisdom* (*Lam rim ye shes snying po*), a *terma,* or treasure, text said to have been concealed by Padmasambhava's consort, Yeshe Tsogyal. As a highly revered teacher who studied with Jamyang Khyentse Wangpo (1820–1892) and Jamgön Kongtrul (1813–1899), Jamdrak would often receive offerings of precious goods, but he paid little attention to their worldly value. Tulku Urgyen recounts the observations of a man named Jokyab, who traveled to see Jamdrak and waited months to receive his teachings on *Light of Wisdom.* The following is an anecdote about the value of a Buddha statue based on Jokyab's observations of an encounter between Jamdrak and the manager of the local monastery:

> During his time with Jamdrak, Jokyab saw many people come to visit, including important lamas and wealthy benefactors. They often gave Jamdrak presents including quite expensive objects and money. Yet the old master was completely free of pretense with regard to these offerings. If an object happened to be beautiful, he would hold it up and say, "Wow, what a lovely little gift! Thank you so much!"
>
> Then, after the person left, regardless of what he had been given, he would simply turn around and toss it into a box behind his seat. Huge chunks of dried meat, chunks of turquoise, sacks of dried cheese, bags of tsampa, priceless pieces of coral—all of it got mixed together. He never looked at an offering twice.
>
> Jokyab noticed that one of the visitors didn't dare to come in. He was a beggar, and it sounded like this wasn't the first time he had come. Instead, he stuck his head in the window. "Eh, Rinpoche! Give me some alms, won't you?"
>
> Each time this beggar came, Jamdrak would reach back, put his hand in the box of offerings and, without looking, grab something and hand it out the window with a loud, "Here you are—enjoy!"
>
> One day, an official from the monastery came by and saw that the beggar had just walked off with an exquisite golden statue. He rushed into the hollow tree and started to complain.
>
> "Rinpoche, you can't just give away things like this. Everything should

be counted and priced first; *then* you can give what is appropriate to someone like that guy."

"Oh dear!" Jamdrak replied, "You want to put a price on the priceless Buddha. I am not able to do that." To which the manager had no reply. (Kunsang and Schmidt 2005, 223–24)

The story of Jamdrak reflects a number of themes found in several traditional Tibetan Buddhist narratives: (1) the value placed on detachment from worldly material goods is reflected in Jamdrak's nonchalant attitude toward his offerings; (2) the polemic against monks who get caught up in business activities and who forget the value of religious practice; (3) the lesson that one should practice nondiscriminatory generosity; (4) the argument against teachers who teach or conduct rituals for money and so make a living from the Dharma; and (5), more specifically, the main point of the story, that one is not able to place a worldly or monetary value on something as priceless as a Buddha statue. Such a position is, in actuality, no different from those articulated by Ngawang Khedrup and Drukpa Künlé and further illustrates the widespread negative attitude toward the commercialization of Buddhist images by vastly different Tibetan religious figures.[11]

A final narrative example, and one of the most famous and often recounted stories utilized by Tibetan teachers to illustrate the heavy karmic weight associated with selling religious goods, concerns Kyergangpa Chökyi Senge (Skyer sgang pa chos kyi seng ge, 1154–1217), a *tertön* (*gter ston*), or treasure revealer, and adept of Avalokiteśvara, who is often listed as the fifth jewel (of seven) in the Shangpa Kagyu teaching lineage.[12] According to one version of the story, one of Kyergangpa's patrons became poor and sold a copy of the *Prajñāpāramitā Sūtra* in one hundred thousand lines. In order to expunge the sin from selling the text, he prepared a lavish meal with the proceeds and invited Kyergangpa and three other monks to partake in it. After consuming the food, Kyergangpa fell violently ill and called upon Avalokiteśvara, who then revealed to him the true reason for his illness as well as a *torma* (*gtor ma*) ritual to remove the bad karma incurred from eating food paid for with the money earned from the sale of a Dharma text. The following account is related by Ngulchu Dharmabhadra (Dngul chu dharma bha dra, 1772–1851) in a ritual text on *drultor* (*brul gtor*), a torma ritual meant for purifying obscurations from the mishandling of religious funds said to have been given directly to Kyergangpa by Avalokiteśvara during his ordeal:[13]

> One evening, while Lama Kyergangpa was staying with the lama [from] Mokchok [Rmog cog], he had a dream of involuntarily eating a pile of shit. While doing so, suddenly, the letter "A" pierced back and forth in [his] stomach. The sharp pains were unbearable. In the morning, a patron from Tölung [Stod lung] had called on the service of four monks headed by Kyergangpa in order to purify [obscurations caused by mishandling the] wealth [*dkor*] [gained] from selling a Dharma book. [But] he [Kyergangpa] did not arrive. Lama Mokchok said, "Now, you should definitely go this once!" And because [the lama] said this, since [Kyergangpa] could not transgress the command [of his teacher], he went [to the patron's house]. He performed the rituals well. He ate, and he became very ill as soon as the monks dispersed. He was at the point of death; medicine and performing healing rituals were of no benefit. Praying to Ārya Avalokiteśvara, at dawn, he appeared directly and said to [Kyergangpa], "Yesterday, that patron [invited] you four spiritual teachers in order to purify the [obscurations caused by mishandling] the wealth from selling scriptures. Since you ate [food] which was bought with the proceeds from selling the Dharma, since you are pure-minded, severe illness has ripened in this lifetime. Your three friends will be born in the Avīci hell [in] their next lives." [Since] Kyergangpa requested a means to recover from his illness in this very life and [to prevent] transmigrating through numerous lower rebirths in [his] next lives, this *drultor* [ritual] was given. He [Kyergangpa] offered [the torma] and [having done so] recovered from [his] illness. This account is based on old documents.[14]

From this narrative we learn several pieces of information which serve to further shape our understanding of how the issue of selling religious goods had come to be articulated by Tibetans. First, we learn that eating food bought and prepared with the money from the sale of a text can ripen into serious illness or can send one to hell, depending on one's level of spiritual maturity.[15] It also reveals the *contagious* nature of the action; that is, even though the person who sells the object is committing the negative act, those who are partaking in the spoils of that act are also at serious risk. Finally, the story reveals (and here recall the statements attributed to Nāropa) that even a highly accomplished master (*siddha*) such as Kyergangpa must experience the effects of his actions, seemingly despite his intention (which was ostensibly to benefit the patron). It is said that while Kyergangpa recovered from his illness in this life as the result of commissioning a *Prajñāpāramitā* text and performing the prescribed torma ritual, the others were reborn in hell in their next lives. Thus, in contrast to the Gampopa story above, the story of Kyergangpa highlights the heavy karmic obscurations that result from this act and their almost inevitable negative consequences.[16]

The above examples reinforce and perpetuate a longstanding and widespread position that selling Buddhist images and texts is to be avoided, is karmically negative and harmful, and (according to some texts) even produces a kind of contagious karmic pollution. Furthermore, we also see that the narrative literature often frames the selling or pawning of these goods as a form of disrespect toward them, as a form of wrong livelihood, and, at least in one case, as an act that may result in the relinquishment of one's refuges. Yet, while these narratives illustrate many of the parameters and consequences of these activities, as well as their potential remedies, the concern with the selling of religious goods became more fully articulated in the path literature. It is within the stages of the path, or lamrim, genre that the most poignant and direct statements against the selling of religious goods are located. More specifically, within this literature, these statements are found in presentations of the refuge precepts and/or preliminary practices, which are understood as the basis for all Buddhist practice. We will now turn to the topic of "going for refuge" (*skyabs 'gro*) and the refuge commitments, which provide further insight into Tibetan attitudes toward selling religious goods.

STAGES OF THE PATH (LAMRIM) LITERATURE—THE REFUGE PRECEPTS

Those who go for refuge to the Three Jewels thereby commit to a number of formal precepts. Refuge (and the precepts this entails) is considered the basis for taking all other vows (e.g., the *prātimokṣa* vows of lay ordination, novice ordination, and full ordination, as well as the bodhisattva and tantric vows; Jamgön Kongtrul Lodrö Tayé 1998, 101). The refuge vows in the Tibetan context are usually taken along with the bodhisattva vows, as the tradition encourages the approach of the Mahāyāna, or Greater Vehicle. Most if not all daily religious practices begin with taking refuge in the Three Jewels and the generation of *bodhicitta* (the aspiration for enlightenment for the benefit of all sentient beings) before proceeding with the main practice. In short, taking refuge wholeheartedly in the Three Jewels is often described as the door or gateway to the teachings and as what distinguishes a person as a Buddhist.[17]

The subject of taking refuge and the refuge vows is a vast topic, and an explication of its various details, details that normally occupy dozens of pages or even entire chapters in texts belonging to the stages of the path literature, would take us too far afield. What most interests us here, however—the precepts that relate to the issue of selling Buddhist religious objects—are located within discussions of the refuge vows under the specific trainings that are prescribed for one who has already taken refuge and refer to how one is to thereafter behave on the path.[18] These trainings are known as the refuge precepts, vows, or commitments pertaining exclusively to refuge and are distinguished from, but understood as prerequisite to, the prātimokṣa precepts. Although the presentation of these trainings vary depending upon the author's school or lineage, generally speaking, part of this advice refers to behaviors that must be rejected and behaviors that must be practiced by the practitioner on the path. More specifically, they include statements that require the practitioner to respect all representations of the Three Jewels. It is precisely in this context that some Tibetan scholars include statements prohibiting the pawning or selling of Buddha images and texts, implying that these are actions that are considered disrespectful.

One important lamrim text that contains statements condemning the pawning and/or selling of images and scriptures within its presentation of the refuge precepts is Tsongkhapa's *Great Treatise on the Stages of the Path to Enlightenment* (*Byang chub lam rim che ba,* or *Lam rim chen mo*), written in the fourteenth century. Here, Tsongkhapa (1357–1419), clarifying his sources for the different sets of refuge vows, categorizes the refuge vows into two parts: (a) how they appear in the *Compendium of Determinations* (*Viniścayasaṃgrahaṇi*) by Asaṅga and (b) how they appear in the oral tradition. He then divides the oral tradition into "special" and "general" precepts and within the special precepts lists three proscriptive precepts (things one must avoid) and three prescriptive precepts (things that one must practice). It is here, under the rubric of special prescriptive precepts that follow the oral tradition, that Tsongkhapa explains the following commitments relating to each of the Three Jewels. According to Tsongkhapa:

> There are three prescriptive precepts. The first is to treat images of the Buddha as objects of reverence—as though they were the Teacher himself—not pointing out their faults regardless of their quality, and not disrespecting them or treating them with contempt by putting them in dishonorable places, *pawning them,* etc. (2000, 194; emphasis mine)

> The second prescriptive precept is never to show disrespect for writings on the teachings, even those composed of as little as four words. Further, you should not pawn volumes of scriptures, treat them as merchandise, place them on the bare ground or in dishonorable places, carry them together with shoes, walk over them, etc. Treat them with respect, as though they were the teaching Jewel itself. (195)
>
> The third prescriptive precept is never to revile or despise members of the community, renunciates, or those who merely possess the symbols of a practitioner of virtue [someone who is dressed as a monk or nun but has no vow]. Nor should you do this to the mere symbols [part of the robes] of these practitioners. Never in any way divide yourself and others into opposing factions and view the others as enemies. Always treat members of the community with respect, as though they were the community jewel itself. (196)[19]

While it was certainly understood, given many of the earlier passages cited, that selling or pawning religious objects was contradictory to one's refuge vows, the statements above, which are based on a short verse from a much older text by Vimalamitra (eighth century) entitled *Six Aspects of Going for Refuge* (*Saḍaṅgaśaraṇagamana*), quite possibly represent the first time the pawning of religious objects is explicitly included among those actions that are considered disrespectful in any explication of the refuge vows.[20] Although earlier scholars (e.g., Atīśa, Gampopa, and Phagmodrupa) writing in the lam-rim genre include discussions of the refuge commitments, not all are as descriptive as regards the ways in which one may show respect or disrespect toward the Three Jewels.[21] However, here in the first two precepts, Tsongkhapa is specific—pawning Buddha images and texts (which may be interpreted here as assigning a monetary value to an image or text, converting them into cash, or putting an image or text up as collateral for a loan) is considered a form of disrespect because such objects are to be seen as the actual Buddha and Dharma Jewel respectively. Not only does Tsongkhapa instruct the practitioner to abide by these precepts, he also paints a rather bleak picture as to the consequences of transgressing them. For example, merely pointing out the faults of Buddhist objects (more precisely those associated with the body, speech, and mind of the Buddha) can result in undesirable rebirths. According to Tsongkhapa,

> *The Kṣudraka Bases of Discipline* (*Vinaya-kṣudraka-vastu*) relates how, after the nirvāṇa of the Teacher Krakuccanda, King Cārumat ordered that a great *stūpa* be built. A workman cursed it twice, exclaiming, "We'll never be able to complete a *stūpa* this huge!" Later, when it was nicely finished, he regretted his curses and used his wages to have a golden bell fashioned and placed on the *stūpa.* As a result, he was reborn as Supriyavat ("Sweet Voice"), with an ugly complexion and a tiny body, but a beautiful voice. Thus, you should never quibble over the quality of images, despise others for using fine materials for images and the like or for making them large, discourage their makers from finishing them, and the like. (2000, 195)[22]

Here, if pointing out the faults of images (or simply having a negative attitude toward them) results in such unfortunate future rebirths (despite feeling regret), we can infer that a behavior such as pawning a Buddha image or text can only bring equal, if not greater, negative consequences.

What is perhaps most significant about Tsongkhapa's presentation of the prescriptive precepts in his *Great Treatise,* however, is the fact that we learn that the pawning of religious objects constitutes a contravention, violation, or a *forsaking* of the refuge vows. Having enumerated a list of the benefits of taking refuge according to the personal instructions, benefits that begin with the statement "you are included among Buddhists," Tsongkhapa lays out the consequences of forsaking the Three Jewels:

> Inevitably you will lose your body, life, and resources. But, if you forsake the three jewels for the sake of these, you will suffer continually throughout many lives. Thus, you should repeatedly vow that whatever happens you will not forsake your refuge—not even mouthing the words in jest. (2000, 206)[23]

Extrapolating from the above precepts then, Tsongkhapa thus seems to be saying here that the pawning and/or selling of the representations of the Three Jewels will not only lead to suffering but is an act that is considered a violation or forsaking of one's refuge precepts. While this association is suggested above in the narrative of Jigten Gonpo Rinchen Pel's father who is said to have sold his refuges as a result of selling a Vajrabhairava text and by the excerpt from the scholar/artist Ngawang Khedrup, Tsongkhapa here appears to make these allusions a concrete, doctrinal fact—pawning religious objects or making such objects items of merchandise is a violation of the very vows that distinguish one as a Buddhist.[24]

Subsequent lamrim works and commentaries on the refuge precepts, as well as texts classified as *lojong* (*blo sbyong*), or mind training, repeat and elaborate the above statements in their own presentations. However, later authors, even modern ones, make little or no exceptions with respect to these commitments. In other words, from Tsongkhapa down to the Fourteenth Dalai Lama, a period of over six hundred years, the general position of these statements appears remarkably consistent and has remained relatively unchanged. We do not find a more relaxed interpretation as the result of, for example, historical events or of modernity (including the events of the Chinese Communist takeover of Tibet in the 1950s). Rather, each author who comments on selling Buddha images and texts as part of their presentation of the refuge precepts reaffirms the traditional perspective that prohibits this activity as a form of livelihood, further qualifying and refining these statements but never relaxing this proscription.

A fuller treatment of this issue, coming several hundred years after Tsongkhapa, is found in a text by Patrül Rinpoche (Dpal sprul rin po che, aka O rgyan 'jigs med chos kyi dbang po, 1808–1887) entitled *The Words of My Perfect Teacher* (*Kun bzang bla ma'i zhal lung*), one of the most significant lamrim works of the Nyingma school. Although written from the Nyingma perspective, Patrül Rinpoche's text has had a profound influence on the Tibetan Buddhist tradition as a whole. In Patrül's scheme, the refuge precepts are treated under the topic of the inner preliminary practices.[25] The following passage is located within a discussion of the three supplementary (refuge) precepts, which are described after an enumeration of the "three things to avoid and three things to accept." Patrül Rinpoche's comments are worth citing in full:

> Nowadays, there are those who consider themselves followers of the Three Jewels, but who do not have the slightest respect for representations of the Jewels. Considering Buddha statues and the scriptures of the Buddha's teachings to be objects of [material] wealth, they sell them off and pawn them. This is called eating the ransom offerings [*sku glud la za ba,* i.e., living off of the ransom offerings given] for the Three Jewels and is a very heavy fault. Furthermore, evaluating [the artistry] of drawn or sculpted images of the Buddha and so forth, saying that they are ugly, except on oc-

casions when one [seeks to] correct their measurements and proportions, is a very severe fault and should be avoided. The volumes of scriptures and texts [should be] raised [up in an elevated place]. Acts such as leaving them uncovered, walking over them, and touching one's fingers to saliva when turning the pages, and so forth, constitute conduct that is disrespectful. All of these actions are exceedingly heavy faults. As the Buddha has stated:

> At the end of five hundred [years],
> I will abide as the body of scriptures,
> Know that I am equivalent to these [teachings]
> And at that time show them respect.[26]

It is a common proverb that one does not place images on top of the words [of the Buddha]. Representations of the Buddha's speech, from among all the representations of the Buddha's body, speech, and mind, demonstrate what is to be adopted and avoided and maintain the continuity of the teachings. Because of that, they are not even slightly different from the actual Buddha and are said, in fact, to be superior.

Furthermore, nowadays, many people do not think the vajra and bell are anything more than temporal necessities. They do not think they are representations of the [Three] Jewels. However, the vajra indicates the five wisdom minds of the Buddha, and on the bell, there exists a representation of a face which, according to the lower tantras, is Vairocana, and according to the higher tantras, indicates Vajradhatvishvarī, aspects of [the Buddha's] body. The syllables appearing on it are actually those invoked by the eight female deities. Moreover [the bell] exemplifies the melodious sound of the Dharma, the Buddha's speech. Thus, they possess all the characteristics of all three representations of the Buddha's body, speech, and mind. In particular, they represent completely all the maṇḍalas of the secret mantra vehicle and are extraordinary *samaya* objects. Since treating them with contempt is a heavy fault, one should be respectful by venerating them always.[27]

Unlike the statements of Tsongkhapa, who merely warns what a practitioner *should* and *should not* do, Patrül Rinpoche's comments appear more direct and specific. The problem, again, is the disrespect afforded to the Three Jewels by treating these representations as ordinary objects to be bought and sold. Like Tsongkhapa, Patrül equates both images and texts with the Buddha himself. While imploring readers not to commit these acts and warning them that such behaviors constitute severe faults, Patrül does not describe the consequences of these actions. However, at least two points stand out from his description. First, Patrül Rinpoche frames the severe fault of selling images and texts (and ritual implements) as one which is known as "eating (or living off of) the ransom offerings" given for representations of the Three Jewels.[28] This statement implies that living on the proceeds or profits gained from selling or pawning religious objects is, in part, what makes this activity negative, a notion which we have seen elsewhere (e.g., in the narratives of Machik Labdrön, Gampopa, Drukpa Künlé, and Kyergangpa). Second, *The Words of My Perfect Teacher* also emphasizes and explains within the refuge precepts that the ritual implements of the bell and *vajra* (*rdo rje dang dril bu*) should be included among those objects worthy of veneration and respect, for they represent the Buddha's body, speech, and mind. Such statements are significant, for among many contemporary merchants in Amdo, a distinction is made between the (negative) act of selling Buddhist images (including statues and thangkas) and scriptures, on the one hand, and selling ritual implements, on the other. The latter is believed by some to be a legitimate business. However, here, Patrül Rinpoche reminds his readers that even these objects, because they represent various sacred characteristics and aspects of the Buddha's body, speech, and mind, are to be shown respect and, we can assume, not sold or treated as merchandise.

We see a further qualification of these statements by Longchen Yeshe Dorje, Kangyur Rinpoche (Klong chen ye shes rdo rje, Bka' 'gyur rin po che, 1897–1975), in his commentary to Jigme Lingpa's *Treasury of Precious Qualities,* entitled *Quintessence of the Three Paths* (*Yon tan mdzod kyi mchan 'grel theg gsum bdud rtsi'i nying khu*). Jigme Lingpa ('Jigs med gling pa, 1729–1798) was one of the most important treasure revealers in Tibet and was believed to have been an incarnation of both Vimalamitra and King Trisong Detsen. His *Treasury of Precious Qualities* (*Yon tan rin po che'i mdzod*), a Nyingma lamrim text written in verse, is considered by the tradition to have been received via direct transmission from Longchenpa (Klong chen rab 'byams pa dri med 'od zer, 1308–1364) in a series of visions at Samyé, Chimpu, in Central Tibet. In a slightly different arrangement of the refuge vows, Jigme Lingpa describes the treatment that should be afforded to Buddha images, texts, and the Saṅgha as a part of the precepts of "causal refuge."[29] In verse 22 of chapter 6 on refuge, he states:

When refuge has been taken in the Buddha, Dharma, Sangha,
Respectively, no honor should be paid to gods
Who, like us, circle in samsara;
We should do no hurt to others, nor befriend those hostile to the Dharma;
With faith we should show reverence to the symbols of the Triple Gem,
And night and day, without forgetting, we should go to them for refuge. (Jigme Lingpa 2010, 57)[30]

Kangyur Rinpoche's commentary then divides this verse into the precepts regarding things to be avoided (the first half of the verse) and the precepts regarding things to be accomplished (the latter half). The following is the gloss provided by Kangyur Rinpoche to the latter portion of Jigme Lingpa's verse:

> One should respect the representations of the Three Jewels, considering them as the actual Jewels. One should abandon selling as merchandise or pawning painted or sculpted images, whether they are of good or poor quality, new or old. This also includes even a single letter of the scriptures, not to mention that [one must abandon] walking over them [i.e., scriptures], directing one's back to them, and smearing them with one's teeth residue. One should avoid scolding not only the general Saṅgha but also those who have poor discipline, and with faith should touch the crown of the head to those who wear the red and gold patched clothing [of monks and nuns]. Setting aside one's forgetfulness and remembering the precious qualities of the Three Jewels from three to six times day and night, or at least once [per day], go for refuge, and introduce this to others.[31]

These statements are obviously similar to those of Tsongkhapa and Patrül Rinpoche and reflect the oral tradition. Yet, interestingly, Kangyur Rinpoche introduces a refinement with respect to selling representations of the Buddha, claiming that there is no difference between selling old and new images. Some Tibetan sellers and artists in post-1980 Tibet believe that selling old (pre-1959) Buddha images is utterly sinful, while selling new images is perfectly acceptable.[32] Part of the reason for this distinction has to do with recent historical events and with the idea that old Buddha images represent "old Tibet"—that is, the society that existed before the Chinese invasion. Selling these images thus represents (for Tibetans who make this distinction) a kind of selling out of Tibetan religious heritage, a further loss to what has already been lost or destroyed. Thus, the sale of older religious objects is considered far more culturally damaging than the sale of newly manufactured ones. Another reason for this distinction has to do with the common Tibetan belief that older images represent and contain the prayers and aspirations of generations of Tibetans and are connected to a particular location, monastery, and/or temple from which they were most likely removed (or stolen). Selling such a precious image is therefore believed by many to be the ultimate insult. On the other hand, newly fashioned images, for these Tibetans, do not contain that history and have not yet been the recipient of prayers and offerings. However, Kangyur Rinpoche's statements here effectively challenge this distinction, one, it might be argued, that was never made until the post-Mao period.[33] According to this perspective, Buddha images and texts, regardless of age, should always be considered representations of their respective Jewels and their sale avoided.[34]

While the above presentations of the refuge precepts represent typical articulations of the concern with the commercialization and general treatment of Buddhist goods, another presentation of these same statements can also be found in the preliminary practices within meditations on refuge. Here, rather than being couched within the proscriptive and prescriptive trainings of refuge (i.e., within the typical list of what to avoid and what to observe), it is assumed that adepts have or will engage in selling statues and texts. One visualizes going for refuge in order to expunge the negative karma already accumulated from these actions in one's current life as well as in one's previous lives.[35] One example of this kind of ritual visualization can be seen in the early nineteenth-century lamrim practice manual entitled *Jorchö, the Six Preparatory Practices Adorning the Buddha's Sublime Doctrine* (*Sbyor ba'i chos drug bya tshul thub bstan lhun po'i mdzes rgyan*) attributed to Ngawang Chöjor (Ngag dbang chos 'byor, eighteenth–nineteenth century).[36] *Jorchö* represents a complete daily recitation and meditation practice manual and is a preliminary ritual meant to be enacted before the meditation on the lamrim. Containing instructions for the three types of individual capacities (small, middling, and great), which is the hallmark of the lamrim genre, it was intended to be used by practitioners of the Geluk school. In the following passage, the practitioner is instructed to visualize the objects of refuge so as to purify the negative karma created by infractions committed against them:

> Reciting, "I go for refuge in the lama" as many times as possible, imagine the blessings of the good qualities and activities of the body, speech, and mind of the lama, which have the essential nature of the body of the Buddha and the lamas who surround him, as five radiant nectars falling continuously, entering the body and mind of yourself and others. All sins and defilements accumulated from beginningless time, particularly those of attacking the guru's body, discounting his speech, disturbing his mind, not believing in him or deprecating him, using his possessions—in short, the sins and defilements associated with the guru, along with sickness or negative influences—are discharged from all of [one's] sense doors and the pores of one's hairs like smoke or liquid charcoal, and go into the gaping, upturned mouth of Yama, the Lord of Death, located beneath the great golden base [of the cosmos]. Furthermore, [imagine] he is satisfied and that you and all other sentient beings come under the protection of the lama. With the exception of some particulars, the refuge [visualization] for each respective [Jewel listed] below, [including] the downpour and purification with the nectars and so forth, should be done in the same way as this.
>
> While reciting, "I take refuge in the Buddha," [imagine] the nectars from the bodies of all the Buddhas [falling] continuously, [entering the body and mind of yourself and others.] All sins and defilements accumulated from beginningless time, in particular, the sins and downfalls of destroying Buddha statues and stūpas, buying and selling statues, analyzing the imperfections of statues, and contradicting the [Buddha's] words [—in short, all the sins and defilements associated with the Buddha, along with sickness or negative influences—are discharged from all of one's sense doors and the pores of one's hairs like smoke or liquid charcoal . . .]
>
> While reciting, "I take refuge in the Dharma," [imagine] the nectars [falling continuously] from the scriptures, [entering the body and mind of yourself and others.] All the sins and defilements dependent upon the Dharma, in particular, those of abandoning the excellent Dharma, buying and selling scriptures, pawning them, placing them on the bare earth, and so forth, [along with sickness or negative influences, are projected from all of one's sense doors and the pores of one's hairs like smoke or liquid charcoal].[37]

Unlike the previous scriptural statements which tend to give the impression that the refuge trainings are somewhat static and removed from the daily life of the practitioner, the refuge meditation highlights the rather prominent role that such ideas played in the context of daily religious practice. The *Jorchö* represents a widespread liturgy that continues to the present day.

In addition, similar concerns with the treatment of the Three Jewels found in the refuge precepts of lamrim texts also appear to have been added to the preliminary practices in later Gelukpa commentaries on the *Seven Points of Mind Training* (*Blo sbyong don bdun ma*), (the preliminaries traditionally being delineated as the first point of the seven points). While *explicit* statements proscribing the selling of representations of the Three Jewels are not a part of the seminal lojong text attributed to Chekawa Yeshe Dorje ('Chad kha pa ye shes rdo rje, 1101–1175) or any of the earlier lojong texts or commentarial literature included in the fifteenth-century anthology known as *Mind Training: The Great Collection* (*Theg pa chen po blo sbyong rgya rtsa*), a subsequent eighteenth-century commentary by Yongzin Yeshe Gyaltsen (Yongs 'dzin ye shes rgyal mtshan, 1713–1793) entitled *Essence of the Seven Points of Mind Training* (*Blo sbyong don bdun ma'i snying bo*) contains a full discussion of the respect to be afforded to the Three Jewels within its section on the preliminaries.[38] According to the text,

> Furthermore, because you have taken refuge in the Buddha, do not seek refuge in worldly deities. Whenever you see a painted or carved body of the Buddha, think "This is an image of the compassionate teacher who liberates us from saṃsāra" and, from the core of your heart, be respectful. Do not be critical of the quality [of an image], place a price or value [on it], or step over it. Do not fall into mistreating [them] at any time. Since you have gone for refuge in the Dharma, renounce all harm toward sentient beings. Do not walk on top of even four words of Dharma or place [texts] on the bare earth. Do not give them to others in return for wealth [i.e., do not sell or pawn them, etc.] In addition to that, do not place any other articles on top of them. Do not carry [texts] together with shoes and do not show them disrespect by smearing them with teeth residue [to mark your place] and so forth. Do not fall into mistreating them at any time.[39]

It is perhaps not surprising that Yongzin Yeshe Gyaltsen, being a Gelukpa scholar trained in the teachings of Tsongkhapa and thus familiar with his presentation of the refuge commitments, should also include these statements in his presentation. Nevertheless, their inclusion here further illustrates how such ideas penetrated important works from leading scholars writing in other literary genres. The belief in the importance of including these particular statements as a part of discussions on the lojong preliminaries does not appear to have waivered over time. An additional contemporary work entitled *Root Text and Commentary on the Seven-Point Mind Training* (*Blo sbyong don bdun ma'i rtsa 'grel*), which makes up volume 7 of a thirty-volume series created to instruct *tulkus* (incarnate lamas) in the People's Republic of China (PRC), contains an almost identical passage to the one cited above.[40] Thus, while earlier lojong literature perhaps took these more extensive explanations of the treatment to be afforded to representations of the Three Jewels as superfluous, the passage above was determined to be important enough by the editorial committee of the series to be included in a modern, standardized presentation of lojong practice.

COMMENTARIES ON THE *GREAT TREATISE ON THE STAGES OF THE PATH TO ENLIGHTENMENT*

While explicit statements condemning the commercialization of religious goods have occurred in major lamrim works and are echoed in lamrim practice manuals as well as in lojong texts, the vast amount of commentarial literature on Tsongkhapa's *Great Treatise* appears to be the primary source for clarification and elaboration on this issue up to the present time. Subsequent lamrim commentaries repeat the overall perspectives of Tsongkhapa. However, the language is often more complex and nuanced, providing further clarification on how these statements were to be understood. For example, the subject is treated in *Liberation in Our Hands* (*Lam rim rnam grol lag bcangs*), the influential commentary to Tsongkhapa's *Great Treatise* by Pabongka Rinpoche Jampa Tenzin Trinley Gyatso (Pha bong kha pa Byams pa bstan 'dzin 'phrin las rgya mtsho, 1878–1941), one of the most famous Gelukpa scholars of the modern era. With Pabongka, the attitude with which one pawns or sells religious goods and the issue of the money earned from this activity and its use appear to become emphasized as determining factors in whether such acts become sinful ones. As with the *Jorchö,* Pabongka's comments are presented within a description of the refuge meditation, which is part of his larger discourse on the six preliminary practices. Here, Pabongka discusses the evil karma associated with selling Buddha images and texts. For example, he states:

> The evil deeds that are related to the Buddhas are [deeds such as] maliciously shedding blood from the body of the Tathāgata, criticizing the

quality of Buddha images, pawning them or buying and selling them *with the idea that they are articles of merchandise,* and maliciously destroying representations of [the Buddha's] mind [such as stūpas]. (Emphasis mine)[41]

Here, we see in Pabongka's statements that the emphasis appears to be on the *way* in which images are pawned or sold (and purchased) and not necessarily on the act itself. Pabongka's language seemingly leaves open the possibility for the legitimate pawning and selling of images (e.g., with the right attitude). However, further glossing his statement, he forecloses on this possibility. Rather than following up this statement by describing a scenario for a legitimate form of exchange or by describing the proper attitude that should be maintained during such a transaction, he instead states:

> Pawning [images] as well as buying and selling them [*nyo tshong byed pa,* i.e., doing business in them] are [activities] that can be seen very often. Such actions must be absolutely avoided.[42]

Thus, while it is suggested that attitude plays a key role, we are nevertheless advised not to engage in the activity (of selling and pawning) altogether. In other words, there is an implicit assumption that pawning or selling images already entails the treatment of images as mere items of merchandise, a negative act.

In Pabongka's comments on evil karma related to the Dharma, he similarly addresses the question of the sale of scriptures. However, here, the issue of the money gained from this activity and its use seems to be central to the accumulation of negative karma:

> The evil deeds that are related to the Dharma are [deeds such as] abandoning the Dharma, treating scriptures as items of merchandise, not respecting the scriptures, and eating the ransom [offering received] for the scriptures [i.e., personal use of money received for scriptures]. These activities are very easy to slip into and are extremely heavy offenses.[43]

On the meaning of his remarks with respect to "eating the ransom" (or the personal use of payment), he states further:

> "To eat the ransom [offering]" means to enjoy or benefit from the money [received] from the sale of scriptures. This is also a very heavy [fault].[44]

Here, we may detect something curious about Pabongka's statement. If one is not supposed to sell scriptures at all, why is there the need to prescribe how one uses the money from their sale? An initial reading of this passage might lead one to believe that Pabongka is, in fact, indirectly supporting the sale of scriptures and is merely concerned with the personal use of the money earned. However, further clarifying this point, he immediately invokes the aforementioned story of Kyergangpa, which illustrates the negative effects of utilizing the payment received from selling scriptures. In Pabongka's commentary, as in Dharmabhadra's ritual text (cited above), Kyergangpa plays the role of innocent bystander who unknowingly consumes a meal paid for with the money his patron earned from selling a copy of the *Prajñāpāramitā Sūtra* and, as a consequence, suffers unbearable pain. Thus, while the language employed here by Pabongka may, in one sense, suggest the condoning of the sale of scriptures, it is far more likely that his statements represent a warning or word of caution, not only against the personal use of the monies gained from directly selling texts oneself—an act that, according to Pabongka, would certainly be considered ethically wrong—but against anyone consciously or even unknowingly enjoying anything (particularly food) paid for from the sale or pawning of scriptures. Thus, it is perhaps safe to assume that, like his comments pertaining to the sale of statues, Pabongka is not condoning the sale of scriptures but providing his readers with good reasons for why one should not sell them in the first place. In short, as in the case of statues, we may understand that selling scriptures should likewise be "absolutely avoided."

Most of the above statements (with the exception of those attributed to Nāropa, who lived in India, and those by Kangyur Rinpoche) were written by authors who lived within a more or less traditional Tibetan cultural and religious context prior to the period of the Cultural Revolution that devastated all aspects of Tibetan life and its religious material culture. The remaining authors that we now discuss have experienced a radically different Tibetan cultural context, one which has witnessed Tibetans undergo unprecedented cultural, economic, and political transformation, and in which the restoration and preservation of traditional Tibetan arts is very much related to the survival of religious *and* economic life. Yet, despite these factors, these authors, most of whom have spent considerable time living in exile, have remained steadfast with respect to the classical position on selling religious goods. Given the unique historical circumstances in Tibet, we might expect to find a reinterpretation or rethinking of this particular issue, such that the trade in religious goods might become an acceptable means of meeting the religious and economic needs of Tibetan Buddhists. But none of the following authors have significantly altered their views from the traditional ones. Rather, what we observe is the continuation of the view that pawning and selling religious goods is a form of wrong livelihood, as well as a growing emphasis on the idea that the personal use of the profits earned from these activities is what makes pawning and selling statues and texts karmically negative.

Of three contemporary commentaries on Tsongkhapa's *Great Treatise,* two express, without qualification, the familiar, rather straightforward view that pawning and selling religious goods such as statues and texts is a form of wrong livelihood that leads to the accumulation of negative karma. This is reflected in the work of the Gelukpa master Shardong Lobzang Shedrub Gyatso (Blo bzang bshad sgrub rgya mtsho, 1922–2001/2002). Shardong Rinpoche studied and practiced at Jakhyung Monastery in Amdo and lived through the Cultural Revolution. Having been labeled a counterrevolutionary, he spent years performing manual labor on a farm but would later go on to teach the first Buddhist studies courses at Qinghai Nationalities University in 1978, when restrictions on religious practice were relaxed under Deng Xiaoping (Arjia 2010, 116). Among his students was Arjia Rinpoche, who later became the abbot of Kumbum Monastery. Having witnessed firsthand the destruction of Tibetan religious life and its subsequent revival, Shardong Rinpoche nevertheless maintains a traditional position toward the issue of selling religious goods despite the changing socioeconomic and religious context. In his work entitled *Adornment to the Intent of the Conqueror Lobzang [Drakpa], a Commentary on the Lamrim Chenmo* (*Lam rim chen mo'i bshad khrid blo bzang rgyal ba'i dgongs rgyan),* we observe his presentation of the refuge precepts as follows:

> Do not disparage a [Buddha] image through claiming it is beautiful or ugly, or made of good or bad materials. Instead, practice according to the advice given in the *Biography of Atīśa* and so on. "Collateral" [*gta' ma*] is something that one gives in return for money that one takes from someone else; this is also called security/pawning. The phrase "and so forth" [in the original text] refers to the fact that one is not allowed to sell such things as scriptures. We have a tradition of selling Dharma texts and images at the time of death. Acts like these are utterly improper. Texts should only be, for

> example, offered to those who are worthy; to treat them as merchandise is very sinful. Nowadays, there are those who count themselves as Buddhists, and who turn images of Buddhas and bodhisattvas and religious scriptures into merchandise and make a lot of profit. Whether they are high or low [in status] this is exceedingly dangerous. (1998–99, 1:490)[45]

What is perhaps most intriguing about Shardong's comments is that they occur well after the implementation of market reforms, the introduction of tourism to many Tibetan areas, and the emergence of the new market for images and texts that filled the vacuum created by the destructive decade of the Cultural Revolution. However, for Shardong Rinpoche, these transformations were not enough to warrant transforming this Buddhist principle.[46]

Another example of this position can be seen in Yangsi Rinpoche's more recent commentary on the *Great Treatise* entitled *Practicing the Path*.[47] Born in Kathmandu in 1968 and educated in India, Yangsi Rinpoche, recognized as the reincarnation of Geshé Ngawang Gendun (Ngag dbang dge 'dun, d. circa 1959), represents a new generation of scholars who have known only life outside of Tibet and who grew up in a market economy. Nevertheless, here, describing the special prescriptive precept requiring one to treat all representations of the Three Jewels with respect, he makes the following statements with regard to the selling the Buddha Jewel:

> Seeing a person selling statues or paintings of buddhas, you may say to yourself that you are not going to purchase anything because that money will become a form of wrong livelihood for this person. It is correct to make this decision in order to prevent this person from accumulating negative karma. On the other hand, you may instead decide to buy the statue or the painting, feeling that it is better off on your altar where you can make offerings to it and accumulate merit than it is sitting in a shop gathering dust. This is also fine. As I mentioned earlier, as long as you have a positive motivation, whatever you decide turns out right, and as long as your motivation is corrupted by negativity or nonvirtue, then whatever you decide will be wrong. Everything is dependent on the quality of your motivation. (2003, 148)

Yangsi Rinpoche's reference to shops that sell Buddha images is obviously drawing on his experience of the modern economic context, either in India or Nepal, or perhaps in the United States, where he currently lives. Many shops in these countries sell Dharma items; something that used to be virtually unknown is now commonplace. Nevertheless, despite the fact that such proscriptions against selling statues developed and were situated historically within a sociocultural and economic context that was entirely different from his own, he considers the selling of images to be a form of wrong livelihood, an action that causes the accumulation of negative karma. In addition, and interestingly, although motivation is mentioned here as a determining factor, it apparently applies only to the buyer and not to the seller. That is, in line with previous perspectives, Yangsi Rinpoche's position on the seller remains rather uncompromising. The seller, it appears, inevitably accumulates negative karma.[48] For the buyer, however, the karmic result is determined by his or her motivation.

In contrast, a third contemporary commentary on Tsongkhapa's *Great Treatise,* while maintaining a similar overall perspective, includes an interesting discussion of the *way* in which religious goods are sold. In his *Steps on the Path to Enlightenment, The Foundational Practices,* Geshé Lhundub Sopa (1923–2014) illustrates the importance of not gaining profit from selling scriptures. Describing how a newly completed canon (Kangyur and Tengyur) was treated with the utmost respect during the ceremony for the reception of the Dalai Lamas, Geshé Sopa explains the reasons for this and why scriptures are not to be sold:

> Scriptures were treated in this way not because they were expensive or beautiful but because they contained the teachings. These teachings are invaluable; you cannot put a price on the explanations you find there. It is through the teachings contained in these texts that sentient beings can be liberated. Losing one is a greater loss than losing millions of jewels. Therefore you should avoid selling volumes of scriptures as ordinary merchandise to make money. Of course, you can buy them at a fair price and later sell them for the same amount that you paid. Or, if you don't need the money, you can give them away to someone who will find them useful. But thinking of them as goods to be bought and sold—and in particular cheating others when you sell them—is called *forsaking the holy Dharma* in the sutras. This will bring you unhappy results in the future. For a little bit of money you give up so much future potential. (Sopa and Patt 2004, 453–54)

Further elaborating on the commitments associated with taking refuge in the Dharma, he later continues his explanation by stating:

> When you go for refuge to the Dharma you should express your esteem for the Dharma in all of its forms: both the Dharma of realization—the path and the cessations—and the scriptures that describe the path. Mindful that you cannot put a price on the explanations that you find in the scriptures, you should honor religious texts and not treat them as ordinary merchandise to sell for profit. (495)

Here, following what was merely suggested by Pabongka Rinpoche, Geshé Sopa, while generally stating that one should not sell scriptures, emphasizes not that one *cannot* sell them, but *how* one sells them. Thinking of them as merchandise and profiting from their sale is forsaking the holy Dharma. However, one can apparently resell scriptures and recoup the money that one spends on buying them without incurring an infraction. Therefore, according to this logic, one could ostensibly operate a not-for-profit enterprise as long as one treated scriptures with respect and resold items at cost. However, any profit gained (and presumably used for one's own livelihood) would be problematic and the act itself karmically negative. It is this perspective—one that represents a fairly significant qualification of the more direct classical perspective—that comes to be reflected in the comments of other contemporary Tibetan Buddhist teachers and which has provided the general governing rationale for many Dharma-related businesses.[49]

STATEMENTS ON SELLING RELIGIOUS GOODS BY OTHER CONTEMPORARY TIBETAN BUDDHIST TEACHERS

A fuller and even more expansive articulation of the ideas presented by Geshé Sopa, which follows this particular rationale with respect to profit, can also be found in the writings of the American-born Tibetan Buddhist nun Venerable Thubten Chodron. In her book *Taming the Mind,* an introductory work on Tibetan Buddhism, Venerable Chodron, within a discussion of the meaning of taking refuge, explains the proper treatment of religious goods and emphasizes the issue of profit when engaging in their sale. However, what is added to the discussion, and which is only implied within Geshé Sopa's remarks, are more specific directives on what one must do with any profits should one acquire them:

> The purpose of Buddha statues is to help us remember the enlightened state and work toward attaining it ourselves. Therefore, we do not use religious objects as collateral for a loan or buy and sell them as someone buys and sells used cars—with the motivation to earn a living. The profit made from selling statues or Dharma books should be used to purchase or produce more Dharma items, not to buy ourselves a good meal or new clothes. (Chodron 2004, 62–63)[50]

Here, in contrast to Geshé Sopa's remarks, which merely emphasize how the *buyer* of scriptures may resell them for the same or lesser amount, Venerable Chodron's statements suggest a kind of businesslike context in which Dharma items are frequently bought and sold. Nevertheless, once again, it is the utilization of the profit earned, and not simply the act of selling, that is framed as the difference and as what determines whether the act results in negative karma. Instead of simply discouraging the activity of selling religious goods altogether in the manner of earlier authors, Venerable Chodron's remarks reflect a workable rationale for a nonprofit business, one which could legitimately function in the service of the propagation of the Dharma without transgressing the refuge precepts.

Not surprisingly, this perspective is echoed by one of Venerable Chodron's primary teachers, Lama Zopa Rinpoche (b. 1946). In a discourse entitled "Advice on Selling Holy Objects," responding to a letter written to him about the sale of prayer wheels, Lama Zopa emphasizes the dangers of selling not only prayer wheels (which contain mantras), but also all holy objects, and of using the profits gained from this activity for personal expenses. He writes:

> Regarding prayer wheels I have some very important advice. First of all the main thing is you should not think that you are selling them. As they are holy objects then if you think you are selling them, thinking that they are just ordinary material, then it is against the refuge precepts. Also the money received from selling holy objects such as prayer wheels can cause very heavy obscurations if it is used for food and so forth. (Zopa 2002)[51]

As with Venerable Chodron's suggestion, Lama Zopa, who is the cofounder of the worldwide Tibetan Buddhist organization Foundation for the Preservation of the Mahāyāna Tradition (FPMT), has stated that the profits earned from the sale of Dharma items should be used specifically for purchasing new Dharma items and for other charitable purposes. In fact, the FPMT website takes this position to its natural conclusion by selling Dharma items through its online store in the context of a not-for-profit business and using the proceeds from the sales for manufacturing new Dharma goods. In a document entitled *Report on Use of Dharma Income for 2007* from their foundation store, the organization is careful to articulate that all income generated by the sale of holy objects is utilized in this prescribed manner. According to this report:

> The main motivation for the FPMT Foundation Store is to make the Dharma available in order to benefit sentient beings. Therefore, while charges may be levied for certain Dharma items that are sold in the Foundation Store, the Buddhist principle that profit should not be made from the sale of Dharma is carefully adhered to in the financial management for the Foundation Store.
>
> Proceeds from sales through the Foundation Store are carefully categorized and calculated to ensure that income from Dharma items is used to make available more Dharma and to further the charitable mission and projects of FPMT Inc. We carefully follow the Buddhist principles for the use of Dharma income and any payments for salaries or food expenses are excluded when calculating the net Dharma proceeds from the Foundation Store. (FPMT 2007)[52]

Thus, FPMT policy makes concrete what had only been suggested by Geshé Sopa and Pabongka Rinpoche: it is not the actual act of selling that is considered negative, but how one sells and, more crucially, how the money is then spent.[53]

Perhaps the most complete elaboration of this approach can be seen in the organization Kechara, founded in Malaysia in 2000 by the Taiwanese-born monk Tsem Tulku (Dga' shar phu khang tshems sprul sku, b. 1965). Tsem Tulku, who studied at Gaden Shartse Monastery in South India, but who grew up in Taiwan and in New Jersey, has embraced the commodification of the Dharma as a kind of *skillful means* (*upāya*) with which to serve his local community, further propagate the Dharma, and serve the poor and those in need. His organization, in addition to making Dharma items available online, has established a total of five retail outlets named Kechara Paradise in malls across Malaysia where people can buy or, as is more appropriately stated on the Kechara website, "invite home" items such as statues, scriptures, and thangkas at fixed prices. According to Tsem Tulku's website, Kechara Paradise outlets "are modern temples, catering for the needs of modern people." Each outlet is conceived of as a miniature temple where people can make offerings to an image consecrated by Tsem Tulku himself. Unlike FPMT, one can also purchase prepriced "puja and blessing packages" for a number of purposes (e.g., bereavement, long life, study, etc.) on the Kechara website, all at the click of a mouse. While Tsem Tulku does not explicitly outline the use of the profits earned by publishing Kechara's financial records in the manner of FPMT, all of the retail activities of Kechara, it is claimed, are done in the spirit of spreading the Buddhist teachings and helping others. According to Kechara's mission statement, all profits are used for charity:

> Kechara Paradise's mission is: To spread Dharma and plant Dharmic seeds to those who are seeking for it; To encourage people in their Dharma practice by providing all the necessities; To help the poor, those less fortunate and the needy from all our proceeds; To serve both the spiritual and non-spiritual customers by providing a retail therapy of beauty and artistry that is authentic to the ethnicity of the Himalayans; To support the age-old traditional artistry and mastery of the Himalayan artisans by making their creations available to all.[54]

Thus, Kechara Paradise presents itself as a nonprofit organization which is sponsored by generous benefactors and staffed by volunteers: "All proceeds go towards Dharma work and to support Kechara's activities including feeding the homeless, upkeep of the Dharma center, and supporting the Sangha of Gaden Monastery in India." Similar statements can be found with respect to Kechara's other ventures which include Kechara Discovery, a travel consultancy which organizes pilgrimages to holy places; Kechara InMotion, a film production house; Kechara Lounge, an information center and lounge near the Boudhanath Stūpa in Kathmandu, Nepal; Kechara Media and Publications; Kechara Oasis, a vegetarian restaurant; and Kechara Saraswati Arts, a Himalayan arts studio in Southeast Asia. While to the casual observer these business activities may appear to be exploiting the Dharma by commercializing it, in essence, by its status as a not-for-profit enterprise, its use of volunteer labor, and its motivation to help others, Kechara appears to be no different than FPMT in its effort to make Dharma items available to practitioners while reinvesting profits in its own Dharma-related activities.[55]

TENZIN GYATSO, THE FOURTEENTH DALAI LAMA

Finally, having surveyed statements from several prominent figures in the Tibetan Buddhist world, both past and present, we conclude this chapter by examining the views of the most authoritative and influential living Tibetan Buddhist figure today, the Fourteenth Dalai Lama (b. 1935). The Dalai Lama has made several statements on this topic that are consistent with other sources concerning the profit earned from the sale of religious goods. His views reflect the modern Tibetan context, one in which the production and dissemination of Tibetan Buddhist material culture has grown exponentially since the 1980s, in response, no doubt, to the previous decades of physical destruction and religious suppression in Tibet as well as to the appeal and spread of Tibetan Buddhism abroad. However, despite his participation in and support for the restoration and preservation of Tibetan arts and literature, his comments on the sale of texts and images still reflect a clear concern for upholding the refuge precepts. While some of his statements include various qualifications similar to those expressed by the authors above (e.g., Geshé Sopa), the Dalai Lama nevertheless maintains the classical perspective that selling religious goods for one's own livelihood is harmful.

In *The Path to Enlightenment*, a discourse given by the Fourteenth Dalai Lama on the lamrim commentary by the Third Dalai Lama, Sonam Gyatso (Bsod nams rgya mtsho 1543–1588), entitled *Essence of Refined Gold* (*Byang chub lam gyi rim pa'i khrid yig gser gyi yang zhun*), his remarks imply the potential dangers of selling scriptures and appear, as do Tsongkhapa's in the *Great Treatise*, within a presentation of the prescriptive refuge precepts related to the proper treatment of texts. He writes,

> The precept to be practiced is to regard all scriptures as being embodiments of the Dharma and to treat them with an according respect. Anyone publishing and selling Dharma scriptures should be careful to do so on the basis of benefit for others and not with thoughts of profit. (Tenzin Gyatso 1995b, 102)

Here, the Dalai Lama's statements do not appear to maintain the position that "one must not sell" but rather reflect an acceptance of the publishing and selling of scriptures as a given reality while emphasizing the importance of *how* one sells and the issue of profit. His comments also appear to be directed toward those individuals and publishers (the word "publishing" being an indication that his statements are directed to the modern context) who are engaged in disseminating and/or preserving the Dharma.[56] While generally in line with what we have already seen, lest these particular statements are interpreted as allowing for the sale of religious goods and the personal use of the income earned, other works by the Dalai Lama provide more definitive remarks. Beyond the fact that one must not have "thoughts of profit," several other of the Dalai Lama's comments state directly that one must not use the income generated by these activities for personal expenses. For example, in *Illuminating the Path to Enlightenment*, the Dalai Lama's commentary on Atīśa's *Lamp for the Path* (*Bodhipathapradīpa*, *Byang chub lam gyi sgron ma*) and Tsongkhapa's *Lines of Experience* (*Lam rim bsdus don*), he frames the activity of selling religious goods as one of wrong livelihood. Wrong livelihoods, he writes, "include killing or abusing sentient beings for a living, *living off of the proceeds* of selling holy objects such as texts, statues and thangkas and so forth" (Tenzin Gyatso 2002, 189n24; emphasis mine). A similar concern with the personal use of profits can also be observed in *Path to Bliss: A Practical Guide to the Stages of Meditation*, a translation of the Dalai Lama's oral teaching on the lamrim text by the First Panchen Lama, Lobsang Chökyi Gyaltsen (Blo bzang chos kyi rgyal mtshan 1570–1662), entitled *Path to Bliss Leading to Omniscience* (*Byang chub lam gyi rim pa'i dmar khrid thams cad mkhyen par bgrod pa'i bde lam*). Here, also within a discussion of taking refuge, he writes, "As a precept of taking refuge, you should never indulge in the business of selling statues and scriptures *for profit*" (Tenzin Gyatso 1991, 123; emphasis mine). A third example of this same injunction is also found in *The Union of Bliss and Emptiness: Teachings on the Practice of Guru Yoga*, an oral commentary on Panchen Lobsang Chökyi Gyaltsen's root text *A Collection of Liturgies to Conduct Offerings to the Gurus* (*Bla ma mchod pa'i cho ga*). In this work, the Dalai Lama's statements are presented in the context of the refuge meditation:

> During all these visualizations of taking refuge, imagine the negativities being purified and especially the negativities committed in relation to the relevant object of refuge. Take, for example, dharma: the negativities of abandoning dharma, putting texts on mattresses or walking over them and

> so forth, and the negativities committed by those who make profit from selling texts and statues and so forth. (Tenzin Gyatso 2009, 49–50)

The issue, again, appears to be one of living on the proceeds from such activities and not the profits themselves.

While the above comments appear cut and dried, other works by the Dalai Lama which include remarks on selling religious goods are not without particular qualifications to these general precepts. In *Stages of Meditation* (*Bhāvanākrama, Goms pa'i rim pa*), his commentary on the root text by Kamalaśīla (713–763), he appears to make exceptions to selling religious goods if the selling party maintains a sincere motivation to spread the Dharma:

> When people treat scriptures and statues or photos of Buddhas as commercial items and do business with them for personal gain, it is wrong livelihood. It is certainly unwholesome and has serious negative consequences. On the other hand, when people work to publish scriptural texts, make statues, and so forth, in order to propagate the Buddha's doctrine, it is a different matter. In such cases, when individuals are motivated to help those in need of such religious support, they are engaged in wholesome activities. (Tenzin Gyatso 2001, 104–5)

While the first portions of this passage are what we might expect given the Dalai Lama's other statements, his latter remarks seem to coincide with the logic provided by Lama Zopa for the work of FPMT, or even the work of such enterprises as the Buddhist Digital Resource Center (BDRC), which, through private donations and public grants, has digitized thousands of Tibetan scriptures and made them available to the public online. Both of these entities are registered nonprofit organizations. Likewise, these statements also seem to acknowledge those Tibetan artists who, by adhering to prescribed iconography and religious protocols, are indeed, according to classical texts, engaging in merit-making activities. At the same time, these particular statements tend to leave open the possibility for publishers and individuals to claim they have a genuine, positive motivation while also making a profit. Clarifying this, other passages in the writings of the Dalai Lama make it clear that transforming these activities into a business for personal income, even when the intentions are good, is considered harmful. In his *Commentary on the Thirty-Seven Practices of a Bodhisattva*, an oral commentary on mind training based on the text called *Thirty-Seven Practices of the Bodhisattvas* (*Rgyal sras lag len so bdun ma*) by Gyalsay Thogmey Zangpo (Rgyal sras thogs med bzang po, 1295–1369), he delivers a stern warning to both those who deal in the market for Tibetan antiquities and those who would attempt to publish scriptures for their own livelihood. Furthermore, clearing away any misunderstanding of how scriptures should be sold, he describes a scenario for how this might be accomplished:

> Nowadays some people trade in images and spiritual texts. These traders will reap heavy penalties in terms of negativities and obstacles if the images and texts they are selling belonged to people who believe in and practise the Dharma. Buying and selling antique images of Buddha and ritual objects for a great deal of money may increase their material possessions, but actually their acts are the same as eating poison.
>
> It is a different case if someone, with a resolute intention to preserve the continuity of the teachings through printing rare texts, takes out a loan for the printing and sells the texts for enough money to cover costs and to print more texts. This is money borrowed and spent in pursuit of wholesome work. But those who sell texts and claim to be serving the Dharma, whereas in reality they are serving their stomachs, are involved in dangerous activity—so be sure not to do such things. (Tenzin Gyatso 1995a, 64)[57]

While the first portion of this passage suggests that a distinction should be made between selling older, antique images and texts, on the one hand, and newly manufactured ones, on the other, given the Dalai Lama's previous statements with respect to profit and wrong livelihood, this is probably not the case. Rather, the Dalai Lama here is most likely drawing on this example in order to illustrate the blatant mistreatment of these objects as merchandise, the art market being seen as the epitome of this activity. More importantly, we can see in the last portion of this passage that the purpose of his comments is to describe an acceptable means of selling. And here we observe that the Dalai Lama's position is consistent with his other statements; it is acceptable to sell religious scriptures as long as that money is utilized for the production and printing of more texts and not for one's personal income.

According to Geshé Lhakdor, the director of the Library of Tibetan Works and Archives in Dharamsala, India, the Dalai Lama has made frequent public statements on this topic at the Kālacakra (Dus kyi 'khor lo) initiations attended by thousands. According to Lhakdor, "I have heard His Holiness say many times that selling sacred objects like images, scriptures, etc., for making profit is very wrong. However, [if] these things are sold not for making profit, but for making them available continuously, then it is fine" (personal communication, March 3, 2011).[58] The Dalai Lama has also stated publicly that he does not accept personal payment for his teachings, explaining that all of the proceeds go to event organizers and to charitable organizations. In 2010, I witnessed a public accounting for all expenditures and profits at the conclusion of a public talk given by the Dalai Lama at the University of California, Santa Barbara. This was done at the Dalai Lama's insistence (and something that is apparently done regularly) in order to fully disclose how much money was spent on the event and where the profits will be distributed. Presumably, it was also to reveal that the money would not be used for personal expenses.

Based on the above statements by the Dalai Lama, we may therefore conclude that his comments are very much in keeping with classical perspectives on selling religious goods. The personal use of profit gained from these activities is considered karmically negative, while at the level of the publisher or organization it is best for that organization to operate with a motivation to help others and/or to propagate the Dharma as a not-for-profit enterprise.[59]

CONCLUSION

The statements which prohibit the sale of religious goods—as they appear both in narrative form within various genres of Tibetan literature and as they appear in the refuge precepts and preliminary practices from Tsongkhapa forward—reveal that the concern for selling religious goods in Tibet was not only widespread (spanning centuries, different schools, and disparate figures) but also remains an important contemporary religious issue. The logic consistently underlying why religious goods are not to be sold, rather than having to do with the fact that they belong to or are the inherent property of the Three Jewels, instead reflects an idea already present in early Indian texts: that selling these objects constitutes a form of mistreatment of them, disrespect toward them, and/or an act of wrong livelihood. According to this perspective, these representations are invaluable because they are believed to represent the actual Buddha, the teacher who taught the law, and the actual Dharma, the teaching, which can lead one to enlightenment. As such, and according to the textual record, representations of the Three Jewels are to be considered worthy of respect, and for this reason they should not be pawned or sold or thought of as a source of livelihood.

Whereas early Tibetan articulations of the proscriptive statements against the sale of religious objects tend to strictly describe pawning or selling such objects as more or less negative, as a form of wrong livelihood, and as an action to be generally avoided, from Pabongka Rinpoche forward, we begin to see, in some discussions, the presence of further qualifications. For example, the language begins to shift toward *how* one sells and, increasingly, to the issue of selling for profit. Crucially, the personal use of that profit, especially for salary or food, while present as a concern in earlier articulations, appears to take on a new, more explicit emphasis. Furthermore, among contemporary scholars, ideas surrounding the appropriate use of the profits gained from selling religious objects (e.g., that they should only be used specifically for such things as the creation of more Dharma goods, or that these activities should be done only in order to further propagate the Dharma) also appear. It is possible that these emphases among more contemporary commentators represent an accommodation for the propagation of the Dharma that is directly related to the modern cultural context in which Tibetans found themselves in the post-Mao era at the end of the Cultural Revolution—amidst the profound loss of their religious material culture and the challenge of reestablishing Tibetan Buddhism at home and in exile. Such a challenge, coupled with the transformation from a mostly barter economy to a market economy, likely required a shift in rhetoric, which allowed for the "sale" of religious goods within a new economic context but was in keeping with the refuge precepts (i.e., that one maintain the idea not to use the profits for personal benefit).[60] This scenario notwithstanding, and despite what appears to be some innovation within more modern articulations of these ideas, what seems clear from the above discussion is that selling Buddhist religious goods and living off of the proceeds has never been viewed as an acceptable practice, but a sinful one.[61]

It is also important to point out that the issue of whether or not a receptacle of the body, speech, or mind of the Buddha has undergone the ritual of consecration (*rab tu gnas pa*), the process through which a statue or image of a buddha, for example, is enlivened with the presence of the deity, does not show up in the textual record as a reason for why Buddhist objects are not to be sold. Such an absence of any mention of this process within the above proscriptions is notable since the presence of a deity seems like an important possible argument for why religious objects should not become items of merchandise. It could of course be argued that the religious objects under discussion in the above excerpts were assumed to have already received consecration, thereby making such an explicit distinction between objects that are consecrated and unconsecrated irrelevant. However, given that none of the preceding historical figures mention the ritual of consecration as being crucial to the issue of the sale or pawning of such goods, and given that even the modern Tibetan Buddhist scholars who do discuss the legitimate sale of Buddhist objects emphasize the danger of the personal use of any profits thereby gained, making no mention of the idea that selling unconsecrated images is a legitimate practice, it seems highly unlikely that the question of whether an image is consecrated or not was ever meant to play a role in this issue. While it is true that some Tibetans today justify the selling of religious objects by appealing to the idea that they are unconsecrated, such a view does not appear to be based on doctrinal norms as they have been outlined in this chapter. Based on the above perspectives, the issue at stake is not whether one can sell an unconsecrated image or not but rather, and more broadly, whether religious objects consecrated or unconsecrated, should become a source of livelihood.

The idea that religious objects were not to be pawned or sold and that selling them was considered a form of wrong livelihood with negative karmic consequences, indeed, had a particular influence on the overall manner in which these objects were exchanged in Tibet throughout history. In the next chapter, in order to more adequately understand the transformations that the exchange in these goods have undergone in the post-Mao era, it will be shown that transactions involving Buddhist religious goods in Tibet took place primarily according to prescribed religious protocols, ones centered around merit creation for both the artist and the patron.

3 | The Exchange of Buddhist Objects in Tibet up to the Cultural Revolution

> In looking at the social life of commodities in any given society or period, part of the anthropological challenge is to define the relevant and customary paths so that the logic of diversions can properly and relationally be understood.
>
> —Arjun Appadurai, *The Social Life of Things*

Arjun Appadurai, in *The Social Life of Things* (1986), claims that commodities can be defined and interpreted as primarily social in nature. They have a life of their own, are born and regulated under particular social conditions, and live a processual existence, having the ability to move in and out of a commodity phase. According to this view, objects circulate within societies according to the meanings and values ascribed to them by that society. Some objects may be restricted or "enclaved" from commodification, while other objects are not.[1] Any diversion of things from their specified, regulated paths—or what we can call normal or socially sanctioned paths—"is always a sign of creativity or crisis, whether aesthetic or economic" (26). Furthermore, according to Appadurai, it is *politics* (which might be interpreted here as the power to determine the circumstances of commodification) that is the link between what he calls "regimes of value" (differing value systems) and specific flows of commodities—that is, whether an object enters the commodity sphere and the details of this, including duration, frequency, and so on (57).

The first part of Appadurai's theory tells us something about how the exchange of Buddhist religious goods in differing sociocultural and historical contexts might have taken place. Indeed, in China and India, for example, recent scholarship suggests that Buddhist images and texts acquired a commodity status during various historical periods. Tansen Sen's *Buddhism, Diplomacy, and Trade* (2003), describing the Buddhism-related commerce that occurred between India and China during the eleventh and thirteenth centuries, suggests that the vast amounts of Buddhist paraphernalia brought from India to China were indeed "religious commodities," the sale of which financially benefited merchants as well as Indian monasteries. In addition, as we have already seen, Jacques Gernet's (1995) work on the relationship between Buddhism and commercial life during the Tang dynasty in China notes the existence of a bustling market in Buddhist religious goods and their open manufacture and sale on the street, an occurrence which later gave rise to an imperial decree outlawing such practices.

While it may indeed have been the case that certain historical periods in China and India became accustomed to the regular commodification of Buddhist objects, this same process does not appear to have occurred historically among Tibetans prior to the Cultural Revolution (1966–76). This event clearly counts as what Appadurai calls a major political and cultural crisis (the latter portion of his theory). It is also one that would change the course of the exchange in religious objects in Tibet. The decade-long Cultural Revolution acted as the "diversion" which, while virtually destroying and emptying Tibet of its religious goods and bringing an end to all new production of religious objects, would dramatically increase the commodification of Tibetan Buddhist objects outside of Tibet in a manner unprecedented. The following historical sketch suggests that up to this tumultuous period, the commodification of Tibetan Buddhist images (statues and thangkas) and texts was neither a widespread practice nor a normative or socially sanctioned one. As will be shown, Buddhist images and texts before this period predominantly followed a pattern of exchange based on commission that was conditioned by and regulated according to specific cultural and religious norms, ones that were actually intended to prevent their commodification. Although Tibetans did sometimes sell these objects in the marketplace, those individuals who participated in making their livelihood from this activity were routinely criticized and marginalized in Tibetan society. In this chapter, we will first examine the exchange of Buddhist images in Tibet before briefly looking at the exchange of religious texts.

THE EXCHANGE OF BUDDHIST IMAGES IN TIBET UP TO THE CULTURAL REVOLUTION

Much has been written about the role that the commissioning of Buddhist images plays in Tibetan culture, for example, its function as a vehicle in personal, familial, and communal merit creation. In addition, numerous artistic manuals, a number of which are located in the portion of the Tibetan canon known as the Tengyur, detail the proper construction and consecration of images. However, there is very little substantive historical information available in Tibetan with regard to the actual exchange of these objects—that is, what took place between the patron and artisan, the nature of this relationship, or how compensation took place. We know that, prior to the Cultural Revolution, Tibet contained over six thousand Buddhist monasteries, which were home to countless images and texts. We may therefore assume that there was a steady process of economic exchange surrounding the creation of Buddhist images at least in Tibet's busiest population centers. But just *how* did this exchange take place? For these answers it is perhaps best to turn first to the relevant texts which detail the creation of images, for these contain at least some clues about the roles and expectations governing patrons and artists and how, at least ideally, these transactions were to occur. Understanding the ideal-typical picture puts us in better position to determine the degree to which these ideals were fulfilled.[2]

Throughout most of the Buddhist world and from the earliest of times, commissioning a Buddha image was viewed as a form of merit making, and Tibet was no exception. Numerous authoritative religious texts influencing the development of Tibetan Buddhism encouraged this practice. For example, Nāgārjuna proclaims in his *Accumulations for Enlightenment* (*Bodhisaṁbhāraka*) that one should "cast statues of the Buddha sitting upright on exquisite lotus blossoms" (Lindtner 1997, 142). In Śāntideva's *Compendium of Training* (*Śikṣāsamuccaya, Bslab pa kun las btus pa*) the commissioning of images is one of the six activities that are an antidote to nonvirtuous actions (Bendall and Rouse 1971, 169).[3] In addition, the commissioning of images is sometimes prescribed for specific purposes in Tibetan literature. For example, in the popular autobiography of Shabkar Tsogdruk Rangdrol (Zhabs dkar tshogs drug rang grol, 1781–1851), Shabkar calls upon the people of

Rebkong to commission images for their own protection. According to this text:

> To stop theft and banditry in Upper Rekong
> And fighting in Lower Rekong
> Everyone should commission paintings of the Blissful Buddhafield,
> Erect statues of the great Compassionate One, Avalokiteshvara,
> And recite the quintessential six-syllable mantra. (2001, 208)

The creation of images was seen to bring merit not only to the patron but also to the artisan. According to the *Verses of Selgyal* (*Gsal rgyal gyi tshigs bcad*):

> Whoever portrays the form of the Victorious One
> Shall achieve an attractive and beautiful body,
> Control of the senses, erudition, sunlike radiance,
> And will be held to be lovely in the world's eye.[4]

The idea that the artist who makes a Buddha image accrues enormous merit has been repeated in modern times. The late Master Pempa Dorjee (1930–2011), who fled Tibet during the Chinese invasion in the 1950s and who was responsible for training generations of new artists at the Norbulingka Institute in Dharamsala up until his death, has stated,

> A statue of no proportions cannot instigate worship from anyone. It will just distract them and be turning off to them. The instigation of such a reaction is a boundless sin. More merit is earned by serving a single monk than by bestowing the five gratifications upon every sentient being. Serving a *bhikṣu*, then earns one more merit than serving a single monk. Serving a holder of the sacred mantra Vajrayāna earns one even more merit. But above all, the creation of the perfect Buddhist statue brings its creator the highest level of merit. (Pempa Dorjee 2011, at 4:48–5:41)

Based on the fact that Pempa Dorjee has taught dozens of artists while living in exile and on the fact that such sentiments were repeated by almost all contemporary artists during my own fieldwork, it is safe to say that such moral attributions are alive and well.

There also exist texts that speak of the proper attitude that the artist and patron should maintain when engaging in transactions. Gega Lama (1931–1996), the master thangka painter of the Karma Gardri school and author of the modern classic *Principles of Tibetan Art*, summarizing various early sources, writes of the artist:

> It is also blameworthy for an artist to be at odds with his patrons, or to exploit a good relationship with them in order to secure personal gain. Any of the following traits are considered shortcomings in an artist's character: being harsh-spoken of [or?] taciturn; coveting others' wealth; demanding remuneration and charging exorbitant fees, even to the point of stealing out of insatiable greed . . .
>
> Regarding an artist's worthy qualities . . . An artist should be of restrained disposition, with respect for the divine he portrays; compassionate and patient in the face of hard working conditions and criticism; skilled in the arts, yet without vanity regarding his skill; slow to anger and suspicion, and with little concern for the wealth and substance of others. He should follow his patron's instructions without deceit. (1983, 57)[5]

Of the patron, in a similar vein, he writes:

> A good patron of the arts by definition understands the value of spiritual principles, and especially understands the importance and function of whatever project he undertakes to sponsor. He will also appreciate the necessity and benefits of whatever wealth is donated to spiritual works of art. He will have great faith and respect in the divinities, and will honour and admire the artist portraying them. No amount of delay will disappoint his strong intent, and he will be very generous in furnishing the necessary supplies for the work. Being easy-going and soft-spoken, he will not begrudge the artist's taking pains with his work; and will not cheat the artist of his due, but will fulfil [*sic*] all his obligations as patron. (1983, 60)

Unlike the behavior associated with the exchange of more mundane commodities in Tibet, in which haggling was a significant feature, instructions such as these undoubtedly served as reminders not only of the attitudes and behavior to be upheld by both parties during such transactions but also of the special nature of religious objects.

Other Tibetan textual sources reinforce this picture of the proper patron/artist relationship and prescribe ways in which to compensate the artist. For example, *The Brief Tantra of Consecration* (*Supratiṣṭhatantra, Rab tu gnas pa mdor bsdus pa'i rgyud*), which was translated into Tibetan in the twelfth century, comments on the proper character and behavior of both the artist and patron of the arts and on the necessity of providing the artist with remuneration:

> Later on, [the patron] makes offerings to the craftsmen with all kinds of ornaments. He should even make offerings to others who assist them. . . . [The patron] should offer the finest of gifts—cattle, horses, wagons, and riches—Furthermore, [the patron], with sincerity, should offer all kinds of resources to [the artist].[6]

Similarly, another source, *A Treatise on the Iconographical Proportions of the Buddha* (*Bde bar gshegs pa'i sku gzugs kyi tshad kyi rab tu byed pa yid bzhin nor bu*) by Menla Dhondrup (Sman bla don grub, b. 1675), speaks of the generous offerings that are to be made to the artist while framing the patron/artist relationship in more spiritual terms:

> Those who are completely altruistic, of utterly wholesome body, who have a sense of decency, are clothed with modesty, are endowed with ornaments, and who have faith and generosity, should honor the artist with a wealth of offerings as if he and the deity were inseparable.[7]

Similar to the guidelines presented by Gega Lama above, such prescriptions were likely intended to reinforce the notion that the act of commissioning an artist was ideally a religious or spiritual matter and, at the same time, to ensure that artists were handsomely recompensed for their services.

Furthermore, similar moral guidelines, albeit from the artist's perspective, can be seen in the work of the aforementioned Mongolian scholar Ngawang Khedrup, who wrote extensively on the proper motivation and ethics of artists engaged in making images. In the same text introduced in the previous chapter, *A Commentary on a Literary Text Composed in the Form of Instructions for Artists*, Ngawang Khedrup draws upon a work written in verse by his teacher Kachen Lama Sherab (Dka' chen bla ma shes rab). Part of Ngawang

Khedrup's commentary explains the appropriate attitude to be maintained by the artist in the context of receiving offerings. Here is Kachen Lama Sherab's verse followed by Ngawang Khedrup's commentary:

> When the offering is large, the goal of both [patron and artist] is
> fulfilled.
> When the offering is small, nonetheless hold [the patron] dear,
> and meditate on joy [while thinking], "What a great thing the patron,
> the spiritual friend, [has done] by inciting me to [practice] virtue."

> If a large offering should be forthcoming, the patron accumulates extensive merit. And since the image maker [also] obtains great wealth, a great purpose for both the artist and the patron is fulfilled. Even if one is offered nothing but a small offering for constructing [an image], do not be unhappy. Hold him dear to you and meditate on joy, thinking, "This is good. It's all right that the spiritual friend, my patron, has not given me a large offering. Having set me on the path of the virtue [involved] in painting such a fine image, he has allowed me to accumulate extensive merit. This is really great! He has shown me great kindness." This is [the meaning of the verse.][8]

As in some of the previous accounts, this verse and commentary reflect the idea that exchanges between the patron and the artist were sites for the accumulation of merit. Furthermore, they reflect the idea that the payment to the artist was based on voluntary offerings in which it was the patron, and not the artist, who determined the extent of what was given.

It is possible that the rules governing such exchanges are rooted in much earlier Indian Buddhist texts, those which contained details about the creation of the Buddhist art form of painting known as the *paṭa*, recognized as the precursor to the Newari *paubha* and the Tibetan *thangka*. According to Matthew Kapstein's analysis of *The Fundamental Ritual Ordinance of Mañjuśrī* (*Mañjuśrīmūlakalpa* or *MMK*), "the paradigms governing the production of Tibetan religious art appear to accord very well with those that may be derived from the *MMK*" (1995, 257). Both Kapstein and, later, Glenn Wallis (2002) point out that this seventh-century Buddhist ritual manual not only contained prescriptions for the proper ritual construction of the *paṭa* but also instructions which discouraged bartering for images, implying that the *paṭa* was to be set apart from all other valuable objects. The Tibetan translation of the *MMK*, *The Root Tantra of Mañjuśrī* (*'Phags pa 'jam dpal gyi rtsa ba'i rgyud*), after describing the attributes to be sought in the weaver of cloth (for the painting), comments on the manner in which the exchange for the cloth should take place:

> One who desires *siddhi* [i.e., yogic accomplishment] should seek for this purpose a weaver of excellent cloth, one who is friendly, of good family, one who is praised, intelligent, and who is exceedingly skilled in crafts. One should request a good weaver of cloth who is particularly outstanding in every way. As the craftsmen say, "The best [craftsmen] will produce the best [crafts], middling ones will produce mediocre ones, [and] inferior ones, with difficulty, [will produce] those that are inferior. The price [for the weaving of the cloth?] should be given right away. Let the first words that come forth be good ones. One who praises the craftsman, and then quickly gives the price [asked for], is called "a heroic merchant." Without regard for [one's own] benefit, accept the price that is asked for [by the weaver]. Cloth [whose price] is established quickly is supremely excellent, and those who do all the work and those who worship it are given the happiness of gods and men. This is what the perfect Buddha taught.[9]

The interpretation of these passages given by both Kapstein and Wallis is that, for the patron, no time is to be lost in bargaining (as one might normally do for common goods) and that the message clearly being conveyed is that "the superior *paṭa* is beyond all price" (see Kapstein 1995, 249).[10] Also seemingly indicated, however, is the idea that a "quick" transaction, one that forfeits any attempt at bargaining, not only affects the cloth (and thus the painting) in a positive way but also benefits the patron and the weaver. As we will see later on, similar ideas are repeated even today by some contemporary Tibetan thangka painters.

The above textual prescriptions at the very least suggest that in earlier times images were constructed by being commissioned, that there was a patron/artist relationship with prescribed roles and expectations concerning particular attitudes and behavior, and that artists were indeed compensated in various forms of wealth, either in the form of receiving a fee or via a voluntary offering (*yön*) bestowed by the patron. Also indicated is the idea that Buddhist images were among those things that, at least theoretically, were to be set apart from other, more mundane commodities. Although it is clear that these textual sources represent ideals, there is convincing evidence that transactions for images on the ground in Tibet typically corresponded to many of the aforementioned guidelines and that images were neither generally considered nor exchanged as mere commodities. This is not only suggested from the practical and religious dynamics involved in their manufacture and exchange but also, and more substantially, from a number of secondary sources and from the accounts of living artists and Tibetan scholars.

That the process of commissioning an artist (i.e., ordering religious goods to be made) was the normal way in which Tibetans acquired Buddhist images historically is generally accepted. However, the logic and details of this process are perhaps less well known. There were practical and religious reasons for commissioning images, which tended to work against their commodification and their presence in the market as premanufactured objects. Commissioning Buddhist images versus preproducing them (and then attempting to sell them in a market) made sense on at least two levels. From a pragmatic perspective, and from the perspective of the artist, making images beforehand in order to sell later on didn't make much financial sense, it being best to have a commission and be sure of remuneration.[11] Some thangkas—and the same can be said of statues—were known to take several months to complete (some taking as long as a year) and could be quite costly to produce. In addition, from the religious perspective, making images beforehand also did not make much sense. Tibetans tended to specify size and detail. Not many patrons would want an off-the-shelf piece, especially in the case of paintings, where the patron usually asked for particular deities and lamas, arranged according to his or her preference. As regards statues, having empty (i.e., unconsecrated) statues lying around was also considered inauspicious, for it was believed that evil spirits could inhabit them. Such beliefs were not merely oral lore but are rooted in canonical texts like *The Brief Tantra of Consecration* (Gyatsho 1979, 73). In addition, the commissioning and creation of images, as already mentioned, were seen as a means to create merit for both the patron and the artist and were considered religious practices. Normally, Tibetans were urged by lamas to create images of particular deities for specific individual needs, goals, or circumstances—to avert misfortune or obstacles, avoid sickness, or acquire longevity, for spiritual practice (to assist practitioners in developing a relationship with a particular meditational deity) or, equally as often, for a deceased individual in order to secure a favorable rebirth. Work generally commenced and was completed on astrologically auspicious days (Lopez 1998). According to Loden Sherap Dagyab, "the commissioning of a work was an act of worship in itself and between the completed work and the patron there existed a very close personal link" (Dagyab 1977, 1:28). For all of these reasons, Tibetans typically did not purchase thangkas and statues ready-made or secondhand, as each image was usually created for a specific purpose and/or individual. Furthermore, the open sale of religious images, or the treatment of them as mundane commodities, as we have extensively seen, was repeatedly condemned by religious injunction, a notion that was likely a major deterrent for those who flirted with the idea of selling or redeeming them in the marketplace. These pragmatic reasons and religious principles were therefore inconsistent with the premanufacture and sale of religious objects in Tibet. Yet, this is not the only evidence to suggest that religious images were not generally sold like common objects; other historical sources and observations also appear to confirm this.

That statues and thangkas did not generally circulate as commodities may be seen in the secondary literature on Tibetan sacred arts, more specifically, in works that comment on the production of such objects and on artists' remuneration. For example, John Clarke, whose research on statue making and metalwork and on the system of exchange that was established in Central Tibet during the seventeenth century—considered a golden age of artistic development—describes an exchange process very much in keeping with that mentioned above. According to Clarke, during this period, Tibet was replete with a number of major centers of artistic production. In Ü and Tsang, for example, there were four major centers of metal-image production: Tsedong (Rtse gdong), Ta nag (Rta nag), the government workshop at Tashi Lhunpo (Bkra shis lhun po), and the government workshop in the capital of Lhasa, below the Potala, known as Shöl (Zhol 'dod dpal). In the east, major craft centers included Markham (Smar khams), Chamdo (Chab mdo), and Rebkong (Reb kong). There were also a number of metalworkers and thangka painters who had settled widely in these regions. Some craftsmen, making up a minority and out of economic necessity, traveled long distances in search of work (Clarke 2002, 116). In Lhasa, the Fifth Dalai Lama embarked on a number of ambitious building projects during this period, including the Potala Palace, all of which required massive amounts of religious artwork. For these purposes, he established artisan guilds, or *zokhang* (*bzo khang*), in all of the crafts in order to supply monasteries with their religious necessities (Alexander 2013, 62). According to Clarke, there were generally two kinds of work performed: that which was done on a compulsory basis for the major monasteries and that which was performed for private patrons. Guild members were paid a daily wage and were required to work for the government for approximately three to four months (2002, 121). Government artists could also do private work during this obligatory period—the pay, it is said, being generally better. Private commissions were usually carried out by local or settled artists at the patron's home and would commonly take up to two weeks to complete. However, sometimes the artist would stay with a patron for six months or even longer (most likely depending on amount of work commissioned) (Clarke 2002, 117). Generally, the artist expected a daily wage, food, and a gift upon completion. Furthermore, according to Clarke, "image makers received the best remuneration of any metalworkers because there existed the belief that if the patron could please the craftsman, the deity would more fully occupy the image. Consequently, in addition to daily wages and presents at the end, the meals provided were particularly good and special cooks might be hired" (2002, 120).[12] Thus, far from the production and sale of ready-made objects for the marketplace, transactions for statues generally followed a pattern of monastic or personal commission in which artists were paid for the work performed. Moreover, according to Clarke's research, there was virtually no change to the systems of patronage of metalworkers until the Tibetan Uprising of 1959 (2002, 129).

According to David and Janice Jackson, thangka painting followed a similar pattern of exchange. In their major study *Tibetan Thangka Painting: Methods and Materials* (1984), in which they draw upon ethnographic work conducted with a number of older Tibetan artists, they describe a situation very similar to that found in Clarke's research. Patrons included monasteries, nobility, and ordinary people—including nomads—who are described as having all the sacred objects one would normally expect on a typical Buddhist shrine (1984, 6).[13] Payment to the artist, in accordance with the above textual prescriptions, was not conceived to be for the completed image per se but for the skilled labor and was considered an offering. According to Jackson and Jackson:

> Traditionally, Tibetan painters were handsomely recompensed for their skills. Although they were sometimes conscripted by the government to do

> compulsory work (*lag khral*) on restoration projects, even then they were usually well paid. And for private commissions their pay was usually even better. These commissions were not supposed to be merely cash transactions. The payment that the patron made to the artist after the completion of the work was thought of as a pious offering, a kind of religious ransom payment (*slu yon*) which allowed the patron then to "invite" (*gdan 'dren zhu*) the sacred image to its new home. Nevertheless, before the work began the patron and artist usually agreed on some minimum payment, as well as on the amount of gold to be used. (1984, 12)[14]

Donald Lopez, borrowing the Jacksons' observations on transactions related to thangkas, suggests that the reasoning behind this method of remuneration was indeed a direct result of Tibetan religious attitudes toward the sale of sacred goods. He writes, "Although artists were generally well paid for their work, their fee was technically considered an offering since trafficking in sacred images was proscribed" (1998, 150).

That Buddhist images were normally acquired by commission (with artists often working at a monastery or at a patron's residence), that the fees or payments to artists were conceived of as offerings, and, moreover, that those individuals who were poor were rarely, if ever, refused if they needed a thangka, were notions that were reinforced by artists during my fieldwork. For example, according to one interview with a metalworker named Jampa conducted in 2006 in Lhasa:

> There was no fixed price for making a statue and we charged the price by asking the patron of this statue to pay whatever he could offer. If [for example] the patron could only offer one yuan to the craftsman, this was still fine, and no one would argue with the patron. But during the making of the statue, the patron had to bring tea and Tibetan *chang* [barley beer] to the craftsman. From the patron's viewpoint, they believed in the preciousness of statues, so they would pay whatever price they could. In the past, if we were invited by a monastery to make a big statue then they would pay us with a daily wage. Materials would be prepared by the patrons. Or, if it was for the monasteries, then they would be prepared by the monasteries.

This same view was confirmed by an eighty-year-old monk and former painter during an interview in Rebkong:

> There is no such specific book [that tells us how to] discuss prices, but there should be mutual respect between both painters and sponsors. There are texts that talk about how the painters are to paint and their motivation. In the texts it says that it [the amount given] depends on the patrons, how much the patron can offer. There is no such thing as artists making decisions on prices. A patron says, "Well, I'll give you this much, so whether there is a profit or not, if what I pay exceeds [your costs], then that is just an offering." Actually, there is such a trust in each other; there is a mutual trust [between the patron and the artist]. Patrons usually pay more than it costs. The patron has faith because he is going to use this for a religious purpose. He doesn't think, "Oh, I'll just pay extra." They have no regret.

This same monk went on to explain that in the past one generally did not refuse the requests made by patrons with little financial means:

> Most of the thangkas were done for the monasteries, not private families. It was pretty rare to get orders from families. . . . Sometimes poor families came to ask for a painting. In this case they [the painters] accepted, and we did it accordingly. They not only accepted the people who could afford it, they [also] accepted from people who could not afford it.[15]

Finally, this same conclusion has been confirmed independently by Eric McGuckin in his work on thangka painting in Dharamsala. Recalling the transactions for thangkas in pre-1959 Tibet, his informants explained that "fees were set according to the patrons' wishes and ability. The poor often paid less than the value of the work, while the rich might pay more" (1996, 34). One particular informant of McGuckin's, Venerable Sangay Yeshi, a thangka master from Kham who once taught at the painting school at the Library of Tibetan Works and Archives, describes this exact scenario:

> We did individual orders and some from the monastery. There was no tradition of asking for money; the fee depended on the client. The patron would say, "I'll give such an amount," and we would have to accept. There was no tradition of turning them down if it wasn't enough. Sometimes they would give four times the cost of the gold in the painting, sometimes a bit less. Normally the clients would bring the gold in themselves. Rich clients sometimes made orders for twenty or thirty painters [paintings?]. The poor usually only one after the death of a relative. (1996, 34)[16]

Thus, beyond the mere fact that thangkas were primarily acquired by commission and were not generally prepared without a patron, according to these accounts, it was typical of the patron (and not the artist) to determine the amount offered. Such ethics, if true in practice, go some way to explain how Tibetans from differing social classes managed to possess religious objects such as statues and thangkas.

In addition to this exchange being conceived of as an offering, other details about these transactions emerged from a number of scholars and artists. For example, a second significant feature of the pre–Cultural Revolution exchange in religious goods, as told by my informants, involved ceremonies or celebrations which reflect a striking resemblance to and continuity with descriptions of ceremonies during the process of constructing and completing temple images provided by Thubten Legshay Gyatsho in *Gateway to the Temple*:

> Accordingly, in the same manner that construction ceremonies are feted, in the course of painting monasteries there are beginning celebrations, middle celebrations, and concluding celebrations, each at their appropriate times, which are hosted on as grand a scale as possible. This can be illustrated by the ceremonies given during the various steps of completion of the temple's main image. On the occasion of the image's "eye-opening", the image is offered a ceremonial silk scarf, and on that day an "eye celebration" takes place. Furthermore, there is also traditionally hosted a "gold celebration" when gold is applied, a "varnish beer" when the murals are coated with varnish and so forth. (Gyatsho 1979, 75)[17]

Similar to this description, Tsering, a metalworker who worked from his home outside the Lhasa city center when I conducted fieldwork in 2006, described the offering of compensation to the statue maker in the past as a three-stage process:

> There was one custom that on the first day of starting a work the patron would give you a party for it and he would give you money wrapped and folded in paper just as a gift and a scarf. In Tibetan we call this "*btsugs don*" [for the benefit of the beginning]. Then the patron would give you a party again when a work was half complete, and he would give a gift the same as the first time. This is called "*bar don*" [for the benefit of the middle]. And finally, after you finished everything and have given this to the patron, he

> would give you big party to celebrate its completion and he would give you a gift like before. And also, depending on [the patron's] family's financial status, they would give you rice, butter, and so on. We call this "*mjug don*" [for the benefit of the conclusion]. This kind of custom not only existed for foundry [statue?] makers but also for those working with other technologies in the past.

That a process of this kind existed is also confirmed by Chögyam Trungpa in his work "*Visual Dharma*" (2004). Here, he describes that the process of remuneration was similar with regard to both thangka painters and statue makers:

> The master and his apprentices were welcomed with a feast and there was a weekly feast for them for as long as it took to complete the work. They were presented with gifts at various times, usually at the time of the feasts. They were paid in commodities, such as cattle, quantities of butter, cheese, grain, jewelry or clothes. . . .
>
> As a social phenomenon, making images was much the same as thangka painting. The art and lore were passed down in families and through apprenticeship. A sculptor and his apprentices having come to a monastery to provide it with a new treasure, were feted, given gifts, and paid just as were the thangka painters. (266–67)[18]

While Tibet mostly maintained a barter economy in the years prior to the Cultural Revolution, in which individuals exchanged commodities for commodities (although some currency did indeed circulate), such exchanges for religious goods were not generally conceived of as a fixed payment, repayment, or trade in kind but rather as a voluntary offering. While a large offering was likely desired by the artist and was perceived of as leading to increased merit for both the patron and artist, the practice of setting prices or goods for images (for example, two cows for a thangka painting of Chenresig) was not the usual practice and would have likely been seen as breach of tradition and, moreover, a sin. Taken together, such a scenario suggests that it would have been unusual to see premade religious images circulating for sale among common goods in the typical Tibetan marketplace, and this picture appears to be corroborated by a number of different sources.

Secondary literature on trade in Tibet scarcely notes any exchange of religious goods. Luce Boulnois's study, "Gold, Wool, and Musk: Trade in Lhasa in the Seventeenth Century" (2003), mostly provides information on trade in Tibet's main imports and exports—musk, gold, hides, medicinal herbs, various animals, precious stones, and so forth—items that Boulnois mentions as being "rare, precious, or curious products that most attracted the attention of foreigners" (145). By the very absence of attention to religious goods, her work suggests that these items were either of no interest to traders or foreign visitors or that these items were not circulating in the markets. While there is, in her study, a brief discussion of a craft industry that included carpets, as well as a discussion of the importance of more everyday products used by Tibetans for religious purposes, such as precious stones for rosaries (146–47), Boulnois does not list in her entire work anything resembling a *trade* in religious images (or texts), either conducted by middlemen or by artists themselves. In her larger work *Silk Road: Monks, Warriors, and Merchants*, she provides insight as to why this absence may have been the case when she writes, "Certain valuable objects, however, such as works of art or ritual objects, form a case apart as they were not intended to be sold again and circulated in different ways, either as gifts or as plunder" (2004, 301). Other major contributions to the study of trade in Tibet, likewise, have little to say about the exchange of or trade in religious goods, focusing instead on standard commodities. Wim van Spengen's significant volume *Tibetan Border Worlds* devotes but a single, albeit ambiguous line in this regard. Describing pilgrimage places as commercial centers, he writes, "Near these power-places sprang up a brisk trade in sacred medicinal plants and religious artifacts, carried on by a host of mendicant monks and itinerant traders" (2000, 72). Such scant attention, although suggestive, hardly represents evidence of the widespread exchange of religious images as a typical occurrence among the Tibetan population or as items to be found ready-at-hand in the marketplaces of major towns. More suggestive documentation of what could be called a "trade" in religious objects in Tibet comes from Gombozhab Tsybikoff, the Mongolian Buryat explorer and scholar. In a report carried out at the turn of the twentieth century for the Imperial Russian Geographical Society, Tsybikoff briefly mentions religious objects as being among the few Tibetan exports. According to his report:

> The articles exported are various objects of cult, as small statues, painted images, religious books, and prints made from carved wooden blocks, incense candles, ribbons, peacock feathers, leaf-shaped seeds "tsampaka,"

> and similar articles that bring high prices only because of the piety of the Mongol lamaist and his reverence for holy things from Tibet. The more famous the person that produces these articles the more eagerly they are purchased and the higher is the price paid. But Tibet also has a trade in cloths, in knit goods, and in the yellow hats of ecclesiastics, and this class of traffic, which depends upon the religious sentiment of the purchasers, as is the case with presents to Tibetan lamas, attains a considerable sum annually. (1903, 745–46)

While Tsybikoff's brief account seemingly implies the commodification of Buddhist paraphernalia, it is difficult to conclude that his description indicates a broad market in religious objects for general consumption in the marketplace. Besides the fact that these goods were destined for export, and not for domestic markets, given the fact that Tsybikoff notes that it was the treasuries of the Dalai Lama and other wealthy incarnates who generally funded such exports, and that such goods were destined for "Mongol lamaists," such a description seems to imply that the particular objects sent to Mongolia were intended for monks and monasteries. Also, the transactions for such objects do not appear to be typical commodity exchanges. Rather, in accordance with many of the accounts mentioned above, the price paid for such objects was apparently dependent upon the piety and/or religious reverence of Mongolian Buddhists, a description that seems more akin to making offerings for such items.[19]

Another source for descriptions of the Tibetan market comes from nineteenth- and twentieth-century European travel narratives, many of which describe the Lhasa marketplace. However, many of these European authors, although fascinated with the collection of artifacts and curiosities of the "other," suggest that there was either a proscription on the sale of religious goods or that these items were, again, nowhere to be found. This is suggested, for example, in Edmund Candler's description of the market in *The Unveiling of Lhasa* (1905), a record of his impressions during the time of the Younghusband Expedition (1903–4):[20]

> British officers haunt the bazaars searching for curios, but with very little success. Lhasa has no artistic industries; nearly all the knick-knacks come from India and China. Cloisonné ware is rare and expensive, as one has to

> pay for the 1,800 miles of transport from Peking. Religious objects are not sold. (200)

Such a description lies in stark contrast to that provided by Tsybikoff above, whose comments were made during the same period. Two decades later, in keeping with this view, Alexandra David-Neel's *My Journey to Lhasa* describes the material goods available in Lhasa's marketplace in a passage that is both telling of her interest in Tibetan material artifacts but also suggestive of a marketplace that was seemingly devoid of religious articles. She writes, for example, "In Lhasa, one does not see the quaint shops and bazaars that offer such an exciting hunting-ground to the collector in China. Nowadays, the most conspicuous articles in the Lhasa market are aluminum wares" (1927, 267). One expects that if Buddhist objects were indeed plentiful in the market, they would appear prominently in the accounts of such Western travelers, especially in the writings of individuals who were actively seeking these kinds of artifacts.[21]

That selling religious goods was considered a taboo in Tibetan society became apparent to some foreign travelers who had spent considerable time in Tibet and its neighboring areas. For example, Hisao Kimura, who traveled in Tibet as a Japanese agent from 1940 to 1950, writing of his experiences in Kalimpong, states that he "knew that religious art was not to be bartered and sold, but only done on commission" (Kimura and Berry 1990, 135). Kimura's memoir also presents an interesting anecdote that reflects the fact that other foreign visitors were well aware of these Tibetan customs. This is revealed in a passage in which he records a conversation between two Englishmen who had just acquired thangka paintings from a lama, Geshé Wangyel, to whom at least one of the men had apparently given a loan. The following is Kimura's record of their conversation:

> "I tried to buy one of these once, but the owner couldn't be found. Instead, I was offered a book on the subject, and told it would come to the same thing."
>
> "I remember that," said his companion. "But we were very innocent in those days even to offer to bargain over a *thanka*."
>
> "That's true. I hadn't learned yet that you should never even attempt to purchase one that is being properly used for religious purposes. It is only

> proper to buy one that is being neglected or that a competent authority is willing to sell. I think we can trust Geshé Wangyel to have exercised proper judgment and I'm certainly happy with these as interest on my loan." (186)

Whether or not it was the intention of Geshé Wangyel for these thangkas to be conceived of as "interest on a loan," or that one could in fact legitimately "buy" a "neglected" image (observations that could well have been the Englishman's own understanding), it is interesting to note that these two men, like Kimura himself, were aware of the existence of religious protocols (albeit perhaps somewhat misconstrued) surrounding the acquisition of Tibetan religious art; these items were perceived to be set apart or treated differently from other, mundane objects. In addition, testimonies deriving from Tibetan scholars as well as from those who lived in Lhasa prior to the Chinese invasion of Tibet in 1950 further support the above picture that religious images were generally absent from the market. Chögyam Trungpa, for example, supports the observations made earlier by Luce Boulnois regarding the circulation of religious objects, stating, "Thangkas were never bought or sold, but changed hands only as gifts" (2004, 268). A similar position is also reported in Dorje Yudon Yuthok's *House of the Turquoise Roof,* an autobiographical account of life in Lhasa during the first half of the twentieth century. Reflecting on the sources of income in her family, she writes, "The priceless antique religious statues, paintings and other ritual objects in the chapels in our Lhasa house and on our various estates were not thought of in terms of financial worth. Religious articles were never sold, but were treasured for their spiritual value" (Yuthok 1990, 167). Furthermore, suggesting that this practice was not just a principle by which wealthy families lived, Loden Sherap Dagyab, author of the two-volume work *Tibetan Religious Art,* has also stated, "there existed no shops where one could buy thangka and religious images" (1977, 1:28). This view was widely corroborated by several informants during my fieldwork, both in Lhasa in 2006 and again in Amdo in 2010.

THE EXCHANGE OF BUDDHIST TEXTS UP TO THE CULTURAL REVOLUTION

Finally, brief mention should also be made about religious texts, considered representations of the Buddha's speech. Like statues and thangkas, numerous early Indian Buddhist works detail the religious merit to be gained specifically from commissioning texts. Such statements, for example, can be found in the *Lotus Sūtra* (*Saddharmapaṇḍarīka Sūtra, Dam chos pad ma dkar po'i mdo*), the *Perfection of Wisdom Sūtra* (*Prajñāpāramitā Sūtra, Yum chen mo*), and *Distinguishing the Middle from Extremes* (*Madhyāntavibhaṅga, Dbus dang mtha' rnam par 'byed pa*), all of which detail the extensive benefits of printing, reading, owning, and/or worshipping texts and likely provided a powerful rationale for funding textual production in Tibet (Schaeffer 2009). Tibetans generated a staggering amount of literature, both before and after the introduction of block printing in the early fifteenth century. But while there has been much research on the content of texts, neither the actual processes of textual production and distribution nor prescriptive information for relationships between patrons and carvers (or patrons and printers) appear to have been recorded as a part of Tibetan historiography or monastic annals. Cabezón's preliminary study of colophons (2001b), in which he examines Tibetan literary production and the concept of Tibetan authorship, has revealed a number of details regarding the commissioning and production of texts. According to Cabezón, in Tibet, "in many instances the production of literature . . . was not the solitary enterprise of the lone scholar . . . , but the communal work of a cluster of individuals . . . [involving] a division of labor, with different individuals responsible for different aspects of the work (teachers, or what today we might call principal investigators, note-takers, research assistants, editors, scribes, proof-readers, and a production crew that included fund-raisers, librarians, printing supervisors, block carvers, and printers)" (237). Those texts or textual collections that were not printed at one of the larger printing houses (*par khang*) required funding from private donations which may have been collected from a number of locations. Furthermore, religious texts, while sometimes written down by a single individual, were oftentimes a compilation of oral discourses, a process that often took place over considerable time and in many different locations with the aid of many donors funding various aspects of production. In terms of the details of the exchange and/or distribution of these texts, however, in the absence of historical records of such dealings, much less is known. Nevertheless, recent scholarship has suggested that at least up to and including the fifteenth century, religious texts changed hands as commodities or were otherwise objects of exchange.

Scholars have frequently characterized the period of translation that occurred in India and Tibet between the tenth and twelfth centuries, known as the *chidar* (*phyi dar*), or "later dissemination of the Dharma," as one of commodification or commercialization. For example, Ronald Davidson notes that during this period "at its very worst the production of Buddhist sacred texts was exactly a commodities business. Certain Indians appear to have shown up with whatever text the market wanted, as long as payment was made with the precious yellow metal that Indians continue to adore" (2005, 234).[22] More recently, however, this framing has been applied to the exchange of texts in Tibet more broadly. Kurtis Schaeffer's work *The Culture of the Book in Tibet*, in characterizing textual exchange in Tibet historically, argues that religious texts (books) were "a significant *commodity* within the premodern Tibetan economy" (2009, 17; emphasis mine). According to Schaeffer, books, while considered priceless from the religious perspective, were nevertheless deeply embedded in economic life and, especially with regard to the manufacturing of the canon, were considered "big business" (26–27). Through his examination of the *Blue Annals* (*Deb ther sngon po*) by Gö Lotsāwa Zhönnu Pel (Gos lo tsā ba gzhon nu dpal, 1392–1481), a historical work considered a veritable microcosm of Tibetan Buddhism up to the fifteenth century, he points out several examples of what he sees as the economics of texts. For example, Schaeffer notes that "a student might serve as a scribe to a teacher as payment for instruction, as when a student copied 40 folios of the *Kālacakra Tantra* to pay for his initiation into the same tantric teachings" (126). Other examples depict the recitation of texts for food, which he notes was a frequent occurrence: "Reciters were also employed as house priests, as in the case of Machik Labdrön, who was hired to recite *Perfection of Wisdom* texts as the house priestess of Drapa Ngonshé" (127). In addition, Schaeffer also notes that the work of translation often required considerable funding, which could be a barrier to its completion. Relating how this was sometimes overcome, in what he describes as "the most explicit statements about the economy of book production," he reports two examples in the *Blue Annals* of prices for translations and/or translated teachings. In the first example, he tells of a Kashmirian scholar named Somanātha who, wishing to spread the *Kālacakra Tantra* throughout Tibet, paid a Tibetan translator named Azha Gyagartsek and his retinue sixty measures of gold and subsidized their living expenses for an entire year while the work was being completed. In a second example, Schaeffer reports that Ra Lotsawa Dorje Drakpa (Rwa lo tsa ba rdo rje grags pa, 1016–1128/1198) even went so far as to set prices for his translations of particular tantras, texts which became known as the "golden books" (195).[23]

While Schaeffer argues that religious texts were important commodities within premodern Tibetan society, I suggest that such a representation may be somewhat misleading when attempting to establish an overall picture of the exchange or circulation of texts in Tibet historically. Such a depiction tends to overlook the important distinctions that were often made by Tibetans between religious objects (specifically those considered representations of the Buddha's body, speech, and mind), on the one hand, and mundane commodities, on the other, as well as the processes, customs, and conceptions that are known to have commonly governed their exchange. In premodern Tibet, religious goods, normatively speaking, were neither perceived as commodities nor were they treated or exchanged like mundane objects. That texts served as objects of exchange—that they were a part of an economy of sorts as sources of livelihood for the monks and artisans involved in their actual production, and that the exchange of wealth for religious teachings and translations occurred—is hardly arguable. However, this did not *de facto* transform Buddhist texts, the commission and exchange of which involved the creation of merit, into mere commercial objects or commodities, subject to the operations of the common market, which contained items that were intended to be *sold* (or resold) for profit and were subject to price and barter. Such practices were reserved for commodities of trade—yak tails, salt, musk, wool, etc.—the exchange of which often took hours of tedious calculation and haggling. The examples of the economics of texts cited by Schaeffer (the copying of folios, the recitation of texts for food, or the translating of books) are not necessarily the same as the commodification of texts. That is, such actions may alternatively be read as payment for work. While it is known that the selling of Buddhist teachings and texts did occur historically among both Indians and Tibetans—a foremost example perhaps being that of Drokmi ('Brog mi lo tsa ba śākya ye shes, 992–1072/1074), who was known to have sold the *Path and Result* (*Lam 'bras*) teachings to his disciples (see Davidson 2005, chapter 5)—such practices were also heavily criticized by figures such as Rog Bande Sherab (Rog bande shes rab 'od, 1166–1244) and others, and may best be viewed not as a mainstream practice but as a marginal one. It is also interesting to note that the author of the *Blue Annals*, Gö Lotsāwa, himself a student of Tsongkhapa (who had pointed out the nonvirtue of selling scriptures), does not critically evaluate or find problematic any of the economic exchanges of texts that he records, suggesting that these dealings were not seen by him to be contradictory to the refuge precepts. Nevertheless, what is of primary concern for our present purposes is not whether texts were an object of exchange but rather *how* one regularly or normally acquired religious texts in Tibet. In other words, the key question is whether texts circulated in the manner of an ordinary, mundane object and whether religious texts were ordinarily an object of the market, available ready-made for a price, or considered a *thing* available for sale or barter. Although historical accounts of such matters are scarce, evidence suggests that, like statues and thangkas, religious texts were primarily acquired as either gifts, donations, or by commissioning them—for example, at a printing house.

That texts were commissioned is evident from the information provided in their colophons. The commissioning of texts—that is, the initial carving of wooden blocks and perhaps the initial printing—was truly a collaborative enterprise, as well as a meritorious one, involving numerous groups of individuals and often numerous donors and patrons. But what was the process of exchange thereafter? How were texts normally distributed or acquired? As Schaeffer points out, texts commonly changed hands through inheritance, as gifts, or via donation. Tibetan texts were mainly the personal property of monks and religious leaders, as well as artists, and were generally handed down from master to disciple. As they were considered valuable property, they were also often transferred through families (e.g., after a death or even between living family members). They were used to secure lines of succession for reincarnate monks and could often serve to forge family ties (Schaeffer 2009, 122). Books were also owned by large numbers of monks, and by the eleventh century it was possible that any given monastic institution had hundreds of monks with their own personal copies of texts (123). Sometimes copies of texts were sponsored by the state and given to monastic institutions as donations. In other instances, wealthy leaders donated books to their students and supporters as well as to their supporting institutions (192). It was also often the case that the distribution of texts was an internal monastic affair. Many of the larger monasteries such as Derge, Kumbum, and Labrang had their own large printing houses through which woodblocks would be carved and texts printed and distributed.[24] According to Rebecca Knuth, "the bigger monasteries produced complete editions of the general collection, the *Kangyur*. Collections of works on philosophy, spiritual practice, medicine, astrology, and other topics unique to a particular school's curriculum would be printed at the principle monastery and copies distributed to branches. For example, Dzogchen Monastery printed a core collection of books that were sent out to 200 affiliated monasteries" (2003, 204–5).[25]

While religious texts changed hands among monks and teachers as gifts or donations or via inheritance as personal or familial property, at the individual level, if one desired a particular text for oneself or wanted to donate copies of texts to a monastery, one achieved this by commissioning the local printing house to produce them. That this process was the typical means by which an individual acquired a work is attested to by a number of scholar-observers. For example, according to Giuseppe Tucci:

> Anyone who wanted a copy of a work ordered it from the monastery where the blocks were stored. Paper could be supplied direct by the monastery or by the person who commissioned the printing. The monks in the printing-shop ran an inkmoistened roller over the blocks, and the pages of the work came off one after another, clear and legible or otherwise according to the degree of wear of the blocks and the quality of the paper. (1967, 199)

The late E. Gene Smith also confirms that the process of commissioning a text's production at a printing house was the primary means of acquiring it. Adding to the above general description, Smith also suggests that this process was not unlike that which existed for statue makers and thangka painters in terms of the manner in which compensation was offered:

> [Blocks were] not commercially distributed. Each page was about a pound and carved on both sides. . . . There were just too many of them. But you had printing houses like Dege and Labrang and Kumbum. . . . People would supply their own paper and ink and it could only be done at certain times of the year. One couldn't print it in the winter because the blocks would crack. You had to take your own paper and your own person who could print. And that is how it was done. If you went to a monastery printing house, you had to sponsor a tea party, which is one of the ways a monastery would make its living, is through the monastic tea party. (Smith 2011, at 6:06–7:24)

Smith's description of the monastic tea party (*ja mgron*) is reminiscent of the way in which statue makers and thangka painters are said to have been compensated at the beginning, middle, and end of a particular commission. Tea parties, according to tradition, not only consisted of the actual distribution of tea but also of food and money, and the extent of what was given usually depended on the patron's financial means. There is also reason to believe that texts did not often change hands as secondhand objects; that is, they were generally not resold or acquired with the intent to resell. According to W. Zwalf in *The Heritage of Tibet* (1981):

> A book was usually ordered afresh, rather than bought from a previous owner; the purchaser often had to supply the ink and paper, and the monks were paid for the work. If the monastery with the required blocks was distant, the costs of the work and those of transport might be greater than the expense of having a text copied from an existing book nearer to hand. In either case, of course, merit was acquired by printers, copyists, and the persons commissioning the work. (121)[26]

Finally, Hildegard Diemberger's article "Holy Books as Ritual Objects and Vessels of Teachings in the Era of the 'Further Spread of the Doctrine' (*Bstan pa yang dar*)," in contrast to the impression given by Schaeffer above, not only reinforces the idea that religious texts in premodern Tibet did not generally circulate as commodities, she also affirms the findings of the above authors by pointing out that commissioning a printing house was the usual path to acquiring a text. According to Diemberger:

> Like relics and consecrated icons, holy books were for a long time outside the realm of traded commodities. Even the introduction of printing did not necessarily imply the immediate rise of a book market. The blocks were kept in printing houses (*par khang*) attached to monasteries or seats of local rulers. If someone wanted a book printed, he or she would go to the printing house with paper and ink, or cover the expenses for procuring paper and ink. Eventually the sponsor would make a lavish donation. The whole enterprise was framed in the morality of merit-making activities and religious patronage: big patrons would provide the bulk of the funding necessary for the carving; small patrons would benefit from the presence of the blocks and sponsor reprints. (2012, 21)

Diemberger's comments about "consecrated icons" being outside the realm of commodities aside (a distinction which I have argued was not relevant to whether they could be sold or not), these descriptions of how one acquired a text are not only fairly consistent but suggest that payment was made for the labor and (if one did not supply them oneself) for materials and was generally considered beyond a mere cash-for-text transaction. Moreover, as payment to the printers appears to have been based on voluntary offerings, the real commodities in these transactions may in fact have been the paper and ink.

The above discussion suggests that up to the Cultural Revolution in Tibet there was a normative system of exchange in religious goods based on the financial means of the patron, which was governed by particular customs or ceremonies of gifting, generously if possible. It was primarily a system of offering, which involved the creation of merit, not one of buying, selling, or even of barter, activities that were the domain of common commodities. Thus, to a significant extent, and based on the above findings, we can say that the reality of the exchange of religious objects on the ground in Tibet was very much in line with the religious protocols governing their exchange as well as with the proscriptions against their sale as outlined in classical Tibetan Buddhist texts. However, while this historical sketch presents a somewhat fixed vision of how statues, thangkas, and texts were exchanged in Tibet in the past, it should not be assumed that the selling of these religious objects *never* took place. Recall that the twentieth-century Gelukpa scholar Pabongka Rinpoche had noted the frequent pawning and selling of such objects during his lifetime—practices, he suggested, which should be "absolutely avoided." There are indeed scattered historical accounts of Tibetans who were involved in the selling of religious goods. Certainly, there are records of purchases of religious artifacts or "curios" from Tibetans by figures such as L. Austine Waddell, who, "realizing the rigid secrecy maintained by the Lāmas in regard to their seemingly chaotic rites and symbolism . . . felt compelled to purchase a Lāmaist temple with its fittings" ([1899] 2005, viii). There are also accounts of purchases by other early (mostly missionary) visitors to Tibet, such as those made by Dr. Albert Shelton and his wife, Flora, for the Newark Museum (Wissing 2004).[27] Yet, these transactions should not be perceived as those that were typical among Tibetans. Rather, such activities should be seen within the context of several converging forces: the colonial project of collecting and categorizing Tibetan objects in the pursuit (and control) of knowledge (as was the case with Waddell; see Harris 1999, 21–32), the desire for personal enrichment and/or the goal of funding further missionary efforts (Wissing 2004, 112), and the numerous social upheavals and wars in Tibet from the late nineteenth through the early twentieth centuries (including the Sino-Tibetan border wars in Kham and Amdo) which motivated many Tibetans to sell religious objects.[28] As Valrae Reynolds writes of Albert Shelton's collection in *From the Sacred Realm,* "the violent political climate provided the conditions under which an outsider such as Shelton could acquire these treasures" (1999, 15).[29] Still, seemingly apart from the "collecting" activities of foreigners, some writers have noted the sale of religious objects in Tibetan markets. For example, Peter Richardus's *Tibetan Lives: Three Tibetan Autobiographies* (1998) reveals that Karma Sumdhon Paul, a Tibetan Christian writing in the early twentieth century, observed "unconsecrated" images for sale in the markets around Lhasa despite his acknowledgment that "Buddhism does not allow Tibetans to buy or sell sacred objects" (135). Likewise, Sven Hedin, writing of Tashi Lhunpo Monastery during this same period, notes that a significant source of income for the monastery came from "the sale of amulets, talismans and relics, idols of metal or terra cotta, sacred paintings (*tankas*), joss-sticks, etc." ([1909] 1999, 358; see also Clarke 2002, 119). While it may be the case that some of what these observers thought was buying and selling might instead have been instances of exchange by voluntary contribution, such instances would nevertheless seem to support the fact that there were indeed exceptions to the general rule against trafficking in religious images.[30] Similarly, in terms of texts, a handful of accounts note the existence of bookstalls and the presence of booksellers in and around Lhasa. For example, similar accounts come from Ekai Kawaguchi (1909) and Heinrich Harrer (1981), who report that one could both order books from a monastery as well as purchase them from bookstalls in the Lhasa Barkhor marketplace. The presence of bookstalls that sold "prayer books, philosophical books, and whatever else one needed for one's education and practice" in Lhasa has also been noted by Geshé Sopa in his autobiography (Sopa and Donnelly 2012, 110). Furthermore, Giuseppe Tucci tells us, after describing the process of commissioning a text at a monastic printing house, that there was indeed a "humble trade" in books during special occasions such as fairs and festivals, mostly consisting of books of interest to the laity (1967, 199–200).[31] Charles Bell also confirms the sale of books in the Lhasa market and provides photographic evidence of a bookseller in his work *Tibet Past and Present* (1992, 92–93).[32] Thus, it appears that religious texts entered the commodity sphere on a much more frequent basis than religious images prior to the Cultural Revolution, an occurrence which was likely facilitated by the technology of printing and the ease with which texts could be reproduced (Diemberger 2012, 21).

FIG. 7. Bookseller in Lhasa (1920–21). Photo attributed to Rabden Lepcha. (The Charles Bell Collection. Copyright Pitt Rivers Museum, University of Oxford. Accession #1998.286.202.1)

Nevertheless, despite the presence of such accounts, it is also the case that attitudes toward those who made their livelihood from such activities remained critical. Such sentiments, as we have seen, were documented in classical Buddhist texts themselves, but these attitudes were also noted by a number of my informants during my fieldwork. For example, an eighty-year-old monk from Sengeshong Mango Gonpa, when asked about the general attitudes toward those who sold religious objects in the past, responded, "During my time, in Lhasa, people who sold such things were considered to be bad people. It was the same in Amdo too. It was rare to see this. But there were some people who still did it. People would look down upon these people.... Especially in Lhasa, if someone sold these things, people wouldn't even eat food from him." That there was indeed a social stigma against selling religious texts for personal profit was also suggested by some of my other informants. One monastic teacher from Kumbum stated, "Traditionally, those businessmen who sold religious goods and butchers were regarded in the same way,

FIG. 8. Books for sale in Lhasa (1920–21). Photo attributed to Rabden Lepcha. (The Charles Bell Collection. Copyright Pitt Rivers Museum, University of Oxford. Accession # 1998.286.201)

as *dik chen* (*sdik chen*), sinful persons." Still another informant, when asked about those who sold religious objects in the past, remarked, "People considered those people who were doing this kind of business to be accumulating negative karma, like drug dealers." Thus, while religious images and texts were indeed periodically sold, those individuals who were involved in these activities were also typically condemned and disparaged in Tibetan society.[33]

Taken together, and given the above evidence, while the selling of religious goods was not unknown in Tibet, it seems clear that this practice was neither the norm nor socially sanctioned. There is overwhelming evidence to suggest that images and texts were primarily acquired by Tibetans either as gifts or through a process of commission and offering and that this was the preferred, legitimate, and prescribed means of exchange. In contrast, the activity of selling these objects for profit, based on accounts from classical religious texts and contemporary Tibetan Buddhist authors, as well as ethnographic interviews, was viewed by the monastic establishment and by Tibetan society more broadly as a form of wrong livelihood, a sin with negative consequences. In any case, the normative pattern of exchange in religious goods that had presumably been in place for centuries would be dramatically disrupted by the Chinese invasion of Tibet, by the failed Tibetan Uprising of 1959, and ultimately by the Cultural Revolution. The Cultural Revolution, an event that brought about the deaths of many millions of Han Chinese and a radical transformation of Chinese society as the result of Mao's failed policies, would also radically transform the whole of Tibetan life, leading to the deaths of thousands of Tibetans, the destruction of countless Tibetan monasteries, and, as a consequence, to the unprecedented commodification of Tibetan Buddhist objects.

CHINESE INVASION AND THE CULTURAL REVOLUTION: DIVERSION TO COMMODITY

The impact of the Chinese invasion of Tibet in 1950 and, later, the Cultural Revolution on Tibetan lives and on Tibet's unique cultural and religious identity was nothing short of devastating. The Tibetan government-in-exile claims that some 1.2 million Tibetans lost their lives between 1949 and 1979—either through warfare (i.e., resistance), direct execution, torture, starvation, or prison labor (Central Tibetan Administration 1996).[34] The Chinese Communists' nationalistic enterprise to bring Tibet into the fold of the "motherland" and to liberate Tibet's "feudalistic" and "backward" society through socialism would eventually lead to the transformation of every aspect of Tibetan life, dismantling its economic, social, and religious foundations. The policies implemented during Cultural Revolution forbade all forms of religious practice and expression so central to the Tibetan worldview and contributed to the systematic removal of almost all symbols of religion and distinct Tibetan Buddhist identity from the landscape. While the extent of human suffering (both physical and psychological) in pursuit of this ideology was the greatest tragedy, this period also marked a significant transformation in the lives of Tibetan religious goods (Appadurai 1986).

One year after Mao Zedong came to power with the Communist Revolution in 1949, the People's Liberation Army (PLA) invaded Tibet, occupying the country. While the Tibetans put up some resistance, they were no match for the PLA, which eventually reached Lhasa that same year. Military skirmishes continued in Kham and Amdo in the early 1950s, and by 1955, as a result of the Chinese Communist Party's (CCP) implementation of land reforms and collectivization, perceived by Tibetans as an assault on their way of life, opposition to these changes mounted. Those whom the Communists identified as among the leaders and the wealthy were subjected to *thamzing* (*'thab 'dzing*), or political struggle sessions, in which Tibetans were forced to confess their "crimes" against the masses (Powers 2007, 199). From 1956 onward, scattered resistance culminated first in a major revolt in Kham, and Tibetans, outnumbered and inadequately armed, suffered significant casualties and material losses. The revolt in Kham was severely repressed and led to the bombing of two major monasteries—Changtreng Sampheling and Lithang. Refugees headed to Lhasa and spoke of the atrocities committed by the PLA to the utter disbelief of the locals. By the beginning of March 1959, another spontaneous demonstration had spread throughout Lhasa. Thousands of people surrounded the Norbulingka, the Dalai Lama's summer palace, demanding to know his whereabouts. Many Tibetans feared the Chinese would either kidnap the Dalai Lama, kill him, or both. They also began to voice their anger and criticism toward the Party leadership and to demand independence. The situation being out of the control of the Kashag (*Bka' shag*), the Tibetan government administration, it was no longer deemed safe for the Dalai Lama to remain in Tibet. Soon after, an escape party was organized, and under the cover of night, on March 17, the Dalai Lama and a small party set out for the Indian border. The Chinese officials in Lhasa, who had been biding their time waiting for the Dalai Lama to quell the demonstrations, finally responded a few days later by launching a full-scale assault to put down the revolt. By all accounts, the result was a massacre of Tibetan soldiers and civilians (Shakya 1999, 202). According to PLA documents confiscated in 1966, eighty-seven thousand Tibetans were killed in the failed uprising (Avedon 1997, 124). The Norbulingka and the Potala were shelled, and the Lhasa government was dissolved (Powers 2007, 201). The Chinese had effectively assumed complete control of Tibet. From 1959 forward, the CCP used the revolt to step up campaigns to eliminate the influence of monasteries (Knuth 2003). These efforts resulted in the arrest and torture of numerous senior monks and lamas and the destruction and/or seizure of monastic properties. The looting, dispersal, and sale of sacred goods that followed this particular period have been described as widespread and systematic. According to Rebecca Knuth:

> Beginning in 1959, the destruction and desecration of rural monasteries in the day was supplemented by the looting of religious treasures at night.

> Truck after truck carried the artifacts of Tibet back to Beijing, and the antique markets in Hong Kong and Tokyo eventually became flooded with Tibetan objects. Throughout the first half of the 1960s, a Chinese-staffed Cultural Articles Preservation Commission inventoried the contents of all the temples, monasteries, shrines, and government buildings. Units of Chinese civilians, including mineralogists and metallurgists, identified objects composed of precious gems and metals, assigned grades of value, and made lists of objects to be sent to China. (2003, 213)

While the suppression of religious institutions continued, by 1962 Mao initiated new, more vigorous social and political campaigns. The Socialist Education Movement (SEM), which focused on battling the economic, political, organizational, and ideological corruption of Chinese cadres on the mainland, was eventually extended to Tibet. In addition, the Three Big Educations (class consciousness, increasing patriotism, and socialist education), a second campaign created for Tibetans, would attempt to mobilize the masses to put an end to the old society and make way for the new order led by the Communist Party (Shakya 1999, 292–293). By 1964, as these campaigns gained momentum, religion was increasingly attacked. There was a massive reduction in the number of monks, and many monasteries were forced to close (300–301). According to reported statistics, between 1959 and 1964 the number of active monasteries dropped from 6,200 to 1,700, and the already diminished number of monks decreased from 110,000 to 56,000 (Grunfeld 1996). The attack on the monastic establishment served to further undermine religious authority and the economic foundations of traditional society. It became increasingly difficult to practice religion, and those who did were subjected to *thamzing*, a practice that was implemented in all Tibetan villages. Religious goods were publicly destroyed both by the Chinese and by Tibetans themselves. Those Tibetans who refused were forced to comply or face being labeled "reactionaries."

In February 1966, religious restrictions in Tibet came to a head with the banning of the yearly Great Prayer Festival (*Mönlam Chenmo*) in Lhasa for the first time since the Chinese had assumed control, a date which, according to Shakya, marked the beginning of the Cultural Revolution for Tibetans (1999, 317). Only months later, a new campaign in mainland China of removing the *Four Olds* (old ideology, old culture, old customs, and old habits) and replacing them with the *Four News* (Mao's ideology, proletarian culture, and

Communist customs and habits), quickly spread to Tibet. Now, any public expression of traditional culture or religious sentiment was viewed as favoring the old society and was banned. Encouraged by endless propaganda to "make room for the new by smashing the old," and motivated to speed up the process of social change in minority regions, the Red Guard troops, a particularly radical faction who saw the cultural distinctiveness of Tibetans as a sign that they were reactionary, descended on Tibet. On August 25, 1966, they stormed the Jokhang Temple in Lhasa, Tibet's main pilgrimage center, and went about destroying centuries-old statues, thangkas, and texts in an initiative that expanded to the three Geluk monastic seats of Sera, Drepung, and Ganden, as well as to the countryside (Craig 1999). Tibetan citizens from every village were forced to remove all images of personal household deities. Images of pure gold or silver that were deemed more valuable disappeared. Those made of lower-quality metals "were ferried to Luyun, from where they were eventually sold to foundries in Shanghai, Sichuan, Tai Yun, Beijing, Tianjin, etc. The foundry called Xi-you Qing-shu Tie (precious metal foundry) situated about five kilometers to the east of Beijing city, alone purchased about 600 tons of Tibetan crafted metals" (Central Tibetan Administration 1996). Monks were forced to walk on and urinate on sacred texts. Other accounts describe texts being shredded and mixed with manure. Statues, murals, and thangkas were destroyed and libraries were desecrated in mass burnings. Many important printing centers, such as Derge, Labrang Tashi Kyil, and Kumbum survived or were only partially damaged. However, others, like Narthang in Tsang, one of the oldest and largest printing houses in Tibet where one of the best-known editions of the Kangyur and Tengyur was compiled, were razed to the ground. According to John Powers, "an estimated one half of Tibet's voluminous religious literature was destroyed, until Chinese authorities belatedly realized that they might be able to make a profit by selling it. As a result, they began shipping loads of books to Beijing, and some of these have been copied and offered for sale" (2007, 206).[35] Many artisans who fashioned images either fled into exile or were forced to give up their craft. Moreover, those artists who remained in Tibet, along with other craftsmen who were involved in the production of traditional or religious culture, were considered "class enemies" and were tortured, used in prison labor, or later died (Clarke 2002, 129). Within Tibet, cultural and religious production ceased, and any semblance of old habits or cultural forms were outlawed and, if witnessed, severely punished publicly. This obliteration of Tibet's material culture and distinctive identity in favor of a policy of total assimilation was accompanied

FIG. 9. A destroyed stūpa at the site of the ruined Sera Gönpasar Hermitage west of Lhasa, a physical reminder of the destructive period of the Cultural Revolution. Numerous ruined religious structures still dot the landscape in Lhasa's surrounding foothills today. Photo taken in 2004 as part of the Sera Monastery Project.

by the public humiliation, torture, rape, and execution of Tibetans that lasted an entire decade.

While Maoist China was, in theory, anticapitalist and anticommodity, especially during the Cultural Revolution, it was this critical period that led to the widespread destruction, confiscation, and dispersal of religious objects and therefore brought about a number of changes with regard to Tibetan religious goods, the most notable being a transformation in their status as commodities. Clare Harris, arguing against Snellgrove and Richardson, who claimed that the increased marketability of Tibetan paintings during the decades that followed the Cultural Revolution was due to the increased knowledge about them and "a revival of interest in the colonial collections in the West," writes that, in fact, it was the chaotic period leading up to and including the Cultural Revolution that brought about the creation of a new market in religious goods:

> From 1959 onwards, as refugees fled from the Chinese incursions into Tibetan territory and began to establish exile communities in India and

> Nepal, many were forced to sell possessions from the homeland in order to survive. The paintings and religious objects which they managed to escape with were eagerly purchased by those whose interest had been triggered by the collecting and documentation of Tibet carried out by such figures as Waddell. . . . Maoist policies of the Cultural Revolution period (1966–1976) also fuelled the market, as the drive to eradicate all tangible traces of Tibetan Buddhism meant that the contents of thousands of Tibetan religious buildings passed to the galleries and dealerships in Hong Kong and further afield. (1999, 36)

While the Western world had collected, bought and sold, and museumized Tibetan religious art and artifacts since the turn of the century, the period immediately before and including the Cultural Revolution dramatically increased their commodification in a manner that was unprecedented.[36] They were now widely distributed commodities and presented as art and cultural artifacts in galleries and museums. Thus, closely related to this transformation toward the commodification of religious goods, the events of the Chinese invasion and Cultural Revolution also simultaneously contributed to their increased aestheticization. Interest grew not in relation to their value as Tibetans themselves viewed it but rather, now, under their new signification as art and antiques. While those who remained in Tibet suffered continued reeducation campaigns, oppression, and starvation and were denied their religious freedoms and distinct identity, many gallery owners who acquired these Tibetan aesthetic and artistic artifacts for low prices returned home and began to sell them at exorbitant prices.[37]

The thousands of Tibetan refugees who followed the Dalai Lama into exile and settled in India and Nepal beginning in the late 1950s would eventually begin the task of remaking their lives and traditions in a foreign land even before the end of the Cultural Revolution. When, fleeing Chinese persecution, they arrived in their new homes, most Tibetans encountered for the first time the idea of Buddhist icons as art and as ready-made commodities, rather than as receptacles for enlightened spiritual energies.[38] While some Tibetans who stayed behind, using a strategy found in Tibetan history in times of religious persecution, resorted to burying their personal religious goods in the hopes of perhaps one day retrieving them, many Tibetans who fled learned that they could get large sums of money for their old paintings and statues.[39] While some managed to preserve them, others, in order to stay alive in the early months in exile, sold their family heirlooms, many of which ended up and remained in the Indian art markets of Darjeeling, Kalimpong, and Delhi until around 1963 (Woodcock 1970, 414–15). Many of those who redeemed their value in the art market turned their profits into establishing businesses such as hotels and restaurants.[40] The rebuilding of Tibetan monastic institutions in Nepal and India and the demand for religious goods created by these new institutions and by the Tibetan diaspora dramatically increased the production and circulation of new religious goods outside of Tibet. Much of the demand for such objects was fulfilled by established Newari artisans and by those Tibetan artists who managed to escape their homeland. While the process of commissioning these goods continued, the influx of Tibetans and Tibetan religious goods would eventually give rise to an increasing number of antique shops and stores selling ready-made objects such as statues and thangkas (only some of which were owned or run by Tibetans) to meet consumer demand and an emerging tourist industry. Some of these would find their way to Tibet after the end of the Cultural Revolution.

CONCLUSION

The above discussion shows that in Tibet, up to the Cultural Revolution, statues, thangkas, and texts were primarily commissioned by patrons, which included monasteries and also individuals, rich and poor. Artists were usually well compensated for their work, as were printers and those involved in textual production. Moreover, religious protocols were very often involved in these exchanges for both parties. Payment was usually offered in the form of either a wage (if working at a monastery) or a voluntary donation, or *yön*, and typically included the giving of other material goods, such as food or even animals. Overall, there was a significant correlation between the prescribed religious protocols for patrons and artists and the proscriptions against selling religious goods found in classical religious texts, on the one hand, and actual transactions (the ways in which images and texts changed hands), on the other. While Tibetans did sell religious goods in Tibet before the Cultural Revolution, such activities were typically condemned, and those who participated in them were seen as being involved in karmically negative behavior and, in another sense, even as spiritually polluted and contagious. The root cause underlying the general absence of these goods from the marketplace likely had as much to do with the religious protocols for artists and patrons as with the religious injunctions against their sale and the negative karmic implications (polluting potential) of such actions expressed in religious literature. The commissioning of religious goods, while of course involving economic transactions, was also, ideally at least, considered a religious activity, an exercise in making merit for both the patron and the artist.[41] The events leading up to and including the Cultural Revolution effectively destroyed most of Tibet's religious material culture and put an end to public religious expression and religious production, now seen by the Chinese communists as anachronistic or as anathema to the goals of socialism. This historic event disrupted the normative pattern of exchange in religious goods. It also emptied Tibet of many of its sacred images and texts (as well as artists) while contributing to the increased commodification (and in the case of images, an increased aestheticization) of Buddhist religious goods outside Tibet. Although some Tibetans in the first few years in exile undoubtedly participated in the selling of religious objects during this period, much of this activity was done in order to survive and occurred under considerable duress.[42]

Following the death of Mao in 1976 and the end of the Cultural Revolution, Deng Xiaoping ushered in a period of reform in China that saw a liberalization of religious restrictions as well as a transition toward a free market economy. While Tibetans, having lived through the previous decade of violence and religious repression met the new religious policies with some skepticism—not knowing where the boundary line existed between what was acceptable and unacceptable—they were allowed once again to publicly express themselves religiously. These freedoms would eventually pave the way for a religious revival. Since the 1980s, and increasingly so in the '90s, despite the long historical record of proscriptions against selling religious goods outlined above and the negative attitudes that were pervasive toward this activity, as well as the reiteration of these proscriptions by contemporary Tibetan Buddhist figures in the post-Mao era, a growing number of self-identified Tibetan Buddhist vendors (i.e., middlemen) within Tibet have begun to participate in the business of selling Buddhist objects for their own livelihoods. Likewise, the number of thangka painters in particular has exploded, and many painters have begun opening their own retail shops in order to sell prepainted (i.e., noncommissioned) thangkas, something that was nonexistent before the Cultural Revolution. While individual Tibetans and monasteries can and still frequently do commission statues or thangkas, thus continuing to participate in more traditional exchange protocols, the growing number of shops selling ready-made religious goods is challenging the traditional means of the production and exchange of these objects and the religious proscriptions against their sale. Many Tibetan vendors of religious objects and painters are now openly engaging in what are, for all intents and purposes, commodification practices (i.e., many are engaging in for-profit, cash-for-goods transactions, at set prices). Many are also serving several different kinds of customers: the Tibetan lay community and pilgrims who need items for religious purposes; monks and nuns in need of a particular book, statue, or thangka for themselves or for their monastery; and an ever-growing influx of tourists, most of whom are Chinese and often non-Buddhist. The next two chapters explore the causes and conditions that have led many Tibetans, despite the religious injunctions against doing so, to openly sell Buddhist religious goods in the marketplace. Taking the context of Amdo as our geographic area of focus, it will be shown that Tibetans' sale of religious objects should not merely be reduced to their embrace of the capitalist free market. Rather, in order to more fully understand Tibetan participation in this activity, it is necessary to also consider the socioeconomic and political context of Tibetans within the PRC since the end of the Cultural Revolution.[43]

4 | The Sale of Buddhist Objects in Amdo

The Socioeconomic Context

Returning to Arjun Appadurai's theory of commodities, Appadurai points out in *The Social Life of Things* that the movement or "trajectory" of an object within its biography illuminates not just the socially constructed nature of the object itself (i.e., the meanings imputed upon it) but also its "human and social context" (1986, 5). By extension, we may say that such movements illuminate the social (including the moral/religious), economic, and political structures that govern their circulation as either commodities or non-commodities in a given society. This, according to Appadurai, refers to the *commodity candidacy* of things—that is, "the standards and criteria (symbolic, classificatory, and moral) that define the exchangeability of things in any particular social and historical context" (14). If we view the commodification of Buddhist objects in Tibet as *processual* (Kopytoff 1986), moving in a temporal trajectory from their status as non-commodities (prior to the Cultural Revolution) toward their widespread, open sale in contemporary Amdo today, what is highlighted in this temporal process is not just a change in the means of their production and exchange (i.e., an exchange largely by commission and voluntary offering toward the increasing sale of pre-priced, ready-made goods) or the potential for these objects to take on new uses and meanings. Also highlighted are the events as well as the social (including religious), economic, and political conditions that help to bring about or that *encourage* their commodification—what Appadurai refers to as an object's *commodity context* (1986, 15).[1] While in the previous chapter it was noted that it was the historical events leading up to and including the Cultural Revolution which effectively disrupted the normative pattern of exchange in Tibetan Buddhist objects, and while the destruction of Tibet's religious material culture during this period undoubtedly helped to fuel a steady domestic Tibetan demand for religious goods after the lifting of religious restrictions in 1978, following Appadurai's suggestion, we must also inquire into the *context* within which Tibetan participation in the commodification of Buddhist objects takes place. Why, now, are a growing number of Tibetans seemingly contradicting a long-held and deeply embedded religious prohibition when as a society—according to the historical record—they largely avoided doing so in the past?

To the casual observer, Tibetans who have opened shops that sell religious goods or who are otherwise engaging in these types of business activities may appear to be doing nothing more than taking advantage of the new opportunities created by the capitalist free market. Indeed, the sight of Tibetan-owned shops selling religious objects, some clearly catering to tourists—with signs in English and Chinese—gives the overall impression that many Tibetans have abandoned the notion that such commercial activity was ever considered a negative practice. Such a view also tends to be supported by recent scholarship, which describes Tibetan participation in these commercial activities. For example, Elizabeth Reynolds's (2011) article on the commercialization of Rebkong thangkas suggests that many Tibetans are indeed catering to a new middle-class Han Chinese taste for Rebkong art and reveals the existence of various sized, but well-established networks of thangka production and distribution between producers in Rebkong and distributors in locations such as Shangri-la, Yunnan Province, and Beijing, all with considerable Tibetan involvement and/or ownership. According to Reynolds, "Tibetan communities such as those in Rebgong are also finding their own ways of adapting to changes in Chinese society, such as by increasing their participation in the new market economy" (92). Rob Linrothe, likewise, has also found that while many monk-artists in Rebkong are kept busy with local demand and perform work in harmony with their ideals (i.e., working on commission and using correct iconography, etc.), many at the same time are also "eager to sell their paintings" (2001, 52). In addition, numerous articles on thangka painting in the Chinese media suggest that many young Tibetans are learning the art form due to its lucrative possibilities, with some authors noting that many painters have begun taking up the craft in order to take advantage of the current market price on the mainland, which is said to have risen tenfold between 2005 and 2010 (Lingui and Chenrong 2010). Indeed, even my own fieldwork in Lhasa and Amdo revealed that some Tibetan shopkeepers are apparently seizing upon this market and are making a very comfortable living, with some sitting on veritable storehouses of product presumably worth tens of thousands of US dollars.[2] However, while it may be possible to locate a number of Tibetans who have fully embraced the capitalist ethic and who have sought to exploit the fact that people (locals and nonlocals alike) want to buy Tibetan religious goods, we should not, for all that, conclude that the causal or motivating factors behind Tibetans' participation in this activity end here. While primary factors for some, to be sure, and while it may safely be said that all of the merchants and painters I interviewed in Amdo were involved in the business in order to make a living, these more obvious reasons tend to mask many of the dynamics and complexities within contemporary Tibetan society which have also served as important motivating factors for Tibetan participation in this activity. Tibetan reasons for engaging in these business ventures have not been homogeneous, merely based on the spirit of opportunism within a context teeming with endless possibilities and in which Tibetans enjoy an even economic and political playing field with China's other ethnic groups, particularly the Han. Rather, many Tibetan participants are often influenced or encouraged by factors that are related, directly or indirectly, to their socioeconomic conditions—conditions that are in many ways an outcome of particular state policies. Importantly, Tibetans are by no means forced to sell Buddhist religious goods; they are, of course, not merely passive agents, but are actively choosing this occupation. However, as will become clear, many Tibetan merchants of religious objects and painters choose or are encouraged to participate as a result of or in response to their current socioeconomic circumstances. Following a description of the emergence of the market in religious objects in Amdo and Tibetan participation in it, we will then turn to a discussion of the economic context and Tibetan motivations for selling religious goods.

THE EVOLUTION AND DYNAMICS OF THE MARKET IN TIBETAN BUDDHIST OBJECTS IN AMDO

By the early 1980s, following Deng Xiaoping's policies of economic reform and the relaxation on religious practice introduced in 1978, a greater degree of autonomy was afforded to Tibetans, and large-scale reconstruction projects to rebuild religious institutions began all over Tibet with the enthusiastic participation of local builders and artists. In Amdo, in particular, while the Chinese Communist government claims to have provided significant financial support for the rebuilding of monasteries and temples, research on the ground has revealed that, while this was true in some cases, local Tibetans predominantly funded this revival.[3] Tibetans' newfound religious freedom had not only seen a return of monasticism and the open display of religious practice—including the performance of rituals, pilgrimage, and the celebration of annual festivals—it also gave rise to renewed religious and cultural production, including a revival of Rebkong arts. According to Rob Linrothe, the rapid pace at which the rebuilding of religious institutions was taking place in Amdo created a huge demand for painters and craftsmen to provide artwork for all existing monasteries and temples (2001, 14). The revival of artistic activities saw the return of old patterns and systems of traditional patronage that existed prior to 1958, as outlying monasteries began once again commissioning Rebkong artists (Fraser 2011, 115–16; Linrothe 2001, 13). Linrothe views the revitalization of thangka painting in Rebkong in particular as nothing less than part of the reassertion of Tibetan Buddhist identity, a force which had been stifled for nearly thirty years under the pressure of "Chinese attempts to submerge it into a generic socialist culture with Chinese characteristics" (2001, 34; see also 41). Following the renewal of religious freedoms and religious and cultural production, however, the revival of the arts has also borne witness to the rise of the commercialization of religious goods generally and of Rebkong arts in particular.

While my own prior preliminary research in Lhasa suggests that the open commodification of religious goods began there in the 1980s with the sale of images of popular lamas, thangkas, and statues from Nepal, and was more or less concurrent with the introduction of tourism, in Amdo, the sale of religious goods, including those produced in the Rebkong area, does not appear to have gained significant momentum until the 1990s.[4] According to one monk from Kumbum Monastery, the earliest commercialization of religious goods in Amdo did not immediately begin with Rebkong arts but with the introduction of mass-produced images from China:

> In the '80s, after the open religious policy passed, religious goods were probably sold, but there were not as many as nowadays. You could hardly see thangkas painted by hand at that time. Then, in the '90s, people started

> selling in the street. There were no painters painting and selling in the streets like nowadays. There were some statues from Nepal, but they were really rare. You could see only a few statues brought from Nepal. There were only some pictures of lamas available in the street and some paper prints available. Then, gradually, I don't know which year it was exactly, there were as many statues made in China as there were stones in the riverbed.

While I have not confirmed that Chinese entrepreneurs and manufacturers initiated the creation of mass-produced religious goods, it is likely that this was the case. Although some Tibetans in more recent years have taken to opening statue production centers, the majority of Tibetans during the 1990s, still relatively impoverished economically, likely lacked the capital, technical know-how, and perhaps even the desire to create mass-produced religious goods, and their participation in this activity seems doubtful at this early date. Furthermore, according to several informants during my fieldwork, it is indeed Chinese manufacturers who today dominate the mass production of religious objects.[5]

Despite this monk's observations, the commercialization of the arts of Rebkong, and in particular of thangkas (including painted and appliqué thangkas, or *gos thang*), appears to have become increasingly widespread in the 1990s. According to Mark Stevenson, who has examined the revival of Rebkong arts since 1978, the beginnings of the commercialization of Rebkong thangkas began around 1991 (2002, 211).[6] This date is corroborated by Elizabeth Reynolds, whose work describes a demand for thangkas outside of Rebkong (in Shanghai) by 1992 (2011, 100).[7] According to my interviews with Tibetan shopkeepers in Xining and Rebkong, however, the earliest Tibetan-owned retail stores exclusively devoted to selling Buddhist religious goods first appeared sometime around 1997 or 1998.[8] In addition, my fieldwork suggests that painters who have opened workshop/galleries for direct sales to consumers in Kumbum, Rebkong, and Labrang are an even more recent phenomenon, occurring only within the last fifteen years or so. Before this time, patrons primarily commissioned images from artists and their families at their homes. Thus, according to my sources, the commodification of Rebkong painting (here referring to the sale of ready-made or noncommissioned images) evolved first as an external market outside of Amdo. Only later did local, privately owned Tibetan stores and galleries appear.[9]

Although it can be assumed that the establishment of an external market for thangkas involved the work of individual painters and/or Tibetan and Chinese entrepreneurs, the Chinese central government also appears to have been at least partly responsible for their commercialization. According to Stevenson (2002), thangka painting in particular has been supported and promoted by the central government ever since the early 1980s—beginning with a state-sponsored exhibition in Shanghai and Beijing in 1982—and the government has indeed played a significant role in the creation of the tourist and/or domestic-external (Han) market. Following the success of this exhibition, the Huangnan TAP party committee and government established the Rebkong Art Gallery, which was administered by the Rebkong Art Research Institute in order to promote and display Rebkong art as well as to preserve and transmit local knowledge of the tradition (Stevenson 2002, 209).[10] While official support has indeed contributed extensively to the promotion and preservation of Rebkong arts and has no doubt benefited a number of Tibetan artists, some scholars have argued that this institutional backing has not been entirely altruistic. Rob Linrothe, for example, has convincingly argued that institutional support has carried with it underlying political and economic motives. According to Linrothe,

> The government pulls all its levers to shift Reb gong painting from monastic control without killing it completely. These levers are financial and institutional power, and they take the tangible forms of an art institute, sinecures for lay artists, publications with glossy color photographs, tourist promotions, and national-level exhibitions. In return for these costly efforts, the potential rewards for the Chinese government are (1) reducing the risk to "national solidarity and the unity of the motherland" from "splittist" identity constructed around Tibetan Buddhism, (2) economic development based on tourism, and (3) the propaganda value of visibly showcasing ethnic culture within the framework of China's borders. (2001, 34)

Other scholars, too, have noted that state support of Rebkong arts has also been driven by the goal of economic development of the region through tourism, as evident by the designation of the town of Rebkong in the Chinese media as the birthplace or homeland of Tibetan art (Stevenson 2002, 197; Marshall and Cooke 1997, 2134).[11] Even according to some Tibetans, however, early government involvement in and support for thangka painting has been aimed at increasing non-Tibetan interest in Rebkong painting and in exploring its potential commercial value. That such was indeed part of the mission of the Rebkong Art Gallery was supported by one painter near Sengeshong Mango Monastery who opened a workshop/gallery in 2009. When asked when the earliest shops selling religious goods first appeared in Rebkong, he replied,

> Nobody had opened a shop here until recently. Some companies used to sell these things, government companies. Before, painters painted at home and just gave [paintings] to them to sell. Now the painters have their own shops. These companies were not so big or really commercial at that time, but usually they did appliqué and gave presents to government officials [to use] for decoration. The companies did mostly advertisement [i.e., promotion]. Their primary aim was to advertise thangka painting in Rebkong for the mainland China market.[12]

While more research is required in order to determine the extent to which the central government has been involved in the beginnings of the commercialization of Rebkong art, if the above comments are historically accurate, it may well be that early government-sponsored institutions and promotional efforts marked not only the beginnings of the commodification of thangkas in Rebkong (perhaps for early tourists) but also provided a link for the establishment of related commercial activities in mainland China. The frequent celebration of the development of the thangka industry and of the profitability of thangka paintings in Chinese newspaper and magazine articles, as well as the government's sponsorship of thangka exhibitions and competitions and its encouragement of collectors, also suggests that the government's early intentions for thangkas may have been part of a plan to develop an external consumer market.[13]

As the introduction of economic reforms in Tibet occurred in the early 1980s and the commercialization of religious goods generally and of Rebkong thangkas in particular is believed to have started in Amdo in the 1990s (with the appearance of Tibetan-owned retail stores appearing toward the end of the decade or later), Amdo Tibetans therefore appear to have entered into the business of selling religious goods relatively late when compared to the opportunities created by market reforms. Such an evolution of the market itself suggests that Tibetans in Amdo were not overly eager to seize upon

FIG. 10. A typical store in the Xining Tibetan market selling statues and thangkas. The owner of this store declined to be interviewed.

FIG. 11. Statues for sale wrapped in plastic sit atop a display case in a recently opened store in the Xining Tibetan market.

the opportunity to sell their religious objects. When I asked my informants about their relatively late participation in the market for religious goods, some noted Tibetans' general lack of business acumen and stated that Chinese and Muslim businessmen were simply better at doing business. Others cited the negative perception of traders and businessmen more generally, as business itself, they explained, involves some degree of cheating and taking advantage of customers. This view is undoubtedly derived from Buddhist teachings, which frequently state that business is not conducive to the spiritual life. Such views can be seen, for example, in Patrül Rinpoche's *The Words of My Perfect Teacher*, in which he writes, "Nothing could be more effective than trade and commerce for piling up endless harmful actions and thoroughly corrupting you" (1998, 106). That Tibetans see (full-time) commerce more generally as un-Buddhist has also been noted by Andrew Fischer as the predominant opinion among rural Tibetans (2008, 24). Still many others, including both middlemen and many monks, agreed that this was chiefly due more specifically to the religious proscriptions against their sale. Nevertheless, despite what may have been a general reluctance among Tibetans to participate in this market, today there is nothing one cannot find in terms of religious goods in the markets of Amdo from Tibetan sellers. The Xining Tibetan market, for example, located across from the main bus station and train station and once dominated by Muslim traders, has slowly seen Tibetan vendors of religious and cultural goods open their doors. There are now over a dozen Tibetan merchants in this market selling various kinds of religious goods—from booksellers specializing in classical religious texts, to those selling appliqué thangkas from Rebkong, to merchants selling statues from Sichuan and Nepal. According to one Tibetan shopkeeper, there are around one hundred Tibetan merchants in total in the market.[14] An official sign designating the commercial area for religious products reads, "Center for the sale and manufacture of bronzes of eastern Tibet [and] gods of wealth as taught in Qinghai Province" (*Mtsho bod nang bstan dzam pa lha gangs can shar li bzo tshong lte gnas*), a sign that certainly would have never existed before the Cultural Revolution.[15] Some of the businesses offering religious goods are family-run or have several members of one family participating with multiple locations in this market. One can also find Tibetan tent manufacturers and Tibetan clothing stores here.

The market surrounding Kumbum Monastery, a major tourist destination, a mere twenty-six kilometers south of Xining, remains dominated by Muslim merchants who sell precious stones highly prized by Tibetans and contains only a very few Tibetan sellers. While there, I counted only four or five Tibetan merchants (this number is probably higher) who sell religious goods as middlemen and only three thangka painters, brothers who owned a small retail shop selling ready-made thangkas but who also accepted commissions.[16]

FIG. 12. The owner of a new shop in the Xining Tibetan market measures the size of an appliqué thangka for sale. This store specializes in appliquéd thangkas from Rebkong and statues from Sichuan. The owner declined to be interviewed.

FIG. 13. A narrow street in the Xining Tibetan market sells a variety of religious paraphernalia: thangkas, statues, monastic clothing, prayer beads, offering butter, prayer wheels, and ritual objects.

FIG. 14. A sign reading, "Center for the sale and manufacture of bronzes of eastern Tibet [and] gods of wealth as taught in Qinghai Province" (*Mtsho bod nang bstan dzam pa lha gangs can shar li bzo tshong lte gnas*), hangs just above the street shown in figure 13.

There is also an entire street northwest of the monastery devoted to repoussé metalwork (a method in which metal is shaped by hammering on the reverse side) and the manufacture of monastery ornamentation. Most, if not all, of this work is done on a commission basis for the renovation of monasteries and temples in the region.

The town of Rebkong, known for the arts historically, contains considerably more retail shops that sell religious goods and is said to contain some twenty-five hundred home-based artists (Lingui and Chenrong 2010). Many thangka shops which sell ready-made thangkas and which accept commissions are located along the highway near the (Upper and Lower) Sengeshong Gonpas and along Dehelong South Road, or Taklung kyil lam (Stag lung dkyil lam), near the main entrance to Rebkong's main monastery, Rongwo Gönchen.

Labrang, which is located in Xiahe County, Gannan TAP, Gansu Province, and is a popular destination on the tourist route for the region—120 kilometers southeast from Rebkong, over a mountain pass—contains only a few stores that sell religious goods on the main thoroughfare headed to the monastery. During the period of my research, I encountered only three major retail shops in Labrang, one of which was owned by an ex-monk (who adamantly refused to be interviewed) on the main road to Labrang Monas-

FIG. 15. Typical stores selling thangkas in the market west of Kumbum Monastery.

FIG. 16. Metalworkers, many of whom are Han, create statues and temple ornaments in street workshops near Kumbum Monastery. Many of these shops had examples out front for passersby to view.

tery. There was also a small Chinese-owned antique shop on the same road, as well as painters who worked primarily on commission and who were located just outside of the monastery. Many smaller towns in the vicinity have at least one or two shops that sell religious goods. One example includes the town of Chentsa, which contained three such shops. While in total I en-

FIG. 17. A thangka painter works on a painting of Mañjuśrī ('Jam dpal dbyangs) in his shop in Rebkong along the road to Rongwo Monastery. Inside are numerous thangkas for sale. This painter explained that most of his customers are Chinese tourists.

countered thirty Tibetan middlemen/sellers who had shops (not including painters who had shops), it was the widespread perception of my informants that the number of Tibetans involved in the sale of religious goods remained low when compared to other ethnicities, such as the Han and Hui. I cannot confirm statistically that this is actually the case, but this perception, which was repeated to me at every turn, is certainly not unfounded, as I encountered several non-Tibetan sellers of Tibetan Buddhist religious goods during my fieldwork. Many claimed that more Chinese merchants who sold Tibetan things (especially thangkas) existed on the mainland.

While this study draws largely upon the views and practices of Tibetan owners of actual retail outlets who act as middlemen/sellers of religious goods and Tibetan painters who have opened galleries and workshops for direct sale to the public, it should nonetheless be briefly noted here, for the purposes of gaining a broader understanding of the location of these participants within the overall distribution structure of the business, that there are several overlapping or interpenetrating markets in Buddhist religious goods in Amdo. While not meant to be an exhaustive or definitive description, it can generally be said that there are two main markets: one internal and one external.

At the most basic level, there is an internal Tibetan market for religious goods which takes place by commission, with paintings or statues moving directly from the artist to the commissioning patron. As previously mentioned, monasteries, both local and more distant ones, frequently commission Rebkong painters and sculptors (or metalworkers) in order to restore old images or to create new ones.[17] The local lay population, likewise, follows this same pattern, although some now also buy ready-made thangkas, statues, texts, and other religious paraphernalia from retail outlets. Reynolds describes the local (lay) internal market for thangkas in particular as small but steady, mainly revolving around life cycle events (2011, 97).

The external market, according to my informants, consists of at least three levels or channels of distribution. First, there are the manufacturers. Aside from thangka painters (which would account for thangka manufacturing), it was widely reported among Tibetan shop owners that the vast majority of the manufacturers of Buddhist religious goods are Chinese-owned and operated companies located in various parts of mainland China, such as Sichuan. While I have not been able to personally verify this assertion, I see little reason to discount these claims of Tibetan merchants, who, after all, purchase items from these agents. Next, there are the wholesalers of religious goods. Many retail sellers said that, with the exception of locally produced thangkas, they indeed purchased their inventory exclusively from various wholesalers throughout Tibet and China. If they sold Nepalese statues, then they either traveled to Nepal themselves or bought them from Tibetan and Chinese trade agents who go to Nepal. According to most of my informants, a high percentage of the wholesalers in this business are, again, Han Chinese traders, although some did note that in Lhasa, in particular, many are Tibetan. Following this, there are, of course, the retailers. At the retail level, there exists what can be identified as an external-local market and an external-remote market. The external-local market may be described as twofold. One is a retail market that is serviced by Tibetans for Tibetans and the occasional tourist. Customers mostly include Tibetan pilgrims, both householders and monks. Items for sale in these shops usually include a whole range of religious goods—from butter lamps and incense, to monastic clothing, to Rebkong thangkas and statues from Nepal and Sichuan, as well as ritual items—and often come from many different locations. The Xining market in particular is an example of this kind of market. Most of my informants who were middlemen/sellers were members of this particular market and claimed that they served a mostly Tibetan clientele. During the period of research, I witnessed no international or Chinese tourists in these shops. The second external-local market is a market in Rebkong thangkas primarily for tourists (although it may also occasionally serve Tibetans), which is a physical retail market located around significant Tibetan Buddhist monasteries. According to Stevenson, the recent local tourist market in thangkas mainly involves young painters who cannot secure larger commissions (2002, 210), and my own observations suggest that this is still the case. Many artists who participate in this market have several pre-painted thangkas available for sale in their stores but also work on a commission basis. Most of the customers for this market are, in fact, Chinese tourists; Westerners, many reported, are interested, but very few actually buy thangkas. Importantly, while the above description of the external-local retail market (both for religious goods more generally and for thangkas specifically) is the case for Tibetans, there are, of course, non-Tibetan retailers of Buddhist religious goods in many of these same areas who primarily service tourists, for it is generally the case that Tibetans prefer to buy from other Tibetans.

Finally, there is what might be described as the external-remote market, consisting of household producer-companies located in Rebkong and immediately surrounding villages that produce thangkas for nonlocal markets. In this case, local and remote businessmen with connections in distant locations commission local Rebkong painters and then resell thangkas to tourists or non-Tibetan collectors in these locations. According to Elizabeth Reynolds (2011), this market is in fact the largest and consists of four types of distribution networks—small businesses, cooperative businesses, mid-sized businesses, and large businesses—which are owned and operated by both Tibetan and Chinese entrepreneurs. The retail point-of-sale for this market is located outside of Rebkong (and even Amdo) at stores in mainland China or in other Tibetan cultural areas.

In addition, it is also of note that the monasteries I visited in Amdo quite consciously did not sell statues or thangkas in their monastery shops. One monk-clerk from Rongwo Gonpa, for example, explained that before they opened their store in 2007 (a shop just inside the entrance to the monastery which mostly contained refreshments and goods for making offerings), each item was carefully scrutinized so as to ensure that no images of buddhas or

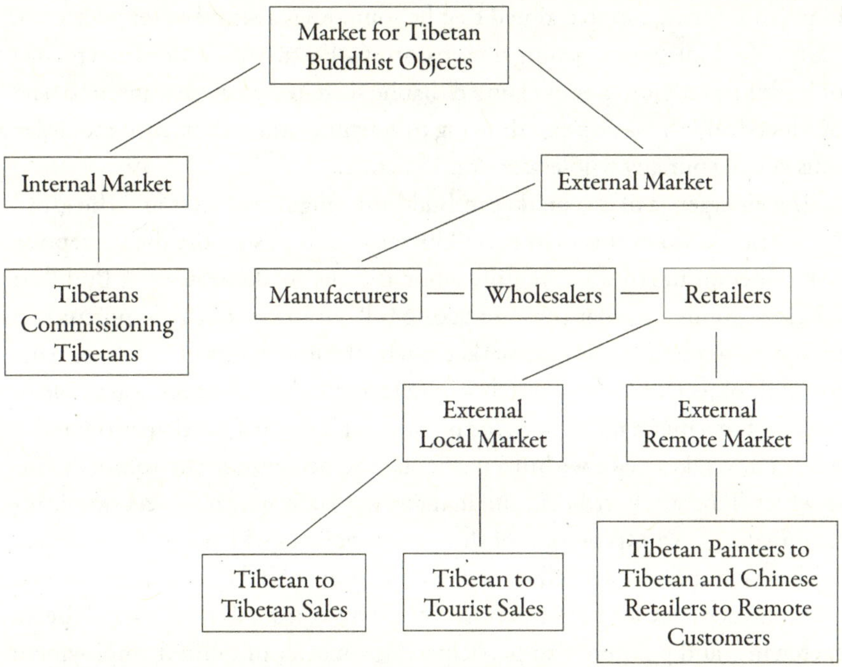

FIG. 18. The general structure of the market in Tibetan Buddhist objects in Amdo (not including books).

bodhisattvas were sold, for to do so, he explained, would be a "violation of religion."[18] On the other hand, some monasteries have been known to sell religious texts at set prices. However, the profits from these sales are apparently recycled and not used for personal expenses. One monk from Kumbum explained that when the monastery was reorganizing in the 1980s, they began to sell religious texts. But shortly afterward they were specifically advised by the current administering monk (which may in fact have been Arjia Rinpoche) not to use the profits for personal expenses but to recycle them for the purposes of producing more texts, a perspective that appears to be directly in line with modern Tibetan scholarly interpretations of how to handle such sales.[19] It has also been my observation that individual monk-painters in Amdo, while they may discuss and negotiate the terms of commissions within the confines of their residences in their respective monasteries, do not generally keep their own residences as retail outlets. As with any market, there are, of course, exceptions to this overall structure and likely much interpenetration of markets. For example, the aforementioned young painter from Kumbum who owned a shop claimed that he sometimes assisted other painters as a kind of middleman in selling their paintings. Furthermore, one Han retailer of Buddhist religious goods claimed that he sketched what he wanted to have produced and then took this drawing to a manufacturer to be made to order, thus cutting out any wholesaler or middleman.

The emergence of the market in Buddhist religious objects and the growing participation in this market by Tibetans tends to support the perception that Tibetans in Amdo have fully embraced the marketization of Buddhist religious goods and that they are taking full advantage of the opportunities presented to them by the free market and by the newer, non-Tibetan demand for such objects. However, such a conclusion, while in many ways true, is only part of a much more complex picture, for Tibetans' participation in this market also takes place within a particular socioeconomic environment, one in which Tibetans have been, and in many ways continue to be, economically marginalized. An exploration of the various policies which have contributed to these conditions, as well as of the reflections of Tibetan merchants and painters on their own participation in the market, reveals that many Tibetan merchants and painters also participate as a matter of limited employment options and out of sense of economic hardship.

THE SOCIOECONOMIC CONTEXT OF COMMODIFICATION AND THE POLICIES OF MARGINALIZATION

From the early 1980s up until the mid-1990s, the Tibet Autonomous Region (TAR) and Qinghai Province were the worst economic performers in the country, with the least-educated minorities and the most rural populations. In response to these conditions, the government began several development projects to stimulate economic growth and to correct economic imbalances between the wealthier eastern coastal regions and the impoverished western provinces (Fischer 2009a, 4). During this period, Amdo underwent rapid economic growth and urbanization. China spent many millions of yuan in subsidies on construction projects and on infrastructure. These initiatives saw numerous Chinese companies venturing west, vying for contracts to partake in this economic boom. Nevertheless, despite government efforts, there remained significant economic inequalities between ethnic groups, largely due to that fact that most Tibetans in Qinghai, as well as in all areas of Tibet, are rural farmers, and expansion and economic growth has been primarily concentrated in urban centers to which the Han Chinese immigrate and where the majority of them live and work (Fischer 2005). These economic disparities and the policies that have fostered them have been the topic of several recent contemporary studies, which have revealed that Tibetans, despite policies seemingly designed to assist them, continue to face particularly challenging socioeconomic conditions. Specifically, education policies as well as economic development policies have, perhaps inadvertently, limited access to the larger pool of employment opportunities within the recent economic boom. The results of these conditions appear to have, at least in part, served as underlying motivating factors for many Tibetans to begin to sell Buddhist religious goods.

STATE EDUCATION POLICIES

Among Tibetans, the practice of sending children to secular schools is a relatively new idea, as education used to be the domain of the monasteries. However, with the modernization of the economy in the 1980s and the central government's drive to promote education as a means of economic development in Tibetan areas, Tibetans have been sending their children to secular schools in the hopes that they will later secure better, nonagricultural employment. During the 1980s, policies were established which supported Tibetan language curricula. The policies established by Deng Xiaoping, which resulted from CCP Secretary Hu Yaobang's visit to Tibetan areas, were set up to train Tibetans for administrative roles (Fischer 2009a, 26). By the 1990s, however, largely as a result of ethnic tensions in minority areas (Johnson and Chhetri 2000), the realities on the ground were quite different, as Tibetan language curricula increasingly gave way to an emphasis on ideological indoctrination and Chinese as the primary language of instruction (Kapstein 2006, 300). The current education policies have been seen by some as exclusionary (Fischer 2005, 2009a; Johnson and Chhetri 2000; Postiglione 1999), for they tend to limit the ability of the majority of Tibetans to advance educationally and thus to compete for available, higher-paying employment. For many Tibetans in Qinghai, where middle schools that teach Tibetan are scarce, formal secular education ends in the primary years, as they find switching from an all-Tibetan curriculum in primary school to a Chinese-language middle school extremely difficult (Kolås and Thowsen 2005, 128). Where Tibetans do attend bilingual middle schools, they receive the benefit of learning both Tibetan and Chinese languages. However, they face the issue of limited class subjects taught in Tibetan, as budgetary constraints often limit the number of Tibetan teachers and Tibetan textbooks in favor of Chinese ones. Subjects taught in Tibetan include arts, mathematics, and Tibetan language and medicine (however, sometimes only Tibetan language), whereas in the Chinese track there are also courses in economics, law, science, business management, forestry, engineering, and agricultural and veterinary studies, subjects more conducive to securing employment in the broader job market (128). These conditions often mean that to compete for government or similar level jobs, one has to opt for the Chinese track. Yet, this presents its own difficulties: learning another language and competing against native Chinese speakers in school (105). Consequently, many Tibetans do not matriculate, and the Tibetans who enter higher education are an extremely small minority.[20]

While a general scarcity of middle schools that teach Tibetan and the difficulties of switching to Chinese as the language of instruction prevent many Tibetans from attending and finishing middle school, cost has become another factor. Beginning in 1985, the central government placed control of education funding in the hands of local governments (Kolås and Thowsen 2005, 106). Since there are imbalances between the wealth of regions, this has meant that some schools are better funded than others. Tibetan areas, which are mostly rural and make up the poorest in all of China, have struggled to attract teachers and to provide children with a decent education. A lack of funds has meant that many of the costs of tuition and books have become the responsibility of students' families. According to Costello, since 1995, students have had to pay the full cost of tuition themselves, a cost which, for many, has proved too burdensome and has been a further cause for dropouts (2002, 225–26).

The rising cost of education coupled with the difficulty of finding employment has, according to Fischer, even prompted emigration from Tibetan areas. According to interviews he conducted with five different families in Qinghai in 2004, all explained that they planned to send one of their children to be educated in India due to the cost of education in Qinghai. Three of the families explained that county-level secondary education was "worthless for obtaining employment after graduation," while four of the families said that the minority education system was contributing to a loss of their culture (2009a, 29).

A third factor with which Tibetans have had to contend has been the end of the job assignment system (*fenpei zhidu*) in 1998, a program in which graduates of middle school were "assured a stable income and social security benefits in a 'work unit' (Ch: *danwei*) that provided for their basic needs" (Kolås and Thowsen 2005, 129). When the system ended, this had a direct impact on enrollment in school among Tibetans, for competing in a job market where placement is no longer guaranteed has discouraged many who know the social realities of discrimination and *guanxi*, the system of social relationships which may assist one in securing a job (Costello 2002, 229).[21] The ending of the job assignment system has also resulted in very concrete exclusionary practices with respect to employment, even for those Tibetans who remain in school and graduate. According to Fischer, planned protests of around two hundred students occurred in Golok (Qinghai) in 2004 in response to the perception that the government was awarding jobs to nonlocal residents and had failed to follow through on their promise of employment. A similar event occurred in Lhasa in 2006 after the government apparently awarded only two jobs to Tibetans out of one hundred available public positions (Fisher 2009a, 30). Fischer sees the educational system as one that is structured for ethnic (Tibetan) exclusion and discrimination. He argues that the education system is set up to advantage Chinese speakers:

> The policy of increasing the use of Chinese language in the education system of Tibet masks an implicit discrimination against Tibetans within the larger provincial society and economy. The dominant use of Chinese in business and the government creates a situation whereby upward mobility depends on fluency in Chinese. Yet the dilemma of Chinese versus Tibetan language medium in education leads the education system into a catch twenty-two of underachievement for Tibetan students, particularly in the monolingual rural areas. This has occurred because up to the mid-1990s, ninety-five percent of primary education was conducted in Tibetan, while secondary education was almost entirely conducted in Chinese, outside certain Tibetan language courses. When education in Tibetan is emphasized at the primary level, students perform better and there is less alienation and dropout, but then students are mal-adapted for secondary education and for the non-farm job market. The switch to Chinese language secondary education has the result that many Tibetan students have difficulty performing. Drop out rates are therefore high. (2002, 34)[22]

In addition, not only do the structural policies of the education system tend to put Tibetans at an educational and thus economic disadvantage, it may also threaten their very identity, which has become increasingly connected to the Tibetan language in the current sociopolitical environment. Those Tibetans who do continue through middle school, opting for the Chinese language track, have little opportunity, beyond the primary years, to learn to read and write Tibetan (Kolås and Thowsen 2005, 130–31). The importance of the language issue vis-à-vis Tibetan identity has been exemplified by demonstrations in Rebkong and elsewhere in October 2010, in which, according to some estimates, thousands of students and teachers demonstrated against government announcements that it planned to end Tibetan-language instruction in schools altogether.[23] A similar act was repeated in March 2012 when around seven hundred students, again in Rebkong, carried out a large protest calling for language rights after they were issued textbooks in Chinese (Tsering 2012). While the central government sees this move toward Chinese language as the sole medium of instruction as preparing students for future employment and as promoting the unity of "one China," many Tibetans see this policy move as an infringement on their constitutional rights to receive instruction in their own language and as yet another attempt by the central government to eliminate Tibetan culture.[24]

For some Tibetans, the challenges to acquiring secondary education and thus the skills necessary to compete for a broader range of nonfarm employment opportunities appear to have had a direct impact on their decision to enter the business in religious goods. My fieldwork suggests that a number of Tibetans who did not continue in school (or who otherwise dropped out) have sought a livelihood as sellers and manufacturers of religious objects. Among my informants who owned and/or operated retail outlets, five were former students who had dropped out of school and had entered or opened businesses primarily serving the Tibetan external-local market. Three people who worked for an appliqué thangka manufacturer in Nyentok Village in Rebkong County had also dropped out of school and worked full time assisting in the manufacturing of thangkas for the local internal market (mostly monasteries).[25] Of these retailers and thangka manufacturers, two explained that their decision to leave school was due mainly to the cost of education. Two other retailers explained that their decision to enter the business was due to their lack of other marketable skills. One young woman from Kumbum, for example, explained that, unlike other jobs, which would require more training and knowledge, and thus more schooling, her business did not require specialized training that other jobs—even other retail jobs selling other products—would necessitate. Being Tibetan, and Buddhist, she explained, she already knew about the products and images, which gave her the confidence to run a small business selling such goods. Another woman who maintained a shop in the town of Chentsa explained, similarly, that the business of religious goods was "all that she knew," as she had no other skills, while a third young woman in Rebkong explained that family poverty and the fact that she had dropped out of school was what ultimately led to her decision to open her business.[26]

In a context in which the path to broader employment opportunities through secular education has become increasingly difficult and costly, as well as a perceived threat to their language and traditional culture, some Tibetans are indeed turning to selling Buddhist religious goods—an opportunity available to unskilled Tibetans which requires little (if any) formal training, requires only a modest investment, and is generally perceived as economically sustainable given the fairly consistent local and tourist demand. Although more research would need to be done to determine the extent to which the rise in educational costs and the end of the job assignment system acted as a catalyst for Tibetans to enter into this business, it is interesting to note that these policies (which took place in 1995 and 1998 respectively) roughly coincide with the appearance of the first Tibetan-owned shops which sold religious paraphernalia.[27] Nevertheless, given the fact that the socioeconomic context is one in which Tibetans do not enjoy equal access to quality, affordable, and competitive education and to employment, for these former students, entering the business in religious goods appears to have been a decision based at least as much on economic necessity and a narrow field of employment options as a decision motivated by mere opportunism.

STATE ECONOMIC DEVELOPMENT POLICIES

While Tibetans must navigate the difficulties of the education system, according to recent studies, the economic development policies and strategies of the central government also have not effectively led to a broader range of employment opportunities for Tibetans.

According to Andrew Fischer, one of the problems faced by rural Tibetans has been the slow growth of the agricultural sector to which the vast majority of rural Tibetan families are tied (Qinghai Tibetans were over 91 percent rural in the 2000 census; 2005, 53 and 136).[28] This slow growth, along with the growth in urban populations and the potential opportunities in urban centers, has led many rural farming Tibetans to search for supplementary income and higher wages in nonagricultural work. This process has been documented in the TAR by Goldstein, Childs, and Wangdui (2008) in what Tibetans have called "going for income" (*yong 'babs la 'gro*), but the same efforts can be observed among Tibetans in Qinghai. According to Fischer, despite Tibetans' attempts to secure such work in urban areas, many find that there is, unfortunately, little opportunity when they arrive in such centers, since the economic boom created by subsidies has also attracted Han and Hui Muslim migrant workers to lower-end jobs in these same areas. Fischer explains,

> Thus Tibetan rural-to-urban migrants and the Tibetan urban poor clash with these out-of-province 'spontaneous' migrants over the residual activities left over from the unproductive boom. Given that the out-of-province migrants generally possess much higher skill levels than the local population and are emigrating from more competitive areas of China, the level playing field between migrants and locals in the urban economy effectively becomes an issue of vastly unequal competition, and thus the confluence of migration flows reinforces social exclusion among the local population. (2005, 133)

Several scholars have noted that during this period immigration was encouraged to speed up the pace of economic development and was facilitated by incentives to resettle in western regions. For example, according to Lustgarten:

> *Hukou*, a residence registration system, was immediately reformed to allow Han migrants to circulate into and around Tibet without restriction. Border checkpoints were eliminated. Business regulations were relaxed, and migrants and officials were offered guaranteed housing, higher wages, tax breaks, and other preferential treatment—such as assured health care and education, which did not exist for indigenous people. (2008, 129)[29]

Given this development scenario, and in the absence of an affirmative action employment policy for Tibetans, which would assist them with securing jobs with investing companies working in Tibetan areas, rural Tibetans must secure employment by themselves and are often marginalized economically in this process with the result that many assume menial or labor-intensive work.[30] For example, it is well documented that the Qinghai–Lhasa railway project, which was completed in 2006 as a major development initiative and touted as bringing prosperity to Tibet, employed a mostly Han, Mandarin-speaking labor force. Only a very limited number of Tibetans were hired for this project, and due to both their lack of skill and their language deficiencies, they participated in the most menial labor—breaking rocks and digging drainage ditches (Lustgarten 2008, 192–93). Fischer likewise finds that even in smaller-scale construction projects, the companies chosen to do the work often come from outside the province and use mostly Han migrant workers (Fischer 2005, 78).[31] He argues that many companies that utilize government subsidies, which could focus on developing the skills of the local population, are instead focused primarily on their own economic growth and on becoming more competitive nationally (79).

Similarly, many scholars have found that tourism, as an economic development strategy, one that is heavily promoted by the Chinese authorities, does not bring the local benefit in the way it has in other development contexts. While sparking some small-scale Tibetan enterprises in the form of tour guides, hotels, restaurants, and souvenir-related businesses, many have observed that the larger share of the tourism industry is dominated by Chinese companies (Cingcade 1998, 15–16). Many tourism services such as travel agencies and hotels are, in fact, run by local tourism departments and other government agencies, a situation which has led to an uneven distribution of profits (Kolås and Thowsen 2005, 168). Yang and Wall in their 2009 article on ethnic tourism, commenting on the level of autonomy afforded to minorities in the context of tourism-related business, write, "Given the fact that managers of tourism enterprises are virtually always Han people and minority people are typically low-paid labourers, 'true' ethnic autonomy does not exist in the Han-dominated tourism industry. Ethnic cultures are regarded as an 'exploitable' resource to make profits for these entrepreneurs, few of whom are willing to share economic power with minority people" (564). Other scholars have also reported this same pattern of economic disparity within the tourism industry. According to Schrempf and Hayes (2009), who trace the development of the tourism sector in Songpan County in Sichuan, while some Tibetans have managed to benefit from the tourism industry—particularly from the new branding and sales of local traditional products, horse trekking, building, and souvenir-related businesses—tourism, especially since 2000 and the "Opening of the West" campaign (*Xibu da kaifa*), has also led to a number of problems, not the least of which is a drop in Tibetan business ownership. They write:

> In urban areas, for private entrepreneurs (shop owners) and for some grassroots businesses, such as the trekking companies, tourism means a real boom. On the other hand, there seems to be a clear and rather alarming shift in business ownership in Songpan town moving towards more Han and less Tibetan entrepreneurs in recent years. According to local Tibetans, there also had been a marked in-migration of Han Chinese happening since 2000 that might have simply outnumbered previous Tibetan ownership by buying them up. Nowadays, the conditions that need to be met for opening up a private tourist agency, for example, are almost impossible to achieve—they require very high capital investments, excellent knowledge of Chinese language, and above all, *guanxi* with local officials and regional tourism offices and companies. (308–9)[32]

Fischer, although referring primarily to the TAR, has found that much tourism investment and revenue functions similarly to the overall subsidization and investment in the western provinces, in that much of the revenue generated by tourism is accumulated by companies located outside of Tibetan areas (2009b, 50). The disadvantages experienced by minorities generally within the context of tourism development in China have been recognized by a number of other scholars. For example, Yang, Wall, and Smith, in their study on ethnic tourism in China (2008), support Fischer's views:

> Minorities are not in a good position to compete with experienced Han developers who are better educated and funded, and have easier access to planning and business intelligence. Training of minorities merely focuses on how to behave around tourists, and does not assist them in becoming economically self-reliant. (766)

This situation has left Tibetans with more jobs that are lower paying within the tourism industry and ones that are primarily reliant on independent, international travelers (Cingcade 1998), who, while making up the majority of tourists to Tibet early on, today constitute a mere fraction of the total number of tourists. Today, most tourists to Tibetan areas are domestic Han

Chinese who prefer larger, highly organized, prepackaged tours and prefer to stay in Han Chinese-run hotels. The result of such patterns is likely that much of the generated revenue flows out of tourist centers (Fischer 2009b, 52).[33] According to Fischer, taken together, the influx of development investment and subsidies, while leading to a slight increase in living standards, has led primarily to the economic exclusion of the majority of Tibetans, who lack Chinese fluency and experience with Chinese work cultures and are not well connected (2009b, 53).

While recent government economic development strategies have tended to foreclose on a broader range of employment possibilities for many Tibetans, it must be noted that some opportunities available in manual labor can actually be quite lucrative. According to Daniel Winkler, one of the main sources of nonfarm income among rural Tibetans has been the collection and sale of caterpillar fungus, or *yartsa gunbu* (*dbyar rtswa dgun 'bu*), literally "summer plant, winter worm." Scientifically known as *Cordyceps sinensis,* it has been cultivated for centuries on the Tibetan Plateau and today enjoys a very high market value. It is used primarily in Chinese medicine for a variety of ailments but is also widely known and used for sexual dysfunction and as an aphrodisiac. According to Winkler (2008a), roughly 40 percent of rural Tibet's total cash income, and in some regions as high as 80 percent, is derived from its sale. This has enabled rural Tibetan families, many of whom have no education whatsoever, to improve their standard of living and to participate in the new commodities-based economy (Winkler 2008b, 303).[34] *Yartsa gunbu* is not all positive, however. In recent years, as the market value has escalated, many young Tibetans spend a portion of the summer collecting this fungus (the collection period is roughly forty days) and make so much money doing so, they often drop out of school and involve themselves in various nonproductive activities. This has contributed to various problems in Tibetan communities—impeding education and even leading to alcoholism among Tibetan youth. It has also led to problems with Tibetans from other regions coming to collect in others' territories and has led to several fights and even murders in recent years. Moreover, there are serious concerns that the economic bubble created by the fungus will burst, for according to some reports, the yield of "*bu*" is much lower than it used to be, and the environmental damage caused by its harvesting may be taking its toll.[35] According to Winkler, should *yartsa gunbu* ever become unsustainable, the Tibetan rural economy would be devastated (2008a, 31). This position is also seemingly supported by Kunga Tsering Lama in his anthropological study of the collection of *yarsta*, "Crowed Mountains, Empty Towns: Commodification and Contestation in Cordyceps Harvesting in Eastern Tibet" (2007). On the importance of *yartsa* to the rural economy, he writes, "even though the seasonal harvesting of *cordyceps* has become a major source of income for rural Tibetans, their heavy concentration on the trade *also* indicates the marginalization of the Tibetans in contemporary China. There are hardly any other viable sources of income for the Tibetans except for the seasonal *yartsa* trade" (33). While the harvesting of caterpillar fungus has, for the time being, provided a much needed boon for rural Tibetans within an economy which offers few other alternatives, the local economy's dependence on this trade only underscores the urgent need for greater economic opportunity and employment diversification.[36]

There are, of course, Tibetans who have managed to navigate the opportunities provided by market reforms and state economic development policies. According to Fischer, those Tibetans who are more likely to succeed are typically those who have acquired secondary education, Chinese fluency, and familiarity with Chinese work cultures and those with connections to government and business networks in China—a population that made up about 12 percent of Tibetans in 2005 (2009b, 53). Nevertheless, according to the above findings, these policies have not necessarily assured that the jobs that are created, even those in Tibetan areas, necessarily go to Tibetans. Instead, Tibetans often find themselves to be less educated and bested in competition with better-skilled and better-educated migrants. While some opportunities in manual labor can, as we have seen, generate an important source of cash income, this source cannot support the entire Tibetan rural population, nor does it suffice to begin to ameliorate the overall educational and economic issues (many of which are structural) facing Tibetans. Thus, government development policies, rather than assisting Tibetans in a transition to improving their skills toward better employment or investing in the development of the *local* economy, have not improved Tibetans' overall ability to assume a broader range of employment opportunities. Even some Chinese officials apparently acknowledge this. According to Fischer, "many officials in West China privately admit that in the end, eastern enterprises may benefit more from western development than the western provinces themselves" (Fischer 2005, 79).

The rather poor economic environment for Tibetans described by the above scholars was reflected in the responses of a number of Tibetans who were involved in the sale of religious goods, as many cited economic reasons as significant factors motivating their participation in this business. Among my informants in Rebkong, for example, three separate individuals claimed that they participated in the business of religious goods as a result of the fact that land previously owned by their families was reduced or confiscated by the government and that income from farming was no longer enough to sustain them. One such response came from two brothers, the sons of a blacksmith (who was also a craftsman of large ornate stūpas), who had recently opened an antiquities shop that sold various items such as stūpas, new statues, thangkas, and jewelry. According to one of the brothers:

> There are so many people who have no jobs, people like him [pointing to a friend]. He used to be on the government staff. He was paid for a while, but due to downsizing lost his job. We used to own some land, but the land was taken away by the government, so now we have nothing to survive on. Since we have no other skills or choices we have to rely on this, even though our parents don't agree. Besides, by selling these things, I provide jobs for those who have lost their jobs.

The aforementioned appliqué thangka maker from Nyentok Village in Rebkong provided a similar response. When asked if he remembered when the sale of thangkas and religious goods started to occur on the street and if there was any community reaction or backlash to openly selling religious goods, he replied by pointing to the larger economic problems associated with the loss of land:

> There was not really a community reaction [to selling religious goods]. Everybody knows. Look at this place. Most of the fields [have been taken] . . . We owned some lands, and nowadays the government took them all. We have no fields anymore. So in order to survive we must depend on something. This is all we have; this is all we depend on. If you want to send your kids to school, you don't have money to send them, so for that reason, sometimes we need to sell it.

Still another painter, just outside Sengeshong Mango Gonpa, who had been painting for ten years and owned a gallery which sold ready-made thangkas to mostly Chinese tourists, said that part of his reason for painting had to do with the fact that income from farming was not enough to make ends meet:

> This is a way of making a living. It is out of necessity. We have really limited lands to cultivate. Actually, it's not enough to produce things to feed us [and] to make a living. Each family owns three or four *mu*. Also, there are so many students going to school, and it's hard to tell if all these students will graduate and get a job. So all these people are trying to find a way to make a living. We cannot make a living only on cultivating lands.[37]

According to these Tibetans, the fact that they were involved in the business of religious goods was directly related to recent transformations in the economy and the reduction or loss of farming income, an issue raised by both Goldstein and Fischer as contributing to a search for nonfarm income, a search that is not always successful. Unemployment, likewise, was noted as a significant problem, as was having the skills to enter other kinds of employment. There was also a keen awareness among the last respondent in this category that schooling no longer guarantees one a job and may be a risky investment. In response to the loss of farm income, and in light of the fact that, according to their perceptions, there were few, if any, available alternatives, these individuals assumed these activities full time, framing their participation by referring to economic or financial difficulties.

Beyond the loss of income from the reduction or loss of farmland, however, other merchants, even those who had completed middle school education, cited economic reasons for their decision to enter the business. For example, one man, who operated a rather successful shop in the Xining Tibetan market selling Nepalese statuary which opened in 1999 and (according to him) was among the first businesses in the market to sell religious goods, explained that when he finished school he could not find a job, a situation which encouraged him to open his own business. A similar reason was provided by another woman merchant in Chentsa who also claimed that she had completed some middle school and had searched for work but could not secure other means of employment. As a consequence, she took over the store for her brother, who had recently passed his middle school exams, suggesting that the business in religious goods is not only one that Tibetans turn to out of a lack of employment options but also one which is sometimes utilized in the pursuit of upward mobility in order to create further, presumably better employment opportunities. Regardless, neither of these sellers' responses suggests that selling religious goods was their first choice of employment. Rather, their inability to secure other work was the primary catalyst that encouraged them to begin selling religious goods.

Two other informants emphasized that they lacked the skills necessary to enter into other kinds of employment and implied that selling religious goods was not necessarily the kind of work they wished to continue to do in the future. One older merchant in Rebkong, for example, a man who was formerly a shepherd and who began selling religious goods in order to improve his livelihood, explained that one of the main reasons he was involved in the business was out of economic necessity and because he did not have the skills or education to perform many other forms of nonfarm work:

> It's not a good thing to sell religious goods. We admit that. But I'm not selling statues. Mainly if you sell statues you create negative karmas. I am not educated. I don't have all this modern knowledge to start another business. We have to live. We have to survive. This is not the best choice. If you are capable of doing something else, then you would do it. But since we are not educated, we can't do it. I think we have to focus on education. Tibetans are obviously backward, from the past up to now, still backward. We should educate the younger generation so they can do something else, not only selling this stuff.[38]

One other seller I encountered in the Xining Tibetan market, who admittedly entered the business with some apprehension due to the negativity associated with selling religious goods, reflected a similar position. While he aspired to move on from the business in religious goods by opening a hotel, he felt that the experience he gained in his current business wasn't really transferable to another kind of business. After relating to me the local government's plans to turn the Xining Tibetan market into a piazza-like space in the future, he explained that if the plans went through, he would not return to selling religious goods.[39] Both of these sellers not only projected ambivalence toward their participation in the commercialization of religious objects but also expressed a dilemma between having limited skills and abilities, on the one hand, and the need to make a living, on the other.

Finally, two younger monks in Rebkong also expressed the problem associated with employment and the generation of income. Today, the vast majority of monasteries in Amdo, and in Tibet more broadly, largely due to changes to the monastic economy, have been compelled to develop creative new ways to earn a living.[40] Monks, besides any family support they may receive or any donations they may earn from performing rituals, have increasingly sought to make a living through various means of employment. In Rebkong, for example, several monks work in general stores operated by their respective monasteries. Others manage China Telecom shops. Still others manage tourism at their respective monasteries, taking tickets and leading tours.[41] One monk from Dechen Monastery (Bde chen) and not from the local Rebkong area, who worked in a shop that sold religious goods, explained his activities to be a matter of economic necessity.[42] When asked about the fact that the shop sold religious goods and whether this was a legitimate means of livelihood, he responded: "There are so many monks in the monastery and there is not much religious freedom now in the country. It is not like it was in the past. That is why we have some [economic] difficulties in daily life. This is a way to raise money."[43]

The same economic concerns were reflected by another young monk-painter from Sengeshong Mango Gonpa who, before I requested an interview with him, approached me to ask if I was interested in obtaining a thangka painting. When asked what he thought of the commercialization of religious goods, he responded: "It's hard to tell because many people are surviving on this. In this society, if you don't have more, it's hard to survive." Furthermore, when asked if he saw the commercialization of religious goods as becoming more socially acceptable, he responded that, for him, the issue was really a matter of being able to support himself financially:

> Well, there are some unacceptable things and acceptable things; there are positive things and negative things. Monks in mainland China are paid a salary, but we are not. Although we know that selling religious goods is considered negative, we have to sell; we are obliged in order to make a living. We have to be self-sufficient.[44]

Whether or not this monk's observations with respect to salaries being paid to Chinese monks is accurate, the above responses reflect the changes to the monastic economy and the fact that today many monasteries and monks in Tibet must often seek outside employment. According to one administrator-monk at Sengeshong Mango, smaller monasteries, including Sengeshong, in contrast to larger monasteries such as Rongwo Gonpa, do not receive government funding, making the search for employment among painters a necessity.[45] Loden Sherap Dagyab, in his work *Tibetan Religious Art* (1977), noted that some painters in exile were compelled to make a living from tourists, having lost the bulk of the source of their patronage (1:28). However, his observations may also apply to many young monk-painters in Amdo, who today may not have access to additional sources of income, may not be able to secure larger commissions from a monastery, and face an increasingly competitive market due to the steadily rising prices and quantity of thangka paintings on the market in recent years (Reynolds 2011, 97). Similar observations concerning monks' need for outside income have also been made by Kunga Tsering Lama in his work on the commodification of *yartsa gunbu*. At Lithang Monastery (in Kham), he found that monks, in a breach of religious injunctions against digging the earth—which is required when harvesting *yartsa*—were in fact contradicting these religious proscriptions. However, he argues that such activities should not necessarily be interpreted as a "triumph of market forces" but largely as a result of the fact that the government policy has required that particular monasteries must be economically self-sufficient. As to the motivation underlying these monks' activities, he writes:

> The explanation appears to lie in the fact that this particular monastery has long had a bad reputation with government officials ever since its resistance against the Chinese in the late 1950s. According to a Chinese NGO worker familiar with the area, the government in some Tibetan parts of Sichuan has been pushing monks to be self-reliant and to find alternative sources of income and not to rely on nearby residents for their livelihood. However, this is selectively enforced. In the case of this monastery in Lithang, the government pressure on the monastery for the monks to be completely self-reliant and not to take any income at all from local donations is strong. This forced self-reliance is less about a free market ideology in this case than the fact that the government does not really want the monastery to exist. Hence, monks harvesting cordyceps here should be understood in the context of these larger political pressures coming into play. (2007, 81)

Thus, while Rob Linrothe has noted in his study of the renaissance of Rebkong painting that many monk-artists are "eager to sell their paintings"

FIG. 19. The Rongwo Gonpa Wholesale Store (Rong bo dgon pa'i sdeb tshong khang) sells general supplies (but no Buddha images or texts). Out front, Tibetan and Muslim men deal in caterpillar fungus as police watch on. Such businesses indicate that even larger monasteries, which are said to have received funding from the central government, participate in generating alternative means of economic support.

(2001, 52), the subtext to this seemingly entrepreneurial move, as implied by the above testimonies, may in fact be that many monks are motivated to a large extent by a very real financial need.

CONCLUSION

Throughout this chapter it has been shown that Tibetans living in Amdo face particularly challenging socioeconomic policies and conditions. Tibetans' educational opportunities in their native language are limited, and due to the structure of the education system as well as rising costs, coupled with the end of the job assignment system, many tend not to complete their education. As a result, many Tibetans fail to be competitive in the job market, which increasingly requires Chinese fluency, familial or *guanxi*-type connections, and familiarity with Chinese work cultures. Rural Tibetans are now also competing with Han and Hui Muslim immigrants who generally have better skills and a higher level of education. In addition, even in areas where Tibetans could ostensibly capitalize on the growing economy—areas such as tourism or construction—such employment opportunities are not always available and (in the case of construction) are often assumed by Han migrant workers. These are by no means normal market conditions, which is to say, conditions in which there are a plethora of opportunities for Tibetans. Rather, they are conditions that are constrained by particular government policies, which tend to limit Tibetans' ability to find employment outside traditional means such as agriculture. The theme that emerges from the above testimonies reflects a preoccupation with these economic realities. Some see their involvement in the sale of religious objects as the only sensible alternative to the loss of land and income from farming. Two sellers in Xining expressed the wish to do something else. Others, having gone to school, resorted to selling religious goods after having unsuccessfully searched for other types of work. While some see their occupation as resulting from their lack of skills and education, others see the business as a stepping-stone in their quest for other, presumably better, employment. Thus, what is emphasized in many of the above testimonies are very significant economic challenges within Tibetan society, something that is confirmed by outside scholars and by Tibetans themselves. Tibetans' own responses suggest that the sale of religious objects is a viable alternative within a context in which they have very few other opportunities. In some cases, the sale of religious objects was even framed as a matter of economic survival. Nevertheless, while we can read some Tibetans' sale of religious goods in Amdo as a response to their economic situation, the question of why Tibetans are participating in this business cannot be reduced to the socioeconomic dimension. In order to more fully understand the causes and conditions which have contributed to the sale of religious goods by Tibetans, we must also consider additional factors, those stemming from their sociopolitical position as an ethnic minority in China.

5 | The Sociopolitical Context of Commodification

As the participation of Tibetans in the sale of their religious goods is becoming increasingly widespread, and as new shops are popping up in the Amdo region, many are discovering that this kind of business activity is not only a sustainable source of income but also (especially for painters) sometimes a significantly lucrative one. However, as we have also observed, Tibetans are not alone in these pursuits but are competing in an open market with other ethnic groups—not ethnic groups touting their own cultural and religious objects, but those that are involved in the manufacturing and selling of traditionally *Tibetan* religious goods. Simultaneously, it is also a fact that tourism, or more precisely, Tibetan ethnic tourism, is a reality in Tibetan cultural areas. It is an industry which aims to attract visitors to experience and consume Tibetan culture, and one in which the central government has been intimately involved in planning, promoting, and actively encouraging Tibetans to participate in as a means of economic development. Thus, on the one hand, for a number of Tibetan merchants and painters, the sale of religious objects in many ways has come to represent an effort to reclaim such goods as distinctly Tibetan in the face of what many perceive to be the appropriation of this market by non-Tibetans and their mistreatment of religious objects. At the same time, the central government's involvement in the development of Tibetan ethnic tourism is also a factor that has played a significant role in influencing Tibetan participation in this market, both by its creation and encouragement of the market for Tibetan cultural/religious products and by its discourse of development. While the preceding chapter has illustrated that Tibetans' sale of Buddhist objects is often related to legitimate socioeconomic issues and concerns, other evidence suggests that many Tibetans are also choosing this occupation as a response to these particular sociopolitical dynamics.

TIBETANS' SALE OF RELIGIOUS GOODS: A RESPONSE TO NON-TIBETAN PARTICIPATION IN THE MARKET

In his seminal and often cited work *Ethnic and Tourist Arts* (1976), Nelson Graburn examines the particular phenomenon of tourist art—art that is created specifically by minority peoples or cultures for tourist consumption but which has been historically disregarded as an inauthentic manifestation of indigenous art.[1] Within Graburn's overall attempt to correct this view, arguing that tourist art is an important means of maintaining and projecting an ethnic identity or image to the outside world (5), he makes a general distinction between art that is created for outsiders, on the one hand (i.e., *tourist art*), and functional/traditional art that is created for internal consumption, on the other, which, while vulnerable to change over time, is typically excluded from commercialization. Furthermore, Graburn argues that what usually occurs when functional/traditional forms begin to be desired by outsiders is that "the local people start to make *near exact replicas* just for sale, adhering to near traditional forms and designs which satisfy their own aesthetic traditions and guarantee some form of 'authenticity' to the buyers" (Graburn 1984, 399; emphasis mine). He goes on to cite particular instances of this practice, which include "the creation of secular figures derived from religious *bulto de santos* in the Hispanic Southwest, the replication of masks and statues in many parts of West Africa, the UNESCO inspired reproduction of ritual *bisj* poles by the Asmat, and so on" (399). To this list, we might also add Australian Aboriginal bark paintings, which are produced for tourists, yet do not contain the secret or sacred forms traditionally associated with them (Belk and Groves 1999).[2] Thus, within Graburn's volume, it is generally assumed that most, if not all, of the ethnic peoples discussed in his work (although now living in a subordinate political position) not only control what is deemed appropriate for selling for themselves (i.e., that they have the ability to collectively withhold their sacred objects from commercialization, or to create near exact replicas of their sacred goods if or when they choose to do so) but that they also maintain exclusive rights over their religious and cultural productions. It is this latter point that is brought into sharp focus in the Tibetan context and that highlights the sociopolitical position of Tibetans within the PRC vis-à-vis Tibetan Buddhist objects. For despite article 4 of the Chinese constitution, which guarantees the equality of ethnic groups as well as regional autonomy for ethnic minorities, Tibetans do not enjoy genuine autonomous status, which would allow them sole governance over their own economic, political, religious, and cultural affairs, not to speak of exclusive rights to their arts and crafts traditions.[3]

Today, in the absence of control over their religious and cultural productions, Tibetans have witnessed the participation of non-Tibetans in the manufacturing and selling of what many perceive to be *their* (i.e., Tibetan) religious arts and crafts. In fact, it was widely proclaimed by Tibetan merchants, painters, and even monks interviewed in Amdo that the vast majority of the manufacturers, wholesalers, and retailers of Tibetan Buddhist religious goods were not actually Tibetans but were predominantly Han Chinese and Hui Muslims. While a thorough verification of these assertions would, of course, require more research into the manufacturing and distribution sides of the business, as well as a broader quantitative survey of the ethnicities involved in these activities, some independent reports appear to substantiate these widely held claims. For example, Alexander Berzin, writing on the relation between Hui Muslims, Tibetans, and Uighurs, has noted:

> The Hui, being very ingenious as well as industrious, have taken over the manufacture and sale of traditional Tibetan goods, and the Tibetans cannot, and do not even seem to want to compete. The Hui are making Tibetan-style jewelry, rosaries, and other religious paraphernalia, equipment for horses, knives, wool, carpets, musical instruments, shoes and noodles, as well as running the ubiquitous restaurants. The Han merchants come only later and sell mostly modern Chinese manufactured goods like toothbrushes and cheap Chinese clothing. (1996, n.p.)

Over a decade later, that much of the Tibetan handicraft industry was still dominated by non-Tibetans has also been noted by an International Campaign for Tibet (ICT) report titled *Interpreting Tibet: A Political Guide to Traveling in Tibet* (2008). According to this document, most of the handicrafts in Lhasa and elsewhere in Tibet are being sold by Chinese traders who "obtain their stock from factories in mainland China" (23). Moreover, these same findings have also been described by artisan organizations on the ground in the TAR. According to the Tibet Artisan Initiative and the Dropenling Handicraft Development Center, a nonprofit organization working to assist artists in preserving their artistic traditions and in finding new markets for their products:

> Although many products in Lhasa and internationally are marketed as Tibetan, most are actually manufactured outside the TAR by non-Tibetan peoples. Moreover, Chinese artisans and business people are settling within Tibet to produce and sell jewelry, statues, prayer wheels and other traditional Tibetan Buddhist items for which there is a steady local demand. Less familiar with enterprise development and marketing, Tibetan artisans are facing difficulty earning income from their crafts skills. (Burkert and Gleason 2008)

Echoing these kinds of reports, an overwhelming majority of Tibetan retailers that I interviewed supported this overall picture of the market, maintaining that they received most of their religious products from Chinese wholesalers or traders. This view was confirmed rather vividly by one Tibetan shop owner from Rebkong, who explained that the amount of goods that are manufactured by Chinese companies versus those that are produced by Tibetans is difficult to compare:

> We get a lot of our goods from China [because] Tibetans don't have that kind of machinery to produce things. Tibetans only produce about one percent of these goods, for unlike the Chinese, they do not have the wherewithal to mass-produce them. You cannot compete [with the Chinese] because of the scale of their manufacturing [capacity].

Furthermore, those Tibetans who sold statues not manufactured in Nepal (which were actually the majority of Tibetans due to the difficulties and expenses involved in acquiring them) claimed that they originated from Chinese-owned factories in Sichuan or elsewhere in mainland China.[4] While an extensive discussion of the important yet complex question of who owns (or should own) the rights to produce and distribute Tibetan sacred arts and crafts is outside the scope of the present study, suffice it to say that for some Tibetans involved in the business of religious goods (many of whom would no doubt assert that Tibetans should own these rights) it is this particular dynamic that has provided an important motivation and sometimes an emotional catalyst for their own participation.[5] More specifically, in response to what some Tibetans see as the misappropriation and mishandling of religious goods by Chinese companies and non-Tibetan retailers and the perceived inability to change the current market conditions due to their political circumstances, at least one response for a number of Tibetans appears to have been to participate in selling. This move not only allows Tibetans to reap some of the financial rewards they know are being enjoyed by other ethnicities but also allows them to attempt to exert their own control or sense of ownership over their religious goods and their concomitant religious meanings and associated practices. Against the manufacture and sale of religious goods by non-Tibetans, Tibetans' desire and ability to treat and sell religious items "appropriately," to serve the Tibetan community, and to mark or claim such religious goods as a fundamental and distinct part of Tibetan identity played an important role in their activities as sellers of religious objects.

One of the more frequent responses given by Tibetans when describing the reasons for their participation in the sale of religious goods was that other ethnicities manufactured and sold these goods. Several of my Tibetan informants (a total of seven) who participated in the business as middlemen or painters, when asked about their involvement in selling, responded similarly: that if Tibetans did not sell religious goods, then other ethnic groups (namely the Han or Hui) would and, almost all added, in religiously inappropriate ways. The most common complaints surrounded the ways in which non-Tibetan manufacturers tended to produce religiously inaccurate goods or, alternatively, how non-Tibetan merchants knew little if anything about Tibetan Buddhist religious goods, mishandled them, grossly overcharged for them, and generally treated them (or mistreated them) like any other mundane objects. Tibetan merchants and painters understood such activities to be not only disrespectful but also damaging to Tibetan religious traditions generally and to those associated with sacred objects in particular. Tibetan responses appeared to reflect a pragmatic rationalization: the very idea that other ethnicities should manufacture and sell Buddhist religious goods in inaccurate and distasteful ways—devoid of religious meanings and values—and that they, being Tibetan Buddhists, should not participate made little if any sense both from a financial perspective and in terms of maintaining the Tibetan Buddhist values and meanings associated with these religious objects. After all, they believed, such objects were intimately tied to *their* religious tradition.

The manufacture and sale of Tibetan religious objects by non-Tibetans, the misappropriation of religious goods for other purposes, the production of religious goods that veered from traditional standards, as well as their mistreatment by non-Tibetan manufacturers and merchants was viewed by many of my informants as a significant problem, yet one that many felt they could do little about. This view was perhaps best expressed by two monks, both of whom framed Tibetans' inability to curb such activities as a result of their subordinate political position. According to one monk from Kumbum:

> Recently, a factory in Chengdu produced shoes with "*nam chu rang den*" [*rnam bcu dbang ldan*, the seed syllable of the Kālacakra tantra] on it. Ever since the monks saw this mantra misused, they said "well, we have to do something in order to prevent this." Now, there is no real movement to prevent this. We have discussed this, but we haven't done anything yet. Likewise, we saw some religious objects on soap as well. It's probably the responsibility of people who are religious followers [to do something about this]. Perhaps it's our fault for not carrying out activities against the misuse of these goods. Sometimes we cannot really bear seeing these sellers sitting on these religious objects, and using religious images on socks, etc. We cannot really bear it . . . If there are shops in the monastery and they produce goods according to the demands of religious people, then this is good, but if it turns into commercialism or if it is sold in the market, then it is involved in negative activity. If it's under the authority of religious people, they can manage the right way to sell it. Now, it is not like this because the authority is in the hands of others, so we cannot control it. If the monastery had its own rights, or if there were an independent ruling on these things, the quality of religion wouldn't be as disgusting as it is nowadays. There are so many religious activities going on, but in reality, the government authorities don't really care what's happening in religious life, and they don't do what they are supposed to do. There are some lamas that are responsible for this, they are trying, but in fact they have no ability to change things. In this case, if monasteries are not really independent or autonomous, then you can't really own things. If you own things, then you can protect or control your properties.[6] If not, they will flow without restrictions. [If we did have more control], in this case, we could control

> the quality and quantity [of religious goods]. But the government only thinks about the growth of the economy, not whether there is progress in terms of religion.

Similar frustrations were also voiced by a well-established monk-painter from Sengeshong Mango Gonpa, who expressed what he saw as a troublesome trend in inaccurate religious goods and the inability to effectively change the course of these events:

> Some factories print *lung ta* [*rlung rta*, or "windhorse"—printed on prayer flags or on small pieces of paper], and they print Buddha images on the *lung ta.* That is completely wrong. It's not supposed to have Buddha images on it. It is supposed to have the windhorse there. But you can't really say anything against these factories because they are powerful and rich and have supporters. In the past, *lung ta* had only the windhorse and the flaming jewels; now there is Buddha and Tāra [on them]. This bothers me. You see these things scattered all over. It is impossible to pick all of them up since there are a lot. Nowadays, they [the factories] put chants on the *lung ta.* This is not something that used to happen. If the manufacturer is a Tibetan, then they would know how to make it, but they are all made by the Chinese. The same thing happens with butter lamp butter. We do not know whether it is clean or even what is it made from.[7]

With respect to the sale of thangkas in particular, this same monk explained that due to the ways in which thangkas are viewed by Han businessmen and Han thangka dealers, these are often sold in ways that are devoid of accurate religious evaluations:

> Chinese businessmen or thangka dealers are not really religious people. They think they [i.e., thangkas] are just products of this area, of a certain ethnic group. They call it *minzu yishu pin*, "the art product of ethnic nationalities."

For these particular monks, the difference between the proper production, distribution, and treatment of religious goods and their misappropriation and/or iconographic inaccuracy and mistreatment seemed to boil down to issues of power and politics. In other words, according to these monks, if

Tibetans had more control or voice in these matters, then the situation would not be perceived to be as unpleasant as it currently was, and perhaps, as noted by the monk from Kumbum, Tibetans would be able to manage to sell them in "the right way." This latter point was a perspective that also appeared to be present in the responses of some Tibetan merchants and painters, a perspective that served, in part, as an underlying motivating factor for their own business activities.

For example, two merchants emphasized that their motivations for selling not only had to do with the fact that other ethnicities sold religious goods, but that non-Tibetans also often sold inaccurate and thus inappropriate goods. One merchant in the Xining Tibetan market, who sold religious texts as well as thangkas, when asked if he was at all apprehensive about opening a business that sold religious objects given the textual religious proscriptions against their sale, explained:

> I was apprehensive [about selling religious goods], but if we don't sell them, some other people will. What we sell is really needed by Tibetans. We have to, we have to sell it. . . . There are some Chinese manufacturers and Muslims [who sell], but they don't really know about these religious goods. For instance, sometimes you find prayer flags in the market. There should not be spaces between the words. They don't know, they just look at it, copy it, and print on it. It should not be like that. So these guys are selling these things without knowledge of them. We are not like that. If we do it, we do it in the proper way.

A similar perspective was shared by another merchant in the Xining Tibetan market, a woman, who emphasized the need for Tibetans to be involved in the business in order to ensure the quality of products. When asked if she had ever heard of the negative associations made with respect to selling religious goods and what she thought of them, she replied,

> Well, most of the Tibetan products are manufactured by Chinese people, and if we don't sell them, the Chinese will sell them. I personally don't agree that Tibetans cannot sell these things or produce them. I think Tibetans should produce Tibetan products. Tibetans should make them and sell them, so this way they are correctly made and [also] so that you can prove that these are Tibetan products. Otherwise, nowadays, most of the

objects that we sell are manufactured by Chinese people, but this is all Tibetan stuff, not Chinese! If we don't sell it, they will sell it. They will produce it and then sell it, whereas we are only selling these things.

According to these particular merchants, the best sellers or custodians of Buddhist religious goods were obviously Tibetans, for they were the most familiar with the products, have the appropriate religious knowledge about them, and can maintain some sense of quality control for their community. Moreover, as expressed by the former merchant, Tibetans know how to handle them appropriately and how to sell them in the "proper" way, the implication being that if Tibetans did not play an active role in the market, not only would they presumably miss out on the potential financial rewards being enjoyed by other ethnicities, but the quality, the proper knowledge about them, their treatment, as well as their association with Tibetan Buddhist practices and meanings, if left in the hands of others, would likely be in jeopardy, a predicament which their very participation in the business attempted to mediate.

Several others, citing similar motivations, focused primarily on the issue of the mistreatment of religious goods by non-Tibetan sellers. At least five others noted that if Tibetans did not sell, others would, and very likely, based on their own observations, in unsuitable ways. This included charging prices for sacred objects which far exceeded what they saw as the acceptable limit for such goods, physically treating religious goods in disrespectful ways, and having the attitude that religious goods were just like any other goods. For example, such a response came from one painter in Rebkong who, after seeing his paintings priced for what he claimed was over twenty times their actual value in mainland China, opened a shop himself. He did this, he claimed, not in order to attempt to earn the same exorbitant profits from his paintings, but because he believed such business practices were unethical and that if anyone should be benefitting from the sale of religious goods, it should be Tibetans. When asked if he thought that Chinese involvement in the sale of religious goods was a reason why many Tibetans were going into the business, he replied:

We don't really like all the businesses that fall to Chinese hands. We have the Rongwo Gonpa here. Since it is our place, since it is a *Tibetan* place,

> why should we let others do the businesses that we can do. Why should we let them take over our business? In the past, it's true that there were not many shops and many religious goods to sell. [But] I think there is an advantage [in this] because now Tibetan people can start earning some money from selling. I would be happy if a Tibetan man or woman would make even one yuan from selling these things because this money goes directly to Tibetans. . . . There are some factories that produce and sell [these goods] just like they were other goods. We don't do that. We sell them for a reasonable price. We try to sell them in the way they should be [sold]. But we have no control. We can't say anything to those manufacturers who sell them. We just let it go. What can you do? The difference is in the way you treat them.

For this particular respondent, not only was there was a sense of resentment toward the fact that other ethnicities were selling and profiting from *Tibetan* Buddhist objects—a point which, in his mind, justified, at least in a pragmatic sense, the sale of religious goods by Tibetans—but also a desire to exert some sense of control or agency upon the ways in which such goods were sold. According to this painter, by participating in the commercial process, rather an avoiding it, Tibetans can benefit financially as well as maintain and perpetuate appropriate relationships to sacred goods by treating them respectfully and selling them at reasonable prices and in ways which are more in line with their religious traditions. This was a point that was emphasized by several others, not only out of a desire to uphold or exert religious principles but also out of a desire to be of service to the Tibetan community, for some Tibetans, many argued, were especially vulnerable to being exploited by non-Tibetan merchants.

Although the desire to respond to the "needs" or "demands" of the Tibetan community was expressed in several merchants' testimonies, the idea that Tibetan involvement in the business was necessary was especially emphasized in the statements of one middle-aged merchant who operated a small shop in the Xining Tibetan market. After explaining a plan to expand the Tibetan market in a different location after a government-proposed piazza was eventually built over the current market, he related the potential consequences to the Tibetan community if Tibetans *did not* participate in the sale of religious goods:

> People in the [Tibetan] community will not let Chinese and Muslims get in [to the new proposed market] because once they get in they break all the laws and all the rules. They also sell so many fake things and so many cheap things, and it damages the reputation [of Tibetan objects or of Tibetans themselves?]. Besides that, they don't really know what they are selling, and they cheat people, especially nomads. They don't know the language, but they just try to cheat people all the time. They are trying to sell religious goods, which they really don't know about at all. And they don't know what they are used for. . . . If we Tibetans don't sell religious goods, somebody will, for instance, Muslims or Chinese. They usually sell them for double the price. And if they do this, then who loses? Of course, [the answer is] the customers: they lose their money. Most Tibetans, if they really want to buy something, they want to buy something from Tibetans, not from others, because this money will go directly to Tibetan businessmen. The Chinese and Muslims don't have a limit on charging. For instance, in Kumbum, there are a lot of Chinese street vendors selling *khatas* [*kha btags*] to Chinese people or to foreigners. They describe a single *khata* as an antique, something that passed from Tsongkhapa's generation up to now. And they exaggerate things, saying "this is precious because this is blessed by blah blah blah blah, and it has been handed down through many generations and that's why it's costly." Maybe a [new] *khata* costs something like six or ten *kuai*, but they will sell it for one hundred. If they are Tibetan, they dare not say [anything] like that. Tibetans' profits are maybe like two or three *kuai*, but they dare not to even say anything like that. That is too far beyond the limitations [of what is acceptable].[8]

This sentiment also seemed to be connected to some Tibetan merchants' notions that they are not "sellers" of religious goods but rather "providers" or "conduits" of such objects. Indeed, at least three merchants described their activities as a *service* to their fellow Tibetans, including monks, all of whom were seeking particular articles or objects for religious purposes. The potential vulnerability of Tibetan consumers in the marketplace was also noted by some of my other informants. For example, one monk-teacher from Kumbum explained that many Tibetans do not know the actual prices of such goods and are often taken advantage of as a result: "Sometimes Tibetans buy these images from Chinese dealers or shopkeepers, and they don't bargain because they [themselves] use them for religious reasons. They think the money that is earned [from the sale] goes to the monastery or [is used] for a religious purpose." As a result, he implied, many Tibetans often pay more than they should. Similarly, the problem with Tibetans being taken advantage of by Chinese or Muslim businessmen was also noted by my interpreter who, upon witnessing two men delight in their recent purchases of pieces of amber in a Kumbum restaurant, explained that the consumption of precious stones is a real problem among poorly educated farmers and herders who purchase stones as status symbols but, unfortunately, are often cheated by savvy Han and Muslim businessmen who sell them fake ones. Thus, part of the motivation for selling, at least for this particular Tibetan merchant, and for those who felt that they were providing a service to Tibetans, involves reclaiming ownership over Buddhist religious goods by selling them in more appropriate ways and in ways which both served and protected the Tibetan community from what they considered unscrupulous Chinese and Muslim merchants.

A third response to the mistreatment of religious goods by non-Tibetan companies and merchants came from a painter from Sengeshong who claimed that while he indeed entered into the business to earn money, he also participated because other, non-Tibetan, merchants were grossly overcharging for thangkas and not treating religious goods in an appropriate manner. Similar to the above painter, his overall goal was not necessarily to earn the same amount from his paintings as was being asked for by Chinese businessmen, a practice which he appeared to view as immoral, but nevertheless to earn a living by charging a reasonable price while treating religious goods "respectfully":

> I have traveled in some of the big cities and I saw my thangkas sold in the shops for about 10,000 yuan [USD (2019) 1,400] per piece. They were extremely expensive . . . so I got the idea to open up my shop from this. I thought, "We are not making any money, so it's better to open a shop ourselves, so we [as the producers] can make some money." . . . Whereas Chinese businessmen treat these things disrespectfully, we think if we produce and sell these things we will [not only] accumulate some positive karma [but] people will see these things and learn about these things. It is a way of spreading Buddhism . . . Mostly, I see those Chinese people sell at prices without limit. If we sell it directly, we don't really play with them; we sell them for a reasonable price and treat them well. Tibetans have a sense of a limit in setting the price, whereas the Chinese have no sense of limit

> in pricing. Chinese businessmen have no limit in cheating people. They don't care about the person. We can't do it. We dare not to do it. Tibetans are not like that. I saw a thangka that cost like 15,000 RMB, however, the price on it was like 60,000–70,000 RMB. Still, they are cheating if you look at the quality. The Chinese try to cheat as much as they can. We can't do it. It's not allowed. Since we are compassionate, it's not enough to be happy ourselves. The other person should also be happy. The Chinese are the other way around. That is why Tibetans are not that rich. If you are rich, you have to deceive. This is what makes Tibetans different from other people. There are limits and controls. You are not going to cheat the other person completely, whereas the Chinese deceive. They charge the customer so much that they "fall into bed." In other words, he will be sick when he realizes he paid too much and was cheated.[9]

While not the only painter to refer to the potential financial benefits that can accrue from selling thangkas or to the possibility for the accumulation of positive karma through these activities, the above comments also illustrate a desire to have some control over how these goods are sold and priced as well as what these goods communicate or symbolize—that they connote accurately Tibetan Buddhist meanings and values (that they may serve to spread the Dharma). Such a response stands as a clear example of a person who is selling not only for financial reasons but also in response to the fact that non-Tibetans are selling and are doing so in inappropriate ways.

Finally, perhaps implicit in all of these responses was a desire to mark (or perhaps to reclaim) such religious objects as a fundamental part of Tibetan identity and to assert or communicate this distinct identity via the sale of religious goods. While Graburn's distinction between the creation of tourist art and functional/traditional art does not appear to pass muster in the context of Amdo, where this line is obviously now blurred by the fact that traditional, iconographically correct religious art is now sold to tourists, his insight regarding the ways in which the artistic traditions of minority peoples may serve to project a sense of identity to the outside world certainly rings true in the Tibetan case. The association that is made between Buddhist religious goods and Tibetan identity can already be seen in many of the above testimonies. The desire of Tibetans for such goods to be treated according to Tibetan Buddhist traditions and values, to be reasonably priced in ways that were more in line with or appropriate to Tibetan religious sentiments and to be sold in the proper manner (i.e., not mistreated, stepped on or over, etc.) with the proper knowledge of them, may be seen as various ways in which Tibetans attempted to claim ownership over what they believed were *their* sacred objects and to mark or distinguish them as distinctly *Tibetan Buddhist* or symbolic of Tibetan identity and culture. Such a desire can perhaps be seen most explicitly in the response of the woman merchant in the Xining Tibetan market who explained that Tibetans should both produce and sell religious goods so that one could not only ensure the quality of products but also "prove that these are Tibetan products." The same concern can also be seen in the comments of the painter who referred to non-Tibetans' sale of religious goods in Rebkong as "our business," or even in the statements of the last painter cited above whose underlying motivation for painting and selling included a desire that "people see these things and learn about these things." Here, there is little doubt that, for this painter, what was to be learned were the meanings, values, and uses of such objects as they are understood according to the *Tibetan* Buddhist tradition. The desire that such religious goods should be seen and understood as associated with Tibetan culture and identity is also supported by the aforementioned monk from Dechen Gonpa who worked in a shop which sold religious objects in Rebkong. After explaining the economic difficulties experienced by many monks today, he added that, for him, selling religious goods was "a way to preserve Tibetan culture."[10] Similar concerns with projecting Tibetan identity via the sale of religious goods have also been documented elsewhere. For example, Elizabeth Reynolds explains that this was the case for one particularly successful merchant and painter in the town of Shangri-la, Yunnan Province. She writes, "As for potential expansion of store locations, Kelsang [one of her informants] explained that they want to keep the stores in Tibetan cultural areas so that thangkas, and the buying of thangkas, can be connected to the idea of 'Tibet' when people buy them as souvenirs" (2011, 99–100). Furthermore, she writes, "By keeping stores in Tibetan cultural areas, Kelsang can effectively manage the meaning of a thangka painting" (100). Such statements suggest that even among successful Tibetan merchants operating in the external tourist market the desire that religious goods represent *Tibetanness* and serve to promote and preserve Tibetan culture also plays a significant role in the sale of religious objects.

Rob Linrothe notes that "one of the answers to the '*why*' or '*why now*' of the Reb gong renaissance of Tibetan Buddhist painting within the larger

A mdo area must be the role religious art plays in the assertion of self-consciously Tibetan ethnic identity" (2001, 34). However, I suggest that such expressions of Tibetan identity can also be found among those Tibetans involved in selling religious goods. Moreover, such expressions may be utilized not only to distinguish *ethnicity* (as Linrothe states) but also to express and reinforce a particular sense of Tibetan *religious* identity. The above examples in many ways reflect responses to what was perceived as the frequent misappropriation and/or mistreatment of religious goods by non-Tibetan manufacturers and merchants, a reality which, as we have observed, was viewed by several Tibetans to be a consequence of their disenfranchised sociopolitical position. Although Tibetans seek to make a living from the sale of religious goods, they *also* desire to be the representatives and caretakers of what they believe are their own religious and cultural objects and to wrest *some* control of the sale of religious goods from the apparent malpractices of non-Tibetan merchants. Tibetans sold Buddhist objects not only for financial reasons but also for the sake of their own traditions, values, and community and, in a larger sense, in order to maintain and preserve the distinct *Tibetan* Buddhist identity of these objects. The alternative, that is to say, to not participate at all, to allow non-Tibetans—nonbelievers—to then dominate the business, and to be dependent upon them for religious objects (which in reality, many merchants already were), was unfathomable.

While the fact that other ethnicities manufacture and sell Tibetan Buddhist religious goods plays a significant role in some Tibetans' participation in this business, we must also briefly consider another key element within Tibetans' sociopolitical context—that of the dynamics of ethnic tourism in China, a force which strongly and actively encourages Tibetans (along with other ethnic minorities) to take full economic advantage of their religious and cultural heritage as a means of economic development.

THE INFLUENCE OF TIBETAN CULTURAL TOURISM AND TOURISM'S DISCOURSE OF DEVELOPMENT ON TIBETANS' SALE OF RELIGIOUS GOODS

Ethnic or cultural tourism, defined early on by Valene Smith (1977) as tourism that is "marketed to the public in terms of the 'quaint customs' of indigenous and often exotic peoples" (2), was introduced to the PRC and to Tibet in the 1980s and has grown over the following three decades to become one of China's "pillar industries."[11] Tourism has, in many respects, contributed to the increased production and commercialization of Tibetan Buddhist religious goods and has created a brand new market for new religious objects and images to be consumed specifically by tourists.[12] Tibetan religious goods, especially thangkas, while they have maintained their religious significance for Tibetan painters and merchants, have now also entered the realm of tourist art, and it is undeniable that tourism is at least partly responsible for the recent increased appearance of Tibetan-owned thangka painting studios and galleries (specifically those which sell ready-made paintings) and at least some Tibetan-owned and many non-Tibetan-owned retail shops that offer a variety of religious goods for sale.[13] However, Tibetan cultural tourism, the impetus for much (although certainly not all) of this business activity, has not been a politically neutral phenomenon. Rather, it is a major government-driven and largely government-controlled economic development strategy and discourse that has not only played a significant role in the creation of and continued support for the commercial market for particular Tibetan religious and cultural goods but also in actively urging Tibetans to participate in the commodification of their traditional religious culture. Thus, while some Tibetan merchants of religious objects have responded positively to the opportunities presented by the free market and the development of tourism, it is nevertheless important to also consider that within Tibetans' current sociopolitical context, the political and ideological discourse of cultural and economic development—which is part and parcel of the dynamics of ethnic tourism—is also uniquely involved in encouraging Tibetans to participate in this business.

A BRIEF SKETCH OF TOURISM IN CHINA, PAST AND PRESENT

Tourism is a relatively recent phenomenon in China, only commencing in the 1980s following the Open Door policy initiated by Deng Xiaoping. Under Mao Zedong, tourism was almost nonexistent. Travel for leisure was viewed as a bourgeois activity, which took away from productive activity (Nyíri 2009, 153–54). Thus, it was not seen as an appropriate form of economic development. However, the policy shifts introduced by Deng initiated several transformations: a transition toward a market economy, the relaxation on policies with respect to domestic movement (154), and a relaxation of policies pertaining to ethnic minorities and expressions of their religion and culture. As a part of this transition, the central government began to look at tourism as a means of speeding up economic development and modernization and as a way to relieve poverty in minority areas.[14]

According to Sofield and Li (1998), the direction in which tourism would develop stemmed from a shift in policy initiated by Deng on the issue of cultural heritage. Deng's perspective on cultural heritage went against the previous iconoclastic policies of Mao, for Deng considered heritage to be a valuable resource that could be utilized not only to further the cause of socialism but also to strengthen national unity while bringing about economic progress (370–71). The passing of the Heritage Conservation Act in 1982, which called for the preservation of—among other things—ancient sites, cultural artifacts, festivals, buildings, and historical documents at the national, regional, and local level, "provided a foundation for early tourism planners to embrace heritage in its development" (371). In addition, substantial efforts to develop new markets related to ethnic culture were also inspired by a speech delivered by Li Zui-han, the director of cultural affairs, at the Thirteenth National Party Congress in Beijing in 1990. In his address to a national meeting of artists, Li encouraged the ethnic minorities to "try to find ways to make money from their heritage" (Sofield and Li 1998, 373). Li's twenty-point speech included thirteen points on how ethnic culture was required to be in the service of socialism (372–73). This meant in no uncertain terms that the development and preservation of ethnic culture via tourism should contribute to economic development and modernization. Li urged artists to "borrow from the old for present use. By giving new meaning to old things, they could form part of socialism's new thinking" (Sofield and Li 1998, 373, citing Li 1990, 109–10). Continuing, Sofield and Li explain: "This attempt to synthesize socialism and modernization with the preservation of minority traditional cultures, while artificial and strained in some respects, nevertheless provided further encouragement to tourism planners (among others) to find ways to 'make culture pay'" (373). As a result of these policy shifts and the new discourse of encouragement, regional governments and tourism planners (many of whom were also entrepreneurs) actively began exploring tourism markets associated with China's cultural heritage. By 1992, this resulted in the development of major tourism companies, the marketing of at least six different tourist routes (including the Silk Road Tour, the Sherpa Trail, and the North-West Minority Cultural Tour; Sofield and Li 1998, 375, citing Wei Xiaoan 1993), as well as the development of commercial markets for potentially lucrative tourism destinations and products. By the late 1990s the push to develop the domestic tourism market manifested as a growing effort to develop *ethnic tourism* in which the unique ethnic characteristics of designated minorities—including their customs, sites, and cultural products—became attractions to be promoted by government tourism bureaus and consumed by tourists.[15] The work of defining ethnic minority characteristics had already been accomplished during the state-building process via the "nationalities identification project" in the 1950s, in which the fifty-five minority nationalities of China were officially recognized and their cultural characteristics (in terms of food, customs, dress, arts and crafts, etc.) carefully categorized (Kolås 2008, 50). This process of ethnicization provided a convenient model for local governments and tourism developers to eventually promote and commercialize particular aspects of minority culture (92).

According to Pál Nyíri, the decision to officially promote domestic tourism came in the late '90s and was triggered by the "Asian financial crisis," a period in which China needed to find a way to increase domestic consumption (2009, 153). As a result, the government initiated the creation of three "golden weeks" of public holidays—one during the spring festival (Chinese New Year), another beginning from Labor Day (May 1), and another commencing on National Day (October 1)—in an effort to increase public spending and expand domestic tourism (Yeh 2006). Furthermore, according to Nyíri, tourism was seen not only as a way to ignite the domestic economy, but also as a "civilizing" strategy. Early on, Chinese writers described tourism as a way to improve the lives of those visited, for it was believed that "through imitation and learning residents of scenic areas can improve and elevate their manners and politeness, speech and bearing, habits of hygiene, thinking and outlook" (Nyíri 2010, 94, citing Jin Hua 1994). Such ideological arguments for tourism, according to Nyíri, were similar to those used in promoting rural-to-urban migration (94). However, tourism was also envisioned as way to promote cultural understanding between nationalities and as a way to display China's cultural diversity and the integration of ethnic minorities (Sofield and Li 1998, 373).

Tourism and tourism planning in the PRC, however, has not generally proceeded in ethnic minority areas in close consultation with local communities or on those communities' own terms. According to recent studies, tourism development in China remains tightly controlled by state and local governments (Cingcade 1998; Yang 2007). Tourism planners often approach tourism development in terms of cultural and ecological "resources" and treat these resources as free for exploitation (Kolås 2008, 17). Yang, Wall, and Smith (2008), drawing on their work on tourism in Xishuangbanna (Yunnan Province), describe how ethnic tourism planning functions in China more generally:

> Governments and tourism entrepreneurs are the main powers in developing ethnic tourism, but few of these are minorities. The dominant Han administrative and commercial involvement in tourism strongly shapes the ways of staging, packaging, and representing culture and influences how minorities participate in the tourism [*sic*].
>
> . . . Entrepreneurs in co-operation with government often control commercially valuable ethnic resources, and create or select the cultural products to be presented in tourism zones. Thus, the culture presented is not determined by the authentic source of the culture—ethnic communities—but by governments and entrepreneurs, usually Han. (764–65)

Echoing this view, Sofield and Li, who have worked extensively on ethnic tourism in the Chinese context, in their studies of state policy and cultural tourism, write:

> Top-down planning is invariably the rule. In western paradigms of development for ecotourism and cultural tourism, community consultations, stakeholder involvement in meaningful dialogue and acceptance of non-governmental organization (NGO) inputs are widely accepted and practiced. However in China the culture of a centrally controlled economy is still deeply embedded in many senior officials and trying to move to a more inclusive approach to tourism planning is simply not present. Much tourism planning takes place in government offices removed from communities and sites, and stakeholders are simply presented with government fiat. Attempts to involve communities in meaningful dialogue for tourism development that has a capacity to maximize benefits for them are often unwelcome, brushed aside or simply met with puzzlement by government officials since communities, especially rural ethnic minority communities by definition in Chinese Communist Party (CP) ideology, are "backward," uneducated and require "uplifting." (2007, 372–73)

The growing number of studies on tourism that have been conducted in Tibetan areas (Klieger 1990; Cingcade 1998; Wenbin 1998; Kolås 2008; Murakami 2008) reveal that tourism planning and development has followed a similar pattern and ideology and, moreover, has tended to benefit the Chinese government and Han businessmen (those who are in a better position to invest) the most.

The promotion of ethnic tourism in Tibetan areas coincided with a shift in rhetoric by state and local governments. Tibetans, while still referred to as "backward" in certain contexts, had become increasingly and simultaneously represented as "mysterious," "pure," and "sacred" in commercial and state representations (Murakami 2008, 61; Yeh 2006). The results of these transformations in policy and discourse have led to an explosion of tourist activity in Tibetan areas, with the number of visitors increasing exponentially every year. Whereas in the mid-1980s and early 1990s the number of international tourists was greater than domestic tourists, today, by far, the majority of visitors to Tibet are urban, middle-class Han Chinese who are drawn to Tibetan areas to experience the "simple," "exotic" culture.[16]

Tourism in the Tibetan context has significantly contributed to the reconfiguring and repurposing of traditional culture. Monasteries were encouraged to accept tourists and to charge entrance fees. Also developed were attractions such as Tibetan homestays and cultural performances, and significant investments were made in the development of Tibetan religious and cultural products. With respect to the handicraft industry in particular, according to Luo Li (2008), a researcher at the Central University for Nationalities in Beijing, between 1980 and 1993, 22 million yuan was invested in infrastructure for the development of the handicraft industry, an industry she describes as the "Flower on the Plateau" (36–38).[17] The handicraft industry itself has been subject to a state discourse of progress and development and reframed as backward and in desperate need of modernization. This historical recasting can be seen in the Chinese foreign ministry's statement on Tibet's national handicraft industry to the United Nations in 1991:

> Tibet's time-honoured national handicraft industry boasts unique craftsmanship. Before liberation, however, it was extremely backward, and chiefly for the benefit of aristocrats and monasteries. Craftsmen and artisans were at the bottom rung of the social ladder, seriously handicapping the development of the industry. Over the past 40 years, with the assistance of the Government, Tibet's national handicraft industry has been rapidly restored and developed. Today, Tibet has 120 national handicraft enterprises, producing more than 1,600 kinds of products. Some of its

> products with distinctive local flavours have entered the international market. In 1989, the total output value of Tibet's national handicraft industry came to 41.07 million yuan. (United Nations Social and Economic Council Commission on Human Rights 1992)

The industrialization and growth of the Tibetan handicraft industry is here celebrated as a tremendous achievement of the Chinese government and its policies, which has brought Tibetans improved living standards and has uplifted them from their "backward," less productive livelihoods.

One of the most prominent objects identified and selected for promotion as an ethnic Tibetan handicraft has been, of course, thangka painting. In an effort to promote thangka painting, the state has attempted to recategorize thangkas from objects primarily associated with Buddhism and Buddhist practice to that of Tibetan *ethnic* handicrafts and/or folk art and has actively supported the production, marketing, and consumption of thangkas in a number of ways (Linrothe 2001). Since 1982, exhibitions, painting competitions, vocational schools, museums, and publications have not only attempted to transform the meaning of thangkas—downplaying their Buddhist origins and shifting them into the realm of aesthetics—but also to mark them and repackage them as a potential financial investment and/or an ideal tourist souvenir.[18] Many descriptions of thangka painting in the local media noticeably minimize its religious dimension while promoting its consumption, strategies that are most likely interrelated and presumably aimed at attracting a wider consumer base. For example, consider how Luo Li's academic publication on Tibet's economy, in a chapter on the development of Tibet's "handicraft industry," frames thangka painting as an ethnic handicraft and tourist souvenir while celebrating the democratization of thangkas as if they were unattainable by poorer Tibetans in the past (a point, as we have observed, that is far from historically accurate):

> Local paintings, carvings, as well as gold and silver jewelry are very unique to Tibet, and are appreciated by domestic and international tourists as souvenirs. As a result of the development of the tourism industry, these arts and crafts have developed too. Qamdo [Chamdo?] is famous for paintings, carvings, gold and silver jewelry. Wazhai in Qamdo has an interesting name "a craftsmen's town", making unique painted scrolls (or Thangka or Thangga), as well as gold and silver wares which are highly valued. . . .

> Today Tibetan arts and crafts as outstanding cultural relics have become ethnic necessities and tourist souvenirs with ethnic style and local characteristics. They are no longer items reserved for religious purposes and for the noble and rich. (2008, 40–41)[19]

Han Chinese and foreigners are also encouraged to buy thangkas as collectors' items and investments. In an article entitled "Experts: It Is a Good Time to Buy Thangka," posted on China Tibet News.com, one anonymous author describes the market in this way: "Generally speaking, for Thangka, those in good condition, with exquisite looks and [a] long history are of high value, especially those by famous monks . . . besides, some works by contemporary artists also deserve collecting. It's a good chance to buy Thangka whose day will come again."[20] In addition, even the modernization of the content of thangkas is encouraged and celebrated as an improvement. According to an article in the *Beijing Review*, "With the development of a new generation of *Tangka* artists, the content of *Tangka* artworks has been enriched. Bodhisattvas are no longer the only theme. In recent *Tangka* paintings, there are various images of contemporary life, such as trains traveling through Tibet, coca-cola tins and even lamas holding telescopes" (Jifang 2007, para. 2). Such statements not only stand as examples of the ways in which the Chinese authorities have attempted to transform the meaning and purpose of thangkas but also the ways in which they have worked to promote and encourage the domestic market in this process.

The promotion of Tibetan ethnic tourism as well as the focus on developing Tibetan cultural or ethnic products for tourist consumption highlights what Kolås describes as "the changing economic relevance of cultural activities in the context of tourism" (2008, 8). However, the creation of the external tourist market for thangkas in Tibetan areas such as Amdo did not simply occur as a result of the veil that was lifted on domestic movement to Tibetan areas. Such a characterization does not fully account for the active involvement of state and local tourism bureaus as well as government officials—including Tibetan cadres—in ethnic tourism planning more broadly and in the creation and encouragement of the market for Tibetan cultural products in particular. The emerging external demand for thangkas is largely the result of a process of object selection, promotion, redefinition, and the politics of display and discourse over a period of time in the creation of the market. Moreover, it is the state that largely determines what cultural objects are deemed worthy of promotion and protection and those that are not, a decision which is based largely on a given object's commercial potential. The state's promotion of thangkas in particular has created an increased external-tourist demand for the art form. These activities have driven prices up in recent years, undoubtedly a major reason (along with, perhaps, the concern with preserving their culture and painting traditions) that has encouraged more young Tibetans (including farmers and herders) to take up painting as a means of livelihood. These activities have also encouraged the government to invest in the building of vocational schools in order to train new would-be Tibetan thangka artists. Such events are often publicized and celebrated in the Chinese media, as is the "unprecedented prosperity" that Tibetans have achieved through their involvement in the painting market. By calling attention to these points, I do not mean to suggest that Tibetans have not willingly participated or benefited both economically and culturally from the market in Tibetan religious and cultural objects such as thangka painting, as indeed they have. Here, I only wish to point out that the state's distinct emphasis on and development of Tibetan ethnic tourism broadly and the market for thangkas in particular goes some way to explain the participation of Tibetans in the commercialization of thangkas. Indeed, the central government likes to take due credit for taking the Tibetan handicraft industry out of the dark shackles of religious use only, once reserved for "the noble and rich," and developing it from a state of "backwardness" into a successful commercial market. Even the deputy head of Huangnan TAP (which includes Rebkong County), Wang Huaping, has stated that the recent popularity of thangkas derives not only from "the rich *cultural* meanings embodied in the thangka arts" but also from government promotional efforts (Yuanfeng, Shuangqi, and Ying 2009, para. 34; emphasis mine). The Chinese government's active role in the process of the creation of the market for thangkas would seem to illustrate the insights of Appadurai on both the entrance of commodities into new regimes of value and the creation of demand. That is, Appadurai argues that the link between regimes of value (i.e., how something is valued and exchanged within a given social context) and "specific flows of commodities," including the "vagaries of demand," has much to do with political processes (1986, 56–58).[21]

What is also important to consider for the present discussion is the fact that Tibetans have *simultaneously* also been subject to the implementation of government tourism propaganda, which actively encourages Tibetans to participate in these activities as a means of cultural and economic development. While the speech by Li Zui-han at the Thirteenth National Party Congress in 1990 signaled a shift in policy and called for the development and preservation of ethnic culture to contribute to goals of socialism, according to the work of Daisuke Murakami (2008), state-sponsored tourism propaganda also encouraged Tibetans themselves to take full economic advantage of their traditional culture as a path out of their economic and cultural "backwardness." Although Murakami's fieldwork was conducted in Lhasa between 2000 and 2002, given the central government's drive to develop and promote tourism across many Tibetan cultural areas, it seems unlikely that such efforts were strictly confined to the TAR. According to Murakami,

> For ordinary Tibetans, the *economic* value of Buddhism, the idea introduced by tourism, is very new. Unlike in Southeast Asia or Nepal, tourism is a relatively new socioeconomic phenomenon for Tibetans. Apart from within a certain section of Lhasa's society (i.e. Tibetan elites, government officials, and entrepreneurs), it is considered inappropriate to associate Tibetan Buddhism with mundane economic values and activities. In some contexts, it is even disrespectful and insulting for Tibetans to make such an association. . . . However, what is different from the previous era, what the development of tourism has brought, is the *systematic* introduction of economic value into the core of traditional Tibetan culture. The commodification of Tibetan religion is naturalised and authorised at the national level for the sake of social and economic progress. Tourism operates as a disseminating vehicle which encourages the Tibetans to re-examine their religious traditions; to consider them as commodifiable. Supporting this newly emerging economic movement is considered a Tibetan ethnic virtue, or even imperative, by the state. These ideas are repeatedly disseminated through a variety of state mechanisms: through local media, including newspapers and TV programmes; through government work units; through schools, universities and religious institutions; and through billboards and banners in the streets. . . .
>
> . . . Through the various state mechanisms such as education institutes and local media, including street banners, Tibetans were repetitively encouraged to pursue and maintain this emerging market. The crucial, underlying message of such propaganda is that Tibetan Buddhist values, Tibetan traditional culture and identity can be transformed into cultivatable eco-

> nomic capital. This view corresponds to an official socialist stance in which Tibetan religion should strictly serve the further modernization of Tibet. (2008, 62–64)

It is questionable that some Tibetans did not already have a sense of the economic potential of their cultural traditions and objects before the emergence of such propaganda campaigns. Nevertheless, Murakami reveals that during the early 2000s the state repeatedly presented Tibetans with a relatively new idea at the level of public discourse: the economic value of their religion and culture and how this was important to their economic and cultural development. Such a discourse resonated with the overall historical framing of ethnic minorities in general and Tibetans in particular as ideologically and culturally backward, an idea that for decades had been (and continues to be) incessantly propagated in Tibetan schools and in political discourse (Kolås and Thowsen 2005).[22] Not only was Tibetan traditional (religious) culture being publicly validated and reconfigured as worthy of preservation, it was now, at least in terms of the perceptions of the state, acceptable, moreover virtuous, to take advantage of or to utilize religious traditions for economic progress and for personal enrichment, a notion which, of course, runs counter to traditional Tibetan Buddhist sentiments.

In addition to more direct attempts by the state to encourage Tibetans to see the economic value of their traditional culture, Murakami (2008) notes that another strategy utilized within tourism discourse has focused on and reinforced the overall *ethnicization* of Tibetan identity. According to Murakami, the Chinese state encourages Tibetans to "perceive and to represent themselves in the language of ethnicity" (64). Such a process, implemented and disseminated via tourism discourse, emphasizes Tibetan *cultural* characteristics, while downplaying Buddhism's role to a mere "flavour of Tibet-ness" (64–65; see also Kolås and Thowsen 2005). Such strategies work to encourage a notion of Tibetanness as distinct from Tibetans' traditional religious identity as Buddhists (*nang pas*), giving primacy to ethnicity and normalizing or legitimating ethnicity as a primary means of identification. Murakami notes that such strategies are likely utilized "to maintain and strengthen the integration of ethnic minorities" (2008, 64). One can likewise observe, however, that the process of ethnicization and the decentralization or minimization of Tibetans' *Buddhist* identity is itself also part of a process of secularization which serves to reinforce the overall idea that Tibetan Buddhist culture may be made commodifiable.

FIG. 20. A weatherworn sign at the entrance to Sengeshong Mango Gonpa depicts tourist activity as part of the new reality in Rebkong.

While Tibetans are certainly not simply passive victims of exogenous discourses, and while it is difficult to determine precisely whether or to what extent such state-sponsored efforts have influenced Tibetans to take part in the commercialization of their traditional culture, I suggest that there are indeed some indications that the discourse of encouragement which seems to derive from the promotion of ethnic tourism-as-development may have influenced at least some merchants to enter the commercial market for religious objects. Although inconclusive, the fact that Tibetan participation itself appears to have been a relatively recent and gradual process, roughly coinciding with the timing of the introduction of Tibetan cultural tourism and the development of new markets for cultural heritage products and destinations, may be one indication of the effectiveness of such a discourse. According to Kolås (2008) and Sofield and Li (1998), such efforts began to a significant extent after the speech delivered by Li Zui-han in 1990. Here we may recall that the beginnings of the so-called commercialization of thangkas in Amdo seems to have occurred not upon the immediate introduction of the free market economy, but (according to the findings of Stevenson and Reynolds) in the early 1990s (i.e., 1991 or 1992), almost precisely around the time of Li's speech. Furthermore, the open sale of religious goods in Amdo among Tibetans is said to have occurred even later than this, with the first shops appearing at the end of the 1990s and with painting studios offering ready-made or noncommis-

FIG. 21. A Chinese couple poses for a photographer (left) in front of Kumbum Monastery (not shown). Kumbum, being only twenty-six kilometers from Xining, is a popular tourist destination and has attracted a number of tourism-related businesses, including the one seen here, to the front entrance.

sioned thangkas opening even later. This suggests that Tibetans did not immediately assume such activities upon the introduction of economic reforms but increasingly did so only after the call to explore and develop markets for cultural heritage in the development of ethnic tourism.

Perhaps more concretely, however, there are more substantive indications that such efforts have had an ideological impact and have been instrumental in encouraging Tibetans to sell religious objects, and this can be seen from the testimonies of some merchants. For example, one merchant in the Xining Tibetan market, who ran a business selling thangkas and religious books, when asked how he reconciled his business in religious products with the textual statements prohibiting such actions, explained, "I don't think what the texts say fits the modern times. If we still followed the texts in a strict way, we [Tibetans] will not *develop*, we will not survive" (emphasis mine). Further clarifying his position, he added, "If you ask this [question] in a place where there is no light, then they might think that selling religious goods is wrong, whereas, if you ask people who have electricity, they might encourage you instead of saying that it is negative." This merchant believed that such religious ideas were no longer completely viable in modern times; moreover, he seemed to believe that the very question of whether selling religious goods was morally wrong reflected the fact that one belonged to a less advanced (backward?) culture, a sentiment akin to government discourse on Tibetans generally and tourism discourse in particular. Similar sentiments were also indicated by two other merchants who, when asked why Tibetans appeared to be late in selling religious goods and in contrast to other merchants who claimed that Tibetans were simply "bad at business," explained that religion had held Tibetans back from participating and succeeding economically. In addition, it may also be the case, at least for some merchants, that the state discourse which describes Tibetan religious objects as primarily "ethnic" or as "folk art" has had some influence over the ways in which Tibetans envision their relationship to such objects. For example, one young girl (an orphan) who sold thangkas and other religious items from a small shop in the Xining Tibetan market in order to raise money for her orphanage, repeatedly referred to the objects for sale in her stall as "our cultural things." Such descriptions suggest that this particular merchant may have understood her wares as *cultural* or *ethnic products* of the Tibetan nationality and thus entirely unproblematic in the commercial world. While such a response may have reflected a limited knowledge of her own religious tradition, it may also indicate the influence of a state discourse which has relabeled religious objects such as thangkas as Tibetan ethnic products, products which can and, moreover, *should* serve as a source of livelihood.

In addition to the above elements, it is also worth considering that what has perhaps made more effective the growth and development of the market in religious objects and the state's discourse of encouragement via tourism propaganda has been a generally limited and/or inconsistent religious or moral counter-discourse from Tibetan religious authorities. Although historically the proscriptions against selling religious objects do not appear to have been instituted in any top-down manner but more generally represented a normative and collective religio-cultural practice, such proscriptions, having their roots within religious texts, were surely supported by monastic institutions. Therefore, it remains significant to our understanding of the causal factors underlying Tibetan participation in the sale of religious goods that within Tibetans' current sociopolitical context the classical ideas associated with selling religious goods do not appear to be widely upheld or effectively reinforced and communicated in any systematic way by religious authorities or religious institutions in Tibet. Although, according to a handful of Tibetan merchants, some monks did attempt to communicate the potential detriments of selling religious goods, based on the testimony of monks interviewed, most did not take any particular active stance on the issue, either publicly or privately, for various reasons.[23] While some who expressed a strong dislike of the current commercialization of religious objects claimed that the issue came down to a lack of political control and autonomy to effectively influence the current situation (one monk at Kumbum even suggested that monks were not allowed to talk about such matters), others were seemingly prevented by serious doubts about the prospect of reversing the tide of the commercialization of religious goods. Furthermore, two additional monks suggested that the economic changes in society had advanced too far and that people "wouldn't listen" even if approached with such ideas. Others feared that Tibetan merchants who are now dependent on such businesses for their livelihoods would get angry or offended at such proposals. Still others maintained religious rationales, which seemingly prevented them from responding to the activities of the market. For example, some explained that one cannot really pass judgment on another person and that selling religious goods ultimately comes down to one's motivation, a theme that will be revisited later on.[24]

Although it was not stated explicitly by any of the monks interviewed, from a broader perspective, it seems very likely that refraining from discussions of such matters as the sale of religious objects also stems, at least in part, from the state's control of monasticism and the state's redefinition of the role of religion and religious institutions. The central government has made it quite clear that monastic institutions must contribute to the goal of economic progress and modernization and not become obstacles to economic development (Human Rights Watch 2002, 279). Additionally, it is important to consider that the limitations and/or restrictions that have been placed on monastic institutions via patriotic reeducation campaigns, most notably since 1996, have likely led to the reprioritization of monastic life, such that religio-social matters and proscriptions pertaining to economics have given way to more important concerns, such as those pertaining to monastic economic self-sufficiency and an increased preoccupation with freedom of religious practice and religious autonomy.[25] Regardless of the reasoning used by monks to account for the general absence of a monastic public discourse on the issue of selling religious goods, this situation has surely only served to encourage rather than discourage many Tibetans from entering the business in religious objects. Evidence suggests that this is indeed the case, for the majority of merchants interviewed claimed they had never been approached by monks (or anyone else) with concerns about their business activities, many instead claiming that they received only support. And among the younger merchants, some claimed to have never heard of the religious proscriptions against the sale of religious goods, a potential sign of the waning influence of these traditional evaluations.

CONCLUSION

As this chapter has attempted to illustrate, in order to further understand Tibetans' participation in the sale of religious objects, we must also consider the dynamics of their current sociopolitical context. Despite the government's use of the terms "autonomous prefecture" and "autonomous region," Tibetans do not enjoy cultural autonomy or a collective political or religious platform that would enable them to control the direction of their own religious or cultural affairs, much less the production and exchange of their religious arts and crafts. As a result, Tibetans have witnessed the manufacture and sale of Tibetan Buddhist religious goods by non-Tibetans, many of whom (it is complained) conduct their businesses in ways considered inappropriate by Tibetan religious standards. Some Tibetans, partly as a response to this situation, have begun selling religious objects. However, elements of their responses reveal that many are not only motivated by economic rewards. Tibetans' desire and ability to treat and sell religious objects in ways that accord with their religious sentiments, to serve the Tibetan community, and to mark or reclaim Tibetan religious goods as a distinct part of Tibetan Buddhist identity also plays an important role in their participation. Moreover, as we have observed, even those who might be perceived to be in the business solely for financial gain—those who participate exclusively in the external-tourist market—remain very much concerned with the perpetuation of the religious meanings associated with Tibetan Buddhist objects and with their status as markers of Tibetan identity.

At the same time, our understanding of Tibetans' commodification of religious objects must also consider the fact that this activity is actively encouraged by the Chinese state, both via their investment and involvement in the Tibetan handicraft industry (in particular the thangka market) and via an ethnic tourism discourse which promotes the commercialization of traditional or ethnic heritage as a pathway to cultural and economic development. Such efforts have created a "context of encouragement," on the one hand, while casting religious and moral counter-narratives as obstacles to both economic and cultural progress and as contrary to the goals of socialism, on the other. As Tibetans in Rebkong are increasing their participation in the new market economy by engaging in the sale and/or creation of Tibetan religious and cultural objects, we should nevertheless recognize that their involvement in this particular domain is in many respects the outcome of central government planning, market creation, and promotion, as well as a manufactured demand through the cultivation of a tourist and collectors' market, all of which have served to channel and incentivize Tibetan employment toward this particular industry. In addition, the testimonies of some Tibetan merchants suggest that the discourse of economic development that is perpetuated via ethnic tourism may also be influencing some Tibetans to participate in the business of selling religious goods. Seen in light of Tibetans' current socioeconomic and political circumstances, such conditions have contributed to a *commodity context* (Appadurai 1986) which has made Tibetans' sale of religious goods, at the very least, difficult to avoid and one in which the alternative—that is, not to participate—no longer seems to make any practical sense. At stake for many are not only the issues of economic survival and cultural identity but also the quality and treatment of such goods and the very meanings and values that are associated with them.

As Tibetans have increasingly begun to participate in the commodification of their religious goods for the external market, there may be yet another reason to suggest that their foray into this business has not necessarily indicated a total triumph of market forces. Even as the commodification of religious objects has become a new source of livelihood in a manner that is unprecedented, the vast majority of Tibetan painters and merchants have not wholly abandoned the religious ideas associated with selling religious goods; as we have already observed, many claim to maintain, to the extent possible, particular traditional ideas and values associated with the handling of these objects. Rather, Tibetans continue to make sense of their activities and the religious proscriptions associated with the sale of religious goods in a number of ways and to various degrees according to their own traditional ideas and values. The next chapter examines Tibetans' current perspectives on selling religious goods, revealing how such activity is viewed by painters, merchants, and monks.

6 | Painters, Merchants, and Monks

Tibetan Perceptions of the Sale of Buddhist Goods

Although the commissioning of religious objects still occurs regularly in Amdo, what the average visitor observes in the regional marketplaces is the open and direct sale of ready-made or preproduced religious goods.[1] In terms of thangka paintings in particular, today, unlike in the past, one can walk into a thangka store or gallery, choose an image displayed on the wall, ask for the price, receive a direct quote from the attending merchant or painter (if the price is not already displayed on the painting itself), and purchase an iconographically correct thangka on the spot. This exemplifies what many painters described as the "new" way of painting—that is, creating thangkas without being commissioned to do so beforehand for the external market. However, beneath the surface of what appears to be a purely mechanistic entrepreneurial activity is a whole host of religious negotiations occurring on a number of different levels. The traditional religious proscriptions against the sale of such goods have not simply disappeared. They persist and continue to play a role in Tibetans' current business activities. While some Tibetan merchants report that they deal exclusively in *ritual* objects (bells, dorjes, bowls, drums, etc.) so as to avoid the negative karma associated with selling statues, thangkas, and texts, Tibetans who do sell these objects have determined that such proscriptions are not as rigid as they appear to be at first glance.[2] For painters and merchants, and even for many monks, the question surrounding the sale of religious objects was not necessarily whether such items could be sold or not, but *how* one sold them.

FIG. 22. A young Tibetan man working on an appliqué thangka in Nyentok Village dons a "Sexy" hat while drawing the eyes on a four-armed Avalokiteśvara (Chenrezig).

Moreover, how one regarded or treated them and the attitude or intention one brought to the transaction was also crucial to whether one was engaging in meritorious or demeritorious activity. Although Tibetans' views on the sale of religious goods varied, took on different emphases, and were at times ambiguous, for the vast majority the negativity traditionally attached to the sale of religious goods was not necessarily predetermined or inevitable. In order to further understand current Tibetan views on the issue of selling religious goods, this chapter addresses the perspectives of painters and merchants (i.e., middlemen) before turning to the perspectives of monks.

PAINTERS' PERSPECTIVES

Among twelve active painters interviewed for the present study, five worked on commission only (these included those who were monks or ex-monks who had built up a clientele or reputation and were therefore kept busy with commissions). The remaining seven fulfilled commissions *and* painted thangkas destined for sale on the open market.[3] But what did painters think of the religious proscriptions against the sale of religious goods (in their case, thangkas)? How, if at all, were these doctrinal ideas relevant to their own activities? And, given the ways in which thangkas were exchanged in the past, how did painters reconcile the new way of creating noncommissioned thangkas and charging predetermined prices with traditional ideas and practices?

FIG. 23. A sign across the street from Sengeshong Mango Gonpa (shown in the distance) advertises a painter's gallery. Signs in Chinese and English indicate the expectation of tourists. The men inside this shop declined to be interviewed.

Despite the fact that some painters were more skilled than others, had more religious knowledge than others, and included monks or former monks as well as laypeople—all of which made for somewhat divergent views—it may nevertheless be said that painters tended to view their activities as beneficial, as acts which served to spread Tibetan religion and culture and generate merit. In support of this position, many appealed to the idea that the act of painting, or seeing thangkas in places where they were not previously found, was a source of tremendous merit, believing that the mere sight of an image of a buddha or a bodhisattva was spiritually beneficial and potentially transformative. This view is well supported by religious texts and was invoked by painters to support their participation in the external market.[4]

Painters, even those who sold premade thangkas, with few exceptions, viewed their own activities as relatively unproblematic from a religious perspective. This is because they believed that, since they were the creators of the paintings, they were entitled to make a living from their work. Most also believed that their dealings with patrons and the associated financial transactions were more or less continuous with the past; that is, many believed that painters in the past calculated a price before conducting their work and presented this to the patron to either accept or reject. Many also noted that the main difference between painters' activities in the past and those of the present was merely a matter of transportation and the availability of materials. Whereas in the past, most of the work was done at monasteries and at the homes of private patrons who would often supply the materials (gold, etc.), today much of the work is done at the painter's home or workshop, with the painter himself supplying these materials, the cost of which is absorbed into the overall cost of producing a thangka. Thus, there seemed to be little acknowledgment of the fact that private transactions for thangkas in the past (as opposed to working for a monastery where one generally received a daily wage) were based primarily on voluntary offerings. Nor did it appear that setting prices for ready-made thangkas posed any type of religious problem. In addition, although painters in Amdo indeed distinguished between the ontological status of unconsecrated and consecrated images, all agreed that selling both types resulted in the accumulation of negative karma, only the relative weight of the negative karma differed, with the selling of consecrated images being substantially more sinful. Painters did not employ this distinction as a strategy or justification for their own activities, perhaps because painters did not generally see themselves as businessmen, involved in the selling or reselling of religious objects.

The most important concern for painters regarding actions with the potential for the accumulation of merit or sin did not revolve around the question of selling at all. Rather, the primary concern of painters was the proper execution of the painting itself and the use of correct iconography and the proper measurements and proportions (*thig tshad*) for deities.[5] There are good reasons for artists to focus on such matters. Descriptions of the benefits and merit earned from the creation of well-proportioned religious images are well documented in classical texts. However, so too are the detriments of painting images without correct proportions and measurements. If executed correctly, an image serves as the basis for the deity when it is invited to enter it in the process of consecration. If done incorrectly, such actions are believed to have dramatic negative consequences. Illustrating the latter scenario, a text entitled *The Lotus Endowed: A Commentary on the Difficult Points of the Great King of Tantras, the Glorious Samvarodaya* (*Dpal sdom pa 'byung ba'i rgyud kyi rgyal po chen po'i dka' 'grel pad ma can* by Ratnarakshita explains:

> An image that possesses the defining characteristics, that is endowed with a charm of peacefulness and so forth, and is made beautiful by its measurements and proportions, such [an image] will become consecrated. Artists

> in this world [who make images] with measurements and proportions that are inferior will become ill, suffer death, and lose their wealth. Likewise, they will lose their friends. [But an image] in which every portion is beautiful is superior for pacifying all [such sufferings]. An image that is neither insufficient nor excessive, and possesses the prescribed dimensions, ought to be worshipped. The deity will approach an image that has the true nature of the deity's body and shape, possesses a compassionate and playful [appearance], and is endowed with the correct background colors.[6]

As such concerns took precedence for painters, most did not see much difference between painting on commission (or upon request), on the one hand, and creating ready-made images in order to sell on the external market, on the other. For some, the commissioned transaction was indeed preferable. For example, some believed that, in this case, a thangka's use as a religious object was more predictable, a commissioned work assisted in a painter's motivation to paint well and allowed the painter to satisfy the patron's wishes more thoroughly, and, thus, they claimed, had the potential to earn the painter more merit. However, the distinction between commissioned work and noncommissioned work did not necessarily make a difference in terms of the potential creation of negative karma for the painter, as both methods were generally viewed as more or less beneficial and merit producing.[7]

The primary concern of painters was therefore correct iconography. However, some painters were also concerned with pricing, believing this to be a possible source of negative karma. According to all painters interviewed, no current artistic manual contains information or advice about pricing (perhaps because, traditionally speaking, payment was based primarily on a *yön*, or offering), nor is pricing a formal part of painters' education or training. Nonetheless, there were unwritten guidelines that centered around the idea that the price of a thangka should not simply be arrived at arbitrarily—the way in which, many argued, merchants (especially Chinese ones) often priced them. Instead, the price of a thangka was ideally based on (1) the time involved in painting, (2) the skill level of the painter, (3) material costs (e.g., the amount of gold used and the quality of pigments, etc.), (4) size, and (5) detail or quality. In addition, the vast majority of painters interviewed, more generally, explained that the price for making a thangka was based on a daily work fee for painters. Moreover, several painters also emphasized that, when it came to price, one had to be honest in one's dealings with a patron. For example, one should not use fake gold and charge for real gold; a painter should fulfill the specifications being requested by the patron, and so forth. The bottom line for many was that the price should be fair and reasonable. Illustrating this process of price calculation, one painter from Labrang explained:

> For me, I personally set the prices into three categories, a high-priced range, a medium-priced range, and a low-priced range. The first [high-priced range] could cost like one thousand yuan [USD (2019) 140.00]. It costs this much because I use a lot of gold and it requires a lot of labor. For the second range, I use less gold and materials and it requires less labor. And the third one costs [even] less because I don't put any gold [on it] and it requires little work. So I just let the customer choose the price. I give all of these options to the sponsor beforehand. I just tell them the true prices and give them the options, and whether they buy it or not is just up to the customers.

Another Tibetan man from Rebkong who had previously worked in Nepal making appliqué thangkas offered a similar response:

> The price is settled according to the work involved and according to the materials used. There are three kinds in terms of textiles [used in appliqué thangkas]. Usually the cost is categorized into three: best, medium, and low quality. The size is also important as well, as is the detail. Take flowers as an example. [In a painted thangka], if you paint more detail, for instance, if there is a flower, and you paint two layers, you use less materials. If there are three, then it looks better, and you use more materials. . . . We don't feel bad about putting a price on it because if someone wants to buy a thangka, he needs it. Without it, he has nothing to look at. And in order to have this, since you can't do it yourself, you need someone else to do it. And if you ask a painter, he or she will not do it for free. It costs [money]. It consumes his time and energy. We are not in another world; we are in this world. We calculate the materials and calculate the time. There is always a guideline or limit in pricing. We don't go beyond it; we set a price that is reasonable.

While the above painters worked mostly on commission, the same pricing arrangements were also mentioned by painters who produced noncommissioned thangkas for the external-local market. The aforementioned young painter from Kumbum explained that he charged a certain amount of money for each day's work. Illustrating this, he explained, "For example, if someone gives me one thousand yuan, then the work can be finished in ten working days. If someone gives me fifteen hundred, then I will do it in fifteen days, and I will add details to the paintings. If you pay one hundred yuan, then there are paintings for that." Similarly, an older painter near Rongwo Gonpa explained that he determined the price according to the time he spends on the painting and according to the materials used: "For example, I might use a lot of gold. If I don't put the amount of gold needed on the thangka, the customers would notice. It would be obvious that I didn't put the amount needed. You can't ask for a high price for an image without gold if it doesn't have any."

Despite what appears to be an internal, moral proscription against overcharging, according to one lay thangka painter who worked at Sengeshong Yango Gonpa, there was really no limit to what a painter could charge for his services. If an artist believed that he deserved a high daily rate due to his skill level, this was seen as acceptable. This particular artist explained that he preferred to work on commission because it assisted in his motivation to paint well. When asked if he ever felt uncomfortable discussing prices with sponsors, he replied:

> I don't feel uncomfortable. I received advice from my teachers and geshés. They told me to do my best in painting. About prices, my teachers told me I could charge as much as I wanted to, but that I must have a good motivation. [They said], "You worked on it, you have a right to determine the prices." And my teachers told me that I can take my daily work fee. I usually charge a high price. The previous geshés and lamas and monks have done it the same way I do. We must do our best when painting. If my ability is not the best, then what can I do? I've tried my best. We have teachers, as you saw the old monk right now [pointing to an elder monk who passes by] he is our *a khu* [i.e., our lama].[8] He teaches us to do it this way. He always advises us to paint in the best way, and he tells us all the rules. Our teacher advises us to make the best thangkas. They will be displayed in places where everybody can see, and they will say, "Oh this is wonderful work." In this way thangka painters will not earn negative karma; they will earn merit. If they earn merit, then it doesn't matter what the price is. The price one gets for the thangka is nothing compared

> to the merit earned—price is temporary. We have our teachers, *a khus*, they always tell us how to do it, and so we know what we are doing. But there are some painters who really know nothing about thangkas; they just paint. They have completely no knowledge of it.

In contrast to the testimony of this painter, however, one clay statue maker, a monk from Gasar Gonpa near Rebkong, expressed the view that it is common for contemporary artists to simply charge 20 percent of the cost of the materials as one's service fee; this is presumably deemed a reasonable amount sufficient to maintain one's livelihood. While admitting that the most ideal transaction is for the patron to pay the material costs plus give an offering, he explained that many patrons these days do not know the traditions associated with such transactions, making the fixing of a price more of a necessity.[9]

Given the criteria involved in determining prices, many painters suggested that what is being priced or sold, if anything, is not the physical painting or the buddha or deity depicted but rather the cost of the materials and the painter's time or labor. Such a notion, as we have seen, is similar to the way in which printers were compensated for the printing of texts. It also resembles the advice given by Lama Zopa to his student regarding the sale of religious objects—namely, that one should not think of oneself as engaged in selling holy objects. In line with many painters' responses, on the topic of earning income from selling religious goods, a more recent FPMT blog post that draws on the teachings of Lama Zopa states, "it is OK for one to collect money to cover the costs of materials and the time spent creating and distributing these holy objects" (FPMT 2018).[10] Representing this view, one painter, a former monk of Labrang, stated, "I consider myself a painter and the cost is the cost of my work fee, not the cost of the thangka. We consider it [i.e., the price or cost] as a *yön,* defined as a salary or wage." While this method and conception of payment (i.e., "for the work") is likely a holdover from past practices in which a painter was invited to a monastery and paid a daily wage, by both conceiving of and determining the pricing of thangkas in such a way, painters, in this sense, avoided the potential pitfalls associated with selling thangkas.

Second, and closely related to the fact that painters did not see their activities as selling, several painters, those who worked on commission as well as those who sold pre-painted thangkas, when speaking about selling and buying religious goods, explained that they preferred to use the word *lu* (*blu ba,* or *glud*), a Tibetan term, as we observed repeatedly in chapter 2, literally meaning "to buy off, ransom, or redeem" and applied in an honorific sense to the buying and selling of religious goods. According to one former monk from Dharamsala, Tenzin Sherab, with whom I had made an acquaintance in the United States and maintained an ongoing dialogue over the course of my research,

> *lu* is basically the honorific word for both selling and buying any Buddhist religious items, especially if it is a sacred object, such as vajra, bell, a text, etc. Whether you sell or buy these, this word is used by faithful people as a symbolic word to symbolize an entire action—which includes the mental motivation, the physical act, and the subsequent dedication—as all being respectful, done out of the purest motivation, for practice and Dharma and not for worldly gains. So, it refers to one complete pure action.

Importantly, according to several painters, to *lu* a painting required a good intention on the part of both the painter and the customer or patron and implied a transaction solely intended for religious purposes, an action believed to be completely legitimate (as well as merit producing) and one which was distinguished from a commercial transaction (*tshong*), understood to be for business purposes only and therefore illegitimate or sinful. A painter-monk from Sengeshong Mango explained this difference by stating,

> If someone who has faith buys [a thangka], we don't call this sell or buy, we call it *lu*. Selling and buying are commercial terms, and *lu* is for religious purposes. Selling and buying is [only] for making profits. If someone is buying by "*lu*-ing" [a verb], there is some offering involved on both sides. The painter also charges according to what the sponsor can afford. It's not like in a shop where if you don't have money, you cannot buy it; it's not like that.

According to this monk-painter, what distinguishes a *lu* transaction is not only that it is meant to be a onetime transaction between the painter and the commissioning patron for religious purposes (i.e., it is not intended to be resold again), but also the fact that—in contrast to haggling over a price—the painter paints, quite literally, according to what the patron wants or is able to afford.

The older monk and *a khu* from Sengeshong Yango Gonpa mentioned earlier, when asked about the difference between *lu* and *tshong*, responded by drawing upon the story of the first image of the Buddha involving the exchange of gifts between King Bimbisāra and King Utrāyaṇa:

> There is a difference between sell and *lu*. Basically *lu* is based on intention. The Buddha itself is priceless. The Chinese emperor, when Buddha was alive, gave some presents—armor that was decorated with precious things—to another emperor, a king in India. And he [the Indian king] said to the Buddha, "[this gift] is really priceless. Even if I give my country to the Chinese empire it wouldn't cover the price of this gift." Then, the Buddha said, "Don't worry." He gave the Indian king a Buddha image and said, "Give it to the Chinese king." The Chinese king was also very knowledgeable and he thought, "Oh this image is priceless!" So he [the Chinese king] said, "The gift I gave to the Indian king is not priceless, its value can be measured. But the Buddha image, you cannot measure the value of it." So, as a painter, one should think of a place where there is no religion, and that if he [the painter] puts this thangka there, people will see it with their own eyes. He should have this kind of intention when painting. For me, for instance, a painter is considered just like a worker and the prices are considered just like wages earned by other people. So he [the painter, should think], "This is my wage per day or for this day." If he [the painter] has the intention of selling the Buddha, it is *dikpa* [a sin]. So, [he thinks], "I needed this much for my work, not for the selling of the Buddha." So when people see this thangka or Buddha, even birds' negative karma will be washed away just by seeing it. . . . It is also dependent on the buyer's motivation. If you as a buyer make it commercial, and think as a buyer that you are going to resell it for *tshong* [in a business transaction], then it is sinful. [But as a painter], thinking that the thangka is for people who want become enlightened is the best intention, and it will be good for this life as well as for the next life. [One should] think that it is something to eliminate the sorrows of all sentient beings. The Buddha renounced all his properties as a prince and eventually he even devoted his body for the sake of all sentient beings, for the sake of enlightenment. These images represent such a person. So the merit is earned by having the intention that every sentient being be free from suffering.

Thus, to *lu* an image, as described above, involves both the painter's intention that an image is seen by many people and serves to alleviate the suffering of sentient beings, as well as the conception that one is merely selling one's time and labor. Having such intentions, as opposed to the intention of selling the Buddha, at least for this particular individual, is a source of potential merit.[11]

Nevertheless, while the above descriptions of *lu* represent its more formal or traditional meaning or usage, in its most basic or common use, *lu* appears to simply be a way of speaking respectfully about the sale of thangkas, in a way that distinguishes this activity from that involving other, common objects. Moreover, its use by many painters when referring to business transactions involving thangkas was seemingly enough to avert the potential karmic damage caused by selling. For example, one young painter from Kumbum appeared to use the term in this more general way, explaining that Tibetans use the term *lu* and not "buy" and "sell" to describe a transaction that involves religious goods. During our interview, he explained that he frequently sold to dealers (those whose business it is to buy and then resell) and often added a few hundred yuan on top of what was apparently the cost price of a thangka for those customers he did not deem to be poor. Furthermore, when asked what he thought about people who buy thangkas and use them for nonreligious purposes, he explained, "People with money take it as just a picture and not anything special. Usually these people have more money. If they can afford it, I ask a higher price. I can tell just from looking at them whether they are Buddhist or whether they are just buying for fun. But there are some people who are really pious but don't have the money, so I will offer it to them for less." For this particular painter, to *lu* a thangka (which he believed he was doing) appeared to involve some flexibility in pricing based on his perceptions of the ability of a customer to pay. However, he did not speak of *lu* as a transaction that was intended for religious purposes only, as one involving a special intention, or as one in which payment was conceived to be for a painter's time and labor. Thus the word *lu*, according to this painter, appeared to be more a manner of speaking about selling religious objects and not much else. Regardless of the presence of the appropriate intention said to be involved in *lu* noted above, or its use as a mere substitute for *tshong* (to sell), the employment of the honorific term *lu* among painters not only symbolically set thangkas as well as their exchange apart from other mundane objects, the use of the word *lu* when describing such transactions worked to absolve or prevent them from becoming entangled in the business and thus the sin of selling religious goods.

Next, although less pervasive as a strategy among painters, yet still worthy of note, four separate painters suggested that the potential for the accumulation of negative karma resulting from selling thangkas (and other religious goods) rested not with the painter but with the consumer/patron and his or her use of the thangka. Such a position was, as we have already seen, indicated by the aforementioned *a khu* from Sengeshong Yango. Illustrating this particular point, one painter who owned a store near Sengeshong Mango Gonpa, while confirming that his paintings were indeed sold, remarked that the potential for negative karma was not necessarily linked to their sale, but to their use and location:

> Nowadays, my paintings are sold, but they are in the temples and monasteries in China, not in public places. So I don't think I am creating negative karma in this sense. . . . My father told me about these things from the negative and positive perspective. My father told me that if I paint a really nice thangka, it would result in positive karma; people will see it and learn about it. In the next life I will take a positive rebirth and will be reborn as a very smart guy. From the positive perspective, if you introduce the thangka to someone who does not know about it, then you can earn merit.

This painter emphasized the potential for the painter's accumulation of merit, further suggesting that any negativity resulting from the transaction was not a matter of its sale but exclusively a matter of where it was displayed and presumably how it was used (for religious purposes). Given that he believed (almost certainly incorrectly) that his paintings were technically in the right location, the possibility for the accumulation of negative karma was minimal or nonexistent.

Likewise, the aforementioned painters from Sengeshong Mango Gonpa also responded not by pointing to the sale of religious goods as the potential problem but rather to their *use* as the real concern. I asked if naming one's price (for example, telling a potential customer that a painting will cost one thousand yuan) poses any religious problem for them. Both agreed that it did not, stating, "There is no religious problem if someone comes to buy a thangka with strong faith." Pressing the issue further, I asked what was considered acceptable and unacceptable with regard to selling religious goods. One of the monks responded by pointing out that the *use* of religious goods such as thangkas (and not the painter's sale) was the real concern when speaking of the accumulation of negative karma:

> It [i.e., selling thangkas] is acceptable because you have the faith involved in selling these things, and it's unacceptable because I recently heard some

> news about the misuse of religious goods. For instance, they put a *maṇḍala* on pavement glasses. So in this case it's unacceptable.[12]

For this particular monk, the painter's intention that a thangka be used for religious purposes plays a role in legitimating the transaction and, in a sense, protects and absolves the painter from incurring *dikpa* (as it is a *lu* transaction); a problem for the painter only appears to arise when that object is put to wrong use. Moreover, this monk reflected a sentiment that many of my informants held regarding the decorative use of religious symbols and images. While a few felt that such uses were relatively harmless, the vast majority of Tibetans interviewed believed that such uses, including the display of images in museums (an act attributed to the actions of the government, primarily for business purposes), were highly inappropriate.[13]

Furthermore, one young Rebkong painter who owned a painting workshop and gallery just outside of Rongwo Gonpa also explained that, regarding the negative karma associated with the sale of thangkas, the onus fell primarily on the consumer. However, in a slight twist to the above examples, he explained that the painter does have some (perhaps initial) responsibility for educating the customer. According to this painter:

> If the person who buys is really in need of it, it is positive. But if the person who buys them puts them to wrong use, then it is negative. If someone buys it from here and puts it in the toilet, for example, that is negative, not positive. . . . As a painter we have to describe [the meanings and uses of thangkas]; we have to tell the consumers. We are responsible for telling the consumers how to treat these things. If the customers use it in the wrong way, then the negative karma [that results from that misuse] can come back to the painter. So it is our responsibility to tell them about these things. About 80 percent of [my customers] know how these religious goods are used.

This painter seems to be suggesting that if the consumer is adequately educated with respect to the appropriate meanings, uses, and display of a thangka and still puts the image to wrong use, the negative karma that is accumulated falls squarely on the new owner. The painter's explanation therefore acts to buffer him from negative karma. Nevertheless, the main point here is that, according to this painter, it is the customer's or patron's use (including the placement of the painting) and not the mere act of selling that determines whether there is resulting negative karma in such transactions.

Moreover, similar to what the *a khu* from Sengeshong Yango Gonpa claimed, one painter and former monk in his thirties from Rebkong who owned a gallery and workshop near Sengeshong Mango placed the fault of selling onto the customer-turned-reseller, remarking that from the painter's perspective it is the merchant or middleman, and not the painter, who is in danger of incurring negative karma. Responding to a question about the proscriptions against selling religious goods described in Tsongkhapa's *Great Treatise*, this painter remarked:

> I have read the *Lamrim Chenmo*. I know what it says. For instance, if I sell a thangka for three thousand [yuan] and that person takes it and resells it for five or six thousand, then it is negative. When I sell this thangka to a person, I charge for all my work on this. I did it myself; therefore, it is not sinful if *I* sell it. If a middleman [however] sells it for five thousand or six thousand, then he is selling this for a business purpose. He is making a business out of it, so it is negative. After I paint all this, if a middleman sells this to others, this has become a business. . . . If I sell a thangka for three thousand, and if [that customer] sells it to another for the same price, there is no sin. If he sells it for five thousand, then this is sinful.

What is being advocated by this painter resembles what Geshé Sopa claimed earlier with respect to the exchange of religious texts. Here, once again, barring any deficiencies in painting, the painter, having completed the actual work, is entitled to make a living from it and is exempt from wrongdoing with respect to the sale of the painting, the price of which is conceived of as a fee for the painter's time plus the cost of materials. Rather, it is the consumer (in this case a consumer-middleman) and his or her use of the thangka that becomes the focus of scrutiny.

Finally, several painters put forward yet another strategy for dealing with the negative karma associated with selling religious goods. They focused primarily on the issue of *motivation,* distinct or separate from the notion of *lu,* as what determines whether one accumulates merit or sin. These painters also stressed the fact that one was required to paint according to the predetermined measurements outlined in religious texts. However, apart from that, they did not claim that sin resulted from the mere act of selling, the price or process of pricing, and even the use by the consumer. Instead, they claimed that the virtue or nonvirtue resulting from selling a thangka depended on the painter's intention—something that, as some explained, was difficult, if not impossible, for anyone except the painter himself to perceive. For example, I asked one lay thangka painter from Sengeshong who opened his shop in 2009 about what he thought of those who believed selling religious goods was a negative activity. He explained his position by drawing a distinction between thangka painters and businessmen:

> Businessmen are different from thangka painters. It depends on how you treat them [thangkas] and consider them and respect them. [For example,] if you think, "Oh, I am going to sell these things just for business purposes," it's completely wrong, but we [as painters] are not doing this. We have these religious things in our home, and we make offerings every day. We are living with these things. If there is no demand, there is no seller.

For this painter, the difference between the accumulation of merit or sin depends on the painter's intention. If a painter solely has the intention to make a business of thangkas, absent of any respect for the paintings or aspirations that thangkas may be of spiritual benefit to the buyer, then such actions are reprehensible and considered karmically negative. This perspective, like others mentioned earlier, creates a distinction between painters and merchants who were not artists. However, if artists sell paintings with the intention that they are for religious purposes, and if the transaction is completed in a respectful manner, with the proper treatment of the thangka and consideration for the patron, then there is nothing but the creation of merit for the painter.

One quite popular and well-established monk-painter who resided at Sengeshong Mango Gonpa also held a similar position. When asked what he thought about the idea that selling religious goods is karmically negative, he responded by confirming that such actions were indeed considered detrimental but explained that motivation played a crucial role:

> It is sinful to sell religious goods, but it depends on one's motivation. Everything depends on motivation. If you look at what the *Lamrim Chenmo* says, you can hardly carry on. Not even laypeople, monks, or geshés can follow this exactly. It is very difficult to carry out what the *Lamrim Chenmo* says. One cannot read the other person. We cannot judge the other person, so it depends on motivation in this case. This is the main issue. You can't judge the person by looking at his or her appearance. As

> a thangka painter, one has to have the Three Jewels in mind. Because we have expenses for this [thangka painting] and we need money to survive, we have to charge an amount of money for these thangkas; we have to charge for our work and the materials. In order to make money for a living, we have to work hard.

According to this monk's response, simply because a painter appears to be selling or is otherwise making a living from thangka paintings does not automatically mean he or she is accumulating negative karma. While acknowledging the existence of particular proscriptions against selling religious goods in the lamrim literature, ultimately, for this painter, such proscriptions appeared to depend on intention. This monk-painter was not the only one to hold such a view; several others did as well. The ex-monk and painter who resided in Labrang provided an even more nuanced explanation of the importance of motivation with respect to the accumulation of sin and merit by drawing on a popular tale from Buddhist folklore. In contrast to the above response, this painter appeared to extend his views to both painters and middlemen:

> Normally, it is sinful to sell all these religious goods, but it depends on one's motivation. If one sells with a bad intention, then it is sinful. Even if a painter thinks he or she has made it properly [i.e., according to the prescribed measurements and iconography], it is possible to incur a sin because it is something related to the body, speech, and mind [of the Buddha]. My teacher said that if one has a good motivation and there is some sin involved [i.e., a mistake in painting], it will be less because one didn't do it intentionally. . . . Sometimes, if the sellers sell it in a place where there are no thangkas, and the buyers also buy thangkas and then they make offerings to the thangkas, then in this case there is also merit earned, not only sin. As we were talking about motivation a story came to mind. There is a story in which two pilgrims were going to Lhasa. One was ahead of the other. And the other was farther back. The one ahead found a statue of the Buddha made of clay and it started to rain. He thought he needed to protect it or it would wash away. He had nothing to protect it except the soles of his shoes. So he covered the Buddha with them and left. The other man came along and was shocked. [To him] this was an act of disrespecting the Buddha, so he took the shoes off and left. Then the rain came and washed the statue away. Later, when asked about the case—of who earned

> the merit, and who earned negative karma—the Buddha said that both earned merit. One thought to protect the Buddha and the other to prevent the Buddha from being disrespected. This story illustrates that motivation is the key to earning merit. Both earned equal merit. . . . As Tibetans, we believe if one sells this for business purposes one accumulates sin that you can never wash away. It's certain that if one's intention is to do business, there is a sin, but I am not able to read his [the seller's] mind [*sems*]. We don't know what his or her intention is; it is hard to predict.[14]

Finally, still another unofficial monk-painter from Labrang who painted on commission in a workshop near the monastery shared these same sentiments; here, as in the above response, he was referring to painters as well as to middlemen-sellers. Moreover, according to this monk, a positive motivation had the power to make the issue of pricing irrelevant such that earning a profit, large or small, was acceptable as long as one's motivation was proper or positive:

> It is not necessarily karmically negative if one sells. There are many ways to sell. If one *only* sells to make profits, then yes [it's sinful]. But you can't say that these people are creating negative karma. Religious images pass on through people. If it is passed on in a proper way, then it is good. People who sell can also earn merit. In Buddhism, we don't measure acts according to price but according to motivation. The price has to be set according to the time, the market price, etc. It [the ethical status of the action] is based on the mind. It is negative or positive due to the quality of the mind. Even if one sells for a high price, but has a good motivation, one is not accumulating sin; one is accumulating merit. One can sell for ten yuan and can earn merit. It has nothing to do with changes in the market or economics. It has only to do with the quality of the mind.

For this group of painters, whether one was accumulating negative karma as result of selling religious goods such as thangkas was not as straightforward as it might appear. Neither the act of selling, nor the price, nor pricing thangkas according to their market value, nor even the use of the profits was the real issue. All of these factors were peripheral to the quality of the painter's and/or seller's motivation. By emphasizing motivation, a well-known Buddhist concept in karmic theory, these painters not only interpreted their own activities as consistent with the Tibetan Buddhist tradition on such matters but also, in a sense, cleared the way for their own and others' legitimate sale of religious goods on the open market.

Despite being a standard view among more savvy or educated painters, not everyone agreed that motivation played such a pivotal role. For example, one clay statue maker in Labrang explained that painters who sold ready-made images were indeed involved in creating sins because they were selling things that were not asked for and were not painting according to patrons' wishes and demands. In this sense, they were treating thangkas like merchandise. Another clay statue maker and monk near Gasar Gonpa in Rebkong expressed this same view. Describing how he created statues on commission, he explained, "If you make it [a statue] beforehand, you have to sell it, and it becomes commercial, and this is against the religion; it's sinful." Furthermore, when asked if there was a legitimate way to sell religious goods in shops, he replied, "No, because they [the sellers] have to make a profit to pay rent." Such responses not only reflect the belief that the commissioned transaction was the more appropriate means of exchange, they also challenge the idea that a proper motivation can save a painter who sells noncommissioned thangkas or a merchant who buys and sells them.

In addition, it should be noted that despite the widespread use of the particular strategies noted above, two different painters and the wife of another artist suggested that their activities contained irredeemably negative aspects. For example, one painter near Sengeshong Mango Gonpa explained, "Well, there is negative karma in doing almost everything we do. About 70 percent of jobs involve negative karma. But in this world everything costs money. So we have to survive. For instance, if you want a cup of tea, you have to pay for it." When asked how he dealt with the fact that selling was traditionally considered a karmically negative act, he responded, "We do daily routine prayers, but we can't completely wash the sins away." Another painter from Labrang, who fulfilled commissions and painted ready-made thangkas, suggested that both the merchant and painter accumulate negative karma: "There is sin in any case. Even though it is negative, it seems that people are still carrying on, still doing it. If you tell them not to do it, then they will do it. This seems to be human nature. If you tell them to do good things, they don't do it. I also feel that I am accumulating sin. And I am thinking of giving up this job and changing my career."[15] Finally, the wife of an appliqué thangka maker in Nyentok Village, who was present during my interview with her husband and who worked on the silk brocade portion of the thangkas, appeared to imply that their activities inevitably created negative karma. This became apparent when she told a story about an incident involving a nomad woman. The wife explained, "A lady who was a nomad came here and asked, 'Are you selling the *Konchok Sum* [*Dkon mchok gsum*; i.e., the Three Jewels]?' To which I said, 'Are you killing all those animals and sheep and accumulating sins? It is just the same. You sell all these animals and they are slaughtered. It's just the same.'"[16] Furthermore, when I asked the wife if they engaged in any particular religious practices to rid themselves of any negative karma that resulted from the business of thangka selling, she replied that indeed they did, stating, "We do this at the end of the year. We take some money from thangka sales and we give it to the monasteries." These responses suggest that despite the use of particular strategies to avert the negative karma associated with selling, some artists still appeared to recognize their activities to be somewhat karmically detrimental.

Aside from the apparent doubts expressed by these particular individuals, painters attempted to avert the sin involved in selling thangkas in a number of ways—whether by appealing to pricing strategies and the idea that they are not selling the actual Buddha but charging a work fee and for material costs; utilizing the concept of *lu*; placing the responsibility on the consumer and his or her use of a thangka; or appealing to the concept of motivation. Such strategies were not without their apparent contradictions and problems. For example, as already pointed out, some painters who appealed to one or another pricing strategy also explained that the price of a thangka was determined by the market, a point which was seemingly at odds with painting according to the patron's ability to pay. In addition, more than one painter, while appealing to the notion of *lu*, explained that they added a few hundred yuan on top of the total cost, inflating the price for customers who appeared to be wealthy. Painters also often knowingly sold to middlemen, which contradicts the idea that the customer's use of the thangka was crucial and that they should not be resold. Finally, even the former monk-painter from Labrang who emphasized the importance of motivation explained that he was once told by a senior monk that his plan to paint a particular thangka to be reprinted for the purpose of raising money for the monastery would be a violation against the Three Jewels, challenging the notion that a proper motivation was what legitimized the sale of thangkas. Nevertheless, for the vast majority of painters, selling as a karmically negative activity was the exclusive problem of merchants, a group that had their own unique perspectives on dealing with these issues.

MERCHANTS' PERSPECTIVES

Merchants, or middlemen, who sold religious goods were often perceived by painters and monks as only involved in the business for the money, and their activity was thus generally perceived to be negative. This was not always the case, however. For instance, some painters expressed a notable disinterest in the activities of middlemen, and, as we will observe later, several monks did not maintain the view that their activity was necessarily negative.[17] However, given that merchants were generally uninvolved in making religious goods but only in buying and selling them, many individuals assumed that middlemen were treating religious goods as merchandise, were making a business of religious goods, and thus were involved in sinful activity. Compared to painters, merchants had relatively fewer strategies for dealing with the negative karma believed to be associated with the sale of religious goods. Nonetheless, they possessed their own unique perspectives on the issue and their own methods for handling it.

Merchants interviewed sold goods such as Buddhist statues, thangkas, texts, or miniature stūpas. They can be divided into those who believed such practices were religiously acceptable and those who believed they were generally negative. More specifically, one group of merchants believed the sale of religious objects as well as the associated negative karma was manageable or negotiable, while the second group believed that this was true only up to a point. The overall perspectives among merchants spanned a spectrum from the view that selling religious goods was acceptable, perhaps even virtuous, to the view that it was indeed negative but was generally not that serious. Those who adhered to this latter view believed that such negative karma could be kept within bounds or reduced by following certain business practices and by relying upon moral or religious atonements.

Of the eighteen merchants interviewed for the present study, twelve believed there was no religious problem with the sale of religious goods. Among these twelve, there were, to be sure, three merchants who claimed to be unaware of such proscriptions. However, according to the remaining nine merchants, if certain conditions were met, and if religious goods were sold in particular ways, then one incurred no negative karma. All of these merchants were aware of the traditional proscriptions against selling religious objects, but many tended to reject such restrictions. Some individuals, as we observed in the previous chapter, saw the textual proscriptions against selling religious goods as a thing of the past or as incompatible with modern times, and some even claimed that such ideas represented an element of Buddhism that has held Tibetans back from economic prosperity. For many of these merchants, while the participation of non-Tibetans in the business or the lack of other employment opportunities may have, at least in part, been used as a reason or justification for their own participation, from a religious or karmic perspective, perceiving and treating religious objects as special or sacred, employing reasonable pricing, and having appropriate knowledge of religious goods was essentially what legitimated their sale. Thus, from these merchants' perspectives, if one fulfilled these criteria, one incurred no sin from the sale of religious objects. The implicit message here was that should merchants treat religious goods like merchandise (disrespecting them by sitting on them, for example), charge exorbitant prices (charging as much as double the price as many claimed Chinese merchants did), or sell without appropriate knowledge of religious objects, such behavior would indeed be considered negative or sinful.

Beyond meeting the above criteria, some members of this group also appealed to additional strategies. For example, one Rebkong shop owner implied that the distinction between the sale of antique versus new objects was a deciding factor in whether one incurred negative karma. When asked whether he was hesitant to open his business, given that it involved the sale of Buddhist objects, he replied: "I never hesitated at all to sell these things except those very old statues or old thangkas and antiques; I might feel guilty selling these things. But I don't hesitate selling new stuff." While not explicitly expressed by merchants in Amdo during my fieldwork, such a distinction was rather widespread among merchants during my research on the sale of Buddhist statues in Lhasa in 2006, and given the profound distaste among Tibetans for those who traffic in antiques from old (i.e., pre-1959) Tibet, it is likely that the majority of merchants in Amdo—both those who acknowledged the possibility of negative karma and those who did not—held similar views. In Lhasa, the distaste for the sale of older religious objects was evident in many ways. For example, one afternoon a group of young Tibetans performed a play reminding the audience that such business activities were offensive to generations of Tibetans who had worshipped these images. That Tibetans continue to have little regard for such merchants was likewise confirmed by one monk from Kumbum who, during our conversation, explained that there was a known businessman in Lhasa who sold a Drolma (Tārā) thangka in order to build a hotel; he is apparently still looked down upon today. Furthermore, according to this same monk, there was more to why Tibetans tended to condemn the sale of old religious objects in particular. He explained that religious objects, when in their original place, give a monastery religious or spiritual value and prevent natural disasters as well as epidemics. Most old religious objects, he remarked, are also blessed by many great religious figures and contain a lot of positive energy, or *chinlab* (*byin rlabs*). Therefore, if one sells these objects to other people, not only does one accrue negative karma but one is also harming others, as such an act negatively impacts those people for whom such items acted as objects of worship.[18]

In addition, while by no means a widespread strategy, two other merchants in this group invoked the fact that the images they sold were not consecrated and utilized this as a rationalization for their legitimate sale. Hence, selling unconsecrated statues was deemed by these two merchants to be religiously acceptable, the logic of course being that since consecration rituals had not been completed, no actual deities were present in the images. This strategy was widespread among statue and thangka merchants during my research in Lhasa in 2006 and is one which Yael Bentor (1993) has also noted was widespread among those who sold tourist thangkas in Kathmandu.

Finally, for some of these merchants, the rationalizations they utilized for entering the market in religious goods were also used as a means of legitimizing their sale from a religious or karmic perspective. That is, many believed the negativity associated with the sale of such objects was ameliorated by the fact that they intended their actions to be of benefit to Tibetans—the idea being that since they were spreading the Dharma, preserving Tibetan religion and culture, or serving the Tibetan community, as well as treating religious objects in respectful ways, this made their actions acceptable from a religious standpoint. Among this group of merchants, eight people held this view, one that (although not stated as such) perhaps most closely resembled an appeal to the idea and importance of one's *motivation* as a way of legitimating the act of selling. For this group, if transactions for religious objects were performed accordingly, then a reasonable profit could be made without the accumulation of negative karma.

In contrast, the remaining six merchants acknowledged that selling religious goods was, from the religious perspective, indeed a karmically negative activity. This group of merchants appealed to many of the same strategies of the first group, although their goal was to minimize what they saw as the inevitable negative karma incurred from the sale of religious objects. Thus, this group emphasized the importance of treating religious objects appropriately and with respect and of offering them at reasonable prices to customers (as opposed to the purported practices used by non-Tibetans). For example, one young merchant in the Xining market, in a move that mirrored a primary concern of painters, explained that if he sold an image that wasn't complete (i.e., iconographically correct) and was missing something, like the leg of a statue or a page of a religious text, then this would be bad. He added that he did not barter or haggle with customers over the prices of religious goods, something he considered inappropriate given the special status of religious objects. However, for this merchant, as well as for other merchants within this group, the idea that selling religious goods was ultimately a negative activity remained, despite the use of various precautions.[19] While at least two merchants within this group adamantly responded that they would never sell consecrated images (one adding, "not even for a million yuan"), none attempted to justify selling unconsecrated objects, for it was widely acknowledged among this group that such a distinction only determined the relative *weight* of the negative karma incurred. In addition, nobody in this group claimed that it was acceptable to sell new versus old religious objects, as selling either was considered to be karmically negative, albeit more so in the case of old objects.

Given the general acknowledgment of the negativity involved in selling religious goods among this second group, another strategy used by three of these merchants—a strategy which distinguished them from the others in this group—was the employment of particular countermeasures to purify the accumulation of the negative karma accrued from selling. The possibility of removing negative karma is an important part of both the Indian and Tibetan Buddhist traditions. It is believed that negative karma can be reduced or even removed via confession, prayers, mantras, or ritual actions.[20] For those who acknowledged that the sale of religious objects resulted in negative karma, the notion that such activity produced extremely heavy obscurations (as indicated in religious texts) did not arise during our conversations, suggesting that for these individuals such actions were not seen to be uniquely harmful when compared to other negative acts. In addition, none of the merchants within this group expressed a knowledge or awareness of expiatory rituals such as *drultor,* the ritual Avalokiteśvara gave to Kyergangpa. Nevertheless, these individuals did believe that their selling activities required some form of remedy.

Examples of these countermeasures took two basic forms—the recitation of mantras or prayers and the practice of making donations to monasteries. For example, one middle-aged merchant in the Xining market, when asked if there were any ways he tried to lessen the negative karma or get rid of it, responded that indeed he did:

> I asked some monk whether I can sell these things or not and he said, "Actually they cannot be sold. But [because] there are so many people who can afford [them] and people who demand them, you have to sell them. But you can sell with a fair price, and you can also chant the mantras in order to reduce the sins." This was his advice . . . I recite all the mantras: the *yig cha* [*yig brgya,* Vajrasattva or "one hundred-syllable mantra"] and the *cham dro* [*skyabs 'gro* or refuge precepts], the invocation . . . I do recite these things to lessen the negative karma. . . . By the time I pay back my [business] loan I'll be an old man and I will probably donate any remaining statues to the monasteries.

A neighboring vendor in the same market also used this same countermeasure. He first responded by explaining that he felt he was providing a service to Tibetans and didn't feel that what he was doing was accumulating any negative karma. He further explained that he charged fair prices and that to charge double the amount would be a sin. However, later in our conversation, he admitted that it *was* sinful to sell religious goods, both those that were consecrated and those that were not. He explained that "there is some sin in selling unconsecrated images, as these things are still images of the Buddha or other deities and not just some lump of clay or piece of paper." Finally, he concluded by adding that he said prayers in order to remove any accumulated negative karma. In addition, a third vendor, the former shepherd from Rebkong, explained that in order to limit the accumulation of the associated negativity, his family made some donations to the nearby monastery, the same strategy for expiating the sin employed by the wife of the appliqué thangka maker in Nyentok Village.[21] Not a single merchant who attempted countermeasures claimed that their atonements completely removed the negative karma, only that it was reduced. Thus, for these merchants, the residue from the negative karma incurred was something that they decided to live with and accept as an occupational hazard.[22]

Not all of the merchants who acknowledged the presence of negative karma as a result of selling, however, claimed to engage in practices to remove such karma. One particular merchant, a farmer-turned-bookseller in Kumbum who had been in the business for seven years, responding to a question regarding whether or not he had heard of the religious proscriptions against selling, replied that he indeed had, but he went on to explain that everything one does involves the creation of negative karma. According to this merchant, "In farming you have to kill insects, for example. So, if you think about this only from the religious perspective, you won't be able to do anything, you won't be able to survive." Finally, he added, "It is up to the individual and his motivation." The perspective of this merchant appeared to epitomize the views of most merchants. That is, for the vast majority of sellers of religious goods, the negative karma associated with such commerce was not unlike that associated with other activities; it did not carry any special weight or character despite the fact that what was being sold were representations of the Buddha. In contrast to this bookseller, two other merchants who acknowledged the negativity of selling religious goods, but who did not cite the performance of specific countermeasures, decided that leaving the business altogether was the best possible option. As already noted, one merchant who operated a corner store in the Xining market, and who acknowledged his awareness of the religious proscriptions against selling, remarked that he agreed with the textual proscriptions and expressed his desire to leave the business in the near future. Another woman from Chentsa County had already recently stopped selling statues and thangkas after having been informed of the heavy karmic misdeeds she would incur as a result. According to the former painter from Nepal whom I interviewed in Rebkong, most sellers of religious goods do not attempt to atone for their involvement in the business. By his estimate, "20 percent of the people who sell try to reduce [their sins] by praying or [making] offerings, but that still leaves about 80 percent who rarely do so. In order to reduce the sin they [the sellers] build monasteries, offer statues, and make stūpas, or else they sponsor monks, recite prayers, and give donations. But there are some people who rarely think of the negative side." Such a statement suggests that most merchants do not view the sale of religious goods as religiously problematic enough to take any specific countermeasures against it.

As is the case with painters, there were apparent contradictions among the perspectives of merchants. For example, many merchants emphasized the proper treatment of religious goods as something that legitimated their sale, yet there were occasions when I witnessed entire bags of thangkas resting on the floor in some stores, which seemed to challenge the notion that one should not treat religious goods as merchandise. But perhaps more telling, while all merchants emphasized respect for religious goods, none used the term *lu* (widely used by painters) when describing their activities. Such an absence of the application of *lu* appears to contrast with merchants' emphasis on the proper treatment of religious objects, which the employment of *lu* (which itself connotes respect and an exchange for religious purposes) surely, at least rhetorically, represents. Moreover, the noticeable absence of the use of *lu* among merchants only highlights the commercial nature of merchants' activities (*tshong*), despite their insistence on respecting religious objects and their motivations to spread the Dharma, preserve religion and culture, serve Tibetans, and so forth.

In sum, the perceptions of the majority of merchants reveal that the selling of religious goods was not believed to be that serious, at least not enough to prevent them from engaging in the activity. Most merchants interviewed believed that selling was potentially negative *only* if certain conditions were not met—for example, if prices were too high (i.e., double) or if images and objects or customers were mistreated. In the end, many of these merchants believed they were helping rather than harming themselves and/or their religion and culture by making religious objects available to Tibetans and others. Thus, most of these merchants saw their activities as essentially beneficial and even virtuous. For those who acknowledged the presence of sin, the same criteria held sway. And while selling was ultimately characterized as a negative activity, several supported the idea that something could be done—on the back end—to purify at least some of the accumulated negative karma. For the first group, the rationalizations and strategies used were essential in transforming an action traditionally thought of as negative into a positive one. Yet, for the second group, this was ultimately deemed impossible, and one had to live with the negative karmic consequences, consequences that were nevertheless not considered to be too severe. Although one monk's suggestion that selling paintings and statues was a negative or harmful activity ultimately led one merchant to stop selling them, such instances were rare. As we will see shortly, this may be due, at least in part, to the fact that not all monks agreed on the ethical status of selling religious goods. While some did appear to hold traditional views, a significant number of monks interviewed emphasized the role of motivation as the critical determinant of whether or not this act contributed to the accumulation of negative karma. Thus, if one maintained a proper motivation, this allowed selling religious objects to become a legitimate livelihood.

MONASTIC PERSPECTIVES

Among twelve monks interviewed from various monasteries in the Amdo region, opinions on the selling of religious goods and the associated religious proscriptions varied but nevertheless fell into roughly two groups. The first group maintained that merchants' buying and then reselling religious goods was always more or less a negative act. Moreover, this group did not believe motivation played a significant role in affecting the karmic outcome from selling. Regarding painters, while all the monks maintained that painters had the right to recoup their expenses, some questioned the right of the painter to request a "work fee."[23] The second group, however, while conceding that selling religious goods was more generally believed to be nonvirtuous, maintained that a seller's motivation indeed played a very significant role in determining whether the act was negative. Specifically, for this second group, if a person (a merchant or a painter) had a positive motivation to benefit others—for example, to either propagate the Dharma or to make these items available for believers to be used religiously—then this intention (being virtuous) made selling religious goods a generally acceptable livelihood so long as the items were treated respectfully. For some, if such criteria were met, selling could even be a potentially virtuous and merit-producing activity. The key factor determining whether selling was appropriate was whether painters or merchants maintained a motivation that went beyond mere profit making.

Five of the twelve monks maintained that reselling religious goods, as merchants do, was always more or less negative; while motivation could play a role, it only reduced the negative karma that one inevitably incurred from selling. Illustrating this first position, one monk-administrator, himself a painter from Sengeshong Mango Gonpa, explained that while the painter has a right to make a living from his work and could legitimately sell paintings that had not been commissioned, because a vendor (i.e., a middleman) of religious goods is involved in such business to earn a profit, this automatically implicated him in negative activity:

> The seller [middleman] sells again to others; that means he doesn't have a good motivation. It's obvious; otherwise he won't sell it. He would buy it from others and then keep it. If he is going to sell, then that means he is going to make a profit. That is why it's not a good motivation. . . . In any case, they accumulate negative karma, no matter what the motivation. He cannot sell.[24]

According to this monk, there was no question as to the motivation of the middleman-seller. His intention, it was assumed, was not to direct the profits to the production of more religious goods for the benefit of others, but obviously to make a living on the proceeds. In this way, this opinion resembled the testimony of the lay painter near Sengeshong Mango who believed that if a middleman sells a religious object for a profit, then the act is negative. Therefore, for this respondent, profit and the use of that profit appeared to be the crux of the issue.

A similar view was also voiced by the eighty-year-old elder monk and former painter from Sengeshong Mango. He claimed that motivation played no role in determining whether the act of selling was ethical or not. Commenting on the difficulty of preventing the sale of religious objects from occurring in today's market environment, he stated:

> Actually, from a religious perspective, these religious goods cannot be sold, but in this modern time you can't go and tell someone that they cannot sell these things. According to the religion, if the buyers respect them and use them for the right purpose, he or she earns merit. But the person who sells is not really doing the right thing. The sellers are the ones who incur the negative karma, but in these modern times you can't say anything. In any case, doing business is always in contradiction to Buddhism. If you are doing business, there is always negativity.

While this particular monk situated the selling of religious goods within the overall negative activity of business—a perspective that, as we have seen, is expressed in classical works such as Patrül Rinpoche's *The Words of My Perfect Teacher*—the view of this monk was rather straightforward: selling religious goods is negative. Recall that the first monk mentioned above generally believed that painters could indeed legitimately earn a living by painting thangkas ahead of time for the external market. By contrast, this second, elder monk suggested that everything he claimed about merchants also extended to painters:

> In the past, there was a tradition that the sponsors came to the painters to paint them a thangka. If it is not asked for and the painters try to sell paintings, then this is considered to be disrespectful; they have bad reputations. Usually those who do this are really unskilled painters. Nowadays, I just heard that people try to sell as much as they can. I don't know; I just heard this . . . I think it would be better if they could follow the traditional way of making thangkas, but I think it won't work. Nowadays, if you make a really good thangka, you get quite a lot of money for it. According to religion, selling things is really not legitimate, but people won't listen.

It is perhaps understandable that monks who are close to the tradition of painting would maintain such views toward merchants, for merchants are, in one sense, competitors and make a living by buying and reselling the work of artists, usually for a lot more money than they acquired it for. But it is interesting to note what may be a generational divide with respect to the ideal activities of painters—the younger monk perceiving a painter's sale of works that have not been commissioned as perfectly acceptable, while the older monk deems it somewhat inappropriate at least from a traditional standpoint. This latter perspective likely stemmed from the fact that painters in the past did not typically determine the prices for thangkas but made their living by relying on the voluntary offerings of patrons.

The perspective that motivation played little if any role in determining the karmic outcome of selling religious goods was not the exclusive position of monks who were closely affiliated with painting or the arts. For example, I asked one middle-aged monk from Gur Gonpa in Chentsa—a monk who was not a painter—whether motivation played a role in deciding whether the selling of religious goods was ethical. He responded, "No, it doesn't have to do with motivation; one cannot sell them. But there could be more or less sin depending on one's motivation." Regarding whether the artist had the right to set the prices for his work, he explained that the artist has the right to recoup his costs and to accept what is given freely (as a *yön* or donation) but should not ask for more or put a price on the object. Moreover, when asked about those artists who today quote a customer a set price, thinking that they will not receive an offering (the common practice among many painters today being to add an additional 20 percent to material costs), he responded by declaring, "these artists are just greedy."

Two monks at Kumbum Monastery responded in a similar way. One of their responses was particularly notable. According to this monk, motivation was indeed important in determining the karmic outcome of a *commissioned* transaction between a painter and a sponsor. However, he did not appear to allow a role for motivation regarding middlemen or merchants of religious goods, whose actions, he implied, were always negative. According to this monk:

> Tsongkhapa said that religious goods cannot be sold merely for the sake of business or [to make] a living, but selling religious goods should have two sides or meanings. He didn't mention that they couldn't be sold at all. For instance, take a Tibetan family. [A Tibetan family may need a religious object] if somebody dies in the family or when all the religious preparations to prevent negative outcomes for the year, called *kurim* [*sku rim*, or *lo gcig sku rim*?] are made.[25] In this case, they might need a statue or image of some buddha. The members of the family cannot make these by themselves. Since they don't have the skill, they should ask some painters or statue makers. So then this family goes to the artists and asks if they can make such a statue for the family. In this case, both the sponsor and the painters usually have a good intention or motivation. So, in this case, intention plays a very important role for both sides—the sponsor and the painter. If the painter paints the thangka with the intention that this thangka will be painted well and will be in a place where people will make offerings, the more offerings and prayers people make, the greater the merit he will earn. There is no need to mention that the sponsors [will also earn merit]. The sponsor is going to have the thangka or statue and gain merit from making offerings, praying, etc. There is such a connection. The painter may ask for the expenses or material costs of the thangka and may ask for a service fee for his work, but I cannot say for sure that he can ask for it. Of course the painter must get his expenses covered, I think he is right to take his expenses. [Anyway,] if it is done in the proper way, both sides earn merit. It's tradition that they [painters] take a *bul* [*'bul*], or offering. [But] if you turn a painting or religious goods into a commercial enterprise, then this is where what the texts are saying is relevant

> and right. . . . We say religious goods cannot be turned into a commercial enterprise. There are some lamas, geshés, and scholars that say it's better to be a butcher than to sell religious goods. This doesn't mean they can't sell other things. This doesn't prevent other businesses. [But] for me, no matter how the social world changes, the fundamental doctrines governing religious goods should not be changed. There could be some changes, but the fundamental doctrines should remain the same.

For this monk it is clear that the ideal method of exchange was that of a traditional commission and that the middleman or merchant who sells religious goods is not engaging in an appropriate livelihood, despite his or her motivation. With regard to the painter, comparing his activities to that of an *amchö* (*a mchod*), a monk who is invited to a home to recite texts and who typically receives a donation in exchange for his services, this monk expressed doubt as to whether a painter charging a fixed amount or fee did not resemble a business transaction.[26]

Finally, perhaps most illustrative of this group, one older monk from Jakhyung Gonpa, who took a keen interest in this topic, vehemently denied any role for motivation in affecting the negative karmic outcome of selling and instead emphasized the magnitude of the negative karma accumulated from this activity. According to this monk:

> Selling religious goods is really sinful. You cannot really sell religious goods in any case. In one of his sermons, the Buddha says that the sins that you have accumulated from selling religious goods is like a pile of sand that you cannot count. It is worse than killing those enlightened *arhats*. You can measure the sin you accumulate from killing, but you cannot measure the sin that you accumulate from selling religious goods. It's totally negative; there is no doubt. If you ask a monastery monk or the common people, they wouldn't be able to answer you because most of them don't know the details. They really don't know what is beyond the sale [i.e., the consequences of selling]. This is just a matter of having knowledge of these religious goods. Nowadays, due to economic development and social changes, you see a lot of people selling these things, but it doesn't mean they can sell it [legitimately]. Most people just keep denying it, because mostly they don't understand what it is that they are selling.

This particular monk appears to be reiterating the doctrines found in the texts reviewed in chapter 2. Selling religious goods, he believed, was an act of "abandoning the Dharma" (*chos spangs kyis las*), a sin discussed under the rubric of "The Greatness of the Teaching" in the lamrim literature.[27] The particulars of the negative karma accumulated from abandoning the Dharma are found in *The King of Concentrations Sūtra* (*Samādhirājasūtra*). According to this sūtra, abandoning the Dharma is an extremely negative act, more so than destroying all the stūpas on Jambudvīpa, and more negative than killing as many arhats as there are sands in the Ganges River, an analogy that seems to explain why some monks compare the selling of religious goods to be the same or even worse than the actions of a butcher. In addition to how such an activity should be categorized in terms of doctrine, the issue of profiting from the sale of such objects was, for this monk, the crucial factor. One could sell an image (a statue or thangka) or a religious text for the amount that one spent in purchasing it, but setting a price beyond that (and using the profit for oneself) he considered an act of abandoning the Dharma. When asked if motivation was a factor in determining the karmic outcome from selling, he responded by denying that motivation played any significant role:

> No, this is not right. We quote the words of Jey Tsongkhapa. "If your intention is good, everything depends on a good motivation. Everything depends on mind." We can take a book as an example. If you have a book to sell—you wrote the book, you bought the papers—then you charge only for the expenses. You have this motivation that if I sell this book, the buyer will benefit from it, so you charge an amount that covers your expenses; that means that you don't lose any money. For instance, if you have an object that has a value of five *kuai* and if you charge more than that, it is not proper; if you charge more than that, it is negative. If you think you are going to make a profit out of it, then it is abandoning the Dharma. The same applies to all the other objects [such as statues, etc.]. If you charge more than the capital you spend on it, then it is negative. In any case, nobody can [legitimately] do business in these religious goods.

Clarifying his point with respect to motivation further, he remarked:

> If someone has an intention to make profits by creating these religious goods, it is [considered] abandoning the Dharma. If someone asks some-

> one else to give teachings and the person gives a teaching for the purpose of getting some money, then it is abandoning the Dharma. If the person has no intention to make money, and has a compassionate motivation, it is positive, even though he is given $10,000 [as an offering]. In this case, both people [the teacher and the student] have accumulated good karma or merit. . . . I have told some people [who sell religious objects about these things], but they say, "Times have changed, we have to live, we need money, and we have to survive." But I say that if you use these religious goods only for a living, then the Dharma loses its value. When you have finished a painting, for instance, and it cost you fifty yuan, and the patron [voluntarily] gives you one hundred, it does not become abandoning the Dharma. This is positive because you have painted it and fulfilled the patron's wishes. Both sides accumulate merit. You can take it [the extra money], and there is no problem. For instance, here, we cannot access the Dalai Lama's teachings. But let's say you bring one of his talks here, and you copy it for three yuan and sell it for three yuan; this is positive. [Alternatively], let's say you know that the Dalai Lama's speech is precious and people wish to hear it. You know there's a market [for this]. If you sell it for the purpose of making a profit, thinking, "I can publish it and make a profit," then this becomes abandoning the Dharma.

Thus according to this monk, any merchant or middleman who sells religious goods in the market cannot have a good motivation, for such activity already implies a profit motive. This monk's perceptions of the motivations of merchants appear to be undeniably accurate, as many merchants (as well as many painters) interviewed explained that they engaged in the business, at least in part, in order to make a living.

One of the few persons to have knowledge of the Kyergangpa narrative discussed in chapter 2, this monk also claimed that the profit gained from such business activities was polluting and should not be used for personal expenses:

> You should not use the money you earn from selling religious goods for daily use or for food. It is just contagious and can affect other people. [For example], you should not eat the seller's food. . . . Those people who are selling those goods are not really Buddhist. We call those people *chirolpas* (*phyi rol pa*), non-Buddhists. As a Buddhist you have to respect religious

goods. Why do we say they are not Buddhist? Because they violate *cham dro* (*skyabs 'gro*), the refuge precepts.

According to the Kyergangpa story, Kyergangpa, himself a highly realized person, fell immediately ill after unknowingly eating food paid for with the money gained from the sale of a *Prajñāpāramitā* text, thus illustrating both the irrelevance of motivation in determining the outcome of selling as well as the polluting nature of the action. As we will see, this idea was not present among those monks in the second group who placed a strong emphasis on the role of the seller's motivation.

As a whole, the above responses appeared more or less consistent with the textual position on selling representations of the Buddha's body, speech, and mind. This view reflects the general perception that the common street vendor of religious goods fully intends and, moreover, expects to make a profit from this business and to live on those profits. Because of this, according to the above perspectives, merchants undoubtedly accumulate negative karma.[28] As for painters, only one monk, himself a painter, expressed a confidence in the legitimacy of a painter's right to request a so-called work fee, a fee calculated by the painter for his time and skill that went beyond the cost of materials in making a thangka. All others either rejected this assertion or harbored doubts about it. Furthermore, for several monks within this group, the growing participation of Tibetans in selling religious goods stemmed less from any socioeconomic or sociopolitical issues or challenges facing Tibetans and more from a general lack of Buddhist education among vendors and, specifically, knowledge about the special status of religious goods. As the monk-educator from Kumbum explained,

> Laypeople usually don't have knowledge of these religious goods, especially the Buddha Jewel. We cannot blame them. It doesn't mean that these people don't believe in the Three Jewels. They just don't have knowledge of [the implications of] selling religious goods. We have a saying, "Even if someone kills his father, there is a reason."[29] Even a monk, if he is not really a knowledgeable person, also has difficulty in understanding this [i.e., the implications of selling]. Everybody hears that religious goods cannot be sold from the time they are small children. But this is just what they heard. They were not really told why these things should not be sold.

Despite the perceived lack of knowledge about the implications of selling religious goods, several informants maintained that regardless of the transformations to economic and social life, such religious ideas should not be altered, nor should they be adapted for modern times.[30]

In contrast to this first group of monks, the second group, consisting of seven monks, saw motivation as the pivotal or crucial factor in whether one accumulated negative karma from selling religious objects. According to this group, if either a painter or merchant maintained a proper motivation, one that went beyond a mere desire for profit, then the sale of religious goods was considered generally acceptable and, according to some, even potentially virtuous. Moreover, for this group, there appeared to be an acceptable amount of profit that the vendor could use for his or her livelihood.

Representing the views of this second group, for example, one older geshé from Kumbum explained that the difficulty in determining whether or not one was accumulating nonvirtue from selling religious objects had to do with the fact that one could not perceive another's motivation:

> One cannot judge the other; one cannot read the other's mind. We cannot say that every [act of selling] involves negative karma. That is why we cannot blame them or point the finger. Maybe he is selling these things and has a good motivation; who knows? Take a painter for example. [Let's say, for instance,] I am a painter and I want to paint something really nice. I want to sell this to people because they want it, and if they pray or use it for religious purposes, I also earn merit. And by the way, I need to make some money for living. But if I sell motivated only by making profits, this is negative karma; this is a sin. . . . So motivation is really important. We cannot really go to those vendors and say that they are creating negative karma. Everything depends on motivation or mind. That is why there is a statement from Tsongkhapa. Since we don't have the capacity to read others' minds, we cannot determine who is right and who is wrong, who is sinful or not, who is positive and who is negative. Some people create negative karma while thinking to do some positive things. In conclusion, if you do something with a good intention, it is positive; if you do it with a bad intention, it is negative. If you do something for the well-being of other beings, that is positive.

Here, this particular monk understood this issue by drawing upon a general understanding of motivation as it applies to karma (actions). For him, positive intention alone—the desire to benefit people beyond merely making a profit—determined whether an action is beneficial. Therefore, according to this view, one could legitimately determine prices and make a profit for oneself as long as that profit was not the only goal, of secondary importance, and a by-product of the action, which was, in the first instance, to benefit others.[31]

Still others made a similar point, further emphasizing the crucial role of motivation while adding that charging a reasonable price also played a significant role in the karmic outcome. For example, according to one monk from Kumbum,

> If the motivation is good, then there is no sin. [As stated by Tsongkhapa], if your motivation is good, the way you take and the place where you end up is also good; if your motivation is bad, the path you are taking is also bad. Everything is based on motivation. If you sell, if you are the vendor and have a good motivation and the buyer has a good motivation, it is positive. If you sell for a high price, then this isn't a good motivation.

Like the views of the first member of this group, not only is motivation the crucial determinant in whether selling religious goods is a negative or positive act, the idea that one can earn a reasonable living (by not charging high prices) is clearly implied.

Other monks held similar views. According to a lama from Maksar Gonpa, the proscriptions against selling religious goods were designed to guard against rampant commercialism, not to suggest that they could *never* be sold. Moreover, whether or not such an activity was to be considered negative depended upon how one treated religious objects and upon one's intention:

> From a long time ago religious goods have been sold and they [those who did so] had good motivations; so you can't criticize them. [The proscriptions came about] because the writers of these texts thought that people would make it commercial and cheat as much as they could. It doesn't matter whether something is sold or not, what is important is compassion and motivation. . . . [The cost] depends on the materials used—if it is made of gold, silver, etc. Upon this [basis] one should make a reasonable profit. [Whether or not selling is negative] depends on motivation. If one has a good motivation with a bad action, then it's negative. [For example], if today a merchant charges double, then his motivation is bad. . . . If one thinks it is just merchandise, it's negative. But if one thinks those [objects] are going to benefit the customers, it's positive for both. It doesn't matter

whether the seller is Chinese or Tibetan; if he considers them [religious objects] as goods, then he accumulates negative karma. If the sellers are Chinese, they don't have knowledge of what they are selling and how to treat them. Booksellers step on books, and they treat them as goods. This is negative.

Once again, for this particular lama, more important than the profit earned and the use of that profit was the intention behind the sale and the manner in which one treated religious goods. Like several of the merchants, he contrasted the appropriate means of selling with the activities of (careless) Chinese vendors, suggesting that Tibetans, being Buddhists, know how to treat religious objects and sell them appropriately. As long as one maintained an attitude that went beyond making profits and did not treat religious objects as mere things to be bought and sold (as commodities), then selling religious goods was acceptable and, moreover, an appropriate way to make a living.

As a final example illustrating the views of this group, another geshé, also from Kumbum, appeared to differentiate between what was acceptable for monks and what was acceptable for laypeople. According to this monk, whereas the sale of religious goods by monks was always inappropriate, for laypersons, such activity could be acceptable if they maintained a proper motivation—and in particular, if they had a desire to promote the Dharma and to help those in need:

We talked about the Buddha, Dharma, and Saṅgha. Representing the Buddha, there are statues and thangkas; for the Dharma, there are books; and for the Saṅgha, there are the monks' robes, etc. As a monk, one cannot sell these things in order to make a profit. There are two different kinds of sellers: one are the monks who sell, the other is the layman who is Buddhist, but not a monk, who sells for a living, for making a profit. It is wrong, not allowed [for these two groups to sell]. That's not the appropriate way. Then there is another group, which is a group of people who don't believe in Buddhism but are businessmen. We believe, from the Buddhist point of view, that if these sellers are selling only to make a profit, they are also committing negative karma. In brief, anyone who sells these religious goods for the purposes of making profits is abandoning the Three Jewels. However, I still have something more to say. It also depends on motivation as well. For example, in our monastery we have a printing house, and we have monks

> who make paintings and statues. If a monk makes a statue and people see it, they can see what a Buddha looks like. They [the monks] have the ambition to spread Buddhism. They think that this is another way to earn good merit. The same applies to books and [monks'] clothes as well. If we publish books, then people can read and study, and it is the same for clothes. So it is the same with the offering material; they do this [sell these] in order to let people know more about Buddhism. If you have a good motivation, making profit is not very negative, it doesn't contradict [the teachings] very much. [This is an exception] because you want to help spread Buddhism. This is okay, but it's not completely okay. In any case, we are not allowed to sell these things in the monastery. [The case of selling with the right motivation] is an exception because people who are not monks, if they sell with the proper aim, have to of course cover their expenses and also make some profit. If they have the idea to take some profit and use this for the right purpose, then in this case it's okay. If they recycle the money [the profit] to again produce [these goods] for the right purpose [to spread the Dharma?], then it's okay.

In contrast to the monk from Jakhyung Gonpa, whose explanation hinged on the profits earned and the personal use of the profits, for this monk, rules that governed the monastic community did not necessarily apply to the lay community, as laypeople could and should not be held to the same standard. Although he apparently begins by claiming that no one should sell religious goods, he ends by claiming that laypersons could legitimately sell such items with the motivation to spread the Dharma. Moreover, far from being an example of abandoning the Dharma, making a reasonable profit was deemed acceptable provided that one took some of those profits and reinvested them for the purpose of propagating the Dharma.[32]

In general, this second group, as we can observe, tended to explain this issue by appealing to motivation. That is, in addition to the proper treatment of religious goods, intention alone, which included a desire to benefit people beyond merely making a profit, had the power to make this action acceptable or beneficial. The more subtle aspects involved in the topic of karma and motivation—for example, the idea that acts committed with respect to the Three Jewels carried greater karmic weight (referred to as the "magnification of karma" in the *Lamrim Chenmo*)—were not considered in this equation.[33] Nor was the issue of profit or its personal use—a notion that, as we have seen, continues to play a central role in popular religious works and modern scholarship—ever considered remotely problematic, as either spiritually polluting or a form of metaphysical contagion. According to this view, one can legitimately make a profit for oneself as long as that profit is limited or reasonable and not the only concern of the seller.[34]

In addition, it should also be noted that for at least one younger monk from Kumbum, motivation seemed irrelevant. He claimed that the textual proscriptions against selling religious goods may no longer be applicable to modern times. When asked whether he thought such statements still apply to today's marketplace, he responded by explaining that the religious proscriptions in this case were incompatible with the current economic context:

> Maybe [these statements were made] according to the time the authors lived. These are very great scholars [who made these statements], but they are not Buddha. So if we take that statement and put it into our context, it cannot be applied. . . . Most of my friends, more than half, have my ideas. The elders would never agree with this—they would follow what the scriptures say. But among my peers I think there will be some people who will have ideas similar to mine. Times are changing, and we have to change and adapt. But the best way [to sell] is to charge the normal price for a working day, how much gold is used [in the production of an image], etc. The reason why there should be criteria is because these are religious goods. You shouldn't make too much money from them.

Further elaborating his particular views, this monk argued that selling religious goods carried certain financial benefits for the sellers:

> If we followed what the texts say, then sellers will have difficulties in making a livelihood. It's possible that their families will have difficulties. [But] I think that it can improve their lives. The Buddha taught that we are supposed to help people. I think the Buddha would agree with selling these things for a living [and not condemn it]. I can't say that Tsongkhapa and Pabongka are wrong, but their statements on this don't apply today.

Such a view not only reflects the government's call for religious institutions to adapt to changes in society, it also indicates what may be a growing acceptance of the idea that selling religious goods is a legitimate livelihood if it can be carried out in particular ways and according to the moral or religious guidelines with respect to treatment, pricing, motivation, etc. We might call this last perspective *accommodationist*. It is a perspective that, while careful not to completely dismiss the classical textual tradition, acknowledges that current conditions are different from what they were in the past and that ethical norms have to accommodate the changing world around us.

CONCLUSION

Despite the obvious business activities of painters and merchants, the classical religious proscriptions against the sale of religious goods continue to play an important role for many Tibetans in the current marketplace. Rather than illustrating a wholesale acceptance of capitalist principles intent solely on profit, the perspectives and strategies outlined above instead reflect a process of negotiation between the preexisting religious and ethical framework rooted in classical religious texts, on the one hand, and the mechanics and expectations of free market processes, on the other. The proper treatment of religious goods as special objects—that these objects are not to be treated as merchandise but with respect—continued to show up in Tibetans' descriptions of their business dealings. Likewise, practices such as restricted pricing—for example, that one should not charge double but could earn a reasonable amount—was also informed by the religious sentiment that what was being sold was unlike other mundane goods. In addition, several painters reported that they attempted to educate customers not to use business terminology such as "buy" or "sell" (*nyos* or *tshong*) and instead to rely on the more culturally appropriate terminology of *lu*. By utilizing various strategies or values drawn from their own religious tradition, the vast majority of Tibetans attempted to set themselves apart from those who engaged in unfettered or unrestricted acquisitive behavior (those who charged as much as they could get from a potential customer) in an effort to avoid treating religious goods as mere commodities, an act that they unanimously viewed as commensurate with blatant commercialism.

At the same time, the preceding discussion also reveals that the selling of religious goods in the Amdo region remains fairly contested. Not all artists agreed on the legitimacy of the practice of making such objects before they are commissioned. Some painters were critical of merchants who made their livelihoods not through creating religious art but through the buying and reselling of thangkas. And monks did not entirely agree on whether painters had a right to claim a work fee or on whether the issue of a seller's motivation mattered in the final analysis. Several monks were nostalgic for the time when such commercial activities did not occur, with some going so far as to warn merchants of the harm involved in their activities and to prescribe countermeasures to limit what they believed were the inevitable negative karmic repercussions of their actions. Even among merchants themselves, while some perceived that times had changed, others believed that selling religious goods remained a somewhat inappropriate livelihood, as evidenced by vendors of ritual objects who consciously avoided selling thangkas or statues, those who were apprehensive about selling them and who planned to seek other employment, and those who performed countermeasures as a remedy against the negative karma they believed they were accumulating from their business activities.

As a whole, however, there appears to be a growing acceptance of the sale of religious objects as a legitimate livelihood among Tibetans. The majority of merchants perceive the selling of religious goods as religiously unproblematic. Monastic interventions are reportedly rare, with many merchants explaining that they have received only encouragement from the community. And a significant number of monks perceive the ethical status of selling such objects as dependent upon one's motivation. The question remains then as to how to interpret or make sense of Tibetans' open sale of religious goods in contemporary Amdo. More specifically, what have been the consequences of the movement of religious objects from their historical status as items that were more or less market-inalienable, set apart, protected, or "enclaved" from commodification, to that which is now saleable?[35] In the remaining chapter we attempt to answer this question by considering some of the various effects of the commodification of religious objects on Tibetan religion and society.

7 | The Impact of Selling Buddhist Objects in Tibet

The Economic, Cultural, and Shifting Moral Dimensions of Commodification

Today, in Amdo, the number of Tibetans who sell ready-made religious objects for their personal livelihoods continues to rise, and articles touting the financial success stories of thangka painters continue to appear in China's mainstream media. The Rebkong cultural region in particular, due to the renown of its artistic heritage, is now a regular stop on the tourist route for visitors to Qinghai, many of whom purchase thangkas as souvenirs. Government-sponsored exhibitions continue to attract painters seeking to build their reputations as well as buyers who are drawn not only by the beauty of thangkas but also by the well-advertised potential value of the art form as an investment. These developments would seem to clearly indicate that Tibetans' commodification of their religious objects has had important economic and cultural ramifications. Indeed, the sale of religious goods has provided Tibetans with a valuable financial resource in an atmosphere of limited opportunity, it has contributed to the continuity and/or preservation of Tibetan culture generally and Tibetan arts in particular, and it has served to strengthen the Tibetan community, acting as a force which has brought Tibetans together in pursuit of their own interests. From this vantage point, we might reasonably conclude that Tibetans' sale of religious objects carries with it particular advantages, empowering Tibetans both individually and collectively. However, as I hope to demonstrate in this final chapter, attending exclusively to these effects yields only a partial picture of the impact of the commodification of religious goods on Tibetan society. For equally as significant, Tibetans' sale of religious objects is also simultaneously transforming the traditional and long-held religious practices, meanings, and values associated with religious objects and their exchange, as well as traditional conceptions of Tibetan Buddhist identity. In the Tibetan case, while we must indeed acknowledge the fact that the sale of religious objects brings with it important practical outcomes that serve to sustain Tibetan culture, we must nevertheless also recognize that such commercial practices have come at a cost. For what is being transformed is not only a way of exchanging religious objects. More broadly, what is being transformed is a way of relating to such objects and thus a way of seeing and experiencing the world. Such transformations should be counted among the effects of the commodification of religious objects in Tibet, as they represent profound historical shifts in thinking and practice.

THE COMMODIFICATION OF RELIGIOUS GOODS: CREATING OPPORTUNITY, PRESERVING CULTURE, AND REINFORCING COMMUNITY

There is little doubt that the sale of Buddhist objects is contributing to a number of significant outcomes for Tibetans. While the argument that the commodification of religious goods has contributed to their democratization is challenged by the fact that common families and even nomads are reported to have owned statues and thangkas before the Cultural Revolution, we must acknowledge that, in fact, the sale of religious objects has indeed given many Tibetans a form of livelihood that they did not previously have.[1] This has been an especially valuable new means of employment in a context where Amdo Tibetans remain both educationally and economically marginalized. It has also served as a welcome alternative and complement to the much more labor-intensive work of farming and herding.

The commercialization of thangkas and the reported steady climb in the prices of paintings over the last decade has enabled many painters to raise their standard of living considerably. Much of this business has, of course, been the result of the central government's introduction and promotion of ethnic tourism, its promotion of thangka painting in particular, as well as a result of the new domestic taste for thangkas among wealthier Han Chinese, a taste which has been driven in part by the exoticization of Tibetan identity in tourism literature and discourse. This has provided lay and monastic painters with a new source of patronage in an environment where much of the restoration work that began in the 1980s is now complete (Reynolds 2011, 94). The high prices that some thangkas now fetch, fueled largely by the recent Han demand, have indeed enriched many painters in the region. Some statistics suggest that the revenue from Rebkong art in 2013, for example, exceeded 300 million yuan (US $49 million), with annual salaries for each craftsman in Rebkong exceeding twenty thousand yuan (US $3,300; Hongxiang 2013).[2] Other reports focusing on individual artists' success stories tell of painters who have earned up to ten times this amount or more annually, sometimes with the earnings coming as a result of the sale of just one painting (Yuanfeng, Shuangqi, and Ying 2009).[3] By comparison, according to China Economic Net, Tibetan farmers and herders earned an average of 6,578 yuan, or US $1,071, in 2013, making painting a much more lucrative and attractive employment option (Xinhua News Agency 2014). According to Mark Stevenson, the success of the painting market has meant that "the painters of Rebkong are wealthy compared to other groups in Tibetan society" (quoted in Wong 2009, para. 17). While of course not every artist in Rebkong is wealthy, such observations were indeed evident to me during my research, as some painters, including some monk-painters, appeared to be relatively well-off materially.[4]

For the smaller but growing number of Tibetans who choose to participate in selling religious objects as vendors or middlemen, the commercialization of religious goods has likewise been financially rewarding. I encountered only a few merchants who actually appeared to be (or had the reputation of being) wealthy. Nonetheless, selling religious objects has allowed Tibetans in the region, many of whom have little or no secular education, to achieve a degree of economic independence and self-sufficiency and has given Tibetans who may have never had prior commercial experience the opportunity to gain valuable transferable business skills, selling objects that they personally use and intimately know.

As an economic resource, the sale of religious objects has not only benefited individual painters and merchants financially but also appears to be contributing to improvements in the livelihoods and standard of living of Tibetans in the region more broadly. For example, the commercialization of the arts is frequently a rallying point to raise funds for various charitable causes, including orphanages and schools. These efforts are illustrated by the young woman in the Xining Tibetan market who sold religious objects to raise money for her own orphanage. These same efforts are further exemplified by some nongovernmental organizations (NGOs), such as the Colorado-based Tibetan Village Project, which trains orphans in various Tibetan handicrafts (including thangka painting) with the goal of providing them with a sustainable source of livelihood (Wangdu 2012). Similar projects have reportedly also been initiated for nomads in Qinghai, who have been relocated to permanent settlements but who have no real marketable skills in their new, less rural environment (Potala Society n.d.). Tibetan painters also frequently utilize their profits to train new generations of painters, assisting others in gaining a new source of income while ensuring the continuation of the tradition. I encountered several reports of painters utilizing their earnings in this way, with some investing substantial sums in the opening of painting schools and in the training and support of young students from poor backgrounds.[5] It also bears repeating that the central government itself is involved in similar activities and has reportedly assisted in the building of thangka training centers and in supporting thangka courses at the university level. There are even cases of Chinese patrons who, wishing to aid Tibetans, have built new painting schools or have assisted in finding new markets for the purpose of helping Tibetans economically.[6] The commercialization of thangka painting has also provided new opportunities for women to develop painting skills, painting being an occupation from which they had been more or less excluded in the past. According to Reynolds (2011, 94), although women painters remain predominantly tied to family businesses, shifting attitudes may open up the possibility for them to become established painters in their own right. While the commodification of religious objects has not created a path toward political freedom or autonomy for Tibetans, and while non-Tibetans, being the main manufacturers and merchants of Tibetan religious objects (as well as the main owners of tourism-related businesses in locations such as Rebkong) are likely the primary beneficiaries of such activity, the commercialization of religious objects and, in particular, thangka painting, is contributing to an overall rise in the quality of life of Tibetans in the region and has become a vital part of the Tibetan economy.

While many Tibetans recognize that they cannot compete economically on equal terms with Chinese and other non-Tibetan manufacturers of religious goods, who, many claimed, own the lion's share of the market, the sale of religious objects among Tibetans has become an important source for cultural reproduction and preservation. Besides the fact that the development of the market for Tibetan religious objects has indeed served to assure the continued production, dissemination, and thus preservation of artistic traditions (although Tibetans would surely debate about the quality of the artistic productions being preserved), such businesses have allowed Tibetans to maintain some semblance of control over the religious and cultural meanings associated with these goods and to conduct transactions on their own ethical terms. Many Tibetans seemed to believe that the consequences of *not* participating in the sale of such goods were far worse than if they did participate, as this would result in a host of problems: higher prices for Tibetan consumers, the misrepresentation and mistreatment of religious goods, as well as an overall decline in their quality and in the correct knowledge about them. The preservation of a distinctly *Tibetan* discourse about the *religious* values and meanings of Buddhist objects has taken on an even greater importance in an environment where state tourism discourse tends to champion their ethnic, aesthetic, and especially their economic value while downplaying their Buddhist evaluations. The opportunity that is created by the commodification of religious objects to disseminate their religious and cultural meanings is reminiscent of Charlene Makley's observations with respect to how tourism at Labrang provided a space for women to exercise traditional narratives about gendered spatial practices (1994). Among Tibetan painters and vendors, the retail transaction, similarly, provides a space to make tourist searches for mere souvenirs or ethnic art into valuable moments of cultural and religious expression, reproduction, and preservation. In addition, such participation, especially given the rise in foreign interest in Tibetan religious art and its consumption by tourists, has also served to reinforce the idea that such objects indeed belong to Tibetans and are important items unique to *Tibetan* religion and culture. That is, the commodification of Tibetan religious objects has contributed to their development as cultural or ethnic markers, signifying their association with Tibetan identity. As some of my informants aptly pointed out (even those who believed selling thangkas and statues for profit was wrong), the marketing of religious goods does provide a vehicle through which more people can be exposed to Tibet and creates a means through which to advertise, promote, and potentially teach others about Tibet's unique religious culture.[7]

Tibetans' participation in the business of religious objects has also, I would argue, served to reinforce a sense of Tibetan social cohesion and community. It has provided a space for Tibetan consumers to acquire religious objects from members of their own ethnic group, without having to deal with or be dependent upon non-Tibetan merchants, many of whom reportedly do not know much about the objects they are selling and have a reputation for unsavory business practices. Likewise, for merchants and painters, participation in the market has not only given them a source of livelihood but also a sense of cultural pride as a community, which, as was often stated, exists in part to serve the religious and cultural needs of Tibetans. The popularity that thangkas enjoy among Chinese tourists in particular has also likely contributed to an increased sense of cultural worth and legitimacy among Tibetans in a context where their very religious and cultural traditions have long been viewed as backward.[8] Furthermore, Tibetan participation in this market has also contributed to the creation of a Tibetan business community, which has, especially in the Xining market, led to solidarity against government decisions that they opposed. The local government's purported plans to build a new plaza where the Tibetan market is located, for example, and for the market's ultimate dispersal united Tibetan merchants as an ethnic business community to act together to confront and deal with the government proposal as a collective. Elizabeth Reynolds's work on the commercialization of Tibetan thangkas in Rebkong also illustrates that the market for thangkas itself—from production, to marketing and promotion, to distribution—is built upon a network of Tibetan social relationships, bringing together a number of individual painters, their families, and merchants, something which has undoubtedly fostered a high degree of social cooperation and unity. As such, the sale of religious objects has served to reinforce and strengthen the Tibetan community vis-à-vis other ethnicities, assisting Tibetans in reaffirming their cultural distinctiveness against a dominant Han ethnic group and against other ethnic groups in a multiethnic region.

Taken together, it is clear that we can identify a number of distinct and very important outcomes from the commodification of Tibetan religious objects that serve to reaffirm and strengthen Tibetan culture. Indeed, a number of authors, likewise, although writing in other disciplines and in various cultural contexts, have reached similar conclusions about the societal effects of commodification. Some have highlighted the fact that commodification promotes prosperity, alleviates social ills, and creates community (Posner 2005). Others have argued that it can lead to the social empowerment of minorities by addressing social and economic inequality (Austin 2005). Still others have maintained that such processes can be liberating, as it signals the public acceptance and legitimacy of subordinated identities (Williams and Zelizer 2005) or, in the context of tourism, that the commodification of cultural products can serve as an economic resource to communities with few options (Kolås 2008) and/or serve as an instrument in constructing, reaffirming, or projecting an identity or the plight of a community to the outside world (Cohen 1988; Klieger 1990). As the above discussion has shown, all of these various conclusions about the effects of commodification certainly apply to some degree to Tibetans' sale of religious objects in Amdo. However, the Tibetan case is unique in that the religious objects that are now commodified in the marketplace have been historically proscribed from being sold by religious injunctions, a view that reaches far beyond Amdo. Moreover, Tibetan Buddhist objects continue to function as part of a meaningful, living, Buddhist moral universe, one which remains connected to notions of sin and merit, and one in which many Tibetans, including many prominent Tibetan teachers, continue to view the sale of such objects as karmically detrimental. I argue, therefore, that beyond the above conclusions, the commodification of religious objects among Tibetans is also contributing to significant transformations in the religious traditions that surround these objects. Such transformations tend to be obscured not only by a lack of knowledge about the traditional exchange practices and prohibitions associated with religious goods in Tibet but also by the sense of normalcy with which the selling of religious goods now occurs in today's marketplace. Specifically, the sale of religious goods has also ushered in changes in the ethical and moral framework associated with their production and exchange, as well as transformations in the norms that have traditionally governed their sale. Moreover, the commodification of religious objects, while in many ways serving to reaffirm and/or signify Tibetan identity, may also be seen as simultaneously contributing to a transformation in traditional notions of Tibetan *Buddhist* identity, such that the sale of religious goods is, for many today, no longer seen as antithetical to being Buddhist. Thus, the commodification of Tibetan Buddhist objects is contributing to significant changes to the traditional or normative Tibetan Buddhist worldview, a worldview that is attached to these objects.

FROM THE MORALITY OF COMMISSIONING TO THE MORALITY OF COMMODIFICATION

Despite their increasing commodification over the past two decades, the religious objects that are produced for the Amdo market have maintained a remarkable degree of integrity. Looking at thangkas in particular, the thangkas produced in the Amdo region today, for example, are still relatively iconographically correct.[9] They have not been subject, in any sustained manner, to the incorporation of modern content, either as a result of individual innovation or as a result of state encouragement.[10] Thangka painting in Amdo has not been substantially threatened by machine mass-production, as there is a thriving market for those that are hand-painted.[11] And while the commodification of thangkas has contributed to what many Tibetans perceive to be a general decline in their overall quality (when compared to those produced in the past) and to the creation of new layers of meaning on top of their traditional signification as sacred objects—for example, as investments, souvenirs, ethnic art products, or more generally as decorative objects—these factors have not led to a significant transformation in the meaning of thangkas for Tibetans, who continue to view them and to use them as functional religious objects.[12] However, the changes in the modes of production and exchange of religious objects from a process based chiefly on commission and remuneration by voluntary offering to their commodification has come at a price: a significant departure from the traditional religious practices, observances, and understandings surrounding these very activities.

Perhaps most obviously, with the sale of premade thangkas at set prices, the traditional religious protocols governing their initial creation are disregarded. For example, the common notion that the painting of a thangka is a collaborative process is going by the wayside. Traditionally, thangkas were created for specific individuals or monasteries according to their particular needs, specifications, predicaments, tastes, and preferences in the number and arrangement of deities and the amount of gold to be used—the latter of which was thought of as an offering in and of itself (Jackson and Jackson 1984, 102). This is disappearing, as these details are predetermined by the artist or, in some cases, by the middleman who places orders and buys thangkas for resale. In the absence of specific patrons, the astrological calculations that typically determine the auspicious dates of production and completion are no longer observed, given that the consumer is not a part of the initial commissioned transaction. The commodification of a thangka also does away with the important religious protocols and ceremonial observances normally associated with traditional commissioned exchanges. On the one hand, the character or comportment of the artist and patron during the process of painting—factors which are said to affect the outcome of a painting and which are considered "conducive to the success of the work"

(Dagyab 1977, 1:27)—have been abandoned. On the other hand, the traditional exchange protocols (briefly outlined in chapter 3) are no longer observed in a market transaction. The patron-turned-consumer often does not even know the artist, only the middleman or salesperson who mediates the sale of the thangka. And the artist fulfills orders for a businessman or company with the knowledge that his (or her) thangkas will likely be resold at a higher price. Furthermore, the dedication of merit after the completion of the thangka, which normally involves the both the patron and the artist, is jettisoned. Thangkas themselves, now displayed in a store or gallery, sit unconsecrated, awaiting purchase, a context that was once believed to have the potentially dangerous consequences of causing them to be inhabited by malevolent spirits. Thus, the painting, even if executed according to the traditional proportions and measurements outlined in religious texts, while still potentially meaningful and significant as an object of worship, loses key components of its initial interpersonal, religious, and cosmological significance. With the commodification of thangkas, the production and exchange process formerly associated with commissioned works ceases, at least from the side of the patron-turned-consumer, to be "an act of religious worship in itself" (Dagyab 1977, 1:28). Moreover, the "close personal link" that is said to develop between the finished object and the patron (and between the patron and the artist) is lost (28).

The testimonies of some Tibetans regarding the importance of the commission type of exchange suggest that there are further consequences to the commodification of religious objects, specifically to the religious objects themselves. For example, one painter who worked exclusively on a commission basis in Labrang explained that the quality of the patron-artist relationship also has a direct bearing on whether or not a thangka can in fact be consecrated:

> The consecration is done after the thangka is finished. When you have finished with a mural, for example, then it is done at the monastery. When you are finished with a thangka for a sponsor, then the sponsor takes it home and does it there. It depends on convenience. If you can't find anyone to consecrate it at home, you just bring it to a lama to have it consecrated. In fact, according to tradition, it is consecrated from the very beginning when the painter starts. This is because painters paint with compassion, and the sponsor treats the painter as his utmost teacher. So the

> spiritual connection between the painter and the sponsor is a kind of consecration. The thangka has already absorbed this consecration. Also, the painter should always be pleased. If he gets annoyed or bored, the thangka itself also gets bored or annoyed. There is a statement in Buddha's teaching that says that the painter and the sponsor should have mutual faith and trust in each other, otherwise there is no consecration. The consecration comes automatically to the thangka by this mutual trust. Otherwise, even if someone does the consecration for the thangka, it rarely receives it. So it is based on the mutual trust between the painter and the sponsor.

My interpreter during this particular interview, a restaurant owner and tour guide, referred to this as a "natural consecration." John Clarke's research on metalwork and statue making mentions a similar notion. There, the idea was that a patron strove diligently to please the artist so that "the deity would more fully occupy the image" (Clarke 2002, 120).[13] The painter I interviewed was not the only person to emphasize the importance of the patron-artist relationship to the outcome of the actual work. One geshé from Kumbum explained that because today many painters (as well as customers) proceed without proper tantric initiations and other religious protocols, paintings are less powerful than they were in the past:

> In the past there were not many religious goods for sale. Especially the painters didn't paint the [tantric] deities. If they were asked to, or if they had to, they would do so. But there would be a kind of ceremony—rituals or meditations—before painting. In the past, you didn't paint *yidams* [tutelary deities] very often. When you were going to paint a *yidam*—for example, Yamāntaka—you went on a retreat. If you could not go on retreat, then there was a mantra that you were to recite. From the beginning, during, and after it was finished, it should not be open for people to view. The other images of the Buddha, for example, you can paint any time. It's fine to paint Buddhas and make Buddha statues and show them. It is not like the case of deities. It is not secret. In the past, painters used to ask if they could paint the Buddha's image. In the tantra, if the sponsor wanted to have a specific [tantric] thangka made, he had to have the transmission of the particular deity depicted in the thangka. The painter and the sponsor both had to be initiated. It is not at all like that nowadays. Today, they paint while drinking and smoking. Usually, if it is done in the proper way

> like it was in the past, you can get nectar from some thangkas; they self-speak, and they cannot be burned. For example, at Kumbum, about one hundred years ago, when there was a fire, many thangkas were not burned because of the blessings they received from the sponsors and painters [who painted them in the proper way, on retreat]. If you do it as people do it now, there is no way these things can happen.

According to this geshé, the commodification of thangkas also had implications for the quality and thus the power or potency of the thangkas themselves:

> The more that street thangka painters sell, the more quality is lost. For example, it's like medicine. In the past, there were fewer kinds and they were very effective. Nowadays, you take this medicine and that medicine and none are very effective. They don't put the adequate dosage today. In the past, they put what was needed. Now they only put a small amount. From the perspective of the power of the thangka, whether or not it has great power or less power depends, like medicine, on the components. Just as medicine in the past was made of fewer and more potent elements, today, because it is made of various ingredients and with less of the potent ones, it is weaker; it is the same for thangkas today. Nowadays, maybe they put as many precious things in a truck full of medicine, but only a match-tip amount of each ingredient. The same thing is true for thangka paintings. Nowadays, painters just paint very fast and make low-quality thangkas and sell them. This is very sad.

Thus, for this informant, not only did the patron-artist relationship and their ritual or spiritual preparation impact the outcome of the artistic product, there was also a direct parallel between the current commodification of thangkas and the loss of quality and spiritual power or blessings that they contained.[14] While I did not follow up further with this particular informant regarding the meaning of his statements, such a position also seems to indicate that the spiritual blessings gained or received from such weakened thangkas are less than those that are made thoroughly and when the patron and artist observe certain religious protocols and maintain appropriate relations. It is also possible that, for this geshé, such thangkas, due to their perceived inferior craftsmanship, are less effective because they inspire little faith.

Other perspectives suggest that there are further implications for the accumulation of merit with the commodification of religious objects. Although it could well be argued that any time a Buddhist gives up something for the sake of religion, even if that is money to pay a set fee, one may earn merit, some sources suggest that more merit may potentially be earned in a commission type of exchange where the patron has greater control over the work being done. Jackson and Jackson (1984) note, for example, that the offering of additional gold for a thangka or the request that the painter depict more deities within a painting were ways in which patrons could increase the merit earned from commissioning a thangka (27 and 102). Some Tibetan scholars also support the position that commissioning an artist may yield potentially more merit. For example, Khenpo Ngawang Pelzang (1879–1941) has stated in a note to *A Guide to "The Words of My Perfect Teacher"* that "books, statues, and paintings increase merit for both artisan and buyer when created and purchased (or commissioned) for the purposes for which they are intended" (Pelzang 2004, 305n138). Echoing this view, the administrator-monk from Sengeshong Mango explained that a commissioned transaction was better not only in terms of the final result—the completed sacred object—but was also better for the artist and patron: "Usually it [the painting] is more blessed because both sponsors and painters agree on it. If it is done on commission, there is more merit and it is more positive for both." One painter in Labrang who worked on a commission basis expressed a similar perspective, claiming that a thangka made for one's own purposes was far better than buying a religious object ready-made. He explained:

> One day a monk came and asked me a question. He was going to buy a thangka or statue for a funeral [i.e., on behalf of the person who died], and he asked me, "Which one would be the best?" So I said, "From my personal point of view, I would make it [a painting] on commission. But since I am a painter, you may not trust me because you might think I am making a business out of this." So I told him that the best thing to do was to go to a lama or geshé and ask, and then decide. I also told him that a painting was better than a statue because it is for yourself, because it is really made for your own purposes. [As a painter] you are also making something that doesn't exist, so you are creating something new for that particular person. When I make a painting, I think that it is made for that particular person. I have to take a cloth and make it from scratch. The intention is different.

> You see, if you buy a statue in a shop, it is not made for you. So between these two [options] there is such a big difference. The intention makes such a big difference. Then the monk went to ask Gendun Gyatso, and he also told him the same thing I did. So I painted a thangka for him. In terms of merit, you can also earn merit from the prices and materials. For instance, there are some statues made from silver. If you commission this, you earn the merit of a silver statue. The same thing exists for gold. Gold costs more and you earn more merit. These are called "price merits," merits earned from the prices you pay.[15]

While it could certainly be argued that this painter's explanation was an attempt to secure himself a commission, for him, a commission type of exchange was preferable or better because working according to a particular patron's needs or specifications aided in a painter's motivation to paint well and to fulfill the customer's wishes (a motivation that, he implied, is not necessarily present when painting for the external market). From the patron's side, having a painting made specifically for one's own purposes was better and fostered the cultivation of a different (more concerned or engaged?) motivation. The result of these motivations in a commissioned transaction, he seemed to imply, also led to the accumulation of greater merit.[16] Such a perspective supports the idea noted by Jackson and Jackson (1984, 102) that the merit earned through thangka painting is ultimately contingent upon the motivation or intention of those involved in a given project. While, according to these informants, the commission type of transaction had religious or spiritual ramifications for the artistic object and for those involved in its creation, it should also be noted that, if considered from the perspective of Marx's theory on the alienation of labor, the traditional Tibetan practice of commissioning artwork, which emphasizes the relationship between the patron and the artist, does not alienate the worker (i.e., the artist). This lies in stark contrast to the commodification of religious objects, where today's tourist typically never meets or knows about the direct producer but deals only with a string of middlemen who exploit the labor of the producer and jack up the prices.

It was also suggested by some of my informants that an artist earned *no* merit in transactions in which he or she determined the prices. Here we may recall the remarks of the monk from Gur Gonpa who explained that artists have the right to recoup material expenses but, above this, should accept only what is freely given, or of the teacher-monk from Kumbum who compared the artist to the *amchö* (the reciter of scriptures), who was expected to take what was voluntarily offered by the patron lest the transaction be perceived as a business matter. In addition, the eighty-year-old ex-painter from Sengeshong Mango suggested that the commodification of thangkas, at least with regard to past practices, was considered antithetical to the accumulation of merit, stating, "In the past, making a thangka was believed to be a means to accumulate lots of merit. That's why painters didn't discuss the price. Nowadays, everything has turned into a business." Some modern Tibetan Buddhist scholars also appear to support this particular view. For example, Venerable Thubten Chodron has made similar remarks about the accumulation of merit with respect to paying fixed prices for Dharma teachings in modern times. In her book *How to Free Your Mind: Tara the Liberator* (2005), she writes that while she understands why some Dharma centers charge these fees, in the case of charging for Dharma, such transactions tend to restrict opportunities for the accumulation of merit. On this, she writes, "first, people don't create positive potential [i.e., merit] and fail to develop the quality of generosity, both of which are essential to progress on the path. When we make a donation, we create positive potential. When we pay a fee, we don't." Furthermore, she writes that in such a market transaction, people tend to "see themselves as consumers, not as spiritual students. In the market economy, the consumer demands and the supplier supplies" (123). According to Venerable Chodron then, charging fixed rates for Dharma forecloses on opportunities for people to express their generosity and thus earn merit and to "free themselves from a mind that constantly says, 'What will I get out of this?'" (123–24). Taken together, such perspectives indeed suggest that even if the commodification of religious objects does not altogether prevent the accumulation of merit, it potentially limits it. The intention behind the two forms of exchange (buying a premanufactured thangka vs. commissioning one) is ostensibly different for both the artist and the buyer as is the potential for the creation of merit. Moreover, in the case of a premanufactured thangka, all of the characteristics of a painting that may play a role in determining merit for the consumer are predetermined by the artist, including, as is now more often the case, the amount of money to be paid (as opposed to voluntarily offered out of generosity) for the religious object.

Not all of my informants suggested that the commodification of thangkas had particular ramifications for the paintings themselves or for the merit earned from thangka painting. Nevertheless, such accounts illustrate the kinds of moral values and conceptions that Tibetans continue to attribute to religious objects, to the commission type of transaction, and to the patron/artist relationship, values that are rooted in religious texts and in historical practice. Many of the traditional exchange protocols associated with religious objects have not completely disappeared within the Tibetan internal market. But as the above discussion makes clear, the commodification of ready-made religious objects is transforming, in a manner that is unprecedented, the traditional moral framework within which these objects and their production and exchange have long been embedded.

FROM PROSCRIBED ACTIVITY TO ACCEPTABLE LIVELIHOOD

While Tibetans' current commodification of religious objects in Amdo is contributing to transformations in the practices and moral framework associated with their production and exchange, their participation in the sale of such goods is also contributing to changes in the traditional understandings of the religious proscriptions against their sale. This is evident in the fact that, when we compare the normative, historical views surrounding the sale of religious objects against those that exist among Tibetans in Amdo today, what emerges is a pronounced shift in how these proscriptions are currently articulated and understood. More specifically, Tibetans who participate in the commodification of religious goods, and even many monks, appear to have transformed the criteria with respect to how one may accumulate negative karma in this activity, making the sale of religious objects an acceptable livelihood under certain conditions.

Early on, in our review of the Tibetan Buddhist literature, we learned how—according to the textual perspective—selling representations of the body, speech, and mind of the Buddha is considered a form of wrong livelihood and a violation of the refuge vows, as it is understood to be a form of disrespect. In all of these accounts, the sale of religious objects is portrayed as a grave misdeed that carries negative consequences. Notable among these textual perspectives is the notion that living off of the profits earned from this activity—that is, using this income for personal expenses or food—leads to accumulation of negative karma. In addition, and a point that will be examined further below, the textual proscriptions against selling such goods are categorical, mentioning no qualifications regarding a seller's motivation. In these texts, the seller's motivation is *always* assumed to be negative, and a positive motivation is never considered as a mitigating factor. At best, Nāropa tells us, in the case of selling texts, "those who are realized, or are dumb, or who act for a purpose, or who are subject to forces greater than they, experience less negative results" (Gyaltsen 2006, 82). Furthermore, the textual record, again, consistently condemns actions such as painters fixing a price for their work. A variety of sources—the Mongolian scholar and painter Ngawang Khedrup, Drukpa Künlé, Yongzin Yeshe Gyalsten, and even contemporary Tibetan scholars like Geshé Sopa—all claim that anyone who places a price on a religious object is committing a negative act.

In addition to the textual record, we also examined how religious objects changed hands on the ground historically. While the selling of religious objects outright was not unknown, the ways in which such objects were normatively exchanged closely corresponded to and reflected both the prescribed protocols for patrons and artists and the associated textual proscriptions against their sale. It was indeed the common practice for artists and patrons to take specific steps in order to avoid the commodification of religious goods, as payment was predominantly achieved through voluntary offering. Several artists revealed that the practice of setting prices or requesting a particular amount of money for the production of religious objects was *not* the regular practice of artists but that whatever was offered (which could have been money, gifts, or a combination of the two) was determined by the patron and his or her financial means and was perceived as a pious gift or donation. Many artists recalled that one was to accept such offerings even if they were perceived to be meager. As we witnessed in our examination of the comments from Ngawang Khedrup and Drukpa Künlé, this attitude toward what one received as an offering was considered a potential source of merit. We have also seen that, historically speaking, Tibetan attitudes toward merchants who sold religious objects were overwhelmingly negative, as such acts were seen to be religiously and socially inappropriate and, moreover, were believed to create a type of spiritual pollution that was potentially harmful and contagious. Several informants commented that, out of concern for such contamination, one did not even accept food from people who sold religious objects. The absence of stores and shops that sold religious objects such as thangkas and statues—although the same cannot be said of texts, at least in the early twentieth century—also attests to the fact that premodern Tibetan interpretations of these proscriptions reflected the understanding that religious objects were not to be sold. All of this evidence supports the fact that the textual proscriptions were, for the most part, reflected in historical practice.

Furthermore, our survey of the writings of contemporary Tibetan Buddhist teachers in the post-Mao era suggests that their perspectives on selling religious objects has remained remarkably consistent with the classical textual position on this issue as well as with historical interpretations of these ideas. As we saw from those earlier discussions, various contemporary Tibetan religious scholars have framed the selling of religious objects *for profit* as acts that constitute wrong livelihood or abandoning the Dharma. The consensus of these contemporary Tibetan scholars was that one must be careful not to utilize any profits from the sale of such objects for personal expenses. Rather, as some suggested, one should reinvest these profits for the sake of spreading the Dharma or, more specifically, for creating new religious objects. Importantly, in all of the modern scholarly interpretations and articulations of these proscriptions, in no instance were the actions of a person who sold religious objects for a living ever framed as anything but potentially dangerous and karmically detrimental. When we juxtapose these textual, historical, and contemporary scholarly perspectives with the present-day interpretations of the proscriptions surveyed in Amdo, however, a number of changes and/or moral shifts become apparent, which serve to transform the selling of religious goods into an acceptable source of personal income.

Transformations to the proscriptions against the sale of religious goods are most clearly observed among the new generation of Tibetan merchants who make their livelihood from selling such items. This group stands as the very embodiment of the changing perceptions of these ideas. Although four merchants acknowledged that the act of selling religious objects was inescapably negative, the vast majority of merchants, twelve of eighteen, viewed their business activities as relatively unproblematic. These merchants negotiated these proscriptions in a number of ways, which, they believed, prevented them from accruing negative karma. For example, some claimed that appropriate or "reasonable" pricing was key in whether one accumulated negative karma; one should not earn "too much money" from the sale of religious objects by charging double, an act which would *then* constitute a sin. Furthermore, for many merchants, the proper treatment of religious objects—not treating them or thinking of them as mundane items—was seen as central to legitimating their sale and to using the proceeds for one's livelihood. Selling for personal profit could even be virtuous if the goal was *also* to help Buddhists acquire religious objects for religious purposes or to spread Tibetan religion and culture. Conducting one's business in opposition to *these* norms, as many claimed non-Tibetans did, was considered a violation of the proscriptions in question. In short, for the vast majority of merchants, provided one followed these business ethics and practices, one could make a reasonable profit from selling religious objects and incur no negative karma, a perspective that is, of course, in direct opposition to textual and historical interpretations of these proscriptions and a view that is a modern invention.

Transformations in the proscriptions against the sale of religious objects can also be observed among painters, especially among those painters who create thangkas for sale on the open market (activities which today occupy the vast majority of painters in the region). As was evident in several painters' accounts, up to the Cultural Revolution, the normative means by which paintings changed hands was on a commission basis and through voluntary offerings. As seen in the comments of Eric McGuckin's informant, Venerable Sangay Yeshi, as well as in the observations of several other artists, in the past there was no tradition of asking the patron for money or setting prices; the fee earned by a painter depended on the sponsor. This practice was likely a response to the religious proscriptions against selling religious goods and a strategy that worked to circumvent the direct pricing and commodification of thangka paintings, activities considered to be inappropriate and reserved for mundane types of goods. Moreover, according to the eighty-year-old monk from Sengeshong Mango Gonpa, historically speaking, a painter who created and sold thangkas that were not requested was regarded as being engaged in activities that were disrespectful and was viewed disparagingly. As we observed, this understanding that such practices ultimately constitute negative acts persists among some artists (e.g., clay statue makers) and monks in contemporary Amdo. Today, however, the vast majority of painters believe that pre-painting thangkas and selling them at a profit (often conceived of as a work fee) is considered a perfectly legitimate practice. For such painters, the sin lies not in selling ready-made paintings at fixed or market prices but almost exclusively in painting inaccurately. Most painters believed, and not without textual grounds, that mistakes made in painting were actions that could result in serious negative karmic consequences. In addition, if one's motivation was governed *solely* by the pursuit of profit, if a painting was unreasonably priced by an artist, or if a painter conceived of the transaction as "selling the Buddha" or the deity depicted, then such an attitude provided a basis for the accumulation of negative karma. However, while such a perspective reflects a continuity with *some* of the moral guidelines associated with painting, it also represents a significant reinterpretation of the religious proscriptions against the sale of religious objects as they were interpreted in the past. Painting with correct proportions and with the intention that a thangka will someday be displayed for all to see—regardless of whether a painting is requested or not (or even sold for a price determined by an artist)—is now perceived as guaranteeing the merit of the act. The notion that one should not create a religious object ahead of time in order to sell it, or fix a price and then sell it in a shop, appears to be disappearing for most painters.[17]

Although further research is required to reach more definitive conclusions, the recent commodification of religious objects may also be contributing to transformations in how even monks understand the classical religious proscriptions against the sale of such goods, and this may be seen through a closer examination of the issue of *motivation*. As has already been noted, a seller's motivation appears to be virtually absent from the textual record as a factor mitigating the sin of selling religious objects, an activity that is always framed as a moral infraction and that assumes a seller's motivation to be negative. In fact, among all of the scholarly perspectives on this issue—both historical and contemporary—that were reviewed for this study, the only discussion of motivation as it pertains to selling religious objects appears to come from Lama Zopa in a lengthy explanation of the refuge vows, and even here it plays a rather unimportant and secondary role. In a talk on a form of Tsongkhapa guru yoga called *The Hundred Deities of Ganden* (*Dga' ldan lha brgya ma*) (1986), Lama Zopa is recorded as stating that if one sells religious objects (an activity he does not recommend if other means of income are available), one must maintain a pure, compassionate motivation, without any regard for one's own self-interest, with the attitude of self-sacrifice, and the knowledge that one will be reborn in the hell (*narak*) realms. Such a view surely reflects the idea that, while motivation does matter and should play a role in this activity, the sale of religious objects is nevertheless a negative act with grave consequences. This same perspective is also reflected in another anecdote related by Lama Zopa in a book entitled *The Lawudo Lama*. There, he describes how he once received biscuits from a known seller of religious texts. In this case, his immediate response to this gift of food was not to assume the seller's motivation was positive but instead to have the biscuits buried at the top of a mountain so as to protect anyone from coming into contact with them (Wangmo 2005, 273). Thus, even in the contemporary context, the role of motivation is understood to be peripheral to the polluting nature of the act of selling religious goods.

The consistency that is shown regarding this issue within the classical religious textual sources is likely the primary reason why five out of a total of twelve monks interviewed in Amdo saw little or no role for motivation as an exculpatory or mitigating factor in the sale of religious objects. It is also surely the reason why some monks have confronted sellers of religious goods about what they believed was the danger of their businesses, why most monasteries explicitly avoided the sale of Buddha images in their gift shops, why some merchants of ritual objects avoided the sale of statues and thangkas, and why advice to avoid the sale of religious goods is frequently given at public gatherings such as the Kālacakra tantra initiations. These actions suggest that, at best, the factor of motivation could only decrease the amount of negative karma that was inevitably accumulated by one who sells religious objects for a living. However, a significant proportion of the monks interviewed, seven of twelve, some of whom were geshés, viewed the selling of religious objects as contingent upon a seller's motivation. According to the members of this group, if a merchant had a motivation that went beyond the mere desire for profit, or if a merchant was motivated to serve others or to spread the Dharma, then this constituted an acceptable motivation and led to the creation of merit for both the merchant and the consumer. Importantly, some implied (and others explicitly stated) that one could earn a reasonable amount of money for one's livelihood without incurring detrimental karmic effects. In short, there was therefore a substantial shift away from the texts and the normative interpretations of these proscriptions in the opinion of the majority of the monks I interviewed.

The emphasis placed by these monks on motivation as mitigating the negativity brought about by selling Buddhist objects raises some interesting questions. Most notably, why do these monks emphasize motivation, and what is the source of this notion? It could of course be argued that these monks were implicitly drawing upon the bodhisattva vow literature, which describes how any ordinarily negative action can be positive for a bodhisattva. Indeed, in his commentary on the *Bodhisattvabhūmi* chapter on ethical conduct (*śīla*), Tsongkhapa states that real bodhisattvas have an obligation to engage in ordinarily sinful actions, even killing, when it will help sentient beings—not only that it is permissible but that it is required (see Tatz 1986, 70).[18] Given this perspective, on the one hand, these monks may have been reticent to condemn sellers of religious objects because they are not aware of who is and who is not a bodhisattva, for slandering bodhisattvas is said to have serious negative repercussions. On the other hand, it is also plausible that those who took motivation into account may have had in the backs of their minds the idea that we live in a more degenerate age, when certain doctrinal accommodations need to be made. But this is of course speculative, for the monks who emphasized the role of motivation did not explicitly suggest that merchants of religious objects *were* bodhisattvas, acting out of a purely compassionate concern for others with no regard for their own livelihood. In fact, such a view did not even appear to be the expectation of these monks, who knew very well that the merchants of religious goods in Amdo personally utilized their profits. Rather, these monks seemed to be claiming that a positive motivation (one not intent *solely* on profit) could in fact transform selling into a meritorious activity and, moreover, a legitimate livelihood. Also, those monks who placed a premium on motivation did not express the issue as one of doctrinal acquiescence in an age of the decline of Dharma but rather as one of doctrinal fact. That is, from their perspectives, the propriety of all actions, even those pertaining to selling religious objects, was determined by one's motivation. Yet, the views of these monks still leave us with a number of unanswered questions. For example, why do texts and a host of scholars—who are also aware of the bodhisattva vow literature—*not* adopt this same interpretation? How shall we account for the personal use of the profits, which appear to be the crux of these proscriptions? And what of the notion of pollution and contagion? The perspectives of these monks do not, in any self-evident way, account for or explain these aspects of the proscriptions, which appear to be left by the wayside in their suggestion that motivation in this matter is pivotal and that a reasonable profit can be made from this activity.

Given these monks' attitudes toward the sale of Buddhist objects, there may be several other underlying causes or reasons behind what appears to be a significant reinterpretation of these ideas. For example, it is quite possible that these monks may be making certain accommodations to Tibetan merchants and painters within their new economic and political environment. Knowing that Tibetans are an ethnic minority who are relatively disadvantaged and who need to make a living, these monks may be reasoning that, ultimately, the sale of statues and thangkas is good for Tibetans religiously, culturally, and economically, as long as one maintains a decent motivation to help others and to spread the Dharma. Nor can we discount the possibility that attitudes toward such practices have changed because of Tibet's rather recent cultural trauma and material losses and because of the political and religious restrictions under which Tibetans now live. In other words, it is quite possible that the goalposts which mark religious norms and observances with respect to these ideas have shifted and that such norms are simply no longer seen to be as relevant as they once were, especially when there are more pressing concerns in Tibetan society, such as political and religious freedom and the preservation of Tibetan religion and culture. Alternatively, and as previously mentioned, we cannot rule out that such transformations may be the result of China's policy on religion as well as the seemingly incessant monastic reeducation campaigns which demand that religion adapt to the views of socialism. This view is not without some ethnographic basis, for at least one monk noted that they are frequently encouraged to "adapt to the current times." This same sentiment is also reflected in the comments of the eighty-year-old monk from Sengeshong Mango, who explained, "With the social changes to society, one cannot tell merchants and painters that they cannot sell religious objects." Whatever the case, the emphasis many monks place on motivation as a factor in selling Buddhist objects appears to be a modern phenomenon. The ideas that the appropriateness of selling religious objects depends on one's motivation, that the personal use of the profits from this activity is no longer polluting or contagious, and that selling religious objects can be a legitimate form of livelihood only appear to arise in the contemporary context. The notion that motivation or intention influences karmic outcomes is, of course, as old as Buddhism itself. Nevertheless, as it pertains to the particular issue of selling Buddhist objects, it does seem to take on a new life in the post-Mao era, and in this context it may be related to the relatively recent social, economic, and political transformations in Tibetan society, as well as to the increasing normalization of the commodification of religious objects among Tibetans.

FROM OUTSIDER ACTIVITY TO INSIDER ACTIVITY

Finally, the commodification of Buddhist objects among Tibetans has other ramifications over and above contributing to transformations in the religious prohibitions against their sale. As the selling of religious objects has now assumed a semblance of normalcy and acceptance in Tibetan society that is historically unprecedented, it is also contributing to changes in long-established notions of Tibetan Buddhist identity.

Traditional religious proscriptions against the sale of religious objects, the historical practices and negative attitudes associated with selling them, and the views of modern Tibetan scholars on this issue all point to the fact that the sale of religious objects for personal profit is quintessentially considered anti-Buddhist. Not only is the selling of religious objects framed as a negative act but, more specifically, as an act that constitutes a form of wrong livelihood and/or an act of abandoning the Dharma (*chos spangs kyi las*), one which violates the very precepts that make one a Buddhist—the refuge vows. As we have observed, some scholars go so far as to explicitly associate such activity with non-Buddhist behavior by referring to those who participate in selling religious objects as people who "claim to be followers of the Three Jewels but do not have the slightest respect for their representations" (Patrül Rinpoche 1998, 186–87), or as those who "pretend to be Buddhist" (Shardong Rinpoche 1998–99, 1:490). Recall that the elder monk from Jakhyung Gonpa even referred to sellers of religious objects (i.e., those who sell for profit) as *chirolpas,* outsiders or non-Buddhists. Historically, the avoidance of commodifying religious goods and the adherence to traditional methods of exchange like commissioning and voluntary offering were not only what set religious objects apart from other, mundane goods but also what served to distinguish Tibetan Buddhists from others. Even if there may have been actual cash involved in premodern transactions, such protocols allowed Tibetans to engage in forms of exchange that circumvented the actual commodification of religious goods and preserved both the singular or special status of such objects (as sacred) as well as participants' own identity as Buddhists (see Taves 2009, 33). Today, however, the vast majority of Tibetan merchants of religious objects and the vast majority of thangka painters believe that preproducing and selling religious objects in stores at market prices for personal profit does not constitute a negative act but a virtuous one. And a significant number of monastic authorities in Amdo now also believe that earning one's livelihood in this way—albeit with a proper motivation—is acceptable and is no longer a spiritually polluting or negative activity. Not only are such attitudes apparent through direct testimony, but the fact that most merchants reported never having received advice or fielded concerns about this issue from the monastic community is also a sign of the prevalence of shifting perspectives. My findings show that many Tibetans in Amdo today see the selling of religious objects for one's livelihood as an activity that is not necessarily anti-Buddhist, as it has long been textually and historically portrayed and understood, but instead—and especially if the goal is also to serve others or to disseminate the Dharma—potentially a very Buddhist one. In fact, today, the notion that selling representations of the body, speech, and mind of the Buddha is antithetical to being a Tibetan Buddhist has now been largely reversed, as their sale has come to be perceived as something that distinguishes or connotes Tibetan ethnic and religious identity. For many merchants and painters, selling religious objects has become a vehicle through which to express one's ethnic and religious identity vis-à-vis other ethnicities and a source of religious and cultural pride. Many of these participants claimed to sell not simply to earn their living but also *because they were Buddhist* and, in contrast to non-Tibetan merchants, knew the appropriate ways to treat and sell religious objects. It is true, from one perspective, that Tibetans' participation in the commodification of their religious objects has served to reaffirm their sense of ethnic and religious identity. Tibetan religious art, especially thangka painting, has become synonymous with Tibetanness, and its presence in the marketplace performs significant cultural work: as an economic resource, as a vehicle for cultural reproduction and preservation, as a means of education, and as a space through which to communicate with the outside world. It is nevertheless also true that the Tibetan identity that emerges and that is reaffirmed through the sale of religious goods entails the negation of another identity that is defined by *not* selling them. While some may argue that Tibetans' commodification of religious objects has become crucial to the survival of Tibetan religion and culture and thus to Tibetan identity, it is also important to recognize that the increasing frequency and normalization of Tibetans' participation in such activities is subordinating a traditional conception of Tibetan Buddhist identity, one which categorically rejects the idea of profiting personally from the sale of religious goods. The tension that exists between these two forms of identity, as we have seen, is not historically new. But the emergence of the Tibetan Buddhist who legitimately sells religious objects as a livelihood in the marketplace is a phenomenon that *is* new and is a direct result of Tibetans' growing participation in the market for Buddhist objects.

CONCLUSION

From one perspective, the commodification of religious goods in Amdo is surely leading to a number of significant material and nonmaterial outcomes for many Tibetans. As the above discussion has illustrated, such activity brings with it much needed economic gains and serves to foster an important sense of community cohesion and cooperation as well as cultural continuity.

It gives Tibetans (as artists and merchants) greater agency in determining and controlling the quality and meanings associated with such objects, an agency that is especially important in a context in which many non-Tibetans participate in the market. It has also aided in the preservation and dissemination of Tibetan religion and culture in general and religious art in particular. And, in its own particularly new way, such objects are increasingly becoming an important source and signifier of Tibetan ethnic, religious, and cultural identity, which serves to reinforce a sense of Tibetan cultural distinctiveness. Yet, as the above analysis has also shown, the various cultural and economic outcomes that Tibetans have derived from the commodification of their religious objects have not come without significant trade-offs—the transformation of long-held traditional religious practices, ethics, and values associated with religious objects. These are not simply transformations in the mechanics of the production and exchange of religious goods but also shifts in the moral framework and practices associated with them. The sale of religious objects has had transformative effects upon traditional notions of sin and merit, notions of spiritual pollution and contagion, ideas of what it means to sell religious objects (i.e., the proscriptive statements themselves), and even notions of Tibetan Buddhist identity. Taken together, such elements are intimately linked to a traditional Tibetan Buddhist worldview, one that has been in place for centuries, and one to which many Tibetans still subscribe.

By attending to the multiplicity of outcomes that have resulted from the commodification of religious objects in Amdo, this chapter has attempted to present a balanced perspective on the effects of this process. By including a discussion of the transformative aspects of commodification in particular, however, it has not been my aim to suggest that such changes have been necessarily negative for Tibetan society. There are, of course, Tibetans who do believe that such changes are objectively negative and who lament what they see as a loss or decline of their religious traditions, an important fact that cannot be overlooked. Rather, my primary aim in attending to the transformative aspects of commodification has been to document the changes that take place when objects that have been traditionally and historically withheld from commodification by religious injunction and exchanged according to prescribed, religiously based protocols are brought into the commodity sphere. My aim has also been, at least in part, to problematize a particular view within the literature on commodification, one which tends to accentuate or highlight certain outcomes that may be derived from it—such as those pertaining to cultural preservation, the reaffirmation of identity, and cultural, economic, and social empowerment—while overlooking, ignoring, or simply not accounting for the potential problems, conflicts, and transformations (especially moral ones) that can also result from this process. The kinds of religious transformations and shifts in moral boundaries that are occurring within the context of Tibetans' sale of religious goods have been seen by some economists and anthropologists as being the very result of the introduction of the capitalist free market to precapitalist societies, where exchange practices typically operate under a different set of social ethics and moral obligations. Authors such as Richard Henry Tawney ([1926] 1998), Karl Polanyi ([1944] 2001), and Michael Taussig (1980), for example, have all in one way or another called attention to the impact of capitalist forms of exchange on the social/moral dimension of life and society and its potential to subordinate or replace preexisting, culturally embedded moral frameworks. In addition, while not emphasizing the effects of capitalism specifically, Arjun Appadurai similarly has observed that "the diversion of commodities from their customary paths always carries a risky and morally ambiguous aura" (1986, 27). And within the context of scholarship on tourism, Li Yang and Geoffrey Wall also remind us that there are potential losses and transformations at stake in the process of cultural commodification, as it "can induce a local people to alter their behaviors to suit the demands of the market, resulting in a loss of traditional activities and other authentic aspects of cultural manifestations" (2009, 562). While the introduction of the free market in Tibet has not led to the kind of moral revolution described by Taussig—many Tibetans continue to maintain traditional protocols with respect to religious objects as well as other, long-standing religious traditions—the work of these authors suggest that there is potentially more at stake in the process of commodification than the advantageous economic or cultural outcomes commonly associated with it.

In the case of the commodification of religious objects in Amdo, an emphasis only on how the sale of such objects may contribute to economic prosperity or to cultural preservation, for example, while certainly true, fails to address the fact that the sale of Buddhist objects in Tibet is also a site of ongoing tension and overlooks the fact that many Tibetans continue to view the buying and selling of these objects as highly problematic and contradictory to their religious traditions. It is also a perspective that, perhaps inadvertently, tends to elide the historical trajectory of how such objects were exchanged in the past and how they entered into marketplace. In Tibet, this entrance has involved a process of invasion, cultural revolution, and massive economic and political transformation, and it continues to involve Tibetan economic and political disenfranchisement. Moreover, such a conclusion fails to recognize the religious transformations and sacrifices that take place in the process of bringing objects that have moral implications associated with their creation and exchange to the marketplace as ready-made religious goods.

Igor Kopytoff, in his essay "The Cultural Biography of Things," writes, "Biographies of things can make salient what might otherwise remain obscure" (1986, 67). It is in this spirit that I have attempted to construct a historical narrative of the commodification of religious objects in Tibet in order to shed light on the various factors influencing Tibetans' current participation in a traditionally prohibited practice and the religious/moral transformations this entails, transformations which might otherwise remain hidden in the absence of a religious and historical perspective on their exchange. Today, there are two diametrically opposed perspectives on the sale of religious objects in Amdo, one that reflects a continuity with past attitudes and practices—that sees selling religious objects as a sinful act (despite motivation)—and another one which, I suggest, is historically newer, that insists that participation in the market for religious objects is not necessarily evil. This latter view sees the sale of religious goods as an acceptable and even virtuous form of livelihood when there exists a positive motivation that extends beyond mere profit making. More research is required to determine whether and to what extent the former, traditional perspective is being eclipsed by that latter view. However, given that a significant number of monks are not opposed to the selling of religious objects as a livelihood or see such opposition as a losing battle, and given that the younger generation of Tibetans appears less inclined to maintain these traditional ideas, it seems fair to conclude that the view which sees the sale of religious objects as an acceptable livelihood and its concomitant notion of Tibetan Buddhist identity is prevailing.

Notes

INTRODUCTION

1. The time in which Rebkong art came of age is disputed. Some have placed the beginnings of the tradition of painting as early as the fifteenth century. However, the general consensus is that this tradition began to flourish in the seventeenth century, coinciding with the Gelukpa monastic expansion in the region.

2. Here, I use the typical English spelling of the word "thangka" (*thang ka*) throughout this book. However, it is pronounced with a hard *t* sound, like in *Tibet.*

3. An exception to my use of generic references involves some cases where I refer to my previous fieldwork in Lhasa. When referring to this work, I have used pseudonyms for the names of my informants.

4. This was especially true at Labrang. At the time of my visit, Labrang had just opened up to tourists after having been closed for political reasons, most likely stemming from the Tibetan demonstrations of 2008. Research among merchants and monks was difficult. Upon engaging one group of monks over lunch in a café, I was told that monks were not allowed to talk to foreigners. Even my interpreter was noticeably anxious, and he did not want to interview monks at the café or the monastery.

5. Although during my research I intended to approach factories that produced Buddhist images, I was repeatedly told by my interpreter that gaining access to such places was next to impossible. His reasoning seemed to revolve around issues of secrecy and/or competition. That is, he suggested that the ways in which such things were produced were considered trade secrets and that the owners of such operations were very protective of them. He was adamant that we would never even find out where such factories were, explaining, "This is confidential. No business trader wants others to sell the same products."

6. Appadurai credits his thinking on paths and diversions to Nancy Munn's work on the kula system of the Western Pacific. See Munn (1983).

1. EARLY PROHIBITIONS AGAINST SELLING BUDDHIST OBJECTS

1. According to Schopen, and based on his reading of the *Mūlasarvāstivāda vinaya,* a shaven-headed householder represented an intermediate type of individual, a layperson in the process of being trained for ordination (2004, 103).

2. *'Dul ba gzhi,* Lha sa bka' 'gyur, 'Dul ba *ga*, fol. 167a.2–167a.5. Unless otherwise noted, all translations are my own. Several sections of the *Mūlasarvāstivāda vinaya* (including the above passage) have been translated into English by Gregory Schopen (2004, 106–21). See also Schopen in Lopez (1995, 473–502) and Walser (2005, 142).

3. According to *The New Tibetan-English Dictionary of Modern Tibetan,* "*shug,*" the present-tense form of "*bshugs*" means "to sell things internally without making a profit" (Goldstein 2001, 1099). Ives Waldo notes that *bshug pa* means sold, bartered, or exchanged.

4. *'Phags pa rin po che'i phung po zhes bya ba theg pa chen po'i mdo,* Lha sa bka' 'gyur, Dkon brtsegs *cha*, fols. 280b.2–281b.2. A more concise version of this passage is found in Śāntideva's *Compendium of Training* (*Śikṣāsamuccaya*). For example, see Śāntideva, *Bslab pa kun las btus pa*, Sde dge bstan 'gyur, Dbu ma *khi*, fols. 36b.6–37a.4. For another translation of this passage from the *Compendium of Training*, see Bendall and Rouse (1971, 57–58). For a translation of the entire fourth chapter of the *Heap of Jewels Sūtra* from which these passages derive, see Silk (2008, 27–32).

5. *'Phags pa rin po che'i phung po zhes bya ba theg pa chen po'i mdo,* Lha sa bka' 'gyur, Dkon brtsegs *cha*, fols. 282a.5–283a.2. See Śāntideva, *Bslab pa kun las btus pa*, Sde dge bstan 'gyur, Dbu ma *khi*, fols. 37a.7–37b.3. See also Bendall and Rouse (1971, 58) and Silk (2008, 32).

6. In Tibet, the theft of monastic property took on equally grave proportions. Kunzang Pẹlden (ca. 1862–1943), in his commentary to Śāntideva's *Engaging in the Deeds of a Bodhisattva* (*Bodhicaryāvatāra*) titled *The Nectar of Manjushri's Speech* (*'Jam dbyangs bla ma'i zhal lung bdud rtsi'i thig pa*), describes the outcome of these actions, writing: "It is said that stealing the property of the sangha, wherever it may be, and especially the provisions directly donated to it constitutes a very grave fault. In short, it is said in the sutras that to steal or traffic the property, great or small, of the sangha, or to appropriate it by dishonest means, cannot be purified even by confession and will surely lead to rebirth in the hell realms" (Pelden 2007, 96). See also Patrül Rinpoche's *The Words of My Perfect Teacher* (*Kun bzang bla ma'i zhal lung*), where this is mentioned numerous times in various case stories. In addition, in China, contracting leprosy was often seen as the result of stealing and selling the property of the monastery. For an example of this, see Leung (2009).

7. *'Phags pa nam mkha'i snying po zhes bya ba theg pa chen po'i mdo,* Sde dge bka' 'gyur, Mdo sde *za*, fols. 277a.7–277b.3.

8. Asaṅga, *Rnal 'byor spyod pa'i sa las byang chub sems dpa'i sa,* Sde dge bstan 'gyur, Sems tsam *wi*, fols. 89b.4–90a.2. This passage has also been translated by Tatz (1986, 71).

9. Vesna Wallace, personal communication, January 1, 2012.

10. Tsuktorchen (Gtsug gtor can; Śikhin), literally meaning the one possessing a head protuberance, is the name of the second of the seven heroic Buddhas in the present age, or *kalpa*. Śākyamuni is known as the seventh.

11. *Smṛtyupasthāna Sūtra,* in *'Phags pa dam pa'i chos dran pa nye bar bzhag pa,* Lha sa bka' 'gyur, Mdo sde *ya*, fols. 156b.2–158b.2. Part of this passage has also been

translated by Erik Zürcher from the Chinese (*Zheng fa nian chu jing*, T 721, 70 *j*). Zürcher's translation is slightly different and runs as follows: "Anyone who, having left the household [and having entered the *saṅgha*], sells Buddha images, whether they be made of ivory, or embroidery, or painted upon cotton cloth, or carved from wood, or made of bronze and other [metals], is a person full of evil and desire. Objects obtained [in this way] shall not be used for religious purposes (lit. in *dharma* [-activities], *fazhong*)" (1995, 8). Zürcher thus concludes that the passage condemns not only the sale but also the use of icons that have been sold commercially.

12. Schopen notes that the *Maitreyasiṃhanāda Sūtra* (T. 310 no. 23) was translated into Chinese in the mid-sixth century and became a part of the *Ratnakūṭa* collection that was compiled by Bodhiruci in the early eighth century. The Tibetan version is also a part of the *Ratnakūṭa*, the Tibetan translation of which Schopen dates to the beginning of the ninth century (2005, 63). However, he also suggests that the *Maitreyasiṃhanāda Sūtra* might be placed much earlier due to the vocabulary and "polemics" it shares with the *Mūlasarvāstivāda vinaya* as well as with other contemporaneous sources, including early Kharoṣṭhī inscriptions, both of which he dates to the beginnings of the Mahāyāna, near the first or second centuries. For an analysis of the dating of this text and the *Mūlasarvāstivāda vinaya*, see Schopen (2005, 63–107).

13. King Prasenajit was the king of Kosala during the time of Śākyamuni Buddha.

14. *Byams pa'i seng ge'i sgra'i mdo,* Stog pho brang bris ma (Leh) bka' 'gyur, Dkon brtsegs *ca*, fols. 208b.2–209b.3. Schopen has also translated part of this passage from the Degé edition. For his partial translations, see Schopen (2005, 65–66). See also, Zürcher (1995, 8–9).

15. According to the *Encyclopedia of Buddhism* (Buswell 2004), the *Brahmajāla* was believed to have been translated from an Indian source by Kumārajīva in 406 CE. However, scholars now believe it was written in China by unknown authors in the mid-fifth century (1:281–82).

16. This is Martine Batchelor's translation. A review of other translations of this passage has yielded an almost identical outcome, implying that all images of Buddhas and bodhisattvas, as well as texts, belonged to or were the property of the monastery or the Three Jewels and should be returned. For example, see Thanh and Leigh (2000) and Seng and Kumārajīva (1981, 38).

17. Zürcher notes that this passage occurs in j. 2, 517a.

18. According to Funayama Tōru, the *Sarvāstivādavinayavibhāṣā,* while containing indigenous Chinese elements, also appears to have been translated from an Indian source (2006, 44–45).

19. This is Zürcher's translation. Zürcher notes that this passage occurs in T1483 and in T1484 (973c and 985b, respectively). It is unclear which version of the Taisho he refers to, as T1484 is often listed as the *Brahmajāla Sūtra* and the passage does not exist in this text. Nevertheless, it should be noted that according to the *Taishō shinshū daizōkyō* on the SAT Daizōkyō Text Database (http://21dzk.l.u-tokyo.ac.jp/SAT/index_en.html), there are two versions of the same text in T1483, vol. 24. In the first version, the passage cited here occurs at 973c16. In the second version, the passage

occurs at 985a29. I owe my knowledge of this bit of information to Eric Goodell, a translator for the Bodhi Foundation for Culture and Education. Tōru believes that the original lecture delivered by Vimalākṣa is not extant but became a text known as the *Scripture of Five Hundred Questions* (*Wubai wenshi jing*). This text was eventually redacted to appear as though it came from the mouth of the Buddha and became the *Scripture of Maudgalyāyana's Questions about Five Hundred Light and Heavy Sins in the Monastic Discipline* (*Mulian wen jielüzhong wubai qingzhongshi jing*). Therefore, according to Tōru, the statement regarding the sale of a Buddha image presented here was originally the instruction of Vimalākṣa.

20. This is Zürcher's translation. Zürcher notes that the *Fo zai jin guan jing fu jing* is quoted in Daishih's seventh-century encyclopedia, *Fayuan Zhulin*, T2122, j. 33 540a, and is listed as an apocryphal work in the *Catalog of Scriptures, Authorized by the Great Zhou Dynasty* (*Da Zhou kandìng zhongjing mulu*), T2153 j.15 472c. See Zürcher (1995, 16n48).

21. Zürcher notes that this text is cited as apocryphal in the *Catalog of Scriptures, Authorized by the Great Zhou Dynasty*, T2153 j. 15 472c, and is quoted in the *Fayuan zhulin*, T2122, j. 33 540a. See Zürcher (1995, 16n60).

22. This is Kyoko Tokuno's translation. This text is located in T2870 vol. 85, 1335c–1338c.

23. According to Tokuno, this text did not originate with the Sect of the Three Stages but rather, due to its content concerning the degenerate age, greatly influenced it (1995, 260).

24. This is Gernet's translation; he notes its location as *Kuang hung-ming chi*, 28.329.b.

25. This is Gernet's translation; the location of this decree is the *Ts'e-fu yüan-kuei*, 159.12a.

26. This evolutionary model—that proscriptions against stealing monastic property eventually became proscriptions against selling representations of the Buddha more generally—is explored by José Cabezón (2001a, 23) as part of a working paper on the commodification of Tibetan Buddhism.

27. One example of this association can be seen in Śāntideva's *Engaging in the Deeds of a Bodhisattva* (*Bodhicaryāvatāra*). In chapter 8 on meditative concentration, he links the act of stealing the property of the Three Jewels with that of motivations for profit and states the negative results of such activity in verse 123: "And for the sake of profit and position, some there are who even kill their parents, or steal what has been offered to the Triple Gem, because of which, they'll burn in hell of Unrelenting Pain" (Shāntideva 2006). This translation is from the Padmakara Translation Group.

2. SELLING BUDDHIST OBJECTS IN TIBETAN BUDDHIST LITERATURE

1. For examples of this narrative about King Utrāyaṇa and King Bimbisāra, see Kunpal (2003, 187–88); Gega Lama (1983, 1:31); Dagyab (1977, pt. 1, 20–21); Rinchen (2006, 95–97); and Jamgön Kongtrul Lodrö Tayé (2010, 396). Some of my

informants during my fieldwork casually invoked this story when speaking of the priceless nature of a Buddha statue or painting.

2. According to the Buddhist Digital Resource Center, the dates for Dorje Dze Ö's life are unknown. He was the disciple of Paldan Ritrö Wang Chuk (Dpal ldan ri khrod dbang phyug), who was himself the disciple of Jigten Gonpo ('Jig rten mgon po, 1143–1217), founder of the Drigung Kagyu lineage. This would seemingly put the dates for his life, and *The Great Biographies of the Kagyu,* between the thirteenth and fourteenth centuries.

3. The text here may be corrupt since these lines make little sense.

4. Rdo rje mdzes 'od, *Bka' brgyud kyi rnam thar chen mo rin po che'i gter mdzod dgos 'dod 'byung gnas* (1985, fols. 60a.3–60b.4). Khenpo Könchog Gyaltsen translates this same passage in *The Great Kagyu Masters: The Golden Lineage Treasury.* Notably, he translates "eating the ransom payment given for the scriptures" as "gain one's livelihood by selling precious texts" (Gyaltsen 2006, 82–83). This opinion is attributed to Nāropa in the *Great Biographies of the Kagyu*. We cannot, of course, assume that this is an accurate attribution. Whether it is the opinion of Nāropa or of someone else, however, is irrelevant to my argument.

5. Ma gcig lab sgron, *Phung po gzan skyur gyi rnam bshad gcod kyi don gsal byed* (2008, fol. 153b.4–153b.5). See also Harding (2003, 266–67). Machik's statements here are in line with certain prophecies of Padmasambhava (ca. 717–762) in a treasure (*gter ma*) text known as *The Legend of the Great Stūpa* (*Mchod rten chen po bya rung kha shor gyi lo rgyus thos pa grol ba*). In this text, the following words are attributed to Padmasambhava: "The belch of the Bon Magician resounds in the Yogin's hermitage and the wealth of the sanctuaries is looted; the scriptures of the Tathagatas, the images of the Buddhas, the sacred icons, the scroll paintings and the stupas will be desecrated, stolen and bartered at the market price—their true worth forgotten; the temples become cowsheds and stables covered with dung" (Dowman 1973, 51). *The Legend of the Great Stūpa* is believed to have been given by Padmasambhava to Yeshe Tsogyal (eighth century), his consort. The text is said to have been first revealed by Lhatsun Ngonmo (Lha btsun sngon mo, twelfth century), re-concealed, and later re-revealed by Yolmo Terton Shakya Zangpo (Yol mo gter ston shākya bzang po, fifteenth century).

6. Surya Das gives this story the title "Gampopa's Business Advice," but it is unclear whether it has an official title. A variation of this story is also found in Patrül Rinpoche's *The Words of My Perfect Teacher,* although that text mentions that the disciple of Gampopa sold only religious texts. See Patrül Rinpoche (1998, 266–67); see also Stewart (1995, 102–3).

7. Interestingly, Patrül Rinpoche's text *The Words of My Perfect Teacher* explains that Gampopa instead prescribes the printing of texts to remove the karmic obstacles caused by selling them (1998, 266). In their translation of this text, the Padmakara Translation Group notes that "the printing and distribution of sacred books is considered a powerful practice for accumulating merit and purifying obscurations, provided that it is done purely as an offering without any profit" (1998, 390n179). Many

Tibetans today justify their ongoing sale of religious objects by stating that they give money to local monasteries. However, one wonders if this was the kind of activity that Gampopa (or the tellers of this story) had in mind when describing how one is to remove the karmic impurities from selling religious objects. The aim of this tale seems to be how one may remove such impurities accumulated from *past* actions and not how one may reasonably continue to sell religious objects for a living. Nevertheless, this karmic balancing act is something that is done in contemporary times, as some Tibetans are known to sell religious objects and then give away some of the proceeds to counteract the negative karma accumulated from doing this.

8. According to Patrül Rinpoche, there are no negative actions that cannot be removed through the power of confession and the four powers (1998, 264). This is in contrast to statements made about taking the property of the Saṅgha, which many authors (Pabongka Rinpoche among them) claim results in negative karma that cannot be removed even by confession.

9. 'Brug pa kun dga' legs pa, *'Brug pa kun dga' legs pa'i rnam thar dang nyams mgur dang zhal gdams sogs* (1978, fol. 32a.4–32a.6). This translation is my own, although I have consulted the translation by Ardussi (1972, 251) as cited in Jackson and Jackson (1984, 13), especially for the expression "e hong," which appears to be unusual. As such, I have retained Ardussi's translation of this phrase as "phooey."

10. Ngag dbang mkhas grub, *Lha 'bri ba'i man ngag lag len du sbyar ba'i gsung rtsom gyi 'grel pa* (1974, vol. 3, fols. 5b.3–6a.2).

11. A similar statement is made by Geshé Rabten (1920–1986) and Geshé Dhargyey (1921–1995) in their book *Advice from a Spiritual Friend,* a commentary on *The Jewel Rosary of a Bodhisattva* (*Bodhisattvamaṇyāvalī*) by Atīśa and *Seven Points of Mind Training* (*Blo sbyong don bdun ma*) by Chekawa. Here, Geshé Dhargyey, commenting on Atīśa's instruction to "abandon all worldly possessions and be adorned by the gems of superiors," writes, "It is inappropriate to be miserly about a religious object since we should not regard it as part of our wealth. If we simply regard it as symbolic of our refuge and, through our veneration for it, as a source of merit, we shall not be concerned by its loss. A true religious object should be considered priceless, but not for its monetary value" (1996, 21).

12. The Shangpa Kagyu lineage is believed to have first descended from the Buddha Vajradhara to Nāropa's consort Niguma and to Sukhasiddhi. They then passed the teachings to Kyungpo Naljor (990–1127), who is believed to have established the lineage. From him, it was passed from teacher to disciple: first to Mokchok Rinchen Tsöndrü, then to Kyergangpa Chökyi Senge, Rigong Sangye Nyentön, and Sangye Tönpa.

13. Dharmabhadra draws upon the earlier work of the First Panchen Lama, Lobsang Chökyi Gyaltsen (Blo bzang chos kyi rgyal mtshan, 1570–1662). The title of Dharmabhadra's text is: *An Instruction Manual that Clarifies the Main Points of [Paṇ chen Blo bzang chos rgyan's] "A Scattered Torma [Ritual]: A Crystaline River that Purifies the [Obscurations Caused by Misusing] Religious Funds* (*Brul gtor dkor sgrib dag byed zla shel chu rgyun gyi 'khrid yig gnad kyi don gsal*). The ritual text of Panchen

Lobsang Chökyi Gyaltsen does not provide a full accounting of this narrative and focuses instead on the actual torma ritual.

14. Dngul chu dharma bha dra, *Brul gtor dkor sgrib dag byed zla shel chu rgyun gyi 'khrid yig gnad kyi don gsal* (1973, vol. 3, fols. 1a.3–2b.1). This story is also found in a number of other works. For example, an almost identical version of this story appears in Pabongka Rinpoche (1990, 153). The same story (while not mentioning Kyergangpa by name) is also referenced in Lama Thubten Yeshe's *Becoming Vajrasattva* and is used to illustrate the notion that money from the sale of holy objects should never be used for temporal needs (see Yeshe 2004, 132). A very brief exerpt of this story can also be found in *A Golden Rosary of Lives of Masters of the Shangs Pa Dkar Brgyud Pa Schools* (*Shangs pa gser 'phreng*) (1970, 237). An alternative version of this narrative exists in *The Nectar of Manjushri's Speech: A Detailed Commentary on Shantideva's Way of the Bodhisattva* by Pelden (2007, 96), and in *Drops of Nectar*, a commentary on the *Bodhicaryāvatāra* by Khenpo Kunpal (2003, 98–99 and 265). In these two works, a patron gives Kyergangpa money to recite the *Prajñāpāramitā Sūtra* in eight thousand lines (*Aṣṭa-sāhasrikā*, *Brgyad stong pa*). However, the story describes how Kyergangpa does not complete this recitation and, as a consequence, suffers pain in his stomach from piercing white syllables. The pain, the story states, was the karmic ripening of not doing the recitation as requested and thus constituted a mishandling of religious funds. This alternative narrative is dramatically different, for rather than framing Kyergangpa as an innocent bystander who suffers because he unknowingly consumed food that his patron bought with the money from the sale of a text, it puts the responsibility directly on Kyergangpa himself and frames his actions as a theft of religious funds, funds which were presumably meant for the Saṅgha at large (and not for his own personal use). This alternative narrative also utilizes a very common definition of the Tibetan word *kor* (*dkor*)—a religious (faith) offering or its misuse. For example, *kor*, according to *Blazing Splendor: The Memoirs of the Dzogchen Yogi Tulku Urgyen Rinpoche*, "refers to material things offered out of faith to a monastic community or an individual lama for the benefit of a living or deceased person, which—when used for another purpose than the intended—have dire karmic consequences" (Kunsang and Schmidt 2005, 384n128). During my fieldwork, when I asked some monks if the selling of religious objects in the marketplace constituted *kor* (*dkor*, i.e., a mishandling of religious funds or faith offerings), several monks argued that it did not. According to them, *kor* followed this latter definition. One monk, however, stated that, indeed, this was *kor*, specifically *dkon mchog gsum gyi dkor*, or *kor* of the Three Jewels. What should not be lost here, however, is that contemporary scholars often draw upon the Kyergangpa narrative to illustrate the severe consequences of selling religious texts in modern times.

15. Spiritually mature individuals are said to experience the results of their karma in this very life, while those who are less mature will have to experience them in the next life, usually in a lower rebirth.

16. The extent to which the ritual of *drultor* is still practiced today remains unclear. During my fieldwork, when I asked some monks if a specific ritual was performed for

infractions related to selling religious objects or misusing the money thereby gained, I was told that one was performed generally for all misdeeds, but not for specific actions such as these. However, there is some evidence that this ritual is still practiced, for Lama Zopa gave a teaching to his students on it in Taiwan in 2007. See Zopa (2007).

17. Illustrating this, Patrül Rinpoche writes, "There are plenty of tīrthikas who avoid harmful acts, meditate on deities, practise on the channels and energies, and who obtain the common accomplishments. But, not knowing the refuge in the Three Jewels, they are not on the path to liberation and will not be free from saṁsāra" (1998, 186). This is the translation by the Padmakara Translation Group. Refuge is often described as a daily practice, to be completed several times a day. According to Jamgön Kongtrul Lodrö Tayé, when practiced properly, "taking refuge includes most of the practices in the gradual paths to enlightenment of the Sutra and Mantrayana" (1977, 59). However, it is also framed within the general preliminary practices (*sngon 'gro*), which include taking refuge, prostration, generating bodhicitta, making offerings, and purification practices, which together are considered precursors to higher tantric practices.

18. This four-part discussion—reasons, causes, methods, and training—is taken from Tsongkhapa's presentation of going for refuge in *The Great Treatise on the Stages of the Path to Enlightenment* (*Lamrim Chenmo*). *The Treasury of Knowledge,* book 5, *Buddhist Ethics,* by Jamgön Kongtrul Lodrö Tayé describes the refuge training as "preconditions not only for the vows of a lay practitioner but also for the purificatory fast and the novice and monk disciplines" (1998, 101).

19. These passages have been translated by the Lamrim Chenmo Translation Committee. For these passages in Tibetan, see Blo bzang grags pa'i dpal, *Lam rim chen mo* (1999, 145–47).

20. Vimalamitra's verse from *Six Aspects of Going for Refuge* reads, "An image, verse, or / Discarded scrap of yellow cloth: / Out of faith and belief, consider it to be the Teacher; / Do not mistakenly deny anything he has said, / Rather place it on the crown on your head; / View pure and impure persons / As though they were noble." This translation is by the Lamrim Chenmo Translation Committee. See Tsongkhapa (2000, 206). For Vimalamitra's verse in the Tibetan, see Blo bzang grags pa'i dpal, *Lam rim chen mo* (1999, 156). See also Sopa and Patt (2004, 496).

21. Early presentations of the refuge precepts within the path literature do not contain specific comments on selling or pawning religious objects as a form of disrespect. For example, Atīśa's *Lamp for the Path to Enlightenment* (*Bodhipathapradīpa, Byang chub lam gyi sgron ma*) and his commentary on this text (*Bodhimārgapradīpaṃpañjikānāma, Byang chub lam gyi sgron ma'i dka' 'grel*)—the basis for the entire lamrim tradition—does not even include specific statements concerning respect for the Three Jewels, much less what behaviors may or may not constitute this. For the section of the *Lamp* which discusses the refuge precepts, see Atīśa, *Byang chub lam gyi sgron ma'i dka' 'grel,* Sde dge bstan 'gyur, Dbu ma *khi,* fol. 248b.1–248b.4. Similarly, there are no statements on selling or pawning religious objects in Atīśa's shorter text

Instructions on Refuge-Taking (*Śaraṇagacchāmideśa* or *Śaraṇagamanadeśanā, Skyabs su 'gro ba bstan pa*). For an English translation of these texts by Atīśa, see Richard Sherburne's *The Complete Works of Atīśa Śrī Dīpaṁkara Jñāna, Jo-bo-rje* (2000). Likewise, Gampopa's *Jewel Ornament of Liberation* (*Dam chos yid bzin gyi nor bu thar pa rin po che'i rgyan*), another enormously influential lamrim text, includes statements that one should have respect for the Three Jewels, yet it is devoid of references to selling or pawning. For a presentation of the refuge precepts in this text, see Sgam po pa bsod nams rin chen, *Dwags po thar rgyan* (n.d., fols. 59a.5–59b.1). See also the translation of these precepts by Khenpo Könchog Gyalsten in Gampopa (1998, 143). In addition, *Engaging by Stages in the Teachings of the Buddha* (*Sangs rgyas kyi bstan pa la rim gyis 'jug pa'i tsul*), a third seminal lamrim text attributed to Phagmodrupa Dorje Gyalpo (Phag mo gru pa rdo rje rgyal po, 1110–1170) specifies the objects to be afforded respect (e.g., Buddha images and texts) but leaves out what acts constitute respect (or disrespect). See Rdo rje rgyal po, *Sangs rgyas kyi bstan pa la rim gyis 'jug pa'i tsul* in *Sangs rgyas bstan rim dang jo nang mdzad brgya* (1977, fol. 20b.4–20b.7). See also Phagmodrupa (2008, 1:58).

22. This translation is by the Lamrim Chenmo Translation Committee. For this passage in the Tibetan, see Blo bzang grags pa'i dpal, *Lam rim chen mo* (1999, 145–46).

23. This translation is by the Lamrim Chenmo Translation Committee. For this passage in the Tibetan, see Blo bzang grags pa'i dpal, *Lam rim chen mo* (1999, 156).

24. It is interesting to note that at the end of his discussion of the refuge precepts, Tsongkhapa states that although there are various opinions about what constitutes a loss of refuge, a loss of refuge only occurs in two instances: (1) when one contravenes the precept not to forsake one's refuge even for the sake of one's life, and (2) when one follows a teacher, teaching, and a community other than the Three Jewels (2000, 206). The former point suggests that if one transgresses the special, prescriptive precepts concerning respect for religious objects for the sake of self-preservation (i.e., one's life), this indeed constitutes a loss of the refuge vows. This view is notably consistent with the comments attributed to Jigten Gonpo Rinchen Pel regarding the loss of his father's refuges as a result of his sale of a Vajrabhairava text during a famine.

25. These include: taking refuge, the development of bodhicitta, the purification of negative karma and the accumulation of positive karma, and guru yoga.

26. Although Patrül Rinpoche does not cite the source of this particular verse, according to Thinley Norbu Rinpoche (2006, 63), it is derived from *The Ornament of the Hearing of Wisdom Mind* (*Snyan gyi dgongs rgyan*).

27. O rgyan 'jigs med chos kyi dbang po, *Khrid yig kun bzang bla ma'i zhal lung* (199?, fols. 142b.5–143b.4.). See also Patrül Rinpoche (1998, 186–87).

28. Padmakara's translation of this line is as follows: "This is called 'living by holding the Three Jewels to ransom' and is a very severe fault" (Patrül Rinpoche 1998, 186).

29. Here, Jigme Lingpa describes two kinds of refuge: (a) causal refuge, corresponding to *Sūtrayāna* refuge and (b) resultant refuge, corresponding to *Vajrayāna* refuge.

30. I have been unable to access Jigme Lingpa's root text in the Tibetan and have relied on the translation of it by the Padmakara Translation Group.

31. Klong chen ye shes rdo rje, *Yon tan mdzod kyi mchan 'grel* (1991, fol. 76a.2–76a.5).

32. The distinction between selling new and old images was related to me repeatedly by statue sellers and artists in Lhasa during my master's thesis research in 2006.

33. Historically, in Tibet, older images were never preserved for aesthetic or art historical purposes but were usually renovated, restored, or painted over whenever necessary. The repair of images and murals is frequently mentioned in religious literature as an opportunity for creating merit.

34. This perspective was repeated by several monks and geshés during my interviews in Amdo. In fact, nobody agreed that there was a distinction to be made in this regard.

35. The assumption of this practice seems to be that even though one may not currently sell religious objects, one has undoubtedly done so in the past. Therefore, these karmic defilements require expunging.

36. The six preparatory practices as outlined in *Jorchö* include: (1) cleaning the room and arranging the objects (of Buddha's body, speech, and mind); (2) acquiring and arranging offerings; (3) posture and generation of thought (including taking refuge, generating bodhicitta, and meditating on the four immeasurables; (4) visualizing the merit field; (5) offering the seven-limb puja—prostration, offerings, confession, rejoicing, supplication, entreaty, and dedication; and (6) supplication.

37. *Sbyor drug bya tshul thub bstan lhun po'i mdzes rgyan* (n.d., fols. 6b.3–7a.3) See also, Ngag dbang chos 'byor (1984, 10–11).

38. While the practitioner is occasionally instructed to be respectful of the Three Jewels in this anthology, extensive elaborations on what this entails appear to be absent. See *Mind Training: The Great Collection,* translated by Thupten Jinpa (2006). Thupten Jinpa identifies the commentary as one of twelve well-known commentaries on mind training (11–12).

39. Yongs 'dzin ye shes rgyal mtshan, *Blo sbyong don bdun ma'i snying bo* (1992, 151–52). This text was given to me by a monk at Jakhyung Monastery as an important source for information on refuge and for statements prohibiting the sale of religious objects.

40. The name of this series is *The Key which Opens the Door to the Complete Knowledge of the Land of Snows* (*Gangs can rig brgya'i sgo 'byed lde mig*). According to the Columbia Online Research Guide for Modern Tibetan Studies, this series was created for *tulkus* living in the PRC in order to give them a complete introduction to Tibetan Buddhism and its religious history. See http://library.columbia.edu/locations/eastasian/tibetan/guide/dictionaries/encyclopedias.html.

41. Pha bong kha pa bde chen snying po, *Lam rim rnam grol lag bcangs* (2009, 117). See also Pabongka (1990, 150).

42. Pha bong kha pa bde chen snying po, *Lam rim rnam grol lag bcangs* (2009, 118).

43. Pha bong kha pa bde chen snying po, *Lam rim rnam grol lag bcangs* (2009, 118).

44. Pha bong kha pa bde chen snying po, *Lam rim rnam grol lag bcangs* (2009, 119).

45. This text, which is located in volume one of two of Shardong Rinpoche's six-volume collected works (*gsung 'bum*), was given to me by a monk at Jakhyung Monastery.

46. While not part of a commentary on the *Lamrim Chenmo,* a similar straightforward presentation of the negative karma associated with selling and pawning statues and texts can be seen in a discourse by another major teacher from this generation, Tsenzhab Serkong Rinpoche (1902–1983), the tutor and debate partner of the Fourteenth Dalai Lama. In his commentary on the lamrim prayer entitled *The Foundation for Good Qualities* (*Yon tan gzhi gyur ma*) by Tsongkhapa, in a section titled "How to Train in Taking a Safe Direction in Life," we read: "When we take safe direction from the Buddhas, the way to train is this. When we see representations of enlightened beings, we never criticize them, saying that the eyes are crooked, the faces are weird looking, or anything like that. We must not be disrespectful. After all, we regard all representations of Buddhas as we would regard the Buddhas themselves. So, rather than criticize the Buddha, we can speak about the artist or the sculpture. We can say that the artist wasn't very skilled, but we leave it at that. In addition, *we must never sell Buddha statues.* Nor should we be disrespectful toward the various representations of the body, speech and mind of an enlightened being. It is better not to walk over them or place things on top of them" (Tsenzhab Serkong Rinpoche 1982; emphasis mine). This passage has been translated by Alexander Berzin.

47. Yangsi Rinpoche is a *tulku* and Lharampa Geshé who graduated from Sera Je and Gyume Tantric College in India. He is the founding president of Maitripa College in Portland, Oregon.

48. A similar position on the seller vis-à-vis the buyer can be seen in statements made by Jamgön Kongtrul Karma Lodrö Chökyi Senge (1954–1992). In a discourse on refuge and the refuge vows given in Palo Alto, California, in 1977, he comments on the prescriptive precept related to respecting all representations of the Three Jewels. He notes, "Particularly, the art market in the West has made it customary to deal with Buddhist art as commercial objects. To treat them as such is totally forbidden by this precept. However, to buy a Buddhist art object for use in one's practice is considered beneficial, because it is like ransoming it from someone who had mistreated it." This seems to be in accord with Yangsi Rinpoche's statements here. The seller, by virtue of the fact that he or she is engaging in a commercial activity with respect to the Buddha Jewel (i.e., making a living from selling), is seen as mistreating the image and inevitably incurs negative karma. Buyers, however, so long as they use the object for religious practice, incur no infraction. See Jamgön Kongtrul Karma Lodrö Chökyi Senge (1977). This same position may also be seen in Chandra L. Reedy's article, "Religious and Ethical Issues in the Study and Conservation of Tibetan Sculpture." Reedy quotes Geshé Thupten Gyatso as condemning the seller of Buddhist sacred objects and not the buyer: "The people who sell the article desecrate it. They commit the bad action (karma) of abandoning Buddha's teaching. But the one who buys the object has no fault, and in fact has accumulated merit in doing so. There is also

nothing wrong with displaying it in the museum; many people will obtain virtue by seeing it, remembering it, hearing the name of the deity depicted, and touching it" (quoted in Reedy 1992, 46).

49. One finds similar presentations in *The Jewelled Staircase* by Geshé Thupten Wangyal (1901–1983), whose description of the refuge meditation includes the purification of obscurations associated with "making a livelihood" from selling Buddha images and scriptures (1986, 101). Likewise, in *The Joyful Path of Good Fortune*, the lamrim commentary by Geshé Kelsang Gyatso (b. 1931), the refuge meditation removes impurities associated with "selling statues of Buddhas for our own financial gain" (Gyatso 1995, 59).

50. For more by Venerable Thubten Chodron on this topic, see her discussion of the forty-six auxiliary bodhisattva vows, especially her commentary to number 12 regarding "wrong livelihoods" under the heading "Selling Dharma Items as Right Livelihood," given at the Dharma Friendship Foundation in 1993 (Chodron 2003). See also "Guidelines for the Practice of Refuge" (2011) and "The Practice of Refuge: Taking Refuge, Part 9 of 10" (1992).

51. For an in-depth discussison of Lama Zopa's views on the topic of selling holy objects, see "Lama Tsongkhapa Guru Yoga (Gaden Lha Gyäma)" (1986) on the Lama Yeshe Wisdom Archive, http://www.lamayeshe.com/index.php?sect=article&id=233&chid=345.

52. See also FPMT's *Foundation Store Policy Regarding Dharma Items* and its *Report on Foundation Store Dharma Income 2018*, https://fpmt.org/wp-content/uploads/organization/pdf/DharmaIncomeReport.pdf.

53. One can also find examples of the influence of Lama Zopa's views on the issue of selling religious objects among some Dharma-related organizations. For example, the Tsa Tsa Studio in Richmond, California, which was a retailer of *tsa tsas* (small clay images of buddhas or deities) as well as a center for tsa tsa practice, stated the following on its website before it went out of operation: "The Tsa Tsa Studio is a center devoted to promoting sacred art and the practice of making tsa tsas, one of the preliminary practices given to many students of Tibetan Buddhism. As instructed by our precious teacher, Lama Zopa Rinpoche, it is important that Buddhists retain their refuge vows and see tsa tsas as manifestations of the Buddha. Our teacher was also very clear that from our side we do not sell the Buddha, but rather we suggest an appropriate donation that goes to support our center and pay for materials. We respectfully request that you treat the tsa tsas made at our Studio as holy objects when you offer them to others, and that whenever possible you use the proceeds to support Dharma activities" (URL was http://www.tsatsastudio.org/trade.htm, but it is no longer available). For examples of Lama Zopa's influence on the way Dharma bookstores and shops operate, see the Kadampa Center, "Is It Appropriate to 'Sell' the Dharma?" (http://www.kadampa-center.org/faq/it-appropriate-sell-dharma), and the Chenresig Institute's gift shop (http://chenrezig.com.au/dharmashop/).

54. For the complete statement on the mission of Kechara Paradise, the retail outlets, see http://www.kechara.com/?p=1678.

55. An interesting statement posted on Tsem Tulku's YouTube channel (www.tsem rinpoche.com/you-tube-channel) describes the rationale of the retail Dharma outlets and suggests the "skillful means" involved. It also contains a statement about the use of the profits earned: "Having Dharma stores makes the Dharma and Dharma items easily accessible to everyone. This is for two reasons—we can open more stores everywhere and in a shopping centre, people don't feel so intimidated about the prospect of walking in and asking questions. They can see the store as a source of knowledge, or they can also see the store as a shop selling works of art. Because they feel more comfortable approaching Dharma this way, they are more likely to be open-minded and feel ready to learn and ask questions. Also, having Buddha statues all over Malaysia in this way, blesses many people who walk by the outlets in the shopping malls. At the Kechara Paradise outlets, people can invite home Buddha statues and other holy items to bless their environment. They can also ask the staff any questions about the items, for example what Lama Tsongkhapa's hat represents or how to use a singing bowl. For Rinpoche, the Kechara Paradise outlets is [*sic*] not about making money. Any income made in the outlets is put back into the Kechara organisation to support our Dharma activities. People who come are not forced to buy anything—in fact, one of the comments we often get is that people are made to feel welcome, and can stay and talk for many hours without being asked to buy anything. This is because Rinpoche only wishes to share the Dharma with others." See paragraph 4 of the descriptive text that accompanies the video "Monlam Goes Kechara Paradise @ Viva Home" (https://www.youtube.com/watch?v=Dn2_CL67FPw).

56. Two of the largest Western publishers of Tibetan Buddhist books began in the 1980s. Snow Lion, which has recently been acquired by Shambhala Publications and no longer exists as a separate entity, opened its doors in 1980, and Wisdom Publications began in 1983. Shambhala Publications began significantly earlier, in 1969, with the publication of Chögyam Trungpa's *Meditation in Action,* but it also publishes other non-Tibetan Buddhist titles. While Snow Lion never claimed to be a nonprofit organization, up until its merger with Shambhala it had probably done more than any other publisher to spread Tibetan Buddhist teachings and assist Tibet and Tibetans. Wisdom Publications and the New York–based Tsadra Foundation, which began in 2000 and publishes Tibetan Buddhist texts in English and French, do identify themselves as nonprofit entities.

57. Once again, these statements are found within a larger discussion on taking refuge as the entrance to practice.

58. A similar statement made by the Dalai Lama at a Kālacakra initiation is also reported in Moran (2004, 79). According to Moran, "When the Dalai Lama taught and bestowed the Kalachakra initiation over a week-long period in Los Angeles in 1989, the $150 fee was, His Holiness explained, to defer the costs of his monastic entourage's travel, the renting of the Santa Monica auditorium and other 'overhead' costs. It is wrong, he said, to profit from the Dharma." Another transcript from this same Kālacakra initiation reveals a similar response from the Dalai Lama to a question about the ethics of charging for religious teachings. According to the transcript, one audience member asked, "Is it appropriate for Dharma centers to charge for

teachings in order to support its directors living expenses or to acquire property?" To this, the Dalai Lama answered, "Money gained through religious activity is a wrong livelihood. It is considered very bad to sell the Dharma. If this is what is happening then this is completely mistaken. For practical reasons you need money. Given human weakness even if at the beginning there is sincere motivation as times passes [*sic*] it can very easily be spoiled. Religious centers must be very cautious. This is very important." See Tenzin Gyatso (1989).

59. Other comments from contemporary Tibetan Buddhist teachers, which are not as specific as regards the use of the monies earned from the sale of Dharma objects, but which nevertheless reject such activities as a form of wrong livelihood, may indeed be found. For example, more recently, a work by Gyumed Khensur Lobsang Jampa (b. 1937), entitled *The Easy Path: Illuminating the First Panchen Lama's Secret Instructions,* a translation and commentary of a seventeenth-century lamrim work by the First Panchen Lama, Lobsang Chökyi Gyaltsen, condemns such actions as karmically negative and describes them as those which are in need of purification (2013, 39). Furthermore, he provides additional statements on this topic within a discussion titled "Practicing between Meditation Sessions." Commenting on the Panchen Lama's root text, which prescribes, among other things, that a practitioner should strive in the yogas of bathing and eating, Khensur Rinpoche writes, "Food should be acquired ethically, which means not purchasing it with money obtained through wrong livelihood or by selling holy objects" (85).

60. The issue of profit earned from selling or pawning religious goods and its use for personal expenses was understood as an important factor from earlier times. Recall the statements by Machik Labdrön which condemn those who achieve wealth and food from the wrong livelihood [of selling] statues, as well as the famous story of Kyergangpa in which the consumption of food paid for with the money earned from selling a text is a central theme. However, the difference between these statements and more modern ones is that the modern statements overtly accept the selling of religious goods under particular conditions—that is, if profits are reinvested, if they are used to further propagate the Dharma, and so on. These conditions are noticeably absent from earlier statements.

61. One exception to this notion may be Tsem Tulku's organization Kechara, which has indicated that the proceeds from all of its activities, activities that include the sale of religious objects, go to charitable causes, including the feeding of the homeless. Of course, this would likely be a controversial prospect for those who maintain that such profits are polluted and that such activity would constitute "eating the ransom" (*sku glud la za ba*) from the sale of religious images and scriptures. However, it is not entirely clear that Kechara does this.

3. THE EXCHANGE OF BUDDHIST OBJECTS IN TIBET UP TO THE CULTURAL REVOLUTION

1. Appadurai adopts this notion from Igor Kopytoff (1986).

2. Tibetan historical accounts of economic activities are scarce. It is believed that

any such records that may have existed were destroyed after the Chinese takeover of Tibet (van Spengen 2000, 137). Other than the artistic activities of important religious figures, we also know very little about the lives and dealings of individual Tibetan artisans (Lo Bue 2003, 188).

3. The remaining five of the six activities that serve as antidotes to nonvirtuous actions are: (1) "reciting the names of the Tathāgatas," (2) "reciting *dhāraṇī* mantras," (3) "reciting sūtras," (4) "meditating on voidness," and (5) "presenting offerings" (Pabongka 1990, 209–10). The *Dharma Sections Entitled "Discourses on the Genuine Benefits of Establishing Images of the Sublime Tathāgata"* (*Tathāgatabimba-parivarta* or *'Phags pa de bzhin gshegs pa'i gzugs brnyan bzhag pa'i phan yon yang dag par brjod pa zhes bya ba'i chos kyi rnam grangs*) is the original source which describes the merit of offering an image upon which Śāntideva draws (Bendall and Rouse 1971, 169).

4. *Gsal rgyal gyi tshigs bcad,* Sde dge bka' 'gyur, Mdo sde *sa*, fol. 201b.3–201b.4. See also Gega Lama (1983, 52 and 58).

5. Gega Lama refers to a number of sources for his *Principles of Tibetan Art.* Among these are the principle text *Music to Delight a Clear Intellect* (*Blo gsal dgyes pa'i rol mo*), which, according to Gega, represents a synthesis of ideas found in works by Mikyö Dorje, Butön Rinchen Drup, Menla Dhondrup, Sangye Gyatso, and Trengkawa Lodrö Zangpo. He also draws upon *Beautiful Ornaments of the Arts* (*Bzo rig mdses pa'i kha rgyan*) by Lobzang Damchö Gyatso, and *Radiant Sun* (*Rab gsal nyi ma*) by Mipham Choklay Namgyal, as well as oral teachings.

6. *Rab tu gnas pa mdor bsdus pa'i rgyud,* Sde dge bka' 'gyur, Rgyud 'bum *ta*, fol. 150a.1–150a.2 and 150a.3. See also Gega Lama (1983, 55 and 60).

7. Sman bla don grub, *Bde bar gshegs pa'i sku gzugs kyi tshad kyi rab tu byed pa yid bzhin nor bu* (1983, fol. 32b.1–32b.2). This passage is also found in Thubten Legshay Gyatsho's *Gateway to the Temple* (1979, 75), a work written in exile as a manual to Tibetan monastic customs, arts, building, and celebrations.

8. Ngag dbang mkhas grub, *Lha 'bri ba'i man ngag lag len du sbyar ba'i gsung rtsom gyi 'grel pa,* in The Collected Works of Nag dbang mkhas grub, Kyai rdor mkhan po of Urga (1974, vol. 3, fol. 6a.3–6a.5). See also Tanaka (1997, 952).

9. *'Phags pa 'jam dpal gyi rtsa ba'i rgyud,* Lha sa bka' 'gyur, Rgyud *tha*, fols. 123b.6–124a.4. See also Glenn Wallis's translation of parts of this passage (2002, 119–20).

10. According to Kapsner and Wynniatt-Husey (1991), a primary source for the religious and behavioral guidelines for artists and patrons derives from the work of Menla Dhondrup, developer of the Menri school of thangka painting, which dates back to 1440 CE. According to these authors, "Menla Dhondrup went on to revise the proportions and composition of religious figures as well as developing new pigments. In addition he defined the religious requirements of both the artist and the patron, demonstrated the need for accurate painting, showing the consequences of inaccurate work and gave instruction in various methods of painting" (291).

11. I owe this bit of insight to Glenn Mullin from an email conversation in 2009. From the side of the potential patron, the desire for new images specifically to replace old ones was virtually nonexistent. Tibetans generally kept images and handed them

down in their families, repairing them only when necessary rather than obtaining new ones—the antiquity or aesthetic quality of an image paling in importance to the meaning associated with it (Dagyab 1977, 28; Lopez 1998, 154).

12. This general view of past transactions between artists and patrons is supported by Loden Sherap Dagyab, who writes that "artists worked either in their own homes, or else got board, and sometimes lodging, and a fee for doing the work at a monastery or in a private household" (1977, 1:28).

13. That common folk and even nomads owned sacred objects is also documented by Thargyal (2007, 127), Charles Bell ([1928], 1994, 70), Yuthok (1990, 66), and by Geshé Sopa in his autobiography. There, Geshé Sopa mentions that "even ordinary families had a hanging scroll, called a *thangka,* or an altar in their houses" (Sopa and Donnelly 2012, 18).

14. That image makers were well paid is the predominant view. However, this stands in contrast to Erberto Lo Bue's comments on artists in his essay "Scholars, Artists and Feasts" (2003, 188). In this work Lo Bue argues that government artists conscripted during the construction of the Potala Palace worked without remuneration, owing taxes to the state. While it is true that the Tibetan government and the monasteries engaged in corvée practices, it is unlikely that corvée labor was the chief mode of production. I believe it is problematic to assume that these artisans—many of whom were not even Tibetan—worked without receiving compensation, at the very least in the form of food and shelter.

15. The idea that a painter ought to fulfill the requests of poorer patrons is still prevalent today. Regarding these requests, another older painter in Rebkong who had been painting for twenty-five years, stated, "My teacher advised me that there are so many different kinds of sponsors—those who are rich and poor. It is not usual, but sometimes you encounter some poor people who ask you to make a thangka. In this case you cannot refuse because they are poor. You should make a thangka anyway in this case."

16. Many of my informants during my fieldwork in Lhasa in 2006 offered similar depictions of what had transpired between the patron and artisan in the past. For example, one clay statue maker who worked from his home just off the Barkhor, referring to these transactions, remarked, "at that time, the price of making [statues] depended on the patron's financial condition. There was no specific price." Another artist, also a clay statue maker, added, "the patron of a statue would bring butter, cheese, and meat when requesting [the artisan] to make a clay statue. There was no bargaining system at that time" (i.e., in these transactions). Although framed in a negative light, a 2013 online article also confirms these findings. According to the piece, one thangka painter named Norbu, referring to the way in which transactions for thangkas took place in the past, proclaimed that "there was no fixed price for a piece of Thangka. If people like[d] it, they [could] buy it at any price, for example, 100, 200 or 300. Nowadays, it's different. The paintings are charged according to the materials we use. More golden pigments, more expensive" (Himalayanglacier.com, "Shanghai Volunteers Work to Promote Thangka Paintings," para. 3, http://www.himalayan

glacier.com/blog/shanghai-volunteers-work-to-promote-thangka-paintings.html; first accessed on CCTV-News.com, December 31, 2013).

17. This is David Jackson's translation. The Tibetan of Thubten Legshay Gyatsho reads: *ces pa ltar ston mo ar ston nang bzhin 'dzugs ston bar ston grol ston rnams skabs skabs de dang der gang rgyas gtong srol/ gtsug lag khang lta bu'i lha'i gtso bor mtshon pas spyan dbye'i skabs lha gtso bo der mjal dar dang de nyin spyan ston dang/ gzhan yang gser ston/ bkrag chang sogs gtong srol yod/.*

18. Yet another account of this form of compensation, this time to smiths for the creation of monastic horns (*dung chen*) for Sakya Monastery, is recorded in *Tibetan Voices: A Traditional Memoir* (Harris and Wardle 1996). The account itself appears to be recalling a time before the 1950s, in the months or years preceding the Chinese invasion of Eastern Tibet from where many of the smiths hailed. Nonetheless, the process of payment described here may have been a typical scenario with respect to religious goods produced for a monastery: "At the end of the summer the smiths had finished six hundred lamp containers and they planned to make the remaining four hundred the following summer at Lhagyal. We held a three-day party in their honor. The long horns had a gorgeous sound. They were very, very good. We thought the men had done a commendable job and they were paid accordingly. Some of the smiths took their pay in yaks, horses, tea, and silk material. We also gave each of them personal gifts. Monks from Lhagyal escorted the smiths back to their homes in various parts of Derge. Some of them sent presents back to us, saying they had enjoyed their work and considered it a contribution that would serve religion for centuries. It was a sad parting. Many of the smiths felt that soon they would be fighting the Chinese and they asked my husband to pray for their protection" (85).

19. That certain symbolic items such as the yellow brocade silk worn by officials were off limits from common merchants is indicated in Rebecca French's book on Tibetan law, *The Golden Yoke* (2002, 34). More research needs to be done to determine whether any of the ancient law codes, such as the Neudong code or the Tsang code, contain any restrictions against selling religious objects.

20. The Younghusband Expedition was an invasion of Tibet by British Indian forces led by Francis Younghusband. It was intended to set up, or rather, force, trade relations between Britain and Tibet. Edmund Candler was an English journalist who witnessed British troops storm and eventually take Gyanste.

21. The literary accounts of these authors are also supported by photographic documentation of the Barkhor marketplace from this period, which suggests an absence of religious images in particular. In "The Tibet Album," an online collection of British photography in Central Tibet from 1920 to 1950, which contains over six thousand images, of the 125 photographs of the Barkhor marketplace and its various shops and vendors, not a single photograph or caption depicts the presence of paintings or statues. See http://tibet.prm.ox.ac.uk/

22. That this particular historical period of translation involved commercial processes is also supported by Alex McKay in *The History of Tibet* (2003, 2–3) and by Snellgrove and Richardson in *A Cultural History of Tibet* (2003, 199).

23. According to the *Blue Annals,* these "golden books" included the *Vajrabhairava-tantra,* the *Kṛṣṇayamāritantra,* the *Eight Tantras of Saṃvara,* the *Six Books of Nag po,* the *Lū yi pa* (*Śrīvajrasattvanāmasādhana*), the *'Jam dpal* (*Bhaṭṭārakamañjuśrīyamā ripūjākramavidhi-nāma*), and the *Zal gñis ma* (*Vajravārahī, Śrī Tattvajñānasiddhi*) (Roerich 1996, 377).

24. Other major monastic printing centers included Narthang (Snar thang), associated with the first Tibetan canon (Kangyur and Tengyur) compiled in the thirteenth century and later indexed by Butön in the fourteenth century. The Narthang edition of the canon was reprinted between 1730 and 1732. Other major centers of printing included Shöl printing house, located beneath the Potala Palace in Lhasa, and Lithang in Kham. It should be mentioned, however, that most monasteries in Tibet had some capacity for printing.

25. This process of intermonastic distribution is also believed to have occurred without the goal of monetary gain. According to the secretary for the Tibetan government-in-exile's Department of Religion and Culture, "Several famous traditional printing houses like the Narthang Parkhang, Lhasa Shöl Parkhang, Dege Pharkhang, etc. printed texts from wooden plates and distributed [them] to the monastery concerned who placed the order. These printing houses used to charge reasonable prices for the materials and services to run the same. They were purely established as a not-for-profit unit." Email correspondence received October 9, 2012, from the Department of Religion and Culture, Central Tibetan Administration, Gangchen Kyishong, Dharamsala, India.

26. John Clarke has also described the process of printing in this way. Writing of the famous printing house at Narthang, he states, "When a copy of a book was to be made, the patron was expected to supply the paper and the monks, working in teams, did the printing" (1997, 60). A similar account of this process was also provided to me by one monk from Kumbum Monastery. He explained, "In the past, for instance, with books, if you really wanted to have something printed, you went to the printing house, brought the materials, and you printed by yourself and you got the book. And as times have changed, they take a *yön* (salary or fee) for printing. In the past it was like that."

27. Other missionary collectors active in Tibet during the early twentieth century included Robert Ekvall, Carter D. Holton, and Robert Roy Service. All of their collections were eventually acquired by the Newark Museum (Reynolds 1999, 15).

28. Even during the late nineteenth and early twentieth centuries there are those who noted the reluctance of Tibetans to part with their sacred objects, observations which further reinforce the notion that such activities were not a typical occurrence. For example, according to George Roerich, "those who have collected Tibetan paintings know how difficult it is to obtain good specimens. A Tibetan will never part with a thaṅ-gka, especially if it is consecrated by some high lama and has the imprint of the lama's hand on its reverse side. . . . To induce a Tibetan to sell a painting to non-buddhists or, as they are called in the Tibetan language, 'outsiders' (phyi-rol-pa, pron. či-rol-pa), is almost a hopeless task. Most of the paintings found in European

public and private collections have been thrown on the market as the result of recent wars and upheavals in Tibet, which brought the destruction of several lamaseries and the ruin of rich families, which were in possession of numerous religious paintings" (1925, 20). Similarly, the reluctance of Tibetans to sell religious goods has been noted by William Gill (1880, 2:233) and Flora Shelton, the wife of Albert Shelton (Wissing 2004, 144; see also 111–12).

29. Of course, it should also be noted that a great deal of what ended up in many European museums and galleries was not that which was "purchased" from Tibetans but rather directly looted, especially as a result of the Younghusband Expedition of 1903–4. Motivated by its desire for a trade agreement with the government in Lhasa, which it eventually secured by force, the expedition elicited the widespread looting of monasteries in Gyanste and Lhasa by British troops. Large amounts of sacred artworks and texts (including manuscripts) were shipped to India and eventually sold off to British museums and collectors. According to Michael Carrington's article "Officers, Gentlemen, and Thieves: The Looting of Monasteries during the 1903/4 Younghusband Mission to Tibet" (2003), in all, over four hundred mule loads of objects left Tibet for Britain and India during this period.

30. The writing of Karma Sumdhon Paul in Richardus (1998) gives us some reason to believe that what may have been perceived as selling was, in fact, exchange by offering. On this topic, he writes, "In Tibet and rDo-rje-gling [Darjeeling] I have come across Buddhist monks who sell precious images containing a gzungs-cugs [mantras placed inside statues for consecration] saying, 'I'm not going to sell it to you, but if you give me a reward, I will hand it to you as a present'" (135). While this monk may have used this language as a strategy to circumvent religious proscriptions against selling statues, we may also observe here how the selling of some religious objects may have been misconstrued, for in this case it is a nondescript donation or offering, and not a price, that is asked for. This kind of request for a donation is employed today by organizations affiliated with FPMT, for example, and is seen as perfectly legitimate.

31. Tucci notes that merchants sold books at fairs and festivals but describes this activity as minor and mostly consisting of less scholastic works. He writes, "The retailers of books thronged to the scene of fairs and festivals. Squatting on the ground they laid out their books before them on pieces of material and offered them to the public. They had had them printed in monasteries on their own account, and sold them on these special occasions for a modest profit. Naturally they only stocked up with works of interest to the laity—lives of the saints, accounts of visions of the other world, guides to holy places—but sometimes I have also seen more exacting works, as diffcult as Tsongkhapa's *Lamrim-chhenmo*" (1967, 199).

32. A most curious case of the selling of Tibetan religious objects is found in Paul Hackett's book *Theos Bernard, the White Lama: Tibet, Yoga, and American Religious Life* (2012). Hackett notes, based on information provided by Bernard, that in order to raise money for modernization efforts, the Lhasa government, during the flight of the Ninth Panchen Lama to Mongolia and China in 1923, seized the Panchen Lama's estates and sold off parts of his properties, which included thangkas and stat-

ues. Much of what was seized was eagerly purchased by European and American entrepreneurs for resale to museums. This story is also found in Nicholas Roerich's book *Shambhala: In Search of the New Era,* originally published in 1930. Roerich, who clearly saw such acts (and Tibetan Buddhism for that matter) as an aberration, writes, "Very recently the Lhassan government put on the market sacred objects which belonged to the Tashi Lama. Into the hands of traders passed the rare ancient Tankas and other sacred images blessed by high priests. Thus was this Blessing regarded by the government which claims to be religious! The Maharajah of Sikhim told us with great pain of this act of barbarism" (1990, 57). If true, such actions, while obviously counter to religious ideals, again, might best be viewed in light of the events of the time—the impending threat from the Chinese, the Thirteenth Dalai Lama's desire to improve the Tibetan military, and the refusal of the Panchen Lama to contribute to these efforts (Goldstein 1989, 110), a situation which would surely be deemed in Appadurai's terms as "a cultural crisis."

33. Regarding the commodification of religious texts in Tibet, Hildegard Diemberger has noted that while texts entered the commodity sphere, their sale would have been a controversial issue. She writes, "More research needs to be done to discover how and when books started to become a regularly traded commodity. Printing undoubtedly facilitated this process but did not determine it. Also, even when books came on the market, through their use as sacred objects they were likely to be swiftly removed from the sphere of normally tradable commodities. They would instead become part of the category of objects for which market transactions were considered to be morally contentious" (2012, 21). Although the content of all books in Tibet was generally religious in nature, one wonders whether certain books, such as temple and monastery guides, prayer books, or those books that were not considered the word of the Buddha, held a different status in the marketplace and were permitted to be sold. One also wonders whether the sale of books at stalls in the Barkhor market was more typical of Lhasa than elsewhere in Tibet. With Lhasa being a major metropolis and a main hub for religious training—being the home of the *densa sum,* the three great monasteries of Sera, Drepung, and Ganden, which collectively housed and trained thousands of monks—it may have been the case that one was simply more likely to find booksellers there.

34. The figure of 1.2 million is, of course, disputed by the Chinese government. Nevertheless, it is a figure that is repeated in popular publications and by various pro-Tibet campaigns in the West. According to Patrick French, this statistic can be traced to the mid-1980s and to an attempt by the Tibetan government-in-exile to come up with a figure in order to satisfy the demands of Western supporters. It was later used in official government publications and in the Dalai Lama's speeches, and was even supported by the US House of Representatives in a State Department authorization bill. According to French, and based on his firsthand research of the relevant documents in Dharamsala, the number of Tibetans who died as a direct result of the Chinese invasion is likely much lower. For his discussion of this issue, see French (2004, chapter 24).

35. Aaron Raverty (1997) also observes that the Chinese authorities eventually went from destroying texts to selling them.

36. This has also been recognized by Valrae Reynolds in her book *From the Sacred Realm* (1999), in which she writes, "The political events of the second half of the twentieth century and the exodus of Tibetans from their homeland have brought Tibetan artifacts into the commercial market in quantities unknown before 1959" (19).

37. According to Chandra Reedy, many of the statues that were brought out of Tibet and that wound up in museums and galleries had their contents removed, an act that is normally seen by Tibetans as a desecration of the image. In her article, "The Opening of Consecrated Tibetan Bronzes with Interior Contents: Scholarly, Conservation, and Ethical Considerations" (1991), she argues that the little information that is gained by removing the contents of Tibetan Buddhist statues does not justify their opening. Furthermore, she argues for increased sensitivity to Tibetan religious sentiments with respect to handling religious images.

38. Personal communication, Glenn Mullin, September 8, 2008.

39. At least one account of an attempt to bury sacred goods can found in the autobiography of Ani Pachen, *Sorrow Mountain: The Journey of a Tibetan Warrior Nun* (Pachen and Donnelley 2000, 140). These hidden artifacts have become part of a religious revival movement that centers on their recovery. See Germano (1998).

40. Those who sold religious objects from "old Tibet," such as thangkas and statues, and who reinvested this money for business purposes are, to this day, viewed somewhat disparagingly in Tibetan society. During my fieldwork in Lhasa in 2006, several people with whom I made an acquaintance were quick to point out who within the neighborhood had done this. Usually such people were quite successful.

41. An interesting distinction can be made here. While Tibetans have been known to compare the activity of those who sell religious goods with the activity of butchers, it is noteworthy that even while one eats the meat of a butcher, he is not considered spiritually polluted in the way that one may become so by eating food or consuming drink that is prepared by a seller of religious goods. The comparison seems to be made merely because butchers are considered low caste and are believed to be performing polluting work.

42. There are some indications that Chinese officials and entrepreneurs were engaging in the sale of Tibetan religious objects even before this time. Jamyang Sakya reports in her autobiography that pictures were taken of her husband, Dagchen Rinpoche, by Chinese photographers and sold at government shops in Jyekundo and surrounding areas (Sakya and Emery 1990, 153–54). In addition, Adhe Tapontsang (aka Ama Adhe) reports in her memoir, *The Voice That Remembers* (1997), that her father, Kunga Gyaltsen Shivatsang, when invited to mainland China for a factory tour in 1953, witnessed thangkas and statues for sale in the markets (50).

43. It may be objected here that even organizations in Dharamsala, such as the Norbulingka Institute, the Tibetan Children's Village (TCV), or the Federation of Tibetan Cooperatives in India (FTCI), sell religious objects, activities which take place apart from the Chinese context. However, the sale of religious images by these

institutions should be distinguished from individually owned and operated, for-profit businesses. The Norbulingka Institute was founded in order to preserve and promote Tibetan art and culture in exile. TCV, likewise, is a government-affiliated nonprofit organization responsible for some ten thousand students. FTCI is also a registered nonprofit, which is involved in a number of charitable activities. Therefore, there is a clear difference between these institutions and privately owned, for-profit businesses. The selling activities of these particular organizations appear to fall into what might be considered the acceptable sale of religious goods as articulated by some contemporary Tibetan teachers; that is, it is not the act of selling itself which is necessarily negative, but the profits and the use of the profits which is the crucial factor to consider. For statements on the nonprofit status of these organizations, see http://www.tcvcraft.org/images/content/handicraftbrochure.pdf, https://www.norbulingka.org, and http://tibeteshop.com.

4. THE SALE OF BUDDHIST OBJECTS IN AMDO

1. According to Appadurai, a commodity context "refers to the variety of *social* arenas, within or between *cultural* units, that help link the commodity candidacy of a thing to the commodity phase of its career" (1986, 15).

2. During my fieldwork in Lhasa in 2006, one young Tibetan merchant, who lived part of the time in Lhasa and part of the time in Kathmandu, showed me two very large storage rooms full of Buddhist statues produced in Nepal. This was in addition to his main showroom on the Barkhor. See Catanese (2007).

3. See, for example, Kolås and Thowsen (2005, 52–53). For other claims that Tibetans largely funded the rebuilding efforts in Amdo, see Linrothe (2001, 15) and Marshall and Cooke (1997, 2137). Kolås and Thowsen have found that many monasteries denied receiving any government funding for restoration, and most amounts received from the government were either exaggerated in official reports or were merely symbolic amounts (2005, 52). They also report that government support was received by larger monasteries deemed important to tourism and by those important to the construction of the Chinese historical narrative. For example, the government contributed aid to Kumbum, which, in 1962, was labeled "one of China's foremost national, cultural, and historical sites" (55). Funding was also given to three temples in Tsolho and Jyekundo (Yushu), TAP, one of which is associated with the Chinese princess Wencheng, known to be one of two brides of the Tibetan king Songsten Gampo (Srong btsan sgam po, r. 617–50). The government has maintained in official histories that the beginning of Chinese reign in Tibet began with this marriage (55). In addition, Stevenson reports that a significant amount of financial support has also come from Hui and Salar businessmen (2002, 210).

4. The exact locus of the early commercial activity in religious goods in Tibet after the passing of religious reforms remains obscure. Yet, as evident from reports of the presence of Nepalese statues in Tibetan markets early on, it is possible that, at least in part, the commercialization of Buddhist religious goods was introduced

to Tibet via Nepal. By the 1980s, Newar and Tibetan artists were already engaged in an artistic renaissance of their own in places like Kathmandu, supplying religious images and artwork for the building of numerous Tibetan monasteries and temples there. In addition, some reports indicate that Nepalese and some Tibetan refugees had already been supplying tourists with religious objects, including thangkas, since the mid-1960s (see Meulenbeld 2001, ix). It is therefore possible that entrepreneurs from Nepal arrived in Tibet in the early to mid-1980s, following economic reforms, seeking new markets and fulfilling the demand for new religious objects.

5. The manufacture of statues in Tibet by Tibetans themselves is still relatively limited and small scale. Although there were casters of statues as well as repoussé (pounded metal) workers living in and around Lhasa in 2006, most of these images were commissioned by monasteries and were never destined for the open market. The vast majority of the statuary for sale in shops in both Lhasa and Amdo comes from Nepal or mainland China. In Lhasa, while an effort to organize local statue makers to create a "made in Tibet" brand of statues for tourists was undertaken by the nonprofit organization Dropenling (an affiliate of the Tibet Artisan Initiative), as of 2008 this effort had stalled due to organizational issues and difficulties with the availability of artists who were working on their own commissions. The civil unrest in Lhasa in 2008 dealt a further blow to these efforts, as tourism dropped significantly, affecting the livelihoods of artists. Dropenling Handicraft Center, whose aim is to assist local artisan communities by providing a crafts market for the tourism industry, began in Lhasa and has now opened a second location in Zhongdian (Shangri-la), Yunnan Province.

6. Unfortunately, Stevenson provides no details as to whether these were sold on the streets of Rebkong or exported to distant locations.

7. In an unpublished version of Reynolds's article, she writes that one of her informants started his business at that time with five hundred thangkas that he sent to Shanghai. Yet, this informant did not consider the full-blown commercialization of thangkas to have begun much before 2000. The published version of Reynolds's work omits this detail.

8. Among Tibetan merchants of religious goods, two explained that Chinese merchants were the first to offer Buddhist statues and other religious paraphernalia in the marketplace. One Tibetan shop owner in Rebkong explained that when he opened his shop in 1997, there were indeed Chinese merchants selling Dharma goods in the area. However, he was the only person to suggest this in Rebkong. Another young man in Xining who ran a store near the bus station likewise explained that some Chinese merchants from Sichuan were the first to offer such items in the wholesale market.

9. The quite recent appearance of painting shops which are open direct to consumers is no doubt in part a response to the increased promotion of tourism by state and local governments but is also driven by the successes of established external markets which resell locally produced thangkas at much higher prices. Several painters noted

that one of the reasons behind the opening of their shops was in order to cut out the middlemen who buy and then resell their paintings for high prices and reap the financial benefits of their artistic work.

10. Huangnan is the name of the autonomous prefecture in which Rebkong County is located.

11. Epstein and Wenbin (1998) also describe the government's goal of economic development through tourism in Rebkong. In their work on the revival of the *luröl* ritual (*glu rol*, lit. "music" or "music festivity"), they note that Rebkong "is, for example, an 'open area' for foreign visitors which already hosts a substantial, if not yet booming, tourist trade that is actively promoted by both state and local interests. Although we do not have statistical evidence, we are under the impression that a not insubstantial portion of the area's income flows from tourism, and discussions with local leaders have led us to believe they are counting heavily on the development of the tourist trade to sustain and finance the area's development" (137).

12. Although it is suggested here by this informant, I have been unable to confirm the existence of other government-owned shops which sold thangkas beyond the Rebkong Art Gallery.

13. While only suggestive of the government's involvement in thangka painting and its role in establishing an external market, in an interesting anecdote, Eric McGuckin (1996) reports that as early as 1981 the central government established a painting institute in Lhasa and invited exiled Tibetan painters to teach as well as to produce thangka paintings. According to one of McGuckin's painter-informants in Dharamsala, a man who had accompanied his father to this institute as an apprentice, by 1986 orders for thangkas came from the Chinese and were carried out so that the government could "improve their image for tourists" (41). He continues, "They only did it for show. I am 100% sure of this, and not because I'm anti-Chinese" (41). Thus, according to McGuckin's informant, government authorities were intimately involved in thangka production, and commissions were carried out for political and/or tourist purposes.

14. According to several shopkeepers in the Tibetan market in Xining, Tibetans were first inspired to go into business there by a Tibetan woman who opened a restaurant in the market. According to one informant, she was motivated to create a place where Tibetans could gather in the market and communicate in their own language. Such a motivation suggests that Tibetan participation in this market was linked to notions of identity and community.

15. The Tibetan of this sign reads somewhat strangely and appears to be a Tibetan rendition of the Chinese.

16. Many of the shops west of Kumbum Monastery were open but nobody was inside, making it difficult to tell whether or not the owner was Tibetan. I did come across young Muslims who sold, among other things, thangkas. This activity appears to be inappropriate from the point of view of Islam. One cleric at Dongguan Mosque in Xining commented that those who sell these goods are not really Muslims.

17. During my fieldwork I encountered two instances of this: one appliqué thangka

maker in Rebkong was fulfilling an order of several thangkas for a local monastery. In another instance, a clay statue maker in Labrang was making a life-sized seated image of a recently deceased lama.

18. The Rongwo Gonpa gift shop did, however, sell a number of other religious items including *khatas* (*kha btags*, ceremonial scarves), *lung ta* (*rlung rta*, prayer flags) *zung shu* (*gzungs gzhug*, mantra rolls for inserting into statues), incense, malas or prayer beads, and ceramic vessels for burial in the ground, known as treasure vases, or *sa-chu* (*sa bcud bum pa*), which are said to make the earth safer and protect it from disaster. None of the religious items sold had Buddha images on them. They also sold other items such as snacks, drinks, and fireworks.

19. It is likely the case that monasteries have varying policies with respect to the sale of images of the Buddha. Whereas Rongwo Gonpa did not sell them, other eyewitness accounts have noted that monasteries such as Labrang did sell them. As I recall from my own visit to Samyé (Bsam yas) in Ü, Buddhist statues were, in fact, sold on the monastery grounds. And at Sera Monastery in Lhasa, one can purchase texts at a bookstore. It may be the case that the proceeds from these sales go back into providing more objects to the public and are not used for food or personal expenses. However, only further research can confirm this.

20. According to Fischer (2005), "drawing a rough line, 15 percent of Tibetans in all of China with secondary education or above in 2002 would account for those who are profiting from the current economic boom, while the 85 percent with no education or primary levels account for those who are struggling on the margins" (xvi).

21. More broadly, *guanxi* refers to the system of networks of influence and relationships between people and is a fundamental part of the functioning of Chinese society. These relationships involve mutual obligations in which, for example, a person may ask another for particular favors, such as resolving problems, finding jobs, etc. In turn, the requester is then obligated to return the favor in some way. Tibetans who know how to use *guanxi* also use it to their advantage at times.

22. Even in cases where Tibetans have received a high level of education and have attained Chinese fluency, ethnic discrimination appears to be yet another factor which has prevented Tibetans from entering into employment appropriate to their level of education. According to Reza Hasmath (2007), in Beijing, where ethnic minority education is well supported and subsidized, and where statistics have shown that university-educated minorities (including Tibetans) have even surpassed the Han in educational achievement, minorities such as Tibetans find it difficult to obtain suitable work in high-wage education-intensive (HWEI) employment, which remains dominated by the Han. Hasmath reports that although one would expect to see a significant representation of ethnic minorities in these higher-wage positions (given their level of education), paradoxically, "only 20% of the ethnic minority population work above the average pre-tax income in Beijing—which virtually comprises only HWEI employment sectors. The remaining 80% of the ethnic minority working population can be found in labour-intensive employment sectors (e.g. farming, forestry and animal; construction; manufacturing; and hotel, restaurant and re-

tail trade" (473). According to ethnographic interviews with university-educated ethnic minorities, Hasmath found that some 64% of his respondents who were employed explained that they were unable to advance because their superiors saw them as ethnic minorities, while 48% explained that they had difficulty finding jobs in the HWEI sectors because they were negatively stereotyped by their would-be employers (474–75). According to Hasmath, "the main stereotypes perceived were language difficulties and vast differences in (family and working) culture" (475).

23. According to an article by BBC News Asia-Pacific, estimates of the number of protesters ranged from one thousand to seven thousand (BBC News 2010).

24. Under the Regional National Autonomy Law for minority nationalities enacted in 1984, article 37 recommends that minority nationalities "shall, whenever possible, use textbooks in their own languages and use their languages as the media of instruction." For the full text of the Law of the People's Republic of China on Regional National Autonomy, see Constitution and Related Laws on the National People's Congress of the People's Republic of China Laws and Regulations Database (http://www.npc.gov.cn/englishnpc/Law/Frameset-index.html). The discrepancies between China's minority language policy and the actual implementation of this policy have been analyzed by Wang and Phillion (2009). The fact that language preservation and instruction in schools is written into the Chinese constitution may be one of the main reasons why Tibetans have felt that it is within their legal rights to publicly demonstrate against this policy.

25. The number of appliqué thangka manufacturers and workers in Nyentok Village in Rebkong who have dropped out of school or who have never attended school is probably much higher. I was informed by the owner of one appliqué manufacturing company that every household in the village was involved in manufacturing thangkas and that nobody in the village "goes outside" for work.

26. It should be noted that Tibetans who graduate high school or college but who cannot attain employment, as well as those who have been laid off from government employment, are actually encouraged to open their own businesses. According to Fischer, as a stipulation for receiving unemployment compensation (150 yuan per month), those students without jobs and former government employees are required to attend workshops on how to start businesses. This has caused further tensions, as many Tibetans do not want to assume work that is beneath their educational level, especially in commerce, which is stigmatized as a lower form of employment and one which has been the domain of Muslims (Fisher 2009a, 28–29).

27. Andrew Fischer notes that in Qinghai the phasing out of the job assignment system had been planned since 1997 and was implemented for college students and high school students in 2001 and 2002 respectively (2009a, 26).

28. According to Fischer, the GDP value of agriculture fell between 1998 and 2000 in Qinghai and Gansu largely because of a severe drought in 2000 and the fact that agricultural land had been taken out of use. Farmland and pastureland was also limited and under pressure from overuse and had made agriculture a slow growth sector

for new employment (Fischer 2005, 54–57). According to Goldstein's study of the TAR, there have been five factors provided by Tibetans which influenced their decision to seek nonfarm employment: (1) households cannot own land and therefore cannot increase yields or profits by purchasing more land; (2) there was a loss of land due to population increase, new housing and road construction, as well as flooding; (3) the prices for farmers' main products had not kept up with inflation; (4) the introduction of the market-based economy resulted in a decrease in government subsidies for education, health care, etc.; and (5) raising yields was not possible due to the already heavy use of fertilizers, nor was there any new land that could be opened for farming (Goldstein, Childs, and Wangdui 2008, 519).

29. Lustgarten's comments are directed mainly to the TAR with reference to the Qinghai-Lhasa railway project, but the same policies appear to have applied to Tibetan areas more broadly. For example, Susan Costello, writing of the context of Amdo, also mentions migration into Tibetan areas as a part of the Great Opening of the Western Regions campaign: "The discrepancy between rural and urban dwellers has been further exacerbated recently by the 'Great Opening of the Western Regions' (*Xibu da kaifa*) policy initiatives, one of which was to give significant pay increases to all salaried government workers, supposedly in the hope that it will trickle down and stimulate the private sector economy" (2002, 227). Kolås and Thowsen, likewise, acknowledge the existence of these same initiatives in Tibetan areas. In particular, they note that in Dechen (Diqing) TAP in Yunnan, preferential policies, including "tax concessions, priority in obtaining loans, and lenient land use fees," were to be implemented in order to speed up the process of the exploitation of resources and to open markets to outside investors, again, as a part of the "Develop the Western Region" campaign (2005, 164–66).

30. Goldstein, Childs, and Wangdui, in their study "'Going for Income' in Village Tibet" (2008), admit that most of the positions created by subsidies have indeed gone to out-of-province Chinese companies, but they argue that state development programs have not been entirely ineffective, for there has been a significant trickle-down effect with Tibetans assuming work as manual laborers, subcontractors, and skilled craftsmen (530). Fischer, however, sees this range of available employment opportunities as indicative of the very problems and exclusionary practices inherent in state development policies (see 2009b). Interestingly, Goldstein, Childs, and Wangdui do not deal with the issue of in-migration to Tibetan areas, and we are left to assume it has not played a factor in their study.

31. Fischer reports two cases in which Han workers were utilized in small-scale construction projects which could have utilized (and improved) the local expertise of Tibetans. In one case he found that houses which were built as a part of village relocation efforts in Nagchu Prefecture in the TAR used teams of Han construction workers from Sichuan. Similarly, in Lhasa, he reports that the renovations on the buildings facing the Potala, which were intended to give the buildings a "Tibetan style," utilized only migrant Han labor and not local labor (2005, 78).

32. Emily Yeh (2006) notes that the same phenomenon exists in Lhasa in the Barkhor marketplace, where Tibetan ownership of stores has gradually shifted to Chinese ownership. This trend, she remarks, is not necessarily linked to trends in tourism.

33. Of course, it is likely the case that at least some of this revenue from tourism does reach the local population. For example, in many monasteries, tickets are sold to tourists and a portion of this revenue goes to support the monasteries. In addition, at least some locals are able to capitalize on tourism as guides, vendors, etc. However, the main point of these authors is that the bulk of the tourism industry is either state-owned or operated by larger, privately owned Chinese tourism companies (many of which are owned by government officials), and absent of an affirmative-action-like policy that would either hire Tibetans for related positions or assist Tibetans in establishing businesses, the revenue from these enterprises tends not to accumulate locally but remotely.

34. It is interesting to note that in Goldstein, Childs, and Wangdui's article "'Going for Income' in Village Tibet" (2008) there is no discussion of *yartsa gunbu* as contributing to rural Tibetans' supplementary income. This may be due to a low incidence of the fungus around Shigatse. According to Daniel Winkler (2008b, 295), the distribution area for *yartsa gunbu* does not reach Shigatse proper.

35. According to a September 2013 report in *China Daily,* the cultivation of caterpillar fungus has declined considerably in recent years and is projected to die out in the next twenty years due to overexploitation. See *China Daily* (2013).

36. Winkler (2008a) observes that there is a general taboo against harvesting *yartsa gunbu* that stems from the belief that one should not disturb the earth spirits. He notes that Tibetans, out of economic necessity, have done away with the general rule that one cannot dig the earth, yet they appear to continue to observe this proscription on sacred mountains (29). This negotiation might be compared to Tibetans' sale of religious goods. Now the selling of religious objects is becoming an increasingly common practice, yet selling consecrated objects such as statues and thangkas or old, pre-1959 objects is still considered off limits by most vendors.

37. *Mu* is a Chinese term for the measurement of an area of land. According to my research, each *mu* is 666.6 square meters. Therefore, according to this respondent, the average household owns a maximum of 2,666.4 square meters of land, which comes to about .66 acres. I assume here that this painter is referring to farming families and not to all Tibetans in Rebkong, for it appeared that not all Tibetan families in Rebkong owned plots of land. A fourth response of this kind came from a young painter in Kumbum, who explained, "Well, we make these [thangkas] because, in the past, [although] religious goods weren't sold, they are sold today because now you have a family, you have limited land to cultivate, now the market price is up. If you are going to buy a piece of clothing you are going to pay at least two hundred [yuan]. Selling thangkas is also partly to make money."

38. While this merchant did not sell statues or texts, he did sell thangkas, miniature stūpas, and various other kinds of religious articles.

39. Upon following up with my interpreter in February 2012, the building of the piazza had not yet taken place.

40. One exception may be Kumbum, where monks are said to receive salaries. The monastery has long been museumized and receives thousands of tourists each year. This is not to say that no learning takes place at Kumbum. During my visit, I witnessed Dharma classes for young monks, many of whom appeared to be well under eighteen.

41. For more on China's efforts to rebuild for the tourism industry, see Cingcade, "Tourism and the Many Tibets: The Manufacture of Tibetan 'Tradition'" (1998). Some of the income from entrance fees presumably goes to the monasteries, but according to my informants, a good portion also goes to the local governments. Kolås and Thowsen (2005) report that in the case of Labrang Monastery, entrance fees go to support the monastery *and* the local government (168). They also report that entrance fees for Lhagang Monastery seemed to be connected to the development of tourism in Kandze TAP (57). On monastery entrance fees and their associated problems, see also Schrempf and Hayes (2009).

42. This monk was probably from one of three monasteries: Dechen Jampaling (Bde chen byams pa gling), Dechen Gonpa (Bde chen dgon), or Dechen Ritrö (Bde chen ri khrod), all of which are in Qinghai Province.

43. The fact that this particular shop which sold religious goods had a monk employee was highly unusual. This was in stark contrast to the Rongwo Gonpa gift shop which sold no Buddha images due to it being (as I was told) considered religiously inappropriate. The monk-clerk at the Rongwo gift shop suggested that perhaps the shop which employed the monk from Dechen was privately owned. The fact that the monk from Dechen was not from the local area and was associated with the sale of religious objects may be indicative of a pattern within the commercialization of religious goods among Tibetans described by Kolås (2008). In her study of tourism in Shangri-la, Yunnan Province, she was told by a friend that, given the fact that many Tibetans view the selling of religious goods as inappropriate, those who sell them often do so away from their home of origin (102). Presumably, this behavior was to avoid being criticized by one's family and one's own community. I did not confirm whether such a pattern existed among my informants.

44. It is my opinion that this particular monk was speaking practically. In his mind he did not actually "sell" thangkas but painted on commission. Nevertheless, his response appeared to reflect the idea that performing work in monasteries was not necessarily always available and that seeking out potential patrons was, in the current economic climate, necessary.

45. Although not directly related to the issue of monastic self-sufficiency, according to one monk-painter at Sengeshong Mango Monastery, at least part of the reason for the nonfunding of some monasteries is actually by the choice of the monks themselves out of a fear that they will actually lose control of their monastery. For example, this monk described his monastery's reluctance to accept any government assistance for renovation, which would then presumably increase tourism and transform the

purpose of the monastery. He explained, "The cultural bureau of the prefecture said that monasteries cannot renovate without permission because it is one of the national cultural heritage places. We don't really want the government to renovate the monastery because if they do, we will have no freedom, no right to use our monastery in our own way. The government so far has probably spent 30,000 [yuan]. They spent this money to make the parking lot in front of the monastery [for tourist buses?]. And that has to be remade after three years."

5. THE SOCIOPOLITICAL CONTEXT OF COMMODIFICATION

1. Graburn, more specifically, defines such peoples as belonging to the "Fourth World"—that is, "the collective name for all aboriginal or native peoples whose lands fall within the national boundaries and techno-bureaucratic administrations of the countries of the First, Second, and Third Worlds. As such, they are peoples without countries of their own, peoples who are usually in the minority and without the power to direct the course of their collective lives" (1976, 1).

2. It was Eric McGuckin who was perhaps the first to point out that such strategies do not appear to be present in the Tibetan case, where *identical* forms of ritual objects used in tantric rituals, such as *dorjes,* or *vajras*, can also be found on store shelves (1996, 31). This, of course, is now also true of religious goods such as thangkas and statues which are offered for sale in Amdo (and elsewhere in Tibet), where the production of such items (by Tibetans at least) is governed by strict canonical rules of iconometry. Making "imitations" of these objects using creative license is generally discouraged. Such objects are not considered religious objects at all—as Yael Bentor (1993) has shown to be the case with tourist thangkas produced in Nepal—or worse, the creator is seen as committing a sin that has negative karmic consequences.

3. Article 4 of the Chinese constitution adopted in 1982 and amended in 2004 reads: "All nationalities in the People's Republic of China are equal. The State protects the lawful rights and interests of the minority nationalities and upholds and develops a relationship of equality, unity and mutual assistance among all of China's nationalities. Discrimination against and oppression of any nationality are prohibited; any act which undermines the unity of the nationalities or instigates division is prohibited. The State assists areas inhabited by minority nationalities in accelerating their economic and cultural development according to the characteristics and needs of the various minority nationalities. Regional autonomy is practiced in areas where people of minority nationalities live in concentrated communities; in these areas organs of self-government are established to exercise the power of autonomy. All national autonomous areas are integral parts of the People's Republic of China. All nationalities have the freedom to use and develop their own spoken and written languages and to preserve or reform their own folkways and customs" (State Council of the People's Republic of China, 2004).

4. Several merchants noted obstacles to obtaining statues from Nepal. One problem had to do with obtaining a passport, which some, including my interpreter,

claimed was almost a hopeless task for Tibetans, especially after the unrest of 2008. Furthermore, according to my informants, the procedure required going through bureaucracy at the county and prefecture levels, a process that often required paying bribes. Restrictions on passports and visas for ethnic minorities in China have been well documented; see, for example, Bodeen (2015) and Chodorow (2015). Another problem was that the Chinese government had seemingly put a ban on importing statues from Nepal. According to a report published by the Tibet Information Network, strong restrictions on the import of religious goods, mainly statues, from Nepal into Tibet, became effective in July 2009. A portion of the report reads, "Although no official reasons have been given for the new policy, many believe that the move by the Chinese authorities was aimed at placing trans-border religious links, and possibly the use of religious funds, under closer scrutiny, while protecting the local markets from Nepali imports" (Canada Tibet Committee 2009).

5. Presumably, such participation by non-Tibetans has been motivated not only by the consistent Tibetan demand for such goods but also by the more recent economic opportunities surrounding tourism to Tibetan areas. In addition, non-Tibetan participation is also likely a reflection of the general absence of effective national protectionist laws or regulations specifically governing the manufacture and exchange of ethnic minority religious goods and arts and crafts, laws and regulations which have been established or are at least debated for various indigenous peoples in a number of postcolonial or multiethnic contexts. Laws and regulations governing the production and exchange of ethnic arts and crafts, indeed, exist in some form for First Nation peoples of Canada, the Maori of New Zealand, Aboriginals of Australia, and Native American groups in North America and were created with the involvement of these communities. Such laws even exist for some peoples in China. As illustrated by Su and Teo in their study *The Politics of Heritage Tourism in China* (2009), the local Naxi of Lijiang (Yunnan Province) since 2003 have been afforded exclusive rights to business licenses to operate tourism services and souvenir-related businesses in town as a result of the problem of encroaching migrants seeking to capitalize on tourism (158). Although it must be acknowledged that the central government has allotted significant funding for the development, preservation, and promotion of ethnic minority arts and crafts traditions (for example, in the Tibetan case, via the construction of museums dedicated to Tibetan arts in such places as Lhasa and Rebkong, the sponsorship of painting exhibitions and competitions, and by adding Rebkong art in particular to the UNESCO list of China's intangible cultural heritage in 2009), this effort appears to have been made primarily for the purposes of economic development and has not extended to the rights of Tibetans to exclusively manage the production and distribution of Tibetan Buddhist religious goods more broadly. While the Chinese authorities recognize Tibetan religious or cultural art forms as uniquely, ethnically Tibetan, such forms are also often framed not as belonging to an autonomous Tibetan culture with rights to its own cultural property but rather—because Tibet and Tibetans are viewed as an integral part of China—as part of China's

overall cultural heritage and, further, as belonging to world heritage. In addition, although it appears that Tibetans have made no such claims to intellectual or cultural property rights with respect to the production and exchange of their cultural or religious objects, one can also see how the rhetoric of national cultural heritage may be used against any such claims. For an example of an article that depicts Tibetan art as belonging to "China's splendid culture" and, moreover, to the world, see "Tibetan Thangka Art" http://english.cri.cn/4026/2008/02/17/1241@323922.htm. February 17, 2008. Similar expressions could also be seen in Lhasa in 2006 on billboards. For example, during one visit, I witnessed a large sign in front of the Jokhang Temple plaza, which read, "National heritage belongs to world heritage."

6. Here, I interpret this monk's reference to "properties" not in the sense that he views religious goods to be literally "owned" by the monastery but rather in the sense that he sees Buddhist religious goods as belonging to the Tibetan community, and due to Tibetans' lack of political power, they are unable to control how religious objects are exchanged.

7. The objection to Buddha images on *lung ta* had to do with the fact that ultimately this was not the tradition and, more crucially, that the images were destined to fall to the ground, something considered sacrilegious. Religious objects such as texts and Buddha images are normally kept in a high place.

8. *Kuai,* pronounced kwai (lit. piece), is a colloquial expression in Mandarin for money, like "buck" in the US or "quid" in the UK. The ICT report on tourism, *Interpreting Tibet: A Political Guide to Traveling in Tibet*, cites one Tibetan blogger who reported similar activities among Han Chinese tourist workers in Kham. According to the blogger, "As soon as you enter the monastery you see company employees wearing all kinds of maroon uniforms looking not quite like monks; they look more like tour guides but they're actually sales assistants. They first give a simple overview of the monastery, and then turn on the sweet talk to try and get tourists to buy *katag* [a white silk scarf traditionally presented as a greeting to visiting guests] and incense, exaggerating what benefits the incense will bring and what disasters will befall [them] if they don't buy and burn incense. Each stick of incense is 200 yuan [$26], around a meter long with the girth of a bowl. Incense like this was never burnt in Tibetan monasteries and people think it is very strange. People are urged to buy a statue of the Buddha, and more exaggerations are made about where the statue came from and what good karma and fortune it can bring. The most calculated bit of business though is getting tourists to buy *thangka* [traditional Tibetan religious paintings]—not to take them home but rather to leave them at the monastery as a kind of meritorious act. The *thangka* is then sold to another tourist, and another and another and another" (2008, 40–41). A similar story about false monks charging exorbitant prices for incense and blessings at Bön monasteries in Shar khog (monasteries which engaged in tourism practices) is also found in Schrempf and Hayes (2009, 305).

9. Two other merchants near the Xining Tibetan market held similar views and emphasized the mistreatment of religious goods by non-Tibetan merchants as motivating factors for their own participation. One younger man who operated a shop

near the bus station remarked, "It is said that it is not good to sell all these religious goods, but if we don't sell them other people like the Chinese and Muslims will sell them instead. . . . These guys don't know the meaning of these statues, and they usually cheat people." A similar response came from another man who ran a store selling Nepalese statuary, who remarked, "I feel I am running an appropriate business. I know about the images, don't step over them, and treat them well, unlike the Muslims and Chinese who don't know them and treat them poorly. If Tibetans didn't do it, then others would."

10. The idea that the sale of religious goods could potentially serve as representations or markers of *Tibetan* culture was also noted by two separate monks during my fieldwork. One monk from Kumbum who, while not condoning for-profit commercial activity in religious goods, explained, "On the one hand, [the exchange of religious goods] has turned into more of a commercial thing, but there might be some advantages to it, because these are part of the culture and arts and crafts of Tibet, and it represents the culture of Tibet. So, since it has become commercial, religious goods have spread all over the world, and when people see these things, people get more knowledge of Tibet. . . . You can also use religious goods as a [form of] media to spread culture . . . like an advertisement." Another monk/painter from Labrang responded similarly by saying, "Tibetan art is part of Tibetan culture, it has to be delivered and spread. It is a unique culture. It would be nice if everyone recognized this. Tibetan art contributes to this."

11. Cingcade reports that although Tibet was officially opened to tourists in 1980, the government did not begin actively promoting tourism until 1985 (1998, 3).

12. Still, in 1981, according to Mullin and Wangyal, a thirty-point Social and Security Law was passed in Lhasa that made the keeping of photos of lamas and the making and selling of religious statues, including pills blessed by lamas, a punishable offense (1983, 19). This seems to contradict a report found in McGuckin (1996) which describes how the central government was involved in establishing a painting institute in Lhasa which began producing thangka paintings as early as 1981.

13. Tourist art is generally understood as art that is created specifically for the tourism market. In Qinghai, many painters work both on commission and create ready-made thangkas for tourists. According to Graburn (1976), the case of thangkas would represent an example of the movement of functional art to commercial art as a result of tourism. However, while Graburn argues that a host society typically creates replicas of their functional art for tourists, in the case of thangkas in Rebkong, paintings are not mere replicas but are understood as authentic sacred images which are painted according to iconographic rules and are suitable and intended for religious purposes. Here, I merely mean to point out that many of the thangkas produced and sold in these locations are not considered "tourist thangkas" but rather real or authentic religious objects. This is not to say that Tibetans agree that the quality of these thangkas is high. One can also find in Lhasa, alongside iconographically correct thangkas, thangkas produced in Nepal that are considered to be of poor quality and are not iconographically correct. In Amdo, most likely due to the proximity and

renown of Rebkong thangkas, thangkas from Nepal or otherwise cheap imitation tourist thangkas are not popular, nor are they widely sold in the markets.

14. Deng Xiaoping entertained the idea of developing tourism in Lhasa as early as 1978 and supported the building of tourism infrastructure such as hotels (Xiao 2006).

15. According to Yang, Wall, and Smith (2008) "ethnic tourism is tourism motivated by a visitor's search for exotic cultural experiences, including the consumption of artifacts, performances, and other products or services" (752).

16. According to Murakami (2008), "In 2005, there were around 1.7 million Chinese visitors to Tibet, more than a dozen times greater than international tourists" (58). At the time, this number was expected to rise significantly in 2006 due to the opening of the Qinghai-Tibet Railway.

17. This work suggests that the so-called Tibetan handicraft industry was known historically as the "Flower on the Plateau." This assertion is tacitly false, for there was no handicraft industry or one by that name in the past. This attempt at creating continuity with the past (e.g., an industry which was ill-formed and has been improved upon with Chinese assistance and modernization) is a clear example of the "invention of tradition" recognized by Hobsbawm and Ranger (1983). Cingcade also notes the Chinese state's use of "invented tradition" by pointing out the state's attempt to link Tibetan and Chinese relations via descriptions of historical sites within tourism propaganda (1998, 10).

18. For more on these efforts, as well as resistance to such efforts, see Linrothe (2001), Kvaerne (1994), and Stevenson (2002).

19. The notion that Tibetan religious objects were only accessible to wealthy Tibetans and nobility is a theme that is repeated elsewhere and appears to be utilized as one justification for state involvement in the handicraft industry and its involvement in the development of Tibet more broadly. Another example of this claims that thangka painting "was once monopolized by monasteries and the nobility." See "Traditional Painting Brings Wealth to Tibetans," http://www.womenofchina.cn/html/news/china/139335–1.htm, March 16, 2012. Yet another article alludes to the same position: "The Huangnan Regong art, designated as the first batch of the country's intangible cultural heritage, was once only made and taught in Tibetan monasteries. However, in recent years, with the industrial development of the art, it has been inherited and made popular among the locals, providing a new way for local farmers and herdsmen to become prosperous. Now, the number of farmers and herdsmen engaging in the art is increasing and the art has witnessed an unprecedented prosperity." See "Regong Thangka Art Thriving," http://www.cctv.com/english/special/tibet/20091012/104048.shtml, October 12, 2009.

20. Xinhua News Agency, China Tibet Information Center, 2009 (this webpage has expired). This article was likely referring to the drop in the sale of thangkas which took place in the region after the Tibetan protests of 2008. After this time, the Chinese authorities closed off areas such as Kumbum, Rebkong, and Labrang to tourism. This "down period" was indeed noted by one of my informants. For substantial as-

sessments of the underlying causes of the 2008 protests in Tibet, see Fischer (2009b) and Barnett (2009).

21. By contrast, while the Tibetan government-in-exile in Dharamsala aims to preserve artistic traditions, provides funding for the training of recently arriving refugees to learn a handicraft, and offers particular religious items for sale through government-sponsored outlets, the promotion of Tibetan ethnic goods, including thangkas, for consumption by collectors and tourists as souvenirs, as well as the celebration of the successful commercial market and the high prices that they can garner, according to informants, does not exist in Dharamsala as a part of a broader campaign for Tibetan economic development.

22. For example, a white paper released in November 2001 by the Information Office of the State Council of the People's Republic of China entitled "Tibet's March toward Modernization" mentions the word "backward" in reference to Tibetans and Tibetan culture seventeen times (State Council of the People's Republic of China 2001).

23. For example, three merchants reported that monks had indeed told them of the potential negative consequences of participating in this market. Such encounters even led one merchant to stop selling them. In addition, three monks mentioned that the abbot of Rongwo Monastery, during a Kālacakra initiation, told the audience in attendance not to sell religious goods, old or new.

24. While other religious factors which may have prevented monks from responding to merchants' actions were not referenced by any of the monks interviewed, there are also various elements within the Tibetan Buddhist tradition which are in tension with any form of criticism against others' negative karmic acts. Such hesitancy may in fact have to do with a broader awareness of how negative and positive karma functions and is expressed in this life and in future lives. Thupten Jinpa points out, for example, that it is impossible to know when and how negative and virtuous karma will come to fruition for an individual, including oneself. He writes, "It is wholly inappropriate to ridicule someone who commits grave nonvirtuous acts and with a complacent heart harbor the pride, 'I do not possess such karma.' You do not know how many karmic imprints you have accumulated since beginningless time that are certain to lead to the hell realms" (2006, 471). That one should recite the refuge prayer, which contains lines to atone for the faults of selling religious objects, follows this logic. While an individual may not be engaged in such activities in this life, one may have done these things in past lives. Yet another possible reason for suspending critical judgment of those who sell religious objects may be found in Śāntideva's *Engaging in the Deeds of a Bodhisattva.* In the sixth chapter on patience, the antidote to anger, Śāntideva writes in stanza 64: "Should others talk badly of or even destroy / Holy images, reliquaries and the sacred Dharma, / It is improper for me to resent it / For the Buddhas can never be injured" (Tenzin Gyatso 1997, 73). This is Thupten Jinpa's translation. The "Chapter on Ethics" in Asaṅga's *Bodhisattvabhūmi*, in a similar vein, states, "The bodhisattva established in the ethics of the vow worries about his own faults and errors, not those of others. He has no thoughts of enmity or resent-

ment for sentient beings who are violent and immoral; based upon great compassion according to the doctrine, the bodhisattva furnishes for them a predominance of mercy and desire-to-do" (Tatz 1986, 52). This translation is Tatz's. While such statements form a part of the bodhisattva ideal, it is possible that these perspectives have influenced monastic thinking on this issue and have prevented more monks from approaching merchants.

25. Patriotic reeducation campaigns refer to government campaigns to attempt to stamp out pro-independence sentiment and support for the Dalai Lama within Tibetan monasteries. Such campaigns were reintroduced in April 1996 across Tibetan areas (the TAR, Sichuan, Gansu, Qinghai, and Yunnan) and resulted in the imprisonment, torture, and disappearance of monks who refused to denounce the Dalai Lama and accept the government's version of Tibetan history. While I was in Lhasa in the summer of 2004, patriotic reeducation campaigns were still happening at Drepung Monastery. For a brief description of what is entailed in such campaigns, see Human Rights Watch (1998).

6. PAINTERS, MERCHANTS, AND MONKS

1. Although shops selling ready-made images are increasing, and the purchase of ready-made religious objects by tourists is the norm given their limited time, according to several informants, tourists also often commission thangkas. According to one monk from Sengeshong Mango Gonpa, some tourists arrive with the name of a particular painter in hand who had been previously employed by a friend or colleague. It should also be noted that the vast majority of painters work from home, ostensibly fulfilling orders for locals and the external-remote market.

2. During my fieldwork, at least two Tibetan merchants who sold only ritual paraphernalia explained that they did not sell images and texts because of the religious proscriptions against doing so. These stores were located near (and in one case right next door to) shops that sold these objects. Many of the shops which sold ritual items, however, did sell bells and vajras, an indication, in line with Patrül Rinpoche's observations noted in chapter 2, that many people may be unaware that such objects are also technically considered representations of the body, speech, and mind of the Buddha.

3. According to most of the painters I interviewed, most buyers of premade thangkas are Chinese. Many painters believe that the Chinese buyers are, in fact, Buddhists, who use them for religious purposes. According to one painter who ran a gallery near Rongwo Gonpa, Chinese people prefer to buy thangkas, and Tibetans tend to buy statues. This preference for painting among Chinese buyers could of course be due to the popularization of thangkas in the media as an ideal souvenir when traveling to places like Rebkong.

4. An example of the benefits of merely witnessing images of the Buddha may be seen in the sūtra known as *The Seal of Engagement in Developing the Power of Faith* (*Śraddhābalādhānāvatāramudrāsūtra*, *'Phags pa dad pa'i stobs bskyed pa la 'jug*

pa'i phyag rgya zhes bya ba theg pa chen po'i mdo). In this text, the Buddha says to Mañjruśrī: "Mañjruśrī, [consider] a son or daughter of a noble family who, on a daily basis, gives a divine meal of one hundred flavors, or gives an offering of robes to pratyekabuddhas equal in number to the grains of sand in the Ganges River and does so for eons equal in number to the atoms in the entire universe. And consider, on the other hand, a son or daughter of a noble family who sees a painted image of the Buddha or one that is fashioned (into a statue). He or she [i.e., the latter] generates an incalculable amount of merit even greater than that [of those who make those extraordinary offerings to the pratyekabuddhas]. If that is the case, what need is there to mention [the merit gained] by one who places their palms together in devotion or offers flowers or incense or butter lamps? He or she accumulates even greater immeasurable merit." Lha sa bka' 'gyur, Mdo sde *ma*, fol. 91a.2–91a.6. For an alternative translation of this passage as well as a discussion of other texts that describe the benefits of creating, seeing, and making offerings to Buddha images, see Lama Zopa's teaching entitled "The Benefits of Having Many Holy Objects" on the Lama Yeshe Wisdom Archive, https://www.lamayeshe.com/article/benefits-having-many-holy-objects.

5. Several painters illustrated the importance of adhering to correct iconography as the crux of the issue regarding the potential creation of positive and negative karma in painting. According to one painter from Kumbum, "The important thing is that I do the opening (drawing) of the eye very carefully, the last step. That's the important part. . . . You have to do the eyes very correctly and you shouldn't miss any icons. These are the most important things to remember." Another painter from Rebkong, responding to a question regarding whether he saw painting as a religious practice, explained, "It is a spiritual practice, if I really make a good thangka, what it is supposed to be. This means I am also practicing religion. I am also doing some kind of positive karma. If you put three eyes, for example, something that is not complete, if you do this, it could be negative. Some painters don't paint properly. In this case, he is not doing something spiritual." Two painters from Sengeshong Mango explained similarly that "if the painter is dishonest and paints a thangka with missing parts or of bad quality (meaning you don't paint according to the payment), in this case, they may be creating negative karma." Finally, one older painter in Rebkong, referring to making mistakes in painting, explained, "According to the texts, it is forbidden and karmically negative, it is very sinful. The sin is not just a normal sin, it is an enormous sin if you don't really make the thangka properly. You shouldn't make any mistakes in it. Of course it is sinful, but you can also earn merit. If you don't paint it, you are not aware of it; there is no way to show images of the Buddha. In this way we also earn merit. There is no way to avoid such negative karma. Actually, as a painter you use saliva [on the brush] and it's sinful, but without using it, it won't come out as good. So you can't say that it's totally negative, nor totally positive. Definitely there is the negative part."

6. Ratnarakshita, *Dpal sdom pa 'byung ba'i rgyud kyi rgyal po chen po'i dka' 'grel pad ma can.*, Sde dge bstan 'gyur, Rgyud *wa*, fol. 89a.2–89a.4. See also, Gyatsho (1979,

72). For a summary of the detriments resulting from misrepresenting various parts of a deity, see Gega Lama (1983, 1:67–68). It should be noted that even while the tradition makes such statements with respect to correct measurements and proportions for deities, it also claims that even poorly executed images are worthy of veneration. This perspective, as we observed in chapter 2, is illustrated by the artist-scholar Ngawang Khedrup, who explains that even those images that are created for the sake of child's play or drawn as simple sketches ought to be viewed as the actual Buddha.

7. This view, as well as the emphasis that is placed on maintaining correct measurements and proportions when creating sacred objects, was supported by one clay statue maker in Labrang, who, when asked about the differences between commissioning and making ready-made images, explained, "You can't just say [that one who makes] statues on commission is not accumulating any sin. It depends on the person. The painter or statue maker has to have a proper motivation. There is a statement from the Buddha, 'One must have thirty-two good motivations.' So in this case, this means that if you do it, you have to do it properly. Otherwise you can incur sin. You might incur it due to making uneven eyes, making one arm long and one arm short, etc."

8. According to the Rangjung Yeshe dictionary, the word *akhu* (*a khu*) is "a polite way of addressing a lama or notable in Amdo." *Rangjung Yeshe Wiki-Dharma Dictionary*, s.v. "a khu," http://rywiki.tsadra.org/index.php/a_khu.

9. That the practice of charging a fixed amount for thangkas is a recent development was confirmed by one painter, an ex-monk, from Labrang. According to this informant, while the traditional protocols involved in commissioning paintings continue to occur among Tibetans—including such acts as the giving of gifts and offerings—he suggested that foreign patrons need or expect set prices. Furthermore, he explained that one cannot tell such traditions to Chinese people because they might think that the painter may charge them more.

10. There is some degree of sense to these methods of pricing besides the logic of the proscriptions against selling representations of the body, speech, and mind of the Buddha. Painters who worked for monasteries in the past were indeed paid a daily wage and were often supplied with the necessary materials. Therefore, it does not appear to be too much of a stretch for painters to calculate the price according to time and materials.

11. While the above responses appear to apply to thangkas that are commissioned, the use of *lu* among painters, it seems, is not restricted to a commissioned work. One young painter near Sengeshong Mango Gonpa, a former monk, referred to his paintings as those intended for *lu*, by which he meant premade ones, and those which were done on commission. However, this remains unclear. Other painters use *lu* to apply to both types of transactions. In such contexts the term *lu* is used synonymously with "invite" (*gdan 'dren zhus*). Traditionally speaking, it is said that one does not or cannot buy or sell but invites a Buddha or deity from one place to another.

12. This monk was referring to the pavement glass or glass block of the kind that

is inlaid into the ground for aesthetic or decorative purposes. This was deemed offensive because tiles were on the ground (which goes against the traditional practice of keeping religious objects and symbols in high and clean places) and were therefore walked upon.

13. Similar objections to the decorative use of religious images and objects have also been made by the Fourteenth Dalai Lama. In *Path to Bliss: A Practical Guide to the Stages of Meditation* (Tenzin Gyatso 1991), a translation of an oral teaching on Panchen Lobsang Chökyi Gyaltsen's *Path to Bliss* (*Bde lam*), for example, the Dalai Lama states, "one should not view one's dharma practice as becoming something decorative, regarding statues and images as material possessions or as furnishings for one's house, or thinking that because there is an empty space on a wall one might as well put up a thangka for decoration. That kind of attitude should not be cultivated" (32–33).

14. This anecdote about the clay Buddha statue is recounted in Patrül Rinpoche's *The Words of My Perfect Teacher.* In Patrül's rendition it involves a clay *tsa tsa*. It is interesting to note, however, that the location of this story in Patrül's work comes almost immediately after his statements that condemn the selling or pawning of Buddhist images and texts. They occur under the rubric of "the benefits of taking refuge." The juxtaposition of the proscriptive statements against selling Buddha images and texts with the story about the importance of intention involving the clay image suggests that the role of motivation, at least according to Patrül Rinpoche, has little to do with the notion that one should not sell religious objects. According to Patrül, it seems that selling representations of the Three Jewels, or "living by holding the Three Jewels to ransom," as he calls it, already entails a negative motivation. For the story about the clay *tsa tsa* in *The Words of My Perfect Teacher*, see O rgyan 'jigs med chos kyi dbang po (199?, fol. 144b.1–144b.6). See also Patrül Rinpoche (1998, 188–89). This anecdote about the shoes is also found in the Tengyur in a text titled *Completely Purifying Mental Obscurations,* in the context of a discussion of how motivation affects action. See Āryadeva, *Sems kyi sgrib pa rnam par sbyong ba zhes bya ba'i rab tu byed ba*, Sde dge bstan 'gyur, Rgyud *ngi*, fol. 107b.1–107b.2.

15. The position of this artist was not unique. This same sentiment was also shared with me during an interview with a clay statue maker in Lhasa in 2006.

16. Here we may note that the logic used by this woman is similar to that expressed in the *Maitreyasiṃhanāda Sūtra,* where the sin of selling Buddha images is compared to the sin of selling animals.

17. For example, one older painter in Rebkong near Rongwo Gonpa remarked, "I have no objections [to the middleman]. You can't really say anything about the middleman. It depends on your [the painter's] ability. If you have the ability, you can sell directly to buyers and a middleman is not needed. If you don't have the ability, then you are dependent on a middleman."

18. A story illustrating this very idea of scriptures is related in Corneille Jest's book *Tales of the Turquoise: A Pilgrimage in Dolpo.* When Jest visited Lang Monastery in

Dolpo in 1961, the custodian there told him the following: "A very long time ago, the sacred volumes of *Dō* and *Yüm* [i.e., the various sūtras of Kangyur and the Perfection of Wisdom Sūtras] had been removed by the traditional leader of Dolpo, who at that time lived in the valley of Barbung. A man of little faith, he sold these manuscripts to a Thakali of Tukucha.

"As soon as this unpropitious action took place, the inhabitants of the Barbung fell seriously ill. The books were then brought back to Dolpo, and were being transported through the valley of Panzang, when a violent wind arose. It was the time of the harvest and the wind carried away the grain with the husk, destroying everything. The books were then taken to Shey, where the monks then fell ill; then to Tra, where the wind burst forth again. Finally the books were packed onto yaks, which of their own accord took the road to Pijor, stopping only at the very door of the temple of Lang!" (1998, 73). This story thus illustrates the calamities that are said to occur as a result of the removal and sale of religious objects which have been installed in a particular location and which have acted as a source of worship. This story is also retold in Kurtis Schaeffer's book *Himalayan Hermitess: The Life of a Tibetan Buddhist Nun* (2004, 20).

19. The notion that a more ideal purchase of religious objects was one that involved no bartering or haggling was also supported by one monk from Kumbum. He explained that when he goes to buy a religious book or text in the market, he simply pays the price that is asked. He explained that if he argued over the price, then this would accentuate the commercial aspects of the transaction.

20. In the *Lamrim Chenmo,* for example, Tsongkhapa speaks of how one can reduce or eliminate the karma from negative actions before it comes to fruition by applying the "four powers." The first power is the power of eradication or regret, which involves the confession of sins. The second power—the power of applying remedies—involves engaging in a number of religious acts. Tsongkhapa mentions six such remedies, which are explained in Śāntideva's *Engaging in the Deeds of a Bodhisattva.* These include: listening and studying the sūtras; meditation on emptiness; recitation of mantras (e.g., the Vajrasattva mantra); making images of Buddhas; making offerings to images or stūpas; and hearing and retaining the names of the Buddhas when they are recited. The third power is the power of turning away from faults. Here, one restrains oneself from engaging in nonvirtuous acts. The fourth is the power of the foundation and involves going for refuge and cultivating *bodhicitta,* the wish to attain enlightenment for the benefit of all sentient beings. For this discussion, see Tsongkhapa (2000, 251–59).

21. According to a woman merchant in Xining, another remedy was reportedly recommended to her by a monk who was also a frequent customer. Upon telling her that selling religious goods was a bad activity, he advised her to offer a statue of Dorje Sempa (Rdo rje sems dpa', Vajrasattva) for free as a countermeasure. This merchant did not acknowledge the existence of the accumulation of negative karma as a result of her business activities nor did she confirm that she carried out the offering.

22. The various countermeasures employed by Tibetan merchants brings to mind

an additional occurrence which took place in Xining. There was one Tibetan man who operated a fairly new shop in the Tibetan market selling appliqué thangkas. After I explained my project to him, he very politely refused to be interviewed. Occasionally, my interpreter and I would pop in to say hello when we were in the market. I would again attempt to ask him some questions, and he would again very politely refuse. Over time, we developed some sense of rapport and would say hello to each other. One day, I asked him if I could photograph and videotape some of the images inside his shop, and he agreed. Before I left, he gave me a thangka of the Medicine Buddha (Sangs rgyas sman bla) for free and refused to accept any money for it. While one could easily chalk this up to the sheer friendliness and generosity of this particular merchant, at the time, I could not help but wonder whether such an act was, in fact, more strategic—a kind of countermeasure against his participation in selling thangkas.

23. This position did not necessarily imply that these monks believed painters should work for free but that they should—in a more traditional way—rely on a donation from the patron.

24. It should be noted that this monk-painter did not consider his own activities to be selling due to the fact that he painted on a commission basis. Therefore, he distinguished his role from that of the middleman, a non-painter who was in business for profit. The middleman rather arbitrarily and illegitimately put a price on an image, which, he explained, is priceless. It can be assumed then that this painter believed that once a person purchased an image it should not be resold at a profit.

25. *Loshi gurim* (*lo gcig sku rim*) refers to end-of-the-year rituals which serve to protect families during the coming year. For an account of this ritual in Sikkim, see Balikci (2008, 213–14).

26. A geshé at Kumbum also offered a similar response. He too appeared to deny a role for motivation. The geshé explained, "A painter has a right to make a living and take a fee but must not go beyond the standard price. But if it turns into a commercial business, then it is a negative thing." Here his statements imply that an artist has a right to make a reasonable living from the creation of religious goods but that a middleman, being involved in buying and selling (*nyo tshong*), is involved in negative activity.

27. For a thorough discussion of this topic, see Sopa and Patt (2004, 59–62).

28. Also included in this group was a teacher at the monastery school at Kumbum who held a comparatively conservative view. When asked about whether recycling the profits made from selling religious goods in order to make more religious goods was legitimate, he replied, "I don't agree. The question is whether using this money again for promoting and preserving or making new ones is okay. But how can you sell them? This is the question. Doing business in religious goods in order to make more religious goods is still a business." Interestingly, further elaborating his position, this monk distinguished between the activities of a monk and those of a layperson, claiming that, in any case, monks especially should not sell religious goods, the activity being totally against the religious rules. Regarding the acceptable means of exchange

for a monk, his response was similar to the position outlined by Geshé Sopa and echoed by the monk from Jakhyung Gonpa: "If they buy something for three *kuai* and sell again for three *kuai*, it's okay." His testimony, once again, reveals that profit is the pivotal factor in the accumulation of negative karma.

29. I interpret this monk's statement to be connected to the sentence that precedes it. It appears to mean that even if one commits a negative act, such as selling religious objects or killing one's father, there is usually some reason for why a person does it. According to this monk, in the case of selling religious objects, one reason for doing so is a lack of knowledge about the consequences of selling them.

30. Other reasons for the apparent lack of knowledge of religious goods among Tibetans were offered, including the encroachment of the scientific understanding of the world and the influence of modern values (including economic ones) which emphasize the accumulation of wealth and a "this world only" mentality as opposed to thinking about one's future lives.

31. Similar to this monk, many of those monks who supported the idea that motivation played a crucial role in selling religious objects attempted to cite a particular verse they attributed to Tsongkhapa about how motivation impacted the results of actions and how it was impossible to judge another's motivation. In this case, the verse may not originate with Tsongkhapa but with another source. The *Sūtra on Obtaining the Roots of Virtue* (*Kuśalamūlasamparigraha*), for example, states, "He then recited the verse, 'Except for the Buddha, a person is not able to measure the progress of another person.'" *Dge ba'i rtsa ba yongs su 'dzin pa'i mdo*, Lha sa bka' 'gyur, Mdo sde *nga*, fol. 271a.3–271a.4. A similar passage can be found in the *Sūtra which Teaches the Non-Origination of All Things* (*Sarvadharmāpravṛttinirdeśasūtra*). Here, it states, "A person should refrain from assessing the capacity of another person. If you assess the capacity of another person, you will injure [yourself]." *Chos thams cad 'byung ba med par bstan pa'i mdo*, Lha sa bka' 'gyur, Mdo sde *pha*, fol. 434a.6–434a.7. The latter passage is also found in the *Great Compendium of Sūtras* (*Mahasūtrasamuccaya, Mdo kun las btus pa chen po*). For the Tibetan, see Atīśa, *Mdo kun las btus pa chen po*, Sde dge bstan 'gyur, Dbu ma *gi*, fol. 22a.1–22a.2. See also, Ngag dbang blo bzang rgya mtsho, *A Commentary on the Three Main Points of the Path* (*Lam gyi gtso bo rnam gsum gyi dgongs 'grel lung rig gter mdzod*) in Ngag dbang blo bzang rgya mtsho'i gsung 'bum (2009, 388).

32. Two other monks held similar views to those maintained by this second group. One monk from Rongwo Gönchen also emphasized the role of motivation. According to him, "If the seller sells for profit, this is called *chos spangs* (abandoning the Dharma). He accumulates negative karma. But the buyer earns merit. The seller [can] sell without accumulating negative karma. If the seller has a good intention, then this could be the way. Of course, he has to earn a profit, but it must be reasonable, with a motivation to spread the Dharma." The potential for selling to be the cause for accumulating merit was also emphasized by the aforementioned older monk (*a khu*) from Sengeshong Yango Gonpa. Further commenting on the element of pricing, he explained, as others did, that the profits earned from selling religious goods could not

be without limit: "Even a lay businessman cannot charge double. He should charge a very acceptable or reasonable price, even if he sells normal things, not to mention religious goods." This particular monk repeatedly stressed the benefits of religious goods and leaned toward the view that creating and selling religious goods could be meritorious: "Even those who don't have faith earn merit by seeing images of Buddha. The fact is that whether we believe in Buddhism or not, whether you have money or not, or whether you have faith or not, seeing pictures of the Buddha or statues has immeasurable positive benefits."

33. For a discussion of the magnification of karma in the *Lamrim Chenmo,* see Tsongkhapa (2000, 211).

34. Here, I by no means intend to suggest that my informants did not know about these aspects of karma, only that such factors were not presented within their explanations and applied to the issue of selling religious goods.

35. Here, I follow Margaret Radin's definition of inalienable. According to Radin, a thing is "market-inalienable" if it is not to be sold or traded in the market (1987, 1).

7. THE IMPACT OF SELLING BUDDHIST OBJECTS IN TIBET

1. At least one painter I spoke with commented on how the recent commercialization of thangkas actually tended to work against those who cannot afford them. By creating a fixed market price, and due to the now rising cost of thangkas, some Tibetans, he explained, may be priced out of purchasing such items. Here, we can see quite clearly how the commissioned transaction, coupled with the traditional ethics of painters—including the idea that a painter should not refuse a patron for lack of financial means—is a mechanism that attempts to avoid such issues.

2. These dollar amounts reflect those found in the source. Of course, the amount of money that has been generated through the sale of thangka paintings may be exaggerated since it is in the government's interest to make such claims.

3. One article in *China Daily* has suggested that the dramatic increase in earnings from thangkas had to do with the inclusion of Rebkong thangkas on UNESCO's list of intangible cultural heritage for China in 2009 (Qian 2010).

4. One monk-painter in Rebkong, whose identity I will not divulge, appeared to own a car as well as a satellite TV, on which he received BBC News and Voice of America.

5. Several examples of painters who have gained some financial success and have paid for the training of students to learn how to paint thangkas can be found in the Chinese media. For such examples, see Wang (2011) and Yuanfeng, Shuangqi, and Ying (2009).

6. See, for example, Nan (2012).

7. Among some monks, the commodification of religious objects was not ideal. Yet some recognized that it does serve to promote Tibetan culture. This perspective appears to have some similarities to one interpretation of the Chinese invasion of Tibet. While the invasion of Tibet ultimately led to the destruction of Tibetan religious and cultural institutions, it has also led to Tibetan Buddhism's dissemination throughout

the world, which many believe has been ultimately positive. For an example of this view, see Chögyam Trungpa (2013, 185).

8. Nelson Graburn suggests that income earned from participation in the creation of art may indeed serve a deeper psychological need to express cultural ownership or cultural pride. According to Graburn, "the arts carry an aura of worth that is not attached to most other means of earning a livelihood; the same income from the arts, in essence, may have a higher psychological value for Fourth World peoples than if it were earned in manual labor or other commercial trade" (1976, 31). I would suggest that, in the Tibetan case, such pride or sense of custodianship is not only present in creators of religious art but also among many sellers of such art.

9. During my fieldwork in Amdo, rarely did I see any thangkas that had been manipulated or falsely aged either to increase their attractiveness or their value. Due to the rising prices of thangkas, especially old thangkas, since the Chinese annexation of Tibet, some sellers have taken to creating thangkas that look like antiques in order to attempt to increase the price. While in Kathmandu and India this was and remains a widespread practice, it was not noteworthy among sellers and painters in Amdo. In all of my visits to stores that sold religious goods, only one Muslim woman merchant in Labrang had such a thangka for sale.

10. This is in contrast to the Kanze (Garze or Ganze) school of New Tibetan Painting (in Kham, now Sichuan Province), in which artists, since the 1980s, have begun to integrate socialist themes into the traditional thangka painting format. For more on this topic, see Kvaerne (1994). According to Mark Stevenson, although such efforts were attempted early on in Rebkong, this practice never took hold among Rebkong painters (2002, 213)

11. While machine mass-produced thangkas are available in the market, they are discouraged and disparaged even by Chinese cultural brokers, who see them as a threat to hand-painted thangkas and to thangka painting as an example of China's intangible cultural heritage. In reality, however, there appears to be no real threat.

12. Rob Linrothe notes that despite the Chinese state's attempt to subordinate the Buddhist meanings associated with thangka painting through exhibitions and the application of the language of folk art to thangkas, Tibetans in Amdo remain largely uninterested in these resignifications, if they are aware of them at all, and have not been affected adversely by them (2001, 40). This discourse has likely affected the views of those who are new to thangkas and know little about them, however, as their first introduction to the art form may in fact be more secular in tone. The fact that tourists are now buying these as souvenirs opens up a number of potential problems in terms of how such objects will be used and understood, questions that are indeed a concern for many Tibetans.

13. There appear to be other types of "natural consecration" that exist within the Tibetan Buddhist tradition. A similar phenomenon has been noted by Kapstein (1995), in which works produced by some artist-yogins are believed to be imbued with a divine agency to the point that no formal consecration is required (260). During my fieldwork, more than one painter suggested that if a thangka is made by a

gelong (*dge slong*)—a fully ordained monk holding 253 precepts—then it is believed that the thangka is already consecrated.

14. This notion of thangkas having a kind of spiritual power is interesting. Kapstein notes that Tibetans have been known to attribute talismanic value (protective power) to some thangkas that are painted by accomplished lamas or yogins (1995, 260n31). I have also come across the idea that a religious object may contain more power or blessings (*chin lap, byin brlabs*) if blessed by particular famous lamas or if a particular object has received many offerings. Thus, there appears to be multiple ways in which a religious object can become powerful. That an object may become especially powerful due to the number of offerings it receives goes some way to explain why older religious objects are said to be more spiritually charged (and why the negative karma from their sale is said to be heavier) than new ones, for they ostensibly have been the object of offerings for generations.

15. It was also explained to me by one clay statue maker and, on a separate occasion, by a thangka painter that the merit earned from commissioning a clay statue is greater than that earned from buying a bronze statue or commissioning a thangka. According to the clay statue maker, the earth holds more positive potential. According to the painter, at least part of the reason clay statues potentially yield more merit than a thangka is due to the fact that it is three dimensional. This ranking of religious objects has also been observed by Glenn Mullin, who has noted that Tibetans and Mongolians "consider appliqué thangkas as being higher art forms than their painted counterparts" (2006, 88). He does not offer an explanation for this, but it is possible that this has to do with the dimensionality of an appliqué thangka or with a special status associated with the materials.

16. This painter was not the only person to stress the importance of intention in painting. According to the aforementioned unofficial monk-painter from Labrang, "there is a big difference between painting on commission and painting in order to sell. For example, as a monk artist, if someone comes and asks for specific things, these are painted according to the patron's wishes. It is made especially for the patron and this helps our motivation. We should cultivate our mind and have compassion before beginning a painting. These ideas make a huge difference between working on commission and working to sell [a thangka] ready-made."

17. It is of course possible that painters who fulfill orders for businessmen who resell them envision these transactions as a more traditional type of exchange. That is, it is quite possible that painters, even though they are aware that their paintings are going to be resold on the open market, conceive of the businessman as a traditional patron who has commissioned them, and thus as long as the patron/businessman is happy, the painter is fulfilling his role and is earning merit. More research needs to be done on how these particular transactions occur and how painters who fulfill these orders see their work.

18. Here we may recall a story from the Buddha's previous life (*jātaka*) that illustrates such a conception. For example, in one tale from the *Upāyakauśalya Sūtra*, or the *Skill-in-Means Sūtra*, the Buddha, as a captain of a ship, kills a man who he

foresaw through his power of clairvoyance was planning to murder five hundred passengers on board. Because the Buddha performed this negative act with the purest compassion, both for the passengers (who, if the plot were exposed, may have committed negative acts themselves in retaliation) and for the would-be killer and the sufferings he would surely face in the hell realms as the result of his heinous deeds, the act of killing became one of virtue.

References

TIBETAN LANGUAGE SOURCES

Ākāśagarbhasūtra. Translated by the Sakya Pandita Translation Group. Sde dge bka' 'gyur, Mdo sde *za*, fols. 264a–283b, 2014. Retrieved from http://read.84000.co/browser/released/UT22084/066/UT22084-066-018.pdf.

Āryadeva. *Sems kyi sgrib pa rnam par sbyong ba zhes bya ba'i rab tu byed ba*. Sde dge bstan 'gyur, Rgyud *ngi*, fols. 106b–112a. Delhi: Delhi karmapae choedhey, gyalwae sungrab partun khang, 1982–1985.

Asaṅga. *Rnal 'byor spyod pa'i sa las byang chub sems dpa'i sa*. Sde dge bstan 'gyur, Sems tsam *wi*, fols. 1b–213a. Delhi: Delhi karmapae choedhey, gyalwae sungrab partun khang, 1982–1985.

Atīśa. *Byang chub lam gyi sgron ma'i dka' 'grel*. Sde dge bstan 'gyur, Dbu ma *khi*, fols. 241a–293a. Delhi: Delhi karmapae choedhey, gyalwae sungrab partun khang, 1982–1985.

———. *Mdo kun las btus pa chen po*. Sde dge bstan 'gyur, Dbu ma *gi*, fols. 1b–198a. Delhi: Delhi karmapae choedhey, gyalwae sungrab partun khang, 1982–1985.

Blo bzang grags pa'i dpal. *Lam rim chen mo*. In *Rje tsong kha pa chen po'i gsung 'bum*, vol. 8. Xining: Mtsho sngon mi rigs dpe skrun khang, 1999.

Blo sbyong don bdun ma'i rtsa 'grel. In *Gangs can rig brgya'i sgo 'byed lde mig*, vol. 7. Beijing: Mi rigs dpe skrun khang, 1988.

'Brug pa kun dga' legs pa. *'Brug pa kun dga' legs pa'i rnam thar dang nyams mgur dang zhal gdams sogs*. Darjeeling: Kargyud sungrab nyamso khang, 1978.

Byams pa'i seng ge'i sgra'i mdo. Stog pho brang bris ma bka' 'gyur, Dkon brstegs *ca*, fols. 148b–218b. Leh: Smanrtsis shesrig dpemzod, 1975–1980.

Chos thams cad 'byung ba med par bstan pa'i mdo. Lha sa bka' 'gyur, Mdo sde *pha*, fols. 420b.4–469a.4. Lhasa: Zhol bka' 'gyur par khang, 194-.

Dge ba'i rtsa ba yongs su 'dzin pa'i mdo. Lha sa bka' 'gyur, Mdo sde *nga*, fols. 1b.1–353b.1. Lhasa: Zhol bka' 'gyur par khang, 194-.

Dngul chu dharma bhadra. *Brul gtor dkor sgrib dag byed zla shel chu rgyun gyi 'khrid yig gnad kyi don gsal*. In *The Collected Works (gsung 'bum) of Dngul chu dharma bhadra*, vol. 3, fols. 1–8a. New Delhi: Tibet House, 1973.

'Dul ba gzhi. Lha sa bka' 'gyur, 'Dul ba *ka–nga* (in their entirety), Lhasa: Zhol bka' 'gyur par khang, 194-.

Gsal rgyal gyi tshigs bcad. Sde dge bka' 'gyur (par phud), Mdo sde *sa*, fols. 201a6–204a4. Delhi: Delhi karmapae chodhey gyalwae sungrab partun khang, 1976–1979.

Klong chen ye shes rdo rje. *Yon tan mdzod kyi mchan 'grel*. Delhi: Shechen Publications, 1991.

Ma gcig lab sgron. *Phung po gzan skyur gyi rnam bshad gcod kyi don gsal byed*, Kathmandu: Sachen International, Guru Lama, 2008.

Ngag dbang blo bzang rgya mtsho. *Lam gyi gtso bo rnam gsum gyi dgongs 'grel lung rig gter mdzod*. In *Ngag dbang blo bzang rgya mtsho'i gsung 'bum*, vol. 15, 377–412. Beijing: Krung go'i bod rig pa dpe skrun khang, 2009.

Ngag dbang mkhas grub. *Lha 'bri ba'i man ngag lag len du sbyar ba'i gsung rtsom gyi 'grel pa*. In *The Collected Works of Nag dbang mkhas grub, Kyai rdor mkhan po of Urga*, vol. 3, fols. 1–7a. Smanrtsis Shesrig Spendzod 46. Leh: S. W. Tashigangpa, 1974.

O rgyan 'jigs med chos kyi dbang po. *Khrid yig kun bzang bla ma'i zhal lung*. Dpal yul rdzong. Tibet: A 'dzom chos sgar par khang, 199-.

Pha bong kha pa bde chen snying po. *Lam rim rnam grol lag bcangs*. In *Gangs can khyad nor dpe tshogs*, pod phreng 32. Lhasa: Ser gtsug nang bstan dpe rnying 'tshol bsdu phyogs sgrigs khang, 2009.

'Phags pa dad pa'i stobs bskyed pa la 'jug pa'i phyag rgya zhes bya ba theg pa chen po'i mdo. Lha sa bka' 'gyur, Mdo sde *ma*, fols. 1a.1–97a.3. Lhasa: Zhol bka' 'gyur par khang, 194-.

'Phags pa dam pa'i chos dran pa nye bar bzhag pa. Lha sa bka' 'gyur, Mdo sde *za*, fols. 171a–516a, *'a* and *ya* (in their entirety) and *ra*, fols. 1b–355b. Lhasa: Zhol bka' 'gyur par khang, 194-.

'Phags pa 'jam dpal gyi rtsa ba'i rgyud. Lha sa bka' 'gyur, Rgyud *tha*, fols. 99b–448b.3. Lhasa: Zhol bka' 'gyur par khang, 194-.

'Phags pa nam mkha'i snying po zhes bya ba theg pa chen po'i mdo. Sde dge bka' 'gyur (par phud), Mdo sde *za*, fols. 264a–283b. Delhi: Delhi karmapae chodhey gyalwae sungrab partun khang, 1976–1979.

'Phags pa rin po che'i phung po zhes bya ba theg pa chen po'i mdo. Lha sa bka' 'gyur, Dkon brtsegs *cha*, fols. 260b–298a. Lhasa: Zhol bka' 'gyur par khang, 194-.

Rab tu gnas pa mdor bsdus pa'i rgyud. Sde dge bka' 'gyur (par phud), Rgyud 'bum *ta*, fols. 146b–150a. Delhi: Delhi karmapae chodhey gyalwae sungrab partun khang, 1976–1979.

Ratnarakshita. *Dpal sdom pa 'byung ba'i rgyud kyi rgyal po chen po'i dka' 'grel pad ma can*. Sde dge bstan 'gyur, Rgyud *wa*, fols. 1b.1–101b.3. Delhi: Delhi karmapae choedhey, gyalwae sungrab partun khang, 1982–1985.

Rdo rje mdzes 'od. *Bka' brgyud kyi rnam thar chen mo rin po che'i gter mdzod dgos 'dod 'byung gnas*. Bir, India: D. Tsondu Senghe, Bir Tibetan Society, 1985.

Rdo rje rgyal po. *Sangs rgyas kyi bstan pa la rim gyis 'jug pa'i tshul*. In *Sangs rgyas bstan rim dang jo nang mdzad brgya*, fols. 1–52a. Bir, India: Zogyam and Pema Lodoe, Bir Tibetan Society, 1977.

Śāntideva. *Bslab pa kun las btus pa*. Sde dge bstan 'gyur, Dbu ma *khi*, fols. 3a–194b. Delhi: Delhi karmapae choedhey, gyalwae sungrab partun khang, 1982–1985.

Sbyor drug bya tshul thub bstan lhun po'i mdzes rgyan. Fols. 1–17a. Tibetan Buddhist Resource Center (TBRC), n.d. http://www.tbrc.org/#!rid=W1PD96301.

Sgam po pa bsod nams rin chen. *Dwags po thar rgyan*. 161 fols. Delhi: Dkon mchog lha bris, n.d.

Shangs pa gser 'phreng: A Golden Rosary of Lives of Masters of the Shangs pa Dkar Brgyud Pa Schools. Smanrtsis Shesrig Spendzod, vol. 15. Leh: Sonam W. Tashigang, 1970.

Shardong Rinpoche. *Lam rim chen mo'i bshad khrid blo bzang rgyal ba'i dgongs rgyan*. In *Rje shar gdong blo bzang bshad grub rgya mtsho'i gsung 'bum*, vol. 1, 1–782, and vol. 2, 1–335. Xining: Mtsho sngon mi rigs dpe skrung khang, 1998–99.

Sman bla don grub. *Bde bar gshegs pa'i sku gzugs kyi tshad kyi rab tu byed pa yid bzhin nor bu*. Gangtok: Bla ma zla ba and Shesrab Gyaltsen, 1983.

Yongs 'dzin ye shes rgyal mtshan. *Blo sbyong don bdun ma'i snying bo*. In *Gangs ljongs rig pa'i dpe tshogs*. Xining: Mtsho sngon mi rigs dpe skrun khang, 1992.

ENGLISH LANGUAGE SOURCES

Adhe Tapontsang. 1997. *The Voice That Remembers: One Woman's Historic Fight to Free Tibet*. Boston: Wisdom Publications.

Alexander, André. 2013. *The Traditional Lhasa House: Typology of an Endangered Species*. Zurich: Lit Verlag.

Appadurai, Arjun, ed. 1986. *The Social Life of Things: Commodities in Cultural Perspective*. Cambridge: Cambridge University Press.

Ardussi, John A. 1972. "'Brug-pa-Kun-legs, the Saintly Tibetan Madman." MA thesis, University of Washington.

Arjia Rinpoche. 2010. *Surviving the Dragon: A Tibetan Lama's Account of 40 Years under Chinese Rule*. New York: Rodale.

Austin, Regina. 2005. "Kwanzaa and the Commodification of Black Culture." In *Rethinking Commodification: Cases and Readings in Law and Culture*, edited by Martha M. Ertman and Joan C. Williams, 178–90. New York: New York University Press.

Avedon, John F. 1997. *In Exile from the Land of Snows: The Definitive Account of the Dalai Lama and Tibet since the Chinese Conquest*. New York: HarperCollins.

Balikci, Anna. 2008. *Lamas, Shamans and Ancestors: Village Religion in Sikkim*. Leiden: Koninklijke Brill NV.

Barnett, Robert. 2009. "The Tibet Protests of Spring, 2008: Conflict between the Nation and the State." *China Perspectives* 3:6–23.

Batchelor, Martine, trans. 2004. *The Path of Compassion: The Bodhisattva Precepts, the Chinese "Brahma's Net Sutra."* Walnut Creek, CA: Altamira Press.

BBC News. 2010. "Tibetan Students in China Protest over Language Policy." Asia-Pacific, October 20, 2010. http://www.bbc.co.uk/news/world-asia-pacific-11581189.

Belk, Russell W., and Ronald Groves. 1999. "Marketing and the Multiple Meanings of Australian Aboriginal Art." *Journal of Macromarketing* 19 (1): 20–33.

Bell, Charles. 1992. *Tibet Past and Present*. 1st Indian edition. Delhi: Motilal Banarsidass Publishers. First published 1924; reprinted 1996, 2000.

———. 1994. *The People of Tibet*. Reprint, Delhi: Motilal Banarsidass Publishers. First published 1928.

Bendall, Cecil, and W. H. D. Rouse, trans. 1971. *Śikṣā Samuccaya, a Compendium of Buddhist Doctrine, Compiled by Śāntideva, Chiefly from Earlier Mahāyāna Sūtras*. Delhi: Motilal Banarsidass Publishers.

Bentor, Yael. 1993. "Tibetan Tourist Thangkas in the Kathmandu Valley." *Annals of Tourism Research* 20 (1): 107–37.

Berzin, Alexander. 1996. "Relations between Hui Muslims, Tibetans and Uighurs 1996." Berzin Archives. https://studybuddhism.com/en/advanced-studies/history-culture/buddhism-islam/relations-between-hui-muslims-tibetans-and-uighurs-1996.

Bodeen, Christopher. 2015. "China Denying Passports to Restrict Critics, Minorities." *Associated Press*, May 20, 2015. http://bigstory.ap.org/article/4e883b19303849d988ba867d59a81b92/china-denying-passports-restrict-critics-minorities.

Boulnois, Luce. 2003. "Gold, Wool, and Musk: Trade in Lhasa in the Seventeenth Century." In *Lhasa in the Seventeenth Century: The Capital of the Dalai Lamas*, edited by Françoise Pommaret, translated by Howard Solverson, 133–56. Leiden: Koninklijke Brill NV.

———. 2004. *Silk Road: Monks, Warriors, and Merchants*. Translated by Helen Loveday. Hong Kong: Odyssey.

Burkert, Claire, and Tony Gleason. 2008. "The Tibet Artisan Initiative and Dropenling Handicraft Development Center." Asianart.com. https://www.asianart.com/articles/dropenling/index.html.

Buswell, Robert E., Jr., ed. 2004. *Encyclopedia of Buddhism*, 2 vols. New York: Thompson Gale/MacMillan Reference USA.

Cabezón, José Ignacio. 2001a. "Singing Bowls and Power Beads: On the Commodification of Tibet." Working paper, University of California, Santa Barbara.

———. 2001b. "Authorship and Literary Production in Classical Buddhist Tibet." In *Changing Minds: Contributions to the Study of Buddhism and Tibet in Honor of Jeffrey Hopkins*, edited by Guy Newland, 233–63. New York: Snow Lion Publications.

Canada Tibet Committee. 2009. "Restrictions on the Import of Religious Items from Nepal." World Tibet News, WTN Archive, July 6. http://www.tibet.ca/en/library/wtn/7004.

Candler, Edmund. 1905. *The Unveiling of Lhasa*. London: Thomas, Nelson, & Sons.

Carrington, Michael. 2003. "Officers, Gentlemen, and Thieves: The Looting of Monasteries during the 1903/4 Younghusband Mission to Tibet." *Modern Asian Studies* 37 (1): 81–109.

Catanese, Alex J. 2007. "Selling the Buddha: The Commodification of Buddhist Statues in Lhasa." MA thesis, University of California, Santa Barbara.

CCTV.com. 2009. "Regong Thangka Art Thriving." Tibet Channel, Culture. October 12, 2009. http://www.cctv.com/english/special/tibet/20091012/104048.shtml.

———. 2014. "Income of Tibetan Farmers, Herdsmen Up in 2013." China Economic Net. March 11. http://en.ce.cn/Business/sdata/201403/11/t20140311_2462411.shtml.

Central Tibetan Administration. 1996. "Tibet: Proving Truth from Facts." CTA white paper, Dharamsala, India. http://tibet.net/1996/01/tibet-proving-truth-from-facts-1996/.

China Daily. 2013. "Tibetans' Caterpillar Fungus Fortune Nearing Exhaustion." September 25. http://www.chinadaily.com.cn/food/2013–09/25/content_16992748.htm.

Chodorow, Gary. 2015. "China's Refusal of Passports to Certain Minorities, Children without Hukous, and Others Impinges on Their Right to Leave and Return." U.S. and China Visa Law (blog). http://lawandborder.com/china-refusal-passports-to-minorities-and-children-without-hukous/.

Chodron, Venerable Thubten. 1992. "The Practice of Refuge: Taking Refuge, Part 9 of 10." http://thubtenchodron.org/1992/02/refuge-guidelines/.

———. 2003. "Commentary on the Bodhisattva Vows, Forty-Six Auxiliary Vows: Number Six through Twelve." Talk, Dharma Friendship Foundation, Seattle, WA, August 4, 1993. http://www.abuddhistlibrary.com.

———. 2004. *Taming the Mind*. New York: Snow Lion Publications.

———. 2005. *How to Free Your Mind: Tara the Liberator*. New York: Snow Lion Publications.

———. 2011. "Guidelines for the Practice of Refuge." http://thubtenchodron.org/2011/12/commitment-three-jewels/.

Chögyam Trungpa. 2004. "Visual Dharma: The Buddhist Art of Tibet." In *The Collected Works of Chögyam Trungpa*, edited by Carolyn Rose Gimian, vol. 7, 259–79. Boston: Shambhala.

———. 2013. *The Path of Individual Liberation*, vol. 1: *The Profound Treasury of the Ocean of Dharma*, compiled and edited by Judith L. Lief. Boston: Shambhala.

Cingcade, Mary L. 1998. "Tourism and the Many Tibets: The Manufacture of Tibetan 'Tradition.'" *China Information* 13 (1): 1–24.

Clarke, John. 1997. *Tibet: Caught in Time*. Reading, UK: Garnet.

———. 2002. "Metalworking in dBus and gTsang, 1930–1977." *Tibet Journal* 27 (1–2): 115–54.

Cohen, Erik. 1988. "Authenticity and Commoditization in Tourism." *Annals of Tourism Research* 15 (3): 371–86.

Costello, Susan E. 2002. "The Economics of Cultural Production in Contemporary Amdo." In *Amdo Tibetans in Transition: Society and Culture in the Post-Mao Era*, edited by Tony Huber, 221–40. Leiden: Koninklijke Brill NV.

Craig, Mary. 1999. *Tears of Blood: A Cry for Tibet*. Washington, DC: Counterpoint.

Crienglish.com. 2008. "Tibetan Thangka Art" (webcast), Feb 17. http://english.cri.cn/4026/2008/02/17/1241@323922.htm.

Dagyab, Loden Sherap. 1977. *Tibetan Religious Art*, 2 pts. Wiesbaden: Otto Harrassowitz.

David-Neel, Alexandra. 1927. *My Journey to Lhasa: The Personal Story of the Only White Woman Who Succeeded in Entering the Forbidden City*. New York: Harper & Brothers.

Davidson, Ronald M. 2005. *Tibetan Renaissance: Tantric Buddhism in the Rebirth of Tibetan Culture*. New York: Columbia University Press.

Diemberger, Hildegard. 2012. "Holy Books as Ritual Objects and Vessels of Teachings in the Era of the 'Further Spread of the Doctrine' (*Bstan pa yang dar*)." In *Revisiting Rituals in a Changing Tibetan World*, edited by Katia Buffetrille, 9–42. Leiden: Koninklijke Brill NV.

Dowman, Keith, trans. 1973. *The Legend of the Great Stupa and the Life Story of the Lotus Born Guru*. Berkeley, CA: Dharma Publications.

Epstein, Lawrence, and Peng Wenbin. 1998. "Ritual, Ethnicity, and Generational Identity." In *Buddhism in Contemporary Tibet: Religious Revival and Cultural Identity*, edited by Melvyn C. Goldstein and Matthew T. Kapstein, 120–38. Berkeley: University of California Press.

Fischer, Andrew Martin. 2002. *Poverty by Design: The Economics of Discrimination in Tibet*. Montreal: Canada Tibet Committee. https://www.tibet.ca/_media/PDF/PovertybyDesign.pdf.

———. 2005. *State Growth and Social Exclusion in Tibet: Challenges of Recent Economic Growth*. Nordic Institute of Asian Studies Report 47. Copenhagen: NIAS Press.

———. 2008. "Subsistence and Rural Livelihood Strategies in Tibet under Rapid Economic and Social Transition." *Journal of the International Association of Tibetan Studies*, no. 4 (December): 1–49. http://www.thlib.org?tid=T5569.

———. 2009a. "Educating for Exclusion in Western China: Structural and Institutional Dimensions of Conflict in the Tibetan Areas of Qinghai and Tibet." Working Paper 69, Center for Research on Inequality, Human Security, and Ethnicity, Oxford, UK.

———. 2009b. "The Political Economy of Boomerang Aid in China's Tibet." *China Perspectives* 3:38–53.

Foundation for the Preservation of the Mahāyāna Tradition (FPMT). 2007. *Report on Use of Dharma Income for 2007*. https://fpmt.org/wp-content/uploads/organization/pdf/DharmaIncomeReport2007.pdf.

———. 2018. "Showing Respect to Holy Objects." Education: The Heart of FPMT. August 2. https://fpmt.org/edu-news/showing-respect-to-holy-objects/.

Fraser, Sarah E. 2011. "Sha bo tshe ring, Zhang Daqian and Sino-Tibetan Cultural

Exchange, 1941–1943: Defining Research Methods for Amdo Regional Painting Workshops in the Medieval and Modern Periods." In *Art in Tibet: Issues in Traditional Tibetan Art from the Seventh to the Twentieth Century*, edited by Erberto F. Lo Bue, 115–36. Leiden: Koninklijke Brill NV.

French, Patrick. 2004. *Tibet, Tibet: A Personal History of a Lost Land*. New York: Vintage Books.

French, Rebecca Redwood. 2002. *The Golden Yoke: The Legal Cosmology of Buddhist Tibet*. 2nd ed. Ithaca, NY: Snow Lion Publications.

Gampopa Sonam Rinchen. 1998. *The Jewel Ornament of Liberation, the Wish-fulfilling Gem of the Noble Teachings*. Translated by Khenpo Könchog Gyaltsen Rinpoche, edited by Ani K. Trinlay Chödron. New York: Snow Lion Publications.

Gega Lama. 1983. *Principles of Tibetan Art: Illustrations and Explanations of Buddhist Iconography and Iconometry According to the Karma Gardri School*, 2 vols. Darjeeling: Jamyang Singe.

Germano, David. 1998. "Re-membering the Dismembered Body of Tibet: Contemporary Tibetan Visionary Movements in the People's Republic of China." In *Buddhism in Contemporary Tibet: Religious Revival and Cultural Identity*, edited by Melvyn C. Goldstein and Matthew T. Kapstein, 53–94. Berkeley: University of California Press.

Gernet, Jacques. 1995. *Buddhism in Chinese Society: An Economic History from the Fifth to the Tenth Centuries*. Translated by Franciscus Verellen. New York: Columbia University Press.

Gill, William John. 1880. *The River of Golden Sand: The Narrative of a Journey through China and Eastern Tibet to Burmah*. 2 vols. London: John Murray.

Goldstein, Melvyn C. 1989. *A History of Modern Tibet, 1913–1951: The Demise of the Lamaist State*. Berkeley: University of California Press.

———, ed. 2001. *The New Tibetan-English Dictionary of Modern Tibetan*. Berkeley: University of California Press.

Goldstein, Melvyn C., Geoff Childs, and Puchung Wangdui. 2008. "'Going for Income' in Village Tibet: A Longitudinal Analysis of Change and Adaptation, 1997–2007." *Asian Survey* 48 (3): 514–34.

Graburn, Nelson H. H., ed. 1976. *Ethnic and Tourist Arts: Cultural Expressions from the Fourth World*. Berkeley: University of California Press.

———. 1984. "The Evolution of Tourist Arts." *Annals of Tourism Research* 11:393–419.

Grunfeld, A. Tom. 1996. *The Making of Modern Tibet*. 2nd ed. New York: Routledge.

Gyaltsen, Khenpo Könchog, trans. 2006. *The Great Kagyu Masters: The Golden Lineage Treasury*. Edited by Victoria Huckenpahler. New York: Snow Lion Publications.

Gyatsho, Thubten Legshay. 1979. *Gateway to the Temple: Manual of Tibetan Monastic Customs, Art, Building and Celebrations*. Edited by H. K. Kulöy. Translated by David Paul Jackson. Kathmandu: Ratna Pustak Bhandar.

Gyatso, Geshé Kelsang. 1995. *Joyful Path of Good Fortune: The Complete Buddhist Path to Enlightenment*. New York: Tharpa Publications.

Gyumed Khensur Lobsang Jampa. 2013. *The Easy Path: Illuminating the First Panchen Lama's Secret Instructions*. Edited by Lorne Ladner. Somerville, MA: Wisdom Publications.

Hackett, Paul G. 2012. *Theos Bernard, the White Lama: Tibet, Yoga, and American Religious Life*. New York: Columbia University Press.

Hanh, Thich Nhat. 2008. *Peaceful Action, Open Heart: Lessons from the Lotus Sutra*. Berkeley, CA: Parallax Press.

Harding, Sarah, trans. 2003. *Machik's Complete Explanation: Clarifying the Meaning of Chöd, a Complete Explanation of Casting Out the Body as Food*. Ithaca, NY: Snow Lion Publications.

Harrer, Heinrich. 1981. *Seven Years in Tibet*. Translated by Richard Graves, with an introduction by Peter Fleming. New York: Tarcher/Putnam. Originally published in 1953.

Harris, Brian, and Heather Wardle. 1996. *Tibetan Voices: A Traditional Memoir*. Rohnert Park, CA: Pomegranate Artbooks.

Harris, Clare. 1999. *In the Image of Tibet: Tibetan Painting after 1959*. London: Reaktion Books.

Harvey, Peter. 2000. *An Introduction to Buddhist Ethics: Foundations, Values and Issues*. Cambridge: Cambridge University Press.

Hasmath, Reza. 2007. "The Paradox of Ethnic Minority Development in Beijing." *Comparative Sociology* 6:464–80.

Hedin, Sven Anders. (1909) 1999. *Trans-Himalaya: Discoveries and Adventures in Tibet*. Vol. 1. Reprint, New Delhi: Asian Educational Services.

Hobsbawm, Eric, and Terence Ranger, eds. 1983. *The Invention of Tradition*. Cambridge: Cambridge University Press.

Hongxiang, Zhang. 2013. "Regong Arts Industry Booming in Qinghai's Tibetan Area." *Xinhua News Agency*. December 18. https://www.chinadaily.com.cn/culture/art/2013-12/18/content_17182305.htm.

Human Rights Watch. 1998. "Human Rights in Tibet." http://www.hrw.org/legacy/campaigns/china-98/tibet.htm.

———. 2002. "China: The State Control of Religion." In *Human Rights and Religion: A Reader*, edited by Liam Gearon, 276–82. Brighton, UK: Sussex Academic Press.

International Campaign for Tibet (ICT). 2008. *Interpreting Tibet: A Political Guide to Traveling in Tibet*. http://www.savetibet.org/wp-content/uploads/2013/05/TibetanChinaTravelGuide.pdf.

Jackson, David P., and Janice A. Jackson. 1984. *Tibetan Thangka Painting: Methods and Materials*. Boulder, CO: Shambhala.

Jamgön Kongtrul Karma Lodrö Chökyi Senge, H. E. 1977. "Refuge and the Refuge Vows, the Bodhisattva Precepts, and the Five Lay Followers Vows." Translated by Matthew Kapstein. Karma Lekshey Ling Institute, Nepal. http://www.dharma

download.net/pages/english/Natsok/0010_Teaching_English/Teaching_English_0019.htm.

Jamgön Kongtrul Lodrö Tayé. 1977. *The Torch of Certainty*. Translated by Judith Hanson. Boston: Shambhala.

———. 1998. *Buddhist Ethics*. Book 5 of *The Treasury of Knowledge*. Translated and edited by the International Translation Committee. Ithaca, NY: Snow Lion Publications.

———. 2010. *Buddhism's Journey to Tibet*. Translation and introduction by Ngawang Zangpo (Kalu Rinpoché Translation Group). Ithaca, NY: Snow Lion Publications.

Jest, Corneille. 1998. *Tales of the Turquoise: A Pilgrimage in Dolpo*. New York: Snow Lion Publications.

Jifang, Zan. 2007. "The Art of Longevity: *Tangka*, the Ancient Spiritual Art Form of Tibet, Has Evolved and Is Finding a New Modern Audience." *Beijing Review*, August 30. http://www.bjreview.com.cn/culture/txt/2007-08/23/content_73678_2.htm.

Jigme Lingpa. 2010. *Treasury of Precious Qualities: The Rain of Joy, with the Quintessence of the Three Paths: A Commentary by Lonchen Yeshe Dorje, Kangyur Rinpoche*. Book 1. Translated by the Padmakara Translation Group. Boston: Shambhala.

Jin Hua. 1994. Cong Wulingyuan kan ziran fengjing kaifaqu de quyu shehui xiaoying [Looking at the Regional Social Impact of Natural Scenery Development Areas from Wulingyuan] *Jingji Dili / Economic Geography* 14, no. 4 (December): 89–92.

Johnson, Bonnie, and Nalini Chhetri. 2000. "Exclusionary Policies and Practices in Chinese Minority Education: The Case of Tibetan Education." *Current Issues in Comparative Education* 2 (2): 142–53. https://www.tc.columbia.edu/cice/pdf/25662_2_2_Johnson_Chetri.pdf.

Kapsner, Matthew, and Tania Wynniatt-Husey. 1991. "Thangka Painting." In *Chö-Yang: The Voice of Tibetan Religion and Culture*. Edited by Pedron Yeshi and Jeremy Russell, 288–301. Dharamsala: Council for Religious and Cultural Affairs.

Kapstein, Matthew. 1995. "Weaving the World: The Ritual Art of the *Paṭa* in Pāla Buddhism and Its Legacy in Tibet." *History of Religions* 34 (3): 241–62.

———. 2006. *The Tibetans*. Malden, MA: Blackwell Publishing.

Kawaguchi, Ekai. 1909. *Three Years in Tibet, with the Original Japanese Illustrations*. Madras: Theosophist Office.

Kimura, Hisao, and Scott Berry. 1990. *Japanese Agent in Tibet: My Ten Years of Travel in Disguise*. London: Serindia Publications.

Klieger, P. Christiaan. 1990. "Close Encounters: 'Intimate' Tourism in Tibet." *Cultural Survival Quarterly* 14 (2). http://www.culturalsurvival.org/publications/cultural-survival-quarterly/china-tibet/close-encounters-intimate-tourism-tibet.

Knuth, Rebecca. 2003. *Libricide: The Regime-Sponsored Destruction of Books and Libraries in the Twentieth Century*. Westport, CT: Praeger.

Kolås, Åshild. 2008. *Tourism and Tibetan Culture in Transition: A Place Called Shangrila*. New York: Routledge.

Kolås, Åshild, and Monika P. Thowsen. 2005. *On the Margins of Tibet: Cultural Survival on the Sino-Tibetan Frontier*. Seattle: University of Washington Press.

Kopytoff, Igor. 1986. "The Cultural Biography of Things: Commoditization as Process." In *The Social Life of Things: Commodities in Cultural Perspective*, edited by Arjun Appadurai, 64–91. Cambridge: Cambridge University Press.

Kunga Tsering Lama. 2007. "Crowded Mountains, Empty Towns: Commodification and Contestation in Cordyceps Harvesting in Eastern Tibet." Master's thesis, University of Colorado, Boulder.

Kunpal, Khenpo. 2003. *Drops of Nectar: Khenpo Kunpal's Commentary on Shantideva's "Entering the Conduct of the Bodhisattvas,"* vol. 2, chap. 2. Compiled and translated by Andreas Kretschmar, edited by Judith S. Amtzis. http://www.kunpal.com/bca2comm.pdf.

Kunsang, Erik Pema, and Marcia Binder Schmidt. 2005. *Blazing Splendor: The Memoirs of the Dzogchen Yogi Tulku Urgyen Rinpoche*. Boudanath: Rangjung Yeshe Publications.

Kvaerne, Per. 1994. "The Ideological Impact on Tibetan Art." In *Resistance and Reform in Tibet*, edited by Robert Barnett and Shirin Akiner, 166–85. London: C. Hurst and Co.

Leung, Angela Ki Che. 2009. *Leprosy in China: A History*. New York: Columbia University Press.

Li, Luo. 2008. *The Economy of Tibet: Transformation from a Traditional to a Modern Economy*. Beijing: Foreign Languages Press.

Lindtner, Christian, trans. 1997. *Master of Wisdom: Writings of the Buddhist Master Nāgārjuna*. Berkeley, CA: Dharma Publishing.

Lingui, Xu, and Jiang Chenrong. 2010. "Lure of Big Money Threatens Sacred Tibetan Scroll Painting." *Xinhua*, September 19, 2010. http://news.xinhuanet.com/english2010/china/2010-09/19/c_13519541_3.htm.

Linrothe, Rob. 2001. "Creativity, Freedom and Control in the Contemporary Renaissance of Reb gong Painting." *Tibet Journal* 26 (3–4): 5–59.

Liu Weiguo, ed. 2012. "Traditional Painting Brings Wealth to Tibetans." March 16. http://www.womenofchina.cn/html/news/china/139335-1.htm.

Lo Bue, Erberto F. 2003. "Scholars, Artists and Feasts." In *Lhasa in the Seventeenth Century: The Capital of the Dalai Lamas*, edited by Françoise Pommaret, translated by Howard Solverson, 179–198. Brill's Tibetan Studies Library 3. Leiden: Koninklijke Brill NV.

Lopez, Donald S., Jr., ed. 1995. *Buddhism in Practice*. Princeton, NJ: Princeton University Press.

———. 1998. *Prisoners of Shangri-la: Tibetan Buddhism and the West*. Chicago: University of Chicago Press.

Lustgarten, Abrahm. 2008. *China's Great Train: Beijing's Drive West and the Campaign to Remake Tibet*. New York: Times Books, Henry Holt and Company.

Makley, Charlene E. 1994. "Gendered Practices and the Inner Sanctum: The Reconstruction of Tibetan Sacred Space in 'China's Tibet'" *Tibet Journal* 19 (2): 61–94.

Marshall, Steven D., and Susette Cooke. 1997. *Tibet Outside the TAR*. Washington, DC: Alliance for Research in Tibet. CD-rom.

Martin, Dan. 2008. Jikten Gonpo Rinchen Pel. *The Treasury of Lives*. http://www.treasuryoflives.org/biographies/view/Jigten-Gonpo Rinchen-Pel/2899.

McGuckin, Eric. 1996. "Thangkas and Tourism in Dharamsala: Preservation through Change." *Tibet Journal* 21 (2): 31–52.

McKay, Alex, ed. 2003. *The History of Tibet. Vol. 2, The Medieval Period: c. 850–1895, The Development of Buddhist Paramountcy*. New York: RoutledgeCurzon.

Meulenbeld, Ben. 2001. *Buddhist Symbolism in Tibetan Thangkas: The Story of Siddhartha and Other Buddhas Interpreted in Modern Nepalese Painting*. Translated by Wanda Boeke. Havelte: Binkey Kok Publications.

Moran, Peter. 2004. *Buddhism Observed: Travellers, Exiles and Tibetan Dharma in Kathmandu*. New York: RoutledgeCurzon Press.

Mullin, Chris, and Phuntsog Wangyal. 1983. *The Tibetans: Two Perspectives on Tibetan-Chinese Relations*. London: The Minority Rights Group. https://minorityrights.org/wp-content/uploads/old-site-downloads/download-1462-The-Tibetans-two-perspectives-on-Tibetan-Chinese-relations.pdf.

Mullin, Glenn H. 2006. *The Dalai Lamas on Tantra*. Ithaca, NY: Snow Lion Publications.

Munn, Nancy. 1983. "Gawan kula: Spatiotemporal Control and the Symbolism of Influence." In *The Kula: New Perspectives on Massim Exchange*, edited by H. W. Leach and E. Leach, 277–308. Cambridge: Cambridge University Press.

Murakami, Daisuke. 2008. "Tourism Development and Propaganda in Contemporary Lhasa, Tibet Autonomous Region (TAR), China." In *Asian Tourism: Growth and Change*, edited by Janet Cochrane, 55–67. Oxford: Elsevier.

Nan, Chen. 2012. "Pious Paintings." *China Daily*, November 26. http://europe.chinadaily.com.cn/culture/201211/26/content_15957911_2.htm.

National People's Congress of the People's Republic of China Laws and Regulations Database. n.d. *Constitution and the Related Laws, Law of the People's Republic of China on Regional National Autonomy*. Accessed January 31, 2012. http://www.npc.gov.cn/englishnpc/Law/Frameset-page.html.

Ngag dbang chos 'byor. 1984. *Jorchö: The Six Preparatory Practices Adorning the Buddha's Sublime Doctrine*. Translated by Losang C. Ganchenpa and Karma Lekshe Tsomo. Dharamsala: Library of Tibetan Works and Archives.

Nyíri, Pál. 2009. "Between Encouragement and Control: Tourism, Modernity and Discipline in China." In *Asia on Tour: Exploring the Rise of Asian Tourism*, edited by Tim Winter, Peggy Teo, and T. C. Chang, 153–69. New York: Routledge.

———. 2010. *Mobility and Cultural Authority in Contemporary China*. Seattle: University of Washington Press.

Pabongka Rinpoche Jampa Tenzin Trinley Gyatso. 1990. *Liberation in Our Hands, Part One: The Preliminaries*. Transcribed and edited by Yongzin Trijang Rinpoche and Losang Yeshe Tenzin Gyatso. Translated by Sera Mey Geshé Lobsang Tharchin and Artemus B. Engle. Howell, NJ: Mahayana Sutra and Tantra Press.

Pachen, Ani, and Adelaide Donnelley. 2000. *Sorrow Mountain: The Journey of a Tibetan Warrior Nun*. New York: Kodansha International.

Patrül Rinpoche. 1998. *The Words of My Perfect Teacher*. Revised edition. Translated by the Padmakara Translation Group. Boston: Shambhala.

Pelden, Kunzang. 2007. *The Nectar of Manjushri's Speech: A Detailed Commentary on Shantideva's Way of the Bodhisattva*. Translated by the Padmakara Translation Group. Boston: Shambhala.

Pelzang, Khenpo Ngawang. 2004. *A Guide to "The Words of My Perfect Teacher."* Translated by Dipamkara, in collaboration with the Padmakara Translation Group. Boston: Shambhala.

Pempa Dorjee. 2011. "Buddhist Statues at Norbulingka Institute: Master Pempa Dorjee and His Apprentices." Norbulingka Institute. Mp4. http://www.youtube.com/watch?v=QEWi7Ukk7uA&feature=player_embedded.

Phagmodrupa. 2008. *Engaging by Stages in the Teachings of the Buddha*. Vol. 1. Translated by Terence Barrett with guidance from Khenchen Konchog Gyaltsen Rinpoche and Khenpo Nyima Gyaltsen. Edited by the Tara Foundation. Munich: Otter Verlag.

Polanyi, Karl. (1944) 2001. *The Great Transformation: The Political and Economic Origins of Our Time*. 2nd ed. Boston: Beacon Press.

Posner, Richard A. 2005. "Community and Conscription." In *Rethinking Commodification: Cases and Readings in Law and Culture*, edited by Martha M. Ertman and Joan C. Williams, 128–32. New York: New York University Press.

Postiglione, Gerard. 1999. *China's National Minority Education: Culture, Schooling and Development*. New York: Falmer Press.

Potala Society. 2014. "Education Project for Tibetan Nomads in Amdo (Qinghai Province China)." Accessed August 19. http://www.potala.cz/en/education-project-tibetan-nomads-amdo-qinghai-province-china.

Powers, John. 2007. *Introduction to Tibetan Buddhism*. Ithaca, NY: Snow Lion Publications.

Qian, Mu. 2010. "Grasping the Intangible." *China Daily*. June 17. http://www.chinadaily.com.cn/cndy/2010–06/17/content_9981615.htm.

Rabten, Geshé, and Geshé Dhargyey. 1996. *Advice from a Spiritual Friend*. Translated and edited by Brian Beresford with Gonsar Tulku and Sharpa Tulku. Somerville, MA: Wisdom Publications.

Radin, Margaret Jane. 1987. "Market-Inalienability." *Harvard Law Review* 100 (8): 1849–1937.

Raverty, Aaron. 1997. "Monastic Interreligious Dialogue: Tibet, Nepal, and Northern India." *Cistercian Studies Quarterly* 32 (2): 245–63.

Reedy, Chandra L. 1991. "The Opening of Consecrated Tibetan Bronzes with Interior Contents: Scholarly, Conservation, and Ethical Considerations." *Journal of the American Institute for Conservation* 30 (1): 13–34.

———. 1992. "Religious and Ethical Issues in the Study and Conservation of Tibetan Sculpture." *Journal of the American Institute for Conservation* 31 (1): 41–50. http://cool.conservation-us.org/jaic/articles/jaic31-01-006.html.

Reynolds, Elizabeth. 2011. "Social Networks and the Commercialization of Rebgong Tibetan Thangkas." *Columbia East Asia Review* 4 (Spring): 89–105.

Reynolds, Valrae. 1999. *From the Sacred Realm: Treasures of Tibetan Art from the Newark Museum*. New York: Prestel.

Richardus, Peter, ed. 1998. *Tibetan Lives: Three Tibetan Autobiographies*. Surrey: Curzon Press.

Rinchen, Geshé Sonam. 2006. *How Karma Works: The Twelve Links of Dependent Arising*. Translated and edited by Ruth Sonam. Ithaca, NY: Snow Lion Publications.

Roerich, George. 1925. *Tibetan Paintings*. Paris: Paul Geuthner.

———, trans. 1996. *The Blue Annals*. 2nd ed. Delhi: Motilal Banarsidass. Originally published in 1976.

Roerich, Nicholas. 1990. *Shambhala: In Search of the New Era*. Revised ed. Rochester, VT: Inner Traditions International. Originally published in 1930.

Sakya, Jamyang, and Julie Emery. 1990. *Princess in the Land of Snows: The Life of Jamyang Sakya in Tibet*. Boston: Shambhala.

Schaeffer, Kurtis R. 2004. *Himalayan Hermitess: The Life of a Tibetan Buddhist Nun*. Oxford: Oxford University Press.

———. 2009. *The Culture of the Book in Tibet*. New York: Columbia University Press.

Schopen, Gregory. 2004. *Buddhist Monks and Business Matters: Still More Papers on Monastic Buddhism in India*. Honolulu: University of Hawai'i Press.

———. 2005. *Figments and Fragments of Mahāyāna Buddhism in India: More Collected Papers*. Honolulu: University of Hawai'i Press.

Schrempf, Mona, and Jack Patrick Hayes. 2009. "From Temple to Commodity? Tourism in Songpan and the Bon Monasteries of A'mdo Shar khog." In *Bon: The Everlasting Religion of Tibet. Tibetan Studies in Honor of Professor David L. Snellgrove*, edited by Samten G. Karmay and Donatella Rossi. Special Issue, *East and West* 59 (1–4): 285–312.

Sen, Tansen. 2003. *Buddhism, Diplomacy, and Trade: The Realignment of Sino-Indian Relations, 600–1400*. Honolulu: University of Hawai'i Press and the Association for Asian Studies.

Seng, Hui, and Kumārajīva. 1981. *The Buddha Speaks the Brahma Net Sutra, Part 2: The Ten Major and Forty-Eight Minor Bodhisattva Precepts*. Burlingame, CA: Buddhist Text Translation Society, Dharma Realm Buddhist University.

Shabkar Tsogdruk Rangdrol. 2001. *The Life of Shabkar: The Autobiography of a Tibetan Yogin*. Translated by Matthieu Ricard. Edited by Constance Wilkinson with Michal Abrams. New York: Snow Lion Publications.

Shakya, Tsering. 1999. *The Dragon in the Land of Snows: A History of Modern Tibet since 1947*. New York: Columbia University Press.

Shāntideva. 2006. *The Way of the Bodhisattva: A Translation of the Bodhicaryāvatāra*. Revised ed. Translated by the Padmakara Translation Group. Boston: Shambhala.

Sherburne, Richard S. J., trans. 2000. *The Complete Works of Atīśa Śrī Dīpaṁkara Jñāna, Jo bo rje: The Lamp for the Path and Commentary Together with the Newly Translated Twenty-Five Key Texts*. New Delhi: Aditya Prakashan.

Silk, Jonathan A. 2008. *Managing Monks: Administrators and Administrative Roles in Indian Buddhist Monasticism*. Oxford: Oxford University Press.

Smith, E. Gene. 2011. "E. Gene Smith Interview Part 2 (with Julie Adler)." TBRC Library Videos. 9 min. 29 sec. (originally recorded in 2007). http://www.youtube.com/watch?v=CUzBQioeETc&playnext=1&list=PLAEB5F29EFA927255&feature=results_video.

Smith, Valene. 1977. *Hosts and Guests: The Anthropology of Tourism*. Philadelphia: University of Pennsylvania Press.

Snellgrove, David, and Hugh Richardson. 2003. *A Cultural History of Tibet*. Bangkok: Orchid Press.

Sofield, Trevor H. B., and Fung Mei Sarah Li. 1998. "Tourism Development and Cultural Policies in China." *Annals of Tourism Research* 25 (2): 362–92.

———. 2007. "China: Ecotourism and Cultural Tourism, Harmony or Dissonance?" In *Critical Issues in Ecotourism: Understanding a Complex Tourism Phenomenon*, edited by James Higham, 368–85. Oxford: Elsevier.

Sopa, Geshé Lhundub, and Paul Donnelly. 2012. *Like a Waking Dream: The Autobiography of Geshe Lhundub Sopa*. Boston: Wisdom Publications.

Sopa, Geshé Lhundub, and David Patt. 2004. *Steps on the Path to Enlightenment: A Commentary on Tsongkhapa's Lamrim Chenmo*, vol. 1. Boston: Wisdom Publications.

State Council of the People's Republic of China. 2001. "Tibet's March toward Modernization." White paper. http://china.org.cn/e-white/20011108/index.htm.

———. 2004. *Constitution of the People's Republic of China*. http://english.gov.cn/archive/laws_regulations/2014/08/23/content_281474982987458.htm.

Stevenson, Mark. 2002. "Art and Life in A mdo Reb gong since 1978." In *Amdo Tibetans in Transition: Society and Culture in the Post-Mao Era*, edited by Toni Huber, 197–219. Leiden: Koninklijke Brill NV.

Stewart, Jampa Mackenzie. 1995. *The Life of Gampopa: The Incomparable Dharma Lord of Tibet*. New York: Snow Lion Publications.

Su, Xiaobo, and Peggy Teo. 2009. *The Politics of Heritage Tourism in China: A View from Lijiang*. New York: Routledge.

Surya Das, Lama [Jeffrey Miller]. 1992. *The Snow Lion's Turquoise Mane: Wisdom Tales from Tibet*. New York: HarperCollins.

Tanaka, Yuko. 1997. "Art as Spiritual Practice: A Study of Three Mongolian Works on the Practice and Sponsorship of Buddhist Thangka Painting." *Tibetan Studies* 2:947–53.

Tatz, Mark, trans. 1986. *Asanga's Chapter on Ethics with the Commentary of Tsong-Kha-Pa, The Basic Path to Awakening, The Complete Bodhisattva*. Lewiston, NY: Edwin Mellen Press.

Taussig, Michael T. 1980. *The Devil and Commodity Fetishism in South America*. Chapel Hill: University of North Carolina Press.

Taves, Ann. 2009. *Religious Experience Reconsidered: A Building-Block Approach to the Study of Religion and Other Special Things*. Princeton, NJ: Princeton University Press.

Tawney, Richard Henry. (1926) 1998. *Religion and the Rise of Capitalism*. Introduction by Adam B. Seligman. Reprint, New Brunswick, NJ: Transaction Publishers.

Tenzin Gyatso (H. H. the Dalai Lama). 1989. "The Thirty-Seven Practices of Bodhisattvas: Preliminary Teachings to the Kalachakra Initiation." Translated by Jeffery Hopkins, transcribed by Phillip Lecso. Kalachakranet.org, English Resources, Other Public Texts. http://kalachakranet.org/resources_english.html.

———. 1991. *Path to Bliss: A Practical Guide to the Stages of Meditation*. Translated by Thupten Jinpa. Edited by Thupten Jinpa and Christine Cox. New York: Snow Lion Publications.

———. 1995a. *Commentary on the Thirty-Seven Practices of a Bodhisattva*. Translated by Acharya Nyima Tsering. Edited by Vyvyan Cayley and Mike Gilmore. Dharamsala: Library of Tibetan Works and Archives.

———. 1995b. *The Path to Enlightenment*. Compiled, edited, and translated by Glenn H. Mullin. New York: Snow Lion Publications.

———. 1997. *Healing Anger: The Power of Patience from a Buddhist Perspective*. Translated by Geshé Thupten Jinpa. New York: Snow Lion Publications.

———. 2002. *Illuminating the Path to Enlightenment*. Edited by Rebecca McClen Novick and Nicholas Ribush. Long Beach, CA: Thubten Dhargye Ling Publications.

———. 2001. *Stages of Meditation*. Translated by Geshé Lobsang Jordhen, Losang Choephel Ganchenpa, and Jeremy Russell. New York: Snow Lion Publications.

———. 2009. *The Union of Bliss and Emptiness: Teachings on the Practice of Guru Yoga*. Translated by Thupten Jinpa. New York: Snow Lion Publications.

Thanh, Minh, and P. D. Leigh, trans. and eds. 2000. *Brahma Net Sutra: Moral Code of the Bodhisattva*. Bronx, NY: Young Men's Buddhist Association and the Sutra Translation Committee of the US and Canada. https://www.ymba.org/books/brahma-net-sutra-moral-code-bodhisattva.

Thargyal, Rinzin. 2007. *Nomads of Eastern Tibet: Social Organization and Econ-*

omy of a Pastoral Estate in the Kingdom of Dege. Edited by Toni Huber. Leiden: Koninklijke Brill NV.

Thinley Norbu Rinpoche. 2006. *A Cascading Waterfall of Nectar.* Boston: Shambhala.

Thupten Jinpa, trans. and ed. 2006. *Mind Training: The Great Collection*. Compiled by Shönu Gyalchok and Khönchok Gyaltsen. Boston: Wisdom Publications in association with the Institute of Tibetan Classics.

Tokuno, Kyoko. 1995. "The Book of Resolving Doubts Concerning the Semblance Dharma." In *Buddhism in Practice*, edited by Donald S. Lopez Jr., 257–71. Princeton, NJ: Princeton University Press.

Tōru, Funayama. 2006. "Masquerading as Translation: Examples of Chinese Lectures by Indian Scholar-Monks in the Six Dynasties Period." *Asia Major*, Series 3, 19 (1/2): 39–55.

Tsenzhab Serkong Rinpoche. 1982. "Staying Mindful of Karma and Ethical Behavior," Part 3 of 6, *Commentary on "The Foundation for Good Qualities."* Transcription of a seminar, Ulverston, England, October 1982. Translated by Alexander Berzin. Berzin Archives. https://studybuddhism.com/en/tibetan-buddhism/path-to-enlightenment/commentaries-on-lam-rim-texts/commentary-on-the-foundation-for-good-qualities-tsenzhab-serkong-rinpoche/staying-mindful-of-karma-and-ethical-behavior.

Tsering, Tendar. 2012. "School Students in Dsala Walk for Tibet Carrying Buddhist Scriptures." *Phayul*. June 8. http://www.phayul.com/news/article.aspx?id=31559&article=School+students+in+Dsala+walk+for+Tibet+carrying+Buddhist+scriptures&t=1&c=1.

Tsongkhapa. 2000. *The Great Treatise on the Stages of the Path to Enlightenment*. Vol. 1. Translated by the Lamrim Chenmo Translation Committee. Edited by Joshua W. C. Cutler and Guy Newland. Ithaca, NY: Snow Lion Publications.

Tsybikoff, Gombozhab. 1903. "Lhasa and Central Tibet." *Annual Report of the Smithsonian Institution for the Year Ending June 30, 1903*, 727–46.

Tucci, Giuseppe. 1967. *Tibet: Land of Snows*. New York: Stein and Day.

United Nations Social and Economic Council Commission on Human Rights. 1992. *UN Secretary-General's Report: Situation in Tibet*. http://www.tibetjustice.org/materials/un/un8annex1.html.

van Spengen, Wim. 2000. *Tibetan Border Worlds: A Geopolitical Analysis of Trade and Traders*. London: Kegan Paul International.

Waddell, L. Austine. (1899) 2005. *The Buddhism of Tibet or Lamaism: With Its Mystic Cults, Symbolism, and Mythology, and in Its Relation to Indian Buddhism*. 2nd reprint, New Delhi: Asian Educational Services.

Wallis, Glenn. 2002. *Mediating the Power of Buddhas: Ritual in the Mañjuśrī-mūlakalpa*. New York: SUNY Press.

Walser, Joseph. 2005. *Nāgārjuna in Context: Mahāyāna Buddhism and Early Indian Culture*. New York: Columbia University Press.

Wang, Clare. 2011. "Giving Thangka a Colorful New Life." *China Tibet Online*.

November 17. http://eng1.tibet.cn/2010home/news/201111/t20111117_1179056.html.

Wang, Yuxiang, and JoAnn Phillion. 2009. "Minority Language Policy and Practice in China: The Need for Multicultural Education." *International Journal of Multicultural Education* 11 (1): 1–14.

Wangdu, Tamdin. 2012. "Tibetan Village Project Establishes Thangka Training Center and School for Children." PRWeb, May 18. http://www.prweb.com/releases/2012/5/prweb9518321.htm.

Wangmo, Jamyang (Helly Pelaez Bozzi). 2005. *The Lawudo Lama: Stories of Reincarnation from the Mount Everest Region*. Boston: Wisdom Publications.

Wangyal, Geshé Thupten. 1986. *The Jewelled Staircase*. Ithaca, NY: Snow Lion Publications.

Wenbin, Peng. 1998. "Tibetan Pilgrimage in the Process of Social Change: A Case Study of Jiuzhaigou." In *Pilgrimage in Tibet*, edited by Alex McKay, 184–201. Surrey: Curzon Press.

Williams, Joan C., and Viviana A. Zelizer. 2005. "To Commodify or Not to Commodify: That Is Not the Question." In *Rethinking Commodification: Cases and Readings in Law and Culture*, edited by Martha M. Ertman and Joan C. Williams, 362–82. New York: New York University Press.

Winkler, Daniel. 2008a. "The Mushrooming Fungi Market in Tibet Exemplified by *Cordyceps sinensis* and *Tricholoma matsutake*." *Journal of the International Association of Tibetan Studies* 4 (December): 1–46.

———. 2008b. "*Yartsa Gunbu* (*Cordyceps sinensis*) and the Fungal Commodification of Tibet's Rural Economy." *Economic Botany* 62 (3): 291–305.

Wissing, Douglas A. 2004. *Pioneer in Tibet: The Life and Perils of Dr. Albert Shelton*. New York: Palgrave Macmillan.

Wong, Edward. 2009. "With Explosions of Color, Tibetan Art Flourishes." *New York Times*, March 29. http://www.nytimes.com/2009/03/30/world/asia/30sengeshong.html?_r=1&.

Woodcock, George. 1970. "Tibetan Refugees in a Decade of Exile." *Pacific Affairs* 43 (3): 410–20.

Xiao, Honggen. 2006. "The Discourse of Power: Deng Xiaoping and Tourism Development in China." *Tourism Management* 27 (5): 803–14.

Xiaoan, Wei. 1993. "The Developing China Tourism." Paper delivered at the Annual Conference of the Travel Industry Council of Hong Kong, June. Beijing: China National Tourism Administration Bureau.

Yang, Li. 2007. "Planning for Ethnic Tourism: Case Studies from Xishuangbanna, Yunnan, China." PhD diss., University of Waterloo, Waterloo, Ontario.

Yang, Li, and Geoffrey Wall. 2009. "Ethnic Tourism: A Framework and an Application." *Tourism Management* 30 (4): 559–70.

Yang, Li, Geoffrey Wall, and Stephen L. J. Smith. 2008. "Ethnic Tourism Development: Chinese Government Perspectives." *Annals of Tourism Research* 35 (3): 751–71.

Yangsi Rinpoche. 2003. *Practicing the Path: A Commentary on the Lamrim Chenmo.* Translated by Tsering Tuladhar. Edited by Miranda Adams. Somerville, MA: Wisdom Publications.

Yeh, Emily T. 2006. "Tourism to Tibet: Context and Recent Trends." *Trin-gyi-pho-nya: Tibet's Environment and Development Digest* 18 (November). http://www.tew.org/editorial-oped/trin-gyi-pho-nya/1106.html.

Yeshe, Lama Thubten. 2004. *Becoming Vajrasattva: The Tantric Path of Purification.* Edited by Nicholas Ribush. Boston: Wisdom Publications.

Yuanfeng, Zuo, Fu Shuangqi, and Bai Ying. 2009. "Commercialize or Die? China's Handicrafts Struggle for Survival." *Xinhua News Agency*, February 16. http://www.lifeofguangzhou.com/node_10/node_33/node_572/2009/02/16/123475092560315.shtml.

Yuthok, Dorje Yudon. 1990. *House of the Turquoise Roof.* Translated and edited by Michael Harlin. Boston: Snow Lion Publications.

Zopa, Lama Thubten. 1986. "Lama Tsongkhapa Guru Yoga (Ganden Lha Gyäma)." Talk, Tushita Meditation Center, McLeod Ganj, Dharamsala, March. Lama Yeshe Wisdom Archive. http://www.lamayeshe.com/article/chapter/refuge-three-jewels.

———. 2002. "Advice on Selling Holy Objects." Tsa Tsa Studio: Center for Tibetan Sacred Art. http://www.tsatsastudio.org/pdfs/AdviceSellingHolyObjects.pdf. Tsa Tsa Studio.org is no longer operational.

———. 2007. Long-life Sutra and Torma Offering (Audio and Unedited Transcripts) "Commentary on Peaceful Torma Purifying Pollution, Part A." Taipei, April 15–16. Lama Yeshe Wisdom Archive. http://www.lamayeshe.com/article/chapter/commentary-peaceful-torma-purifying-pollution-part.

Zürcher, Erik. 1995. "Buddhist Art in Medieval China: The Ecclesiastical View." In *Function and Meaning in Buddhist Art*, edited by K. R. van Koolj and H. van der Veere, 1–20. Groningen: Egbert Forsten.

Zwalf, W. 1981. *The Heritage of Tibet.* London: British Museum Publications.

Index

Italicized page numbers refer to illustrations.

Traditions and Transformations in Tibetan Buddhism

This series will investigate the stability of Tibetan religious culture from its historical beginnings in the sixth century through the modern era as well as how the religious tradition has changed in reaction to historical realities, technological transformation, and social unrest. To facilitate an interdisciplinary approach, the series publishes projects on four interconnected themes: ritual traditions and textual transformations, Tibet in its historical milieu, Tibet and the modern world, and Tibetan Buddhism in diaspora.